W9-ADY-516

MAR 2 8 1991

Republic of Fear

Republic of Fear

*The Politics
of Modern Iraq*

Samir al-Khalil

UNIVERSITY OF CALIFORNIA PRESS
Berkeley · Los Angeles

University of California Press
Berkeley and Los Angeles, California

© 1989 by
The Regents of the University of California

Second Printing with New Preface 1990

Library of Congress Cataloging-in-Publication Data
Khalil, Samir.
  Republic of fear.
  Includes index.
  1. Iraq—Politics and government.   I. Title.
DS79.65.K494   1989   956.7'04   88-10759
ISBN 0-520-06442-9 (alk. paper)

Printed in the United States of America

2 3 4 5 6 7 8 9

The paper used in this publication meets the minimum
requirements of American National Standard for Information Sciences—Permanence of Paper for Printed Library
Materials, ANSI Z39.48–1984. ∞

Contents

░░░ COMMUNITY COLLEGE LIBRARY

Preface

On Violence

Since I finished writing *Republic of Fear,* the chamber of horrors that is Saddam Husain's Iraq has mushroomed into something that not even the most morbid imagination could have foreseen. The war with Iran ended in the summer of 1988 on favorable terms for Iraq. But did the violence stop, or even abate? On the contrary, it turned in on itself as it had done before, from 1968 to 1980, the year the war started.

The day after the ceasefire came into effect, Iraqi warplanes went into action with chemical weapons against Kurdish villages. Between August 25 and 27, several thousand helpless civilians died.[1] The attacks continued on a systematic basis all through September. It had of course been done before, in the town of Halabja in March 1988, where around 6,000 perished. This one the world noticed (because the Kurds got Western television reporters into the town).[2] But no one noticed in May, in June, or in September of 1987. And all the times before that. How many died in these attacks? We may never know. Tens of thousands of army deserters had collected since 1980 in the marshes region of southern Iraq.[3] They were given an ultimatum. What happened to those who handed themselves in? We only know what happened to those who didn't; they were gassed.

Then there are the truly grisly stories. Reports reached Amnesty of hundreds of children whose eyes were gouged out to force confessions

---

1. Middle East Watch, *Human Rights in Iraq* (New York: Human Rights Watch, 1990), 144.

2. At the time Red Cross officials who visited the site put the dead at around 5,000. See ibid., 160. Writing later, Edward Mortimer estimated 6,350 dead. See *The Financial Times,* March 16, 1989.

3. See the report by Helga Graham, *The Guardian,* September 14, 1988.

from their adult relatives.[4] There are rumours of giant vats of acid in a Baghdad suburb used for the disposal of bodies at a rate faster than nature can provide for. Poison was administered to a whole meeting of Kurds by a Kurdish Mata Hari double agent who risked life and limb ten times over to poison some forty Kurdish leaders. Six died.[5] Her family was held hostage in Baghdad. There is no glamour in the violence of the Baʿth.

In Baghdad there is a labyrinthine family intrigue that would make the Borgias pale. Consider, for instance, the tale of Saddam Husain's eldest son, Uday, who in full public view stomped and clubbed to death his father's official food taster, Kamel Hana Geogo. The President was furious and saw in this the hand of his wife, Sajida. Why? Because between Geogo's food-tasting functions, it was his job to vet the many women who wrote in asking to see the President as part of his "meet the people" program. One of these, it is rumoured, he secretly married. The affair comes to a climax of sorts with the death in a helicopter "accident" of Khairallah Tulfah, a leading pillar of the regime, the father of Sajida and uncle and foster-father of Saddam Husain.[6]

The stories go on and on. And they get even more bizarre. Fortunately, for the first time, the horror stories themselves are beginning to be chronicled, documented, and recorded. A new human rights monitoring group, Middle East Watch, has produced a major 235 page report (published in February 1990).[7] More Iraqis are willing to go to organizations like Amnesty International than ever before. Some are going public at great personal risk and founding human rights organizations and refugee assistance programs. The BBC Everyman program has produced "Enemies of the State," the first extended television documentary on human rights abuses in Iraq. The regime of Saddam Husain in Iraq is slowly but surely being exposed as the number one human rights violator in the world.

But not by everyone. Western governments looking towards lucrative

4. The practice goes back at least to the early 1980s. See the circular entitled "Iraq's War on its Children," by Amnesty Action, March/April 1989, 6. Also see the report by Frances Williams in the *Sunday Times*, March 5, 1989.

5. See the report by Hazhir Teimourian in *The Times*, January 13, 1988.

6. When stories about the affair started to leak in Syrian newspapers, Saddam Husain decided to turn it to his advantage. His son was arrested and the President demanded the full measure of the law to be brought against him despite appeals for clemency from his own ministers and (a nice touch this) from the father of the murdered man. Iraqi newspapers played up Saddam's implacable demand for justice beside the emotionalism of the father's appeal. Finally and reluctantly he concedes and Uday is packed off to Switzerland as ambassador. There, however, he beats up a Swiss policeman, is declared persona non grata, and is shipped back to Iraq. Today he is reinstalled as a leading figure of the regime. For a glimpse into the details, see the report in the *Sunday Times*, May 7, 1989.

7. See note 1 above.

markets in the near future (for oil prices are expected to rise) are not doing enough. They turn a blind eye to the worst excesses when these do not involve them directly. More ominous is the active support Saddam Husain's regime receives from the Arab world—from regimes in particular but also from public opinion.

In the wake of the execution of Farzad Bazoft, for instance, the Iraqi President's prestige rose as that well-worn call to confront Western and Zionist designs was recited to Arab audiences once again. Not a word of condemnation of the indiscriminate use of poison gas to eliminate a civilian population has appeared in the Arabic press. Worst of all, however, is the terrible silence of the intelligentsia both inside and outside the Arab world, a silence which is in such stark contrast to the clear voices of their counterparts in Latin America or Eastern Europe; no Arab versions of Vaclav Havel or Christa Wolf have called Saddam Husain to account.

Describing Violence

Republic of Fear is first of all about how such horror stories became the norm inside an otherwise ordinary corner of that great political misnomer, "the Third World." The book describes a Kafkaesque world before the meat grinder of the Iraq-Iran war. I focused on the nature of the regime that started it. Nothing that came out of that eight-year experience could, of course, be quite as "normal" as what went in. If Ba'thi Iraq wasn't normal in the early 1980s, it is even less so now. Today the reality of Saddam Husain's world is even stranger than Kafka's fiction.

Is *Republic of Fear* still relevant? Glancing over the pages in order to write this preface, I realized that the text is overwritten and long-winded in many places. But I think it got the most fundamental things right. Violence has played an extraordinarily important role in Iraq since 1968; it forms the language of politics and it is the key political question facing the population in the foreseeable future. The relevance of this central strand of the book has grown in importance. In the case of Iraq the level of violence is on a steeply rising curve; and the silence of the Arab intelligentsia indicates that there are political issues involved here which remain profoundly unresolved for the culture as a whole.

Description is the first and most fundamental act of resolution: ruthless, relentless, unforgiving description. Even when their conditions seem to utterly disintegrate, like some kind of China syndrome, human beings are able to exercise a degree of control through the power of description. Telling horror stories is the first step towards dealing with the rule of violence. But it is not enough. *Republic of Fear* tries to go beyond that. Horror has shape and form. And horror repeats itself; it follows patterns and beats to a certain rhythm. Farzad Bazoft's televised confession of spying has a long pedigree. The Ba‘th cemented their rule with a spate of such confessions, followed by public hangings, twenty-one years before the Bazoft affair (see "The First Spectacle," chapter 2 of this book). This history needs to be explicated, to be digested, to be systematized. Events like the execution of Bazoft need to be seen not as isolated incidents but as the bizarre way in which this particular system of government sustains and reproduces itself.

The mechanics of violence translate into horror through sensual experience. We inflict violence upon one another, but we experience the full shock of horror in privacy. It is therefore a matter of feeling, or rather a matter of cultivating feeling through description so as to stick on the consequences of political violence that label—horror—and not some other (violence as "necessary evil," for instance, or "the midwife of history"). Shunning the label (because it is too "moralistic" or "subjective") is as much a political statement as adopting it. The horror has to be relentlessly confronted, if for no other reason than to come to terms with it. Kafka retains his relevance for contemporary Iraq because he understood this better than any other writer of this century.

Unlike horror, violence is instrumental and objective. It is structured through particular institutions and these are in turn transformed by their specialization. They work through precedents and contingencies. Personal quirks, levels of resources, varying degrees of intelligence, these all have a place in the determination of what the agents of violence look like, how they behave, and what scale of damage they inflict upon the population. What kinds of jobs do these people do and how do they go about doing them? Through description, to whatever extent the facts allow, such organizations can be stripped naked and understood. Moreover, the act of scrutiny, endlessly repeated, paralyzes them. Focusing upon these instruments, describing their inner workings, and confronting their horrific work also transforms the scrutinizer's priorities. For instance, it becomes possible to understand why Iraq is not your normal garden variety type of dictatorship, a little bit more ruthless than the others; it is a consistently criminal state, one which ought to be treated as such by the world community of states.

Responsibility and Violence

Although violence is always instrumental, requiring armies, police, weapons, and networks of informers, it has to be justified and legitimated by the ends it pursues. In this, Saddam Husain's violence in its origins is no different from the policies of other rulers. There must be people out there willing and prepared to implement the policies on behalf of those who are telling them what to do. No normal human being can kill or maim another without some way of rationalizing the act. No war was ever fought other than for the cause of peace (through victory). Peace, on the other hand, requires no justification.

The special problem of Baʿthi violence begins with the realization that hundreds of thousands of perfectly ordinary people are implicated in it. Even Saddam Husain's torturers and elite police units who do the dirtiest work are by and large normal. There are too many of them for it to be otherwise. From being a means to an end, violence has turned into an end in itself, into the way in which all politics (finally no politics) is experienced by the public in Iraq. Still, the violence has to be justified. Certainly no government bureaucracy can pluck out the eyes of its children without providing itself with reasons for such behaviour. But, like a snake eating its own tail, justification is itself now manufactured through the fear of violence, not by way of consent or even of deception. The system functions like a concentration camp: inmates are played off against one another (enemies are invented) and children are tortured (for a "higher" purpose) as the whole thing spins wildly out of control in a closed world all of its own making. This is the peculiarity of violence in Iraq and the reason for its seemingly detached "Kafkaesque" nature. The regime that achieved all this is a totally indigenous phenomenon, imposed by no outside force, wholly a product of the culture that sustains it. The days of Western-imposed monarchies have been left far, far behind. Here is the most troubling part of the reality that *Republic of Fear* tries to come to grips with. Looking for a monster or a master-criminal called Saddam Husain, who himself enjoys acting out the part, is too easy, too childlike.

Saddam Husain was born in 1937. This is the generation that made possible the rule of the Baʿth in Iraq. It does not matter whether what remains of it is part of the state machinery in Iraq, or is scattered in exile, or consists of tired and burnt out Iraqis who once had high ideals for their country which they saw metamorphose into the horrors of today. The Baʿth generation in Iraq is not made up of the hundreds of thousands of young men in their teens and twenties who died in the Iraq-Iran war. Similarly the generation that made possible the Lebanese civil war is not made up of the mountain and peasant thugs who are still slugging it out in the ruins of Beirut. These are the children of violence for whom violence has become a way of life. They are easy to understand. It is the previous generation of cosmopolitan intellectuals, of spinners of grand theories and the activists who believed in those theories, usually for the noblest of motives, who are both responsible for the current state of affairs and central to understanding it. The best of them escaped and emigrated abroad either into the dead end of exile politics, or to become diehard cynics who bring to the word disillusionment a new dimension. So perhaps it is no wonder that the Arab intelligentsia is silent.

Republic of Fear looks closely at the set of ideas which moved the Ba'th generation, the generation of Saddam Husain and the 1960s in Iraq. It examines the historical roots of those ideas and argues that they legitimated the rule of violence. But does that go far enough? Many well-wishers of the book think that on this score it fails, and that objective factors like ethnic diversity, tensions between social classes, between the city and the countryside, historical particularities, or the stage of development of Iraq must somehow be brought into the foreground of the analysis.

Violence, however, "took off" in some countries and not in others, and always in different ways. There are no general rules; there is only pseudo-objectivity. Consider, for instance, the example of the Algerian revolution, where the whole question of violence in relation to the politics of decolonization was first posed as an intellectual problem of the first order. Franz Fanon celebrated the role of violence in his immensely moving book, *The Wretched of the Earth,* and from then on the phrase became a recurring motif in "Third World" politics. "Only violence pays," the starving Algerian peasant discovers.[8] And by acting accordingly, he is thought to have freed himself, not only of the mechanical facts of oppression, but politically and even spiritually. "The colonized man finds his freedom in and through violence."[9] The lesson of violence, Fanon is telling us, has been learnt from the colonizers themselves, from the way they behaved in Algeria as occupiers and settlers. But what about the case of Indian decolonization and the Gandhi phenomenon?

Fanon's way of thinking became very widespread in the late 1960s and 1970s. When Sartre wrote the preface to Fanon's book in 1963, he got carried away with the idea of "man recreating himself" through violence. "No gentleness can efface the marks of violence; only violence itself can destroy them."[10] Fanon was incapable of writing something as stupid as that, but the worst interpretation of his work was widely taken up in the Arab world.

The most striking thing about the Algerian revolution is that this way of putting the question did not correspond to the way in which independence was actually achieved. Puny pinpricks of Algerian violence were met by massive levels of French violence. One million Algerians died, yet the Algerian FLN won. And they achieved independence after the French had succeeded through systematic torture techniques in breaking up their organized networks (think of the film *Battle of Algiers*). The historical memory of colonial violence is much fresher and more real in Algeria than it is in a country like Iraq, which has been independent

8. Franz Fanon, *The Wretched of the Earth* (New York: Grove Press, 1968), 61.
9. Ibid., 86.
10. Ibid., 21.

since 1932. Yet Algeria is nowhere near as despotic as Iraq, in which the ideology of employing violence in politics *followed* independence. Certainly, no Baᶜthist militant ever died fighting the British. Different choices were made.

In other Arab countries, like Lebanon, where violence is as much a part of public life as in Iraq, it has a completely different physiognomy: a regime of rampant anarchy in which betrayal is the rule, versus one of the greatest despotism in which the demand for loyalty is suffocating beyond belief. Yet Lebanon used to be called the "Switzerland of the Middle East." Today these are two of the most violent countries in the world, yet what is most interesting is the contrast between them, not the similarities.

Such examples point to the ways in which I would respond to my critics. First, no account of political violence in Iraq will be satisfactory that does not situate it in the broader frame of Arab political culture. Second, singular genetic theorizations regarding the peculiarity of Iraq are bound to be unsatisfactory because counterexamples from other parts of the world which did not result in the same levels of violence are always likely to be found. Third, a great deal more concreteness and facing up to hard facts is required of Arab writers in particular before any "patterns" can be adduced. We just don't know enough about things like the role of violence in the Algerian revolution, or the damage done to Palestinian aspirations by the ideology of armed struggle. Most important of all we don't know enough about that great laboratory experiment in violence, where every form, shade, variety, and justification imaginable was tested out: the Lebanese civil war. The best accounts we have are by Western journalists. No Lebanese writer has so far been able to deal with the searing trauma of his country's experience in anything like the depth that it demands. For that matter *Republic of Fear* barely scratches the surface of what happened in Iraq. It was written abroad and is based on pockets of information and testimony about the regime between 1968 and 1980. What patterns, linkages, and historical connections behind Iraqi violence might yet become apparent if comprehensive direct evidence from large numbers of victims, former Baᶜthis, and eyewitness observers were forthcoming?

The use of violence for political ends has been part of the human drama since the dawn of civilization. One must not be sanguine about the complexities involved. In the context of Arab political culture, the relevance of *Republic of Fear* is that it is a counter text to *The Wretched of the Earth*. Its premises are totally different, but like that book it takes its stand in that important gap which always exists between past and future, the gap in which human volition, responsibility, commitment, and a sense of anger or shame can decide the course of events. We all still stand in that gap, unable to take our distance from it. The bodies have not stopped accumulating in Iraq. The stench of slaughter rises daily.

One day the books will be opened and even more terrible stories will come tumbling out. Then the even more wrenching problems of who did what to whom and why will be on the agenda. They are asking those kinds of questions today in Romania, as they asked them yesterday in Argentina. When violence has so permeated a culture its force must not be diluted by "objectivizing" it away from the moral heart of public life.

In the end many "descriptions" and "explanations" of violence in Iraq are bound to emerge. They will operate at different levels, come at different times, and serve a whole variety of purposes. Each generation will want to understand things in its own way. No matter how different one explanation is from the other, if pursued with integrity on the premise that for a while at least the central problem is or was violence, they will complement one another and add to our "knowledge." But knowledge of what? Of the world or of the potential in ourselves? I believe the latter, for finally there is a profound enigma in violence of the sort described in *Republic of Fear*; that enigma is the reason we are so driven to want an explanation, and so unsatisfied the moment we think we have put our fingers on it.

May 1990

Note to the Reader

This book is not a history of the Baʿth regime established in 1968 in Iraq. It is an enquiry into its meaning. No doubt there are many different ways of making such an enquiry. My preoccupation throughout is the country's prewar experience with a politics rooted in violence and high ideals. I choose to look at the Baʿth through the prism of their violence because I believe this to be the central problem in that unhappy country for the foreseeable future. My prejudices in this regard give rise to a particular interpretation of Iraqi Baʿthism. The validity of this interpretation can partly be judged on the basis of the facts and arguments deployed. The other part must finally rest on the worth of my prism in the eyes of the people directly affected.

Some of my general assumptions about political behaviour are relevant to the styles of reasoning employed and the kinds of evidence adduced in their support. First, what leaders, parties, and citizens think and expressly say about politics matters. The words that people use are not a "reflection" of some hidden reality; they are themselves part of that reality. The problem always resides in how words and actions correspond. Hence an important somewhat neglected source of information on the Baʿth can be found in speeches, party political programmes, and the whole body of ideological artifacts.

Second, despite the proclivity of those in public office to propaganda, rhetoric, chicanery, and lies, on the whole even they usually end up saying what they mean and meaning what they say.

Third, I vigorously eschew all variations of the conspiratorial view of history, particularly as these are applied to relations with the West. Instead, I single out for consideration the demonstrably inverted relation between the common Iraqi perception of the pervasiveness of a hateful Western influence and the factually diminishing ability of the West to influence local events in the modern period.

Fourth, political trends that held true in the past because of certain reasons may not hold true in the future even if most of the reasons remain in place. People will change their minds; occasionally political behaviour rests simply on that. I am not searching for historical processes, nor am I engaging in a spurious science. Nothing, therefore, should be imputed from this book concerning the future stability of Baʿthism in Iraq. In the event that war brings down the Baʿthist edifice tomorrow, Iraqis would still be faced with the problem of coming to terms with what made it become by 1980 the most powerful and stable regime in the country's modern history.

Every writer on post-1968 Iraq has to work with severely inadequate information originating in an obsessive official attitude towards "national security." In choosing to focus on institutions like the secret police and the politics of fear, this book inevitably suffers from this liability more than others. My way around the problem has been to make explicit every source, and not to discard a story or a circulating rumour merely because it has no firmer basis in fact. A feature of Baʿthist Iraq is that sometimes the truth content of a particular story is less important than the fact that people have come to believe that it is true.

The same obsession has personal ramifications as well. I owe a handful of very dear friends a great deal in the writing of this book. But things being what they are under the Baʿth, I can no more mention their names than I can write under my own.

—March 1988

PART ONE

The Baᶜthist Polity

i

Institutions of Violence

The Secret Police

Salim was about to sit down to dinner when the knock came. The two men did not come in or identify themselves. They confirmed Salim's identity and politely told him to accompany them for a few questions. His wife asked too loudly whether anything was wrong, what was the problem, they hadn't done anything, and so on. Salim reassured her as though he knew all about it; he stepped outside with the men, and gently pushed the door shut in her face. Salim remembered his hands turning clammy in the car, although it was not hot, and feeling his stomach had caved in on itself although he was no longer hungry. The car stopped at the local *Amn* headquarters.

In the early 1970s, Baghdad was divided into security zones, the planning of which required citizens to sell their properties in certain areas at a price set by the government. The headquarters of such zones were surveillance centres, routinely checking on movements within and between zones. Many a casual visitor to Baghdad has confirmed their surprising efficiency upon being questioned for taking snapshots of the Tigris at sunset, or some other such offence (cameras are sold in Iraq, but photography is suspect without the written authorization of the Ministry of Interior). Some of these centres are hooked to video cameras concealed on roof tops or built into statues and public monuments. The cameras cover the major roads, intersections, and roundabouts forming a comprehensive network for each zone and enabling the centre to monitor its area visually. Salim was escorted into such a building.

He remembered waiting for a long time. Although still ignorant of the reasons for his being there, he was becoming more and more afraid. Eventually he was ushered into an enormous office. Screen monitors dotted the entire space, and their flashing images impressed him more than anything else about the room. Whether they were there for effect or for function made little difference.

Salim was offered tea and spoken to politely throughout. An important-looking man, whose office this was and whose name he never found out, looked at some papers before him and asked where he had been on a particular day many months ago. Salim didn't remember. He listed a few license plate numbers, only one of which Salim recognized as being his own. Dates and numbers were now being combined into single questions, and Salim was becoming so frightened he could not retain the different parts of each question, much less put them together into a coherent answer. Finally he was caught out: the interrogator demanded to know how he could have been at work on that particular day if his car had been left at home. They knew he always drove to work.

Now it dawned on him. Those were the weeks he had been laid up with a leg fracture. When he was well enough to go to work, a cousin had picked him up in the mornings. The children were taken to school by someone else; and his wife had rearranged her schedule. These and other details could not tumble out of his mouth fast enough, and he caught himself saying nonsense but he did not think the important-looking man noticed. To his astonishment the explanation appeared acceptable; in fact it seemed to come as no surprise. More questions followed as though to pin down the matter, and then the interrogation was over. Relief covered Salim's face until the bombshell struck.

The important-looking man wanted Salim and his family to vacate their house within ten days—clothes, furniture, and all. Salim was to drop his keys at another office in the building and register his new address; he would be contacted when his story had been checked out. Further questions and polite remonstrations were ruled out; the man's demeanour began to show irritation. Salim was escorted to the street and returned home.

The house was vacated, and the keys delivered. Months later a telephone call from Salim's local *Amn* headquarters informed him that he could collect his keys from the office where he had deposited them and return to his house.

Not a single official piece of paper was proffered, or for that matter asked for. Salim, having recovered from the mechanics of his tribulations, shoved the matter aside as one might the weather or a natural disaster of some kind, and pressed on with his otherwise perfectly mundane life.[1]

From the standpoint of ordinary citizens like Salim, the secret police rules in Iraq and is all-pervasive. The public perception of police omnipotence and omniscience is resisted as a topic in books on the post-1968 Baʿthi regime, in part because so little is known about these institutions. But they rest on a central truth of Iraqi politics.

All anyone has to work with regarding the secret police are a failed 1973 coup, a few passages from the 1974 Political Report, reports on documents leaked in 1979, the publicity surrounding overseas operations that go awry, the observations of a handful of informed outsiders, hints from indiscreet party members, individual experiences passed along by word of mouth, and finally a book written by a man reputed to be the new head of the *Mukhabarat,* the party intelligence network. Apart from a few published laws regulating movement and prescribing the multitude of permissions required of citizens, published information on the role and purpose of policing agencies does not exist. The only statistics on the police date back to the monarchy, and even these lump together traffic control with the repressive institutions of the state. Prior to the Baʿthist coup of 1968, a police tradition remotely comparable with today's did not exist.

From this limited pool of information, I surmise that the agency that Salim encountered in the late 1970s originated in a special unit of the Iraqi branch of the Arab Baʿth Socialist Party (ABSP) conceived in clandestinity sometime between 1964 and 1966 and called *al-Jihaz al-Khas,* the special apparatus. Its code name was *Jihaz Haneen,* or the instrument of yearning. *Haneen* was a shadowy entity selected from the most committed cadre who became specialists in intelligence matters. These units of armed men were in the thick of events during the 1968 Baʿthi coup.[2]

From the start *Haneen* was created as a party-based alternative power to that wielded by the officer cadres of the Baʿth and deriving from their strategic location in the state. The first Baʿthi regime in 1963 was overthrown when the military men of the party sided with fellow officers to oust the civilian Baʿthi National Guard. A similar occurrence in Syria

1. A true story, the details of which have been changed.
2. David Hirst referred to *Haneen* in *The Guardian,* November 26, 1971. *Jihaz Haneen* is also mentioned in the semiofficial biography by Amir Iskander, *Saddam Husain: Munadhilan, wa Mufakiran wa Insanan* (Paris: Hachette, 1981), 101, 104–5.

left deep divisions throughout the Arab organization. In 1964 at the instigation of Michel ᶜAflaq, the founder of the Baᶜth, Saddam Husain was elevated into the Regional Command, the highest decision-making body of the Iraqi branch of the ABSP. This appointment marked a new beginning for the Baᶜth in Iraq because Saddam Husain was the architect of *Jihaz Haneen* and always oversaw its various metamorphoses into the complex and ever-so-secret policing institutions of the second Baᶜthi experience.

The first chief of Internal State Security was Nadhim Kzar, a 1969 appointee of Saddam Husain's. He was a hard and ascetic man who joined the party as a student in the 1950s and became one of the few Shiᶜis to occupy a position of real power. Kzar figured prominently in the excesses of the first, 1963 Baᶜthi regime. He nurtured a reputation for ruthlessness and sadistic practices, which struck terror inside the party itself. For instance, he had a penchant for conducting interrogations personally and extinguishing his cigarette inside the eyeballs of his victims.[3] Kzar invigorated an organization that was inefficient and subservient to army dictate between 1958 and 1968.

Under Kzar, the secret police was responsible for the torture and unpublicized killings of possibly a few thousand people, principally communists and Kurds. In 1971, for instance, one faction of the Iraqi Communist Party (ICP) issued a list with the names of 410 members who had died in the aptly named *Qasr al-Nihayyah*, Palace of the End.[4] Kzar favoured settling the Kurdish question by force, and his agents attempted to assassinate Kurdish leader Mulla Mustapha al-Barazani at least twice. Both operations were undertaken shortly after the signing of the March 1970 autonomy accords, which, according to the Baᶜth, were to bring peace and autonomy to the Kurdish people.

We know as much as we do about Nadhim Kzar's tenure as police chief because in July 1973 he was executed along with thirty-five others after a summary party tribunal presided over by members of the Revolutionary Command Council (RCC), the supreme authority in the post-1968 state (notionally elected from the Regional Command). Still, only a few facts were given by the regime, and clearly there is more behind the whole affair. Kzar took hostage the ministers of interior and defence and is said to have planned the assassination of the president, Ahmad Hasan al-Bakr. When this failed he attempted to flee with a loyal escort

---

3. See the perceptive report by ᶜAli Hashim in *al-Nahar*'s July 8, 1973 issue, p. 8.
4. Ibid.

to the Iranian border. Cornered by his pursuers, he shot both ministers. The affair was used to instigate a widespread purge of the party.

The 1974 Political Report of the ABSP, an important benchmark for Baʿthi rule in Iraq, made an unusually frank assessment of previous Baʿthi practices; in particular it made this self-criticism of the Kzar reign in the secret police:

> The state security service, though reinforced throughout by Party members and independent patriots, was an immense machine which, under previous regimes, had used blackmail against the party and other national movements, and thus had evolved a peculiar psychology. To reform it, to make it adopt new values and practices was therefore very difficult. It has indeed made serious mistakes during the period under review [1968–73], to the detriment of the Party's reputation and policy in various fields. . . . the leadership was at fault in allowing this sensitive organization to operate without rigorous and careful control. Some officers of this service abused the confidence placed in them by the Party, to the extent of conspiring against the Party, as in the plot of 30 June 1973. This criminal enterprise alerted the Party to the dangers of inadequate control, and extensive changes were made.[5]

The regime was badly shaken by the Kzar episode. Moreover, that a "peculiar psychology" had indeed surfaced in the new state security services became evident in the course of a bizarre series of crimes that occurred right after the purges mentioned in the Political Report. The crimes rattled the party almost as much as the coup. The Baʿth had taken great pride in the fact that the crime rate was down in Baghdad; *Shurtat al-Najdah,* the emergency police, was reputed to be able to arrive at any point in the city within minutes. But this confidence was visibly shaken by a succession of house robberies in which whole families were hacked to death. The perpetrator, nicknamed *Abu al-Tubar,* the hatchet man, ran a gang made up of old hands in the Kzar police service. It transpired at the trial that the gang's ability to elude capture derived from their knowledge and expert use of secret radio frequencies to mislead the police.

Kzar's coup and Abu al-Tubar's crimes were preceded by oil nationalization decrees (March 1973) and followed by the overthrow of the Allende government (September 1973). To readers not versed in the synthetic method of Baʿthism, these might seem like separable events. In a September 24th speech, however, Saddam Husain analysed the situa-

---

5. The document was adopted at the eighth regional congress of the ABSP held in Baghdad in January 1974. I am quoting from the English translation, *The 1968 Revolution in Iraq: Experience and Prospects* (London: Ithaca Press, 1979), 106. Henceforth, referred to as ABSP, *Political Report.*

tion by contrasting Iraq and Cuba, which took imperialism by surprise, with Chile, where the "concealed reserves" of imperialism crushed the experiment:

> We know that imperialism realised finally and particularly in 1972 that the Revolution in Iraq had gone past the state of the "permitted revolution" which it was accustomed to see in the countries of the Third World. . . .
>
> We have objective evidence that imperialism was surprised by the many fundamental methods of the policy followed in this country. It had previously been surprised by several earlier experiences [in Cuba]. . . . However hard imperialism may now look for its concealed reserves [in Iraq] it will never be able to compel our Revolution to retreat and collapse. . . . Some people may imagine that the Revolution is unaware of what is happening around it. The Revolution has its eyes wide open. Throughout all its stages, the Revolution will remain capable of performing its role courageously and precisely without hesitation or panic, once it takes action to crush the pockets of the counter-revolution. All that we hear and read about, including those crimes which have taken place recently, are new devices to confront the Revolution and exhaust it psychologically. These are not sadistic crimes as some imagine; they are crimes committed by traitorous agents.
>
> Those who have sold themselves to the foreigner will not escape punishment. . . . Those who are committing these deeds are individuals who have been hired and exploited in certain ways in the midst of the difficult phase through which we are passing. However, it is not enough to speak loosely about our forces' capabilities and concepts or about imperialism. We must know, learn, and accurately monitor the movements of imperialism. We must calculate with foresight the probable developments of its plans, forces and reserves both inside and outside our frontiers. We must be prepared. The plans, concepts, views, internal forces and reserves we used up to the 1st of March 1973, the day on which the monopolistic companies knelt down and recognized our nationalization, are no longer enough to confront imperialism with its newly conceived and developed plans. We know on this basis that when imperialism was surprised by the revolutionary moves and measures of 1972, it re-examined the situation in order to launch a counter-attack. Thus we prepared additional forces for which imperialism had not allowed in its plans. We can assure our patriotic brothers, . . . they will not make an Allende of us.[6]

The speech was a restatement of the reasoning behind having a powerful secret police at a time when confidence in the agency was at an all-time low. The "eyes" of the Revolution, the "unmasking" of enemies, and the various "preparations" can only be functions of an intelligence-gathering capability. Throughout, the stress is on what the Baʿth "know,"

---

6. Saddam Husain, *On Current Events in Iraq* (London: Longman, 1977), 17–18. Speeches are translated by K. Kishtainy.

or have "objective evidence" for. Such knowledge does not originate in loose talk and abstract ideological analysis, but from accurately monitoring the furtive movements of this thing, imperialism, and its "concealed reserves" inside Iraq; only a politically motivated police also working furtively can provide it.

While notions of secrecy and conspiracy shade into one another in Saddam Husain's speech, a completely new conception of treason is highlighted. Treason is the magic word that brings together Abu al-Tubar's exploits and the outside world; it invests his crimes with a public significance they might not otherwise have had. For some countries, including pre-Ba'thi Iraq, treason was a more specific offence involving, for instance, selling state secrets to a foreign state, promoting a coup, or violating the person of the monarch. Punishment for treasonous acts when so defined was more procedural and lenient.

But now Ba'thist legitimacy derived from "the people" and the "Revolution" made in their name. The new state and its mission were virtually synonymous with "the Arab nation" or "the people," conceived as an undifferentiable collective noun. As it became harder for an individual to offend against this collectivity through specific acts (peoples have no secrets, nor do they have "bodies" except in the form of tired metaphors), it became easier to offend against *the idea* of its sovereignty. In the Ba'thist mind, violating the whole "people" was an even more monstrous version of old-fashioned treason; it assaulted their source of authority, much as a coup attempt assaulted the authority of the individuals at the helm of state. Somehow we have all come to feel that an affront to the dignity of "the people" is worse than an affront to yet another seedy regime, however little it may mean politically. Another type of regime, less entangled in the embrace of so many people, might have shunned this association between Abu al-Tubar's actions and treason, not least because he and his cronies had been state functionaries. Such a regime would choose to prosecute on criminal, not treasonous grounds. But all the people were genuinely terrified by Abu al-Tubar and his actions; and the more they talked about it, the more frightened they became. An unprecedented situation had to be accounted for; a reason for this fear had to be found that would ultimately justify Ba'thism, and not turn into the focus of attacks on it. Saddam Husain set out to find that reason working from conviction and not from cynical intent.

His speech was designed to make treason grow more vague and abstract; now it could be found in people's thoughts, not only their deeds. At the same time its monstrousness was made palpable and concrete

through Abu al-Tubar's sadism. This thinking derived from Baʿthist ideology and was of course consistent with broader twentieth-century
ideological trends, originating in Europe at the turn of the century. In
light of the precedents that culminated in the interwar years in fascism,
Nazism, and Stalinism, Saddam Husain was an imitator, not an inno-
vator. Nonetheless, his legacy has already been assured by the consistency and determination with which he brought such trends to bear inside Iraq. Above all, his particular achievement was the placement of an
inordinate emphasis on a revised conception of political crime, one that
made it ever more loose and all-inclusive. Treason in his hands was a
much larger offence, directed at the whole people, and a much less specific one. Once treason was ensconced in this fashion, police work logically became the substitute for all politics.

In the following year, the Political Report placed the blame for Kzar's
actions on "some officers" and the inherited bureaucracy of the service.
This contention was less tenable than Saddam Husain's because it presented itself in too factual a guise, eschewing the appeal of a teleological
explanation of human affairs. After all, who was Kzar if not the creature
of the party that had spawned him? Was the psychological profile mentioned in the Political Report an old or new phenomenon? Are men like
Nadhim Kzar and Abu al-Tubar not mirror images of one another? Is it
any wonder that the cronies of the one were the cronies of the other?

But where are the same sort of questions for those who are already
motivated by faith in abstractions like imperialism, the ubiquity of its
presence, concealed reserves, and a politics singularly confined to the
distinction between treason and virtue? There are none, because all
facts are necessarily buried in the secrecy required by the explanation. A
strong and *secret* police provides the only way to "be prepared" and get
at the facts that are needed to defeat imperialism. Even asking a question about Abu al-Tubar thus becomes grounds for casting suspicion of
treacherous intent on the part of the questioner.

If the aftermath of the Kzar affair suggests a police going out of control, the background to the story highlights important institutional tensions that became manifest in the new regime because of the escalating
power of the police.

Kzar's formal position was ambiguous. He had been granted a military title without ever having been in the army (later Saddam Husain
would do the same without the resentments that had accompanied
Kzar). In a country that had been ruled by army officers (1958–68), it
was still deemed necessary to have the appearance of an army man in

charge of the police. Kzar's department was theoretically under the combined jurisdiction of the interior and defence ministers whom he had taken hostage; however, his party rank greatly exceeded that of the two men, both of whom were officers who had hitched their fortunes to the rising star of the party after 1968. Moreover, Kzar was known to harbour resentments against the growing Sunni domination of the party, and had been arguing for restriction of all ministerial appointments to members of the Regional Command (the ministers taken hostage were not on this body and owed their position in the state to their services during the coup). He wanted a purge of all rightists and careerists in the party.

Alongside Kzar's problems with his ministers, a conflict was brewing between the head of the Ba'th Military Bureau (executed with Kzar) and the same defence minister who had disregarded a number of directives coming from the bureau.[7] In short, a conflict of authority between party and state had arisen. This translated in the conditions of the early years of Ba'thist rule into a power struggle between an increasingly assertive secret police and the long-standing political authority of the army. Kzar's failure suggested that this conflict was being resolved in favour of the army and to the detriment of the civilian wing of the party. But even if true, it proved to be a temporary outcome.

Saddam Husain, then assistant secretary-general of the ABSP and deputy chairman of the RCC, was Kzar's immediate party superior. Probably his position weakened for a while, as rumours circulated that he was behind Kzar. The provisional constitution, for instance, was quickly amended to give the president, Ahmad Hasan al-Bakr, much greater powers. Bakr's credentials were well-suited for a resolution of the crisis. He was secretary-general of the Ba'th Regional Command from 1965, a party man from its earliest and most isolated days, and its most respected member since 1964 when his elevation into the leadership brought the internal factional struggles to an end. Moreover, he was a much respected former member of the Free Officers organization that overthrew the monarchy in 1958. These qualities combined in no other person in Iraq.

Bakr assumed control of the Ministry of Defence, thus alleviating the further escalation of party-army tensions. Saddam Husain's position could not have eroded all that much, in part because he had close family connections to Bakr (both are Takritis from the same tribal subsection,

7. See *al-Nahar*, July 8, 1973, p. 8.

related yet again through marriage). The pair also had a close working relationship since 1964 when they forged a leadership team based on Saddam's control of the party, and Bakr's prestige in the country and army. Yet all of this might not have been enough to save Saddam were it not for three steps taken by him in the course of the Kzar affair.

First, he implicated his most popular rival in the party, ʿAbd al-Khaliq al-Samarraʾi, a leading ideologue considered the third most powerful man in the country (after Bakr and Saddam). Samarraʾi was tried on the flimsiest of evidence, but Bakr refused to ratify his execution order. He was imprisoned, only to be summarily shot in 1979, after Bakr himself was purged (see Appendix 1).

Second, Saddam acted decisively to resolve the confusion that had spread through the ranks of the party militia, many of whose local commanders were torn between loyalties to Kzar, party bosses further up the line, and the authority of their state against which Kzar was clearly aligned. Saddam personally took command of loyal units of this militia, gave these a high visibility in Baghdad, used them in hot pursuit of Kzar, and sealed and stormed suspected Kzar strongholds. The army was excluded. However weakened the secret police may have been by whatever happened in June–July 1973, the army's political position had at the very least been checked by Saddam's resolute actions. Under his leadership the party put its own house in order.

Third, Saddam Husain administered the restructuring of the secret police by himself. The institution that Salim and his family encountered originated in this overhaul. The outcome was three agencies, independently responsible to the RCC.

1. The *Amn* or State Internal Security, Kzar's old department, was transformed and modernized. By the end of 1973 Saddam Husain had hammered out a secret intelligence agreement with Andropov, then head of the KGB, on the strength of certain clauses in the Iraqi-Soviet Friendship Treaty signed in 1972 (also negotiated by Saddam Husain). The agreement, leaked to the West by dissident Baʿthis after the 1979 purges, provided for[8] a) reorganization of all aspects of internal security on the recommendations of the KGB; b) supply of sophisticated surveillance and interrogation equipment; c) training for Iraqi personnel in KGB and GRU (Military Intelligence) schools in the Soviet Union; d) exchange of intelligence information; and e) provision of assistance

8. Extracts from these documents received a sensationalist coverage in the London magazine, *NOW!*, September 14, 1979, pp. 54–62.

by Iraqi embassy personnel to Soviet agents operating in countries where the Soviet Union has no diplomatic relations.

2. The *Estikhbarat,* or Military Intelligence, controls most of the operations against Iraqi or other nationals resident abroad. It employs embassy personnel, in particular the military attaché's office. Presumably it has a brief for duties inside the army, but no information is available on this.

In 1979 a forty-page document by Khalil al-Azzawi, director of operations of the *Estikhbarat,* was also leaked. The Strategic Work Plan set the goals of the overseas branch of the agency. These read like something out of a cheap thriller. For example, the military attaché's office, say in London, is instructed to provide regular reports on "nuclear, bacteriological and chemical warfare institutions and installations, giving as detailed information as possible on their capacities and stockpiles." Within this rubric the document demands information on particular experiments, cross-country cooperation, data on the "personal tendencies" of individual scientists who work in these institutions, and full specifications of naval bases accompanied by plans and aerial photographs.

In a separate section of the Work Plan on NATO, Ba'thist agents are instructed to uncover no less than the "structure of NATO's forces. . . . Its air, land and sea bases throughout the world, and particularly in the Mediterranean area. The armaments of its conventional and nuclear forces. The objectives of its forces in the Middle East, and their movements." Iraqi agents are recommended tactics that "suggest that the authors of the plan are not convinced that their men in foreign capitals will know how to buy a newspaper unless every detail of the transaction is spelled out for them." [9]

Still one should not dismiss such agencies too lightly. After Saddam Husain threatened in February 1980 that "the hand of the revolution can reach out to its enemies wherever they are found," several opposition leaders were assassinated in Beirut and at least one attempt was made in Paris.[10] The *Estikhbarat* assassinated Abdul Razzaq al-Nayef in London (see Appendix 1) and provided training and logistical support for the Iranian London embassy siege in May 1980. Their involvement in the assassinations of Palestinian leaders by the Abu Nidhal group through 1980 is also likely. When the Palestine Liberation Organization (PLO) tried to return the favour to Abu Nidhal while he was undergoing

9. Ibid.
10. Reported in *al-Ghad,* London, no. 6 (April–July 1980): 18.

medical treatment in a London hospital in 1979, they could not get at him because "the Iraqis had turned the hospital into a fortress."[11]

The Guardian exposed an agent of the *Estikhbarat* as having been the ringleader of the attack on Shlomo Argov, the Israeli ambassador to London, an event that provided the pretext for the Israeli invasion of Lebanon, and also revealed the existence of six separate death squads sent from Baghdad to murder Iraqi political exiles in Egypt.[12] "Death lists" uncovered in Britain prompted a Home Office investigation and demands for the protection of Iraqi students whose names were on the lists.[13] Baʿth is also suspected in the death of Napolean Bashi, an anti-Baʿth journalist of Iraqi origin assassinated in Detroit on January 11, 1983, and three other assassinations in the Detroit area between 1977 and 1980 (one student, two recent immigrant activists).[14] Prominent non-Iraqi personalities, like Ismet Vanly, a Swiss national of Kurdish origin, have also been the target of assassination attempts.[15]

Another ominous example of the methods of the *Estikhbarat,* is the case of Hans Melin, chief of the police immigration unit in Sweden. Melin was arrested on February 5, 1979, for passing classified information to Iraqi embassy officials, three of whom were expelled from Sweden that day. Melin had access to the files of some 150,000 foreign nationals living in Sweden among whom were many Kurdish political refugees. Collating information, particularly on Kurds resident in "target countries," featured prominently in the Strategic Work Plan.[16] Another foreign official, Norwegian diplomat Arne Treholt, was convicted of spying for the Soviet Union and Iraq and sentenced to twenty years.[17]

3. The *Mukhabarat* or Party Intelligence, the most powerful and feared agency among the three, is a meta-intelligence organization de-

---

11. From the *Sunday Times,* August 29, 1982. For more on Iraqi connections to these operations, see *The Economist,* October 9, 1982, p. 36, and *The Guardian,* March 7, 1983.

12. *The Guardian,* March 7, 1983; March 8, 1983; and March 2, 1972.

13. The Iraqi Students Society in the United Kingdom has done a great service by compiling into a single volume more than seventy items on four years of Baʿthi attacks on Iraqis inside Britain. See *The Iraqi Embassy Agents and the Baʿthist NUIS—Terrorist Attacks on the Members of the ISS: A Documented Diary* (London, November 1982). Many reports on the death lists appear in this collection.

14. See CARDRI, *Iraq Solidarity Voice,* London, no. 10 (Spring 1983); and *Nahnu Nudeen* (Paris: French Committee Against Repression in Iraq, 1981): 83–84. The latter source documents repressive acts of Iraqi agents abroad in many countries; see pp. 75–89.

15. Vanly, who was severely wounded, described the incident in *People Without a Country: The Kurds and Kurdistan,* ed. G. Chaliand (London: Zed Press, 1980), 204.

16. See *NOW!,* September 14, 1979, p. 59, on the Melin affair and the singling out of Kurds in the Strategic Work Plan.

17. See *New York Times,* June 21, 1985, p. A3.

signed to watch over the other policing networks and control the activities of state and corporate institutions like the army, government departments, and the mass organizations (youth, women, and labour). A section of the *Mukhabarat* called the Special Security Section commands the armed party militia headed by Saddam's younger brother and Sa'doun Shakir, a member of the Regional Command. The *Mukhabarat* developed directly out of *Jihaz Haneen*, Saddam's creation during his years in the political wilderness. The paucity of information at our disposal on this institution makes it impossible to establish what relation, if any, Nadhim Kzar had to it, and whether it played a role in the 1973 affair. Nonetheless, in Ba'thist affairs political weight increases with secrecy. To the best of my knowledge, the only published acknowledgment of the *Mukhabarat*'s existence are two paragraphs in the 1974 Political Report:

> At the beginning of the Revolution, the Party undertook to build a special security apparatus [*jihaz khas*], at first known as the General Relations Bureau, later as the General Intelligence Department [*Da'irat al-Mukhabarat al-'Amah*]. It also tightened its control over the Security and Police services [*al-'Amn wa al-Shurtah*] by appointing Party members or independent patriots to sensitive posts inside them, and by reorganizing and reeducating these services in accordance with the concepts of the Revolution and the requirements of the new stage.
>
> This special security apparatus, manned entirely by Party members, has in the last few years been a model of efficiency, loyalty to the leadership, and precision in accomplishing its party security tasks. Although the personnel of this apparatus has no formal experience of security work before the Revolution, these comrades learned the arts of this work through absorbing certain aspects of the party's activities before the takeover of power through trial and error. They proved highly efficient in unmasking foreign and internal plots, and in repressing and liquidating them. This apparatus also played a crucial role in liquidating the espionage networks.[18]

Unlike other policing agencies, the *Mukhabarat* is a distinctly *political* body, not merely a professional organ of the state charged with safeguarding national security. Its first members combined professional *inexperience* with political *knowledge,* not mere loyalty. We are told that their abilities and skills as agents originated in how political they were,

18. I translated these passages from the Arabic original, because the Ithaca edition does not translate the phrase *al-Jihaz al-Khas*, the Special Apparatus. This was the name of *Jihaz Haneen* before 1968. Moreover, the Ithaca translation compounds the problem with an error in the second paragraph. See the ABSP publication, *Thawrat 17 Tammuz: al-Tajribah wa al-'Afaq* (Baghdad: ABSP, January 1974), 139.

not how unqualified they may still have been in the subtler aspects of, say, modern electrical stimulation techniques.

To sum up: under Kzar, the *Amn* conducted its operations with the brutishness that characterized Ba'thist behaviour in 1963 when untrained National Guard thugs, operating out of improvised headquarters, picked up anyone denounced as a communist or Qassem sympathizer. In 1968 these methods were reworked using the old state security apparatus headed by Ba'thist appointees. The Ba'th were small and, as the 1974 Political Report makes clear, had a hard time filling important state posts with technically competent cadres.[19] In such a setup when a boss like Kzar went sour, the whole enterprise was threatened.

In Saddam Husain's reorganization, the boss became a faceless party bureaucrat. The new system was less brittle, more complex and nuanced; instead of one big chief, it embraced a whole hierarchy of bosses controlling those below and keeping an ever watchful eye on those above. The result was virtually absolute control by the party through its own intelligence and the formalization of a system of spying on spies. Any distinctions between the *Amn* and the *Mukhabarat* under Kzar were soon blurred. All policing agencies under the Ba'th today are political, in the sense just described. The party has consumed the state, rather than the reverse. Liveliness is maintained in the system through a permanent condition of fear and insecurity that grips not only the people being serviced, but the personnel of the secret police themselves at every level of authority. Privileges and large financial bonuses can be showered upon lowly agents or their bosses at one moment, and revoked the next. The strange world of experiences that enveloped Salim and his family is also the norm inside the very institutions that ensnared them.

Our final piece of evidence on the secret police comes from a book by Dr. Fadhil al-Barak on Jewish and Iranian schools in Iraq, published in 1984. Rumour has it that Barak was appointed the new head of the *Mukhabarat* after the ouster of Saddam's half-brother, Barazan al-Takriti, in 1982. If true, his appointment speaks volumes on the scope of the reorganization undertaken by Saddam Husain; gone are chiefs whose qualifications originated in pure thuggery, and even family ties have been shunted aside. Instead, we have the true intellectual, an author who continues to write even as he presides over the most demanding job.

Barak draws attention to the unique scientific opportunities made

19. See *Political Report*, 40–42, and 110–11.

possible to him by his personal experience as an academic and member of the party, and "by virtue of the position which I am honoured to be responsible for."[20] His book was published on the direct authority of the Diwan of the Presidency and draws its material from extensive police files all carefully referenced in the bibliography. No matter how one looks at it, this is an intellectual effort of the secret police and demonstrates a capability that no such agency ever had before in Iraq. The idea for the book, Barak says, originated in a 1979 speech by Saddam Husain that drew attention to the "social and political means of sabotage practised by evil expansionist forces inside Iraq." Saddam singled out education as the preferred arena for the "mental and spiritual enslavement" of Iraqi youth by forces that included Iranian and Jewish schools in Iraq.[21]

The study notes that Jewish and Iranian schools were conceived to achieve long-range political goals. In the case of Iraqi Jewry, Zionist sources prove that since the seventh century B.C., the yearning for the land of Zion "was the principal force which suffused the soul" of every Iraqi Jew in every historical period, leading them to side with the British during the various stages of their presence in Iraq. For the modern period, Barak relies on the anti-Semitic forgery of the Tzarist police, the Protocols of the Elders of Zion. Freemasonry, he says, was the crucial link between the ambitions of the world Zionist leadership, British imperialism, and the activities of local Iraqi Jews in the service of this foreign triumvirate. But Freemasonry itself was led by the same Elders who had signed the Zionist protocols in Basle, Switzerland. They conspired to use education in the form of false ideas as the principal means by which to spread the conspiracy against Iraq. Barak's secret-police sources show that "on the road to executing the Zionist plan for the occupation of Palestine, Iraqi Jewish schools placed great and vigorous attention, albeit indirect, on education in military and espionage affairs."[22] A simi-

20. Fadhil al-Barak, *Al-Madaris al-Yahudiyya wa al-Iraniyya fi al-'Iraq* (Baghdad, 1984), 13. Barak, who obtained his Ph.D. in the Soviet Union, wrote his dissertation on the 1941 experience of pan-Arabism in Iraq. See Chapter 5.

21. Ibid., 12. Ba'thi racism is sometimes breathtaking in its crudity. For example, in 1981 Dar al-Hurriyya, the government publishing house, widely circulated a pamphlet whose title in translation is *Three Whom God Should Not Have Created: Persians, Jews and Flies*. The author is Khairallah Tulfah, former governor of Baghdad, and foster-father, uncle, and father-in-law of Saddam Husain. Persians, Tulfah says, are "animals God created in the shape of humans." Jews are a "mixture of the dirt and leftovers of diverse peoples," and flies are a trifling creation "whom we do not understand God's purpose in creating." Quotations are from a reprint in *Nahnu Nudeen*, 64–72.

22. All quotations are from *Al-Madaris*, 20, 26, and 48, respectively.

lar tale is spun about an Iranian fifth column, which is deemed to have been conspiring against the Arabism of Iraq since 539 B.C.[23]

Policemen the world over read events in their own image, and the pan-Arab vision of history as the conspiratorial machinations of outsiders was done more professionally by an earlier generation of ideologues. Barak is a policeman for whom history is merely the contextual backdrop to his real job, and it takes up a mere 10 percent of his nearly three hundred pages. What then is the main purpose of this book?

Fundamentally Barak is in the business of naming people and making lists. He provides personal information in written or tabular form on teachers, administrators, and employees in Iranian schools in Iraq (553 names accompanied by all personal particulars); a discussion attempting to establish the foreign origin of these people; a listing of every Jewish and Iranian school since Ottoman times with a history of each including numbers of graduates in various years; the names of the benefactors or trustees of these schools; the names of Jews accused of terrorism or spying for Zionism and their relationship to the Jewish schools; the names of individuals who crossed the Iranian border generations ago and illegitimately obtained Iraqi nationality for the express purpose of occupying key positions of influence in government, commerce, and the opposition; the property holdings of these "economic saboteurs"; their role in financing the fundamentalist Daʿwah party in recent years; a discussion on how 140 people of Iranian origin who had infiltrated the Central Bank and other financial institutions went about sabotaging the economy; the numbers of Jewish and Iranian merchants in different periods, classified by type of merchandise, locale, and influence on the economy; the conspiracy that led Jewish merchants to sell out to Iranian merchants in the early 1950s in Iraq; the names and activities of Zionist and Iranian secret societies; a table listing personal information on 245 Jewish members of the ICP; and so on.

Names belong to families in Iraq, not individuals; hence, we must keep in mind that the numbers of people implicated by such a book is far greater than the 1000 or so fully identified individuals. Moreover, when Barak fixes a number—for example, he says there were 3,245 Iranian merchants in Baghdad alone in the 1970s—one must assume the existence of files on 3,245 families, all of whose members are deemed part of a much larger community of fifth columnists. Barak himself em-

---

23. This particular spectre goes under the heading of shuʿubiyya (hatred of Arabism from within), a tenet of Baʿthi doctrine; see Chapter 6.

phasizes that fifth columnists placed their children and other relations in strategic locations where they could do the most damage.

This effort at sorting, naming, and classifying people must be set against the background of successive waves of deportations carried out by the Ba'th. The first of these involved about 40,000 Shi'i Kurds (called Faylis) in 1971–72. This community was a minority inside a minority and could even be excluded for being "Iranians" because they lived in the border areas. In the second half of the 1970s, up to 200,000 more people deemed to be of "Iranian origin" were denounced as fifth columnists and a spearhead for Iranian ambitions inside Iraq. These deportations started before the Iraq-Iran war, and the evidence suggests that the people involved were Arabic speaking. Barak himself implicitly admits this by telling us that many carried the Iraqi nationality obtained "illegally for the most part." [24] For some, this "fact" confirmed by Barak might be the cause of legal or moral anguish; but for him it is definitive proof of how insidious and far-reaching the real intentions of these people were. By way of illustration he provides short biographies but does not even bother to construct an individually tailored "proof" of treacherous intent and behaviour. Presumably this is given by the ideological "analysis" with which he embarked on his study. Here is a typical saboteur:

> The Iranian Ibrahim Muhammad: He entered the country in 1954, working at first as a porter [hammal] in the Shawrjah district. He began buying and selling empty wooden boxes and jute sacks. He joined up with an acquaintance to open a small shop behind the Damirchi building. After 1958 he worked as a tea importer. His business grew because of monopolistic practices with a special kind of tea that was very popular at the time, called Abu Ghazalah. He used false religious practices as a cloak to expand his influence and cover up his illegal practices. He used to hold pageant mourning ceremonies in his enormous house in the 'Utayfiyyah district. Before his deportation he owned 100,000 dinars and a large house worth another 100,000 dinars as well as a new Mercedes Benz 280S model.[25]

A distinction must be made between a secret police whose very existence assumes the presence of a genuine criminal or political counterpart, and one that does not. In the case of the American FBI and CIA, or

---

24. Barak, *Al-Madaris*, 143. For Ba'thism's conception of citizenship, see Chapter 4, "The Source of Authority." The estimate of Shi'ite deportees is taken from K. McLachlan and G. Joffe, *The Gulf War: A Survey of Political Issues and Economic Consequences*, Economist Intelligence Unit, special report no. 176 (London, 1984), 34.

25. Barak, *Al-Madaris*, 157.

even the defunct Iranian SAVAK and the Egyptian *Mukhabarat*, somebody had to be out there, however many lies were spread around about
what they were really doing or intended to do. Even the actions of agents
provocateurs who "make" the crimes they blame on others presuppose
that arrest and punishment on the grounds of suspicion alone are insufficient.

By contrast the post-1975 secret police in Iraq invent their enemies.
They do not behave as provocateurs because their victims no longer
have to do anything to become suspects. Real organized political opposition had been done away with by the time the secret police emerged
as the most powerful institution in Iraq. The Kurds were crushed in
1975 following the Algiers accord; and the leaders of the ICP, their organization a shell of its former self, were booted out of the offices they had
been given in return for recognizing the Baʿth in 1973 as the vanguard
party of a socialism they had once championed.

Today, suspects do not have to do anything to be victimized. They
are "chosen by the revolution" as Saddam put it in 1978:

> The revolution chooses its enemies, and we say chooses its enemies be-
> cause some enemies are chosen by it from among the people who run up
> against its program and who intend to harm it. The revolution chooses as
> enemies those people who intend to deviate it from its main principles and
> starting points. As for those people who protect the revolution, they are
> chosen by it to be friends.[26]

It is not unreasonable, therefore, to inform future suspects who "in-
tend" harm of what lies in store for them. Barak tells us that his book is
only the first instalment. Apparently another volume is planned on "the
presence of other foreign schools which played a despicable role in our
society—the American schools, Hikma university and other schools
and institutes—by alienating the Iraqi from his inner self for the purpose of weakening the moral spirit of our nation."[27] Turning ideological
fiction into reality is a truly Herculean task.

In the end Salim was wrong; the secret police do not actually rule
contemporary Iraq. They merely appear to do so because they alone enjoy the full confidence of the highest political authority. In fact they are
the executors of this authority's most cherished policies; this is what dis-
tinguishes the Baʿthist secret police from other less-trusted institutions.

26. Saddam Husain, *Al-ʿIraq wa al-Siyasa al-Duwaliyya* (Baghdad: Dar al-Hurriyya, 1981), 164.
27. Barak, *Al-Madaris*, 13.

Barak did not choose whom to cast as the internal enemy; this was given by Ba'thist ideology as articulated by the Leader, Saddam Husain. However, he did translate a general ideological proposition that might have gone unnoticed into lists of names. By this act he gave shape to the enemy. Henceforth, the public would know whom to shun and finger, and, more important, every citizen would know that suspects always existed, even for crimes that had not yet been committed. This gave substance to what Saddam had said in 1979 and, hence, "proved" his perspicacity, which was that much in advance of all knowable facts. No policing bureaucracy under any previous Iraqi regime had come even close to such a remarkable accomplishment.

The Army

For six decades the Iraqi army acted as an agent for internal repression. Before the Iraq-Iran war, its only engagement with a foreign power was in May 1941 when the army failed to repulse a small British force that invaded Iraq. Contributions to Arab-Israeli wars have been nil (1956), or purely token (1948 and 1967). In the October 1973 war, two divisions and a part of the air force fought on the Syrian front; but the bulk of the army was held back for deployment against Iraqi Kurds. Much has been made by the regime of its contribution to the October war, largely to conceal the embarrassing inaction of its units in Jordan during the September 1970 war against the Palestinian movement. Since independence the only army successes have been against tribesmen and defenceless civilians, events that have formed the mentality of the Iraqi officer corps in a very specific way.

The Arab world's first military coup in 1936 was led by Bakr Sidqi, the Iraqi officer who had instigated and directed the massacre of the Assyrian community three years before. A succession of coups followed until the British attack in 1941. The monarchy then reasserted control by breaking up the armed forces. In 1941, there were 1,745 officers and 44,217 soldiers; by 1943 hundreds of officers had been imprisoned or pensioned, and the soldiery was down to 30,000, two-thirds of whom were deserters.[28] In the decade following the 1948 war, the armed forces

28. In 1941–42, 324 officers were pensioned off, and by 1948, 1,095 other officers had been discharged from military service. See Hanna Batatu, *The Old Social Classes and the Revolutionary Movements of Iraq: A Study of Iraq's Old Landed and Commercial Classes and of its Communists, Ba'thists, and Free Officers* (Princeton: Princeton University Press, 1978), 30. The emergence of a politicized army bound up with the problem of Iraqi-Arab identity is discussed in Chapter 5.

were modernized once again. But, as long as the conditions that brought the army into politics remained, it seemed no amount of purging was enough. Many of the principal actors in post-1958 Iraqi politics were men who had escaped the purges of 1941. 'Abd al-Karim Qassem, the prime mover behind the monarchy's overthrow in 1958, had served as a soldier under Sidqi whom he greatly admired; Ahmad Hasan al-Bakr, the president under the second Ba'thi regime, had joined the army in 1938 and graduated from the Military Academy in 1942.

Between 1958 and 1968 there were more than ten coups and attempted coups, two armed rebellions, and a semicontinuous civil war against the Kurds. Military men held between 25 and 35 percent of all cabinet posts and "monopolized from one-half to two-thirds of the top policy-making positions. The three presidents of the republic, all prime ministers except one, all vice-presidents except one, almost all ministers of interior and defense, and many ministers of information have been ex-military men."[29] Officers were appointed to run the State Industrial Organization, factories, and act as undersecretaries to the Ministry of Industry. Such men took over key positions straight from the barracks, on the basis of a lifetime experience limited to training manoeuvres, bawling out recruits, and killing other Iraqis. With the exception of Bakr and a few other officers, they did not pass through political parties, much less civil service bureaucracies. Between 1958 and 1966, the army doubled its budget, while expenditure on development projects remained stationary or declined.[30] Expenditure on the army increased in direct proportion to the decline in military professionalism, a decline brought into sharp focus by the 1967 war.[31] The malaise highlighted by the six-day war played an important role in the Ba'thist critique of the military regime, contributing to its overthrow and the installation of the second Ba'thi regime in 1968.

What happened to the army under the second Ba'thi regime? Through the mid-1970s, the army's principal function of internal repression was accentuated by a major escalation in the levels of violence directed at the Kurds, which took on "the character of a racist war of extermination" in the words of the Kurdish Democratic Party.[32] One incident at the vil-

29. Phebe A. Marr, "The Political Elite in Iraq," in *Political Elites in the Middle East,* ed. George Lenczowski (Washington, D.C.: American Enterprise Institute, 1975), 125–26.
30. Ibid., 127–28.
31. For one observer's comments on the condition of the forces dispatched to the front from Iraq in 1967, see Edith Penrose and E. F. Penrose, *Iraq: International Relations and National Development* (London: Ernest Benn, 1978), 348.
32. Quoted in Lorenzo Kent Kimball, *The Changing Pattern of Political Power in Iraq, 1958 to 1971* (New York: Robert Speller and Sons, 1972), 156.

lage of Dakan in the province of Mosul on August 8, 1969, was brought
to the attention of the United Nations: sixty-seven women and children
were knowingly burnt alive in a cave where they had sought refuge from
artillery shelling.[33]

The last phase of the Kurdish war broke out in March 1974. In the
first month the towns of Zakho (population 25,000), and Qalaᶜat Diza
(20,000) were razed to the ground. Planes napalmed and bombed Kurdish villages and districts systematically. Hundreds of thousands of Kurds
fled the plains and their towns for refuge in the mountains,[34] including
teachers, workers, doctors, lawyers, schoolchildren, and whole families.[35] Waves of arrests, deportations, summary executions (for instance,
five Kurdish students at Baghdad University), assassinations, and public
hangings (eleven Kurdish dignitaries in Erbil) immediately followed the
outbreak of hostilities. Apart from the thousands of combatant casualties during the one-year war, Turkish news sources claimed that up to
five thousand women, children, and men too old to fight died in the
scramble to escape Iraqi Kurdistan following the collapse of the resistance. One thousand Pesh Merga fighters were shot down in cold blood
after surrendering to government troops.[36] Yet more refugees poured
into Iran.

> ᶜAli Abbas was a Pesh Merga, a soldier in Mustafa Barazani's rebel army.
> Along with thousands of his comrades he fled to Iran with the collapse of the
> revolt. He ended up in Isfahan as a hunting companion for Iranian officers. But
> there he named his new-born daughter *Ghariba*, Stranger, and when in Au-
> gust this year the Iraqi government renewed its offer of an amnesty he de-
> cided to return home. His, and some 20 other families, only just made it. . . .
>
> He had a weary and hunted look about him as he crossed. He knew that
> the Iraqi government had been deporting thousands of homecoming Kurds
> to the deep, exclusively Arab south. But, as he told the official "reception
> committee," the risk he deemed himself to be running was not just that; it
> was detention, torture, or even execution. Such, he said, were the fears of all
> returnees. He obviously could not quite believe official assurances that the
> fears were groundless, and that he would be dispatched, that very day, to his
> own village.[37]

33. Ibid., 155–56.

34. "Out of an estimated population of one and a half million, between 600,000 and
750,000 are believed to be displaced persons. Well over 100,000 have crossed the frontier
into Iran." See Edward Mortimer, *The Times*, November 27, 1974.

35. "Most of them are going through this experience for the first time. . . . their decision to come was not taken light-heartedly. For many of them, it was dictated by fear of
being made to choose between active cooperation with the Baᶜthist regime and prison or
even death." Mortimer, *The Times*, November 28, 1974.

36. See the report in the *Financial Times*, April 1, 1975, and also the March 24, 1975
issue for the condition of the refugees entering Iran.

37. David Hirst, "Rebels without Recourse," *The Guardian*, December 7, 1976, p. 2.

The measure of a regime of terror is the victims of its peace, not the casualties of its wars. Kurdish resistance crumbled following the abrupt withdrawal of the Shah's support in the wake of the March 1975 Algiers accords with Iran. And the army was now going to carry out the party policy of mass Kurdish deportations to the southwestern desert region of Iraq. Families of Kurds were bundled up in army trucks and transported to large hastily improvised camps or to Arab villages west of the Euphrates where they were settled in small groups. In areas designated for deportations by the "Higher Committee for the Affairs of the North," presided over by Saddam Husain, troops placed the villagers on trucks to be carried off at night in long caravans along sealed routes. Having reached their destinations families were supplied with a tent, and grouped in fives in so-called villages. Movement was prohibited except for official business. The men were assigned jobs at a fixed pay.

Eighty-five percent of all those Kurds and their families who returned to Iraq on the strength of the general amnesty, or who were driven out by the Shah's troops, were sent to these desert camps. The Ba'th tried to relocate all Kurds from the provinces of Diyala (the districts of al-Sa'diyya, Khanaqin, Shahraban, Mandali), Kirkuk (Kifri, Tuzkhurmatu), and Mosul (Safin, Sinjar, 'Ain Zaleh). Stories began filtering out of soldiers serving in these camps who broke down in emotion at the sight of this proud mountain people scrambling in the dust after the water trucks trundling along prescribed routes and doling out the precious liquid in officially prescribed amounts.[38] The number of people affected by this policy will not be known until the files are opened. Estimates range from 50,000 given by *The Economist*, in an article that praised the Ba'th for "being generous with internal reforms," to 300,000 to 350,000 given by Kurdish and Iraqi opposition sources.[39] That a crime of this magnitude is still shrouded in ambiguity speaks volumes on the nature of the Ba'thi regime.

38. This description of the deportations is summarized from a fifteen-page handwritten report by eye-witnesses obtained from Kurdish opposition sources. The document also describes Ba'th party organization in Iraqi Kurdistan, naming the bureaucrats in positions of authority wherever known. It touches upon the reverse practice of Arabizing the depopulated areas and the new laws promulgated to effect these demographic changes, and concludes with the deterioration in the health of families incarcerated in the desert camps.

39. *The Economist*, November 27, 1976, p. 85. Hirst notes that the 50,000 figure was given to journalists by a Kurdish stooge, Bakr Pizhdari, a less reliable source than the Ba'th themselves. He goes on: "The most Iraqi officials will admit is that villages have indeed been removed from a 10-kilometre security belt along the Iranian frontier. . . . They do not admit that the same thing is happening on the Syrian frontier. It is, nonetheless. The village of Fishkabur, reports a western pipeline engineer, was untouched on his first visit there, but a deserted ruin on his next." *The Guardian*, December 7, 1976, p. 2.

But the army that carried out party policy in the second half of the 1970s was different from the one that waltzed in and out of governments in the 1960s. It had metamorphosed into a creature of the Baʿth party. Three things account for this.

The first change was the comprehensive series of purges of all influential high-ranking officers (see Appendix). The purges began with those outside the party and potentially least enthusiastic about the new regime (Nayef, Daud, Ansari, Uqaili); then affected party members whose power had originated in the armed forces (Hardan al-Takriti, ʿAmmash, Naqib, Nasrat); and finally reached Ahmad Hasan al-Bakr himself and his supporters in 1979 (see Chapter 2). Out of thirty-five names, at least sixteen were officers of the highest rank. The sequence, therefore, graphically depicts the stages of the institutionalization of the Baʿth in Iraq.

Purging the first group was a foregone conclusion; one can but stand in awe at the naiveté of officers like Nayef and Daud who played an important role in the overthrow of the ʿAref regime, had no intention of becoming Baʿthists, and actually believed Baʿthist promises. Among the second group, the crucial link was Hardan al-Takriti who served as commander of the air force in the 1963 Baʿthi regime and became chief of staff and minister of defence in 1968. Like Bakr and Saddam Husain, he came from the town of Takrit. In 1963 he sided against the civilian leadership of his own party. The device employed in his ouster was the encouragement of rivalry between him and ʿAmmash, another very prominent Baʿthi officer in charge of the Ministry of Interior. The civilian wing of the party, instigated by Saddam Husain, backed ʿAmmash, the weaker personality of the two. With the exacerbation of tensions, Bakr became convinced of the need to assert his own leadership in the interests of party unity. ʿAmmash and Takriti were both appointed vice-presidents on April 3, 1970. This outward promotion concealed their loss of the two most sensitive positions in the state (Defence and Interior). The coup-de-grace was delivered to Takriti while he was abroad in the form of a dismissal and an ambassadorial appointment, which he contemptuously rejected (later purgees learnt the wisdom of swallowing their pride). Shortly after, he was gunned down in Kuwait by four assailants who were never caught.[40] Other officer Baʿthists fell more easily. Purges of junior officers and even soldiers were also common in the early years. A party member once confided to David Hirst that "when I saw hundreds of professional soldiers being dismissed, I was worried about

---

40. Majid Khadduri, *Socialist Iraq: A Study in Iraqi Politics Since 1968,* (Washington D.C.: The Middle East Institute, 1978), 57–61.

our army's fighting abilities, but the October war and the campaign against the Kurds showed how wrong I was."[41]

The 1974 Political Report drew this balance sheet of the policy of purges inside the armed forces:

> From the earliest days, the Party had urgently . . . to consolidate its leadership in the armed forces; to purge them of suspect elements, conspirators and adventurers; to cultivate Pan-Arab and socialist principles among the soldiers; to establish the ideological and military criteria which would enable the armed forces to do their duty as well as possible and would immunize them against the deviations which the Kassem and Arif regimes and their military aristocrats had committed in the army's name; and thus to integrate the armed forces with the people's movement, directed by the Party.[42]

The second change leading to the consolidation of the party was the establishment of a new system of accountability in which party men could thwart the orders of their senior non-Ba'thist officers if they suspected them. Party members who generally had secondary-school education received intensive training at the Military College for six, twelve, or twenty-four months, depending on their location in the military hierarchy. Inside the army they remained under discipline not to carry out important orders without party approval. The officer elite was atomized by this parallel authority, and its ability to maintain a group identity not subordinated to party policy disintegrated.

> The Party has managed in the last few years to install its own, very substantial and effective organization in the armed forces. Supervised by the Party leadership, it has played its part as an avant-garde. Our military comrades have given proof of their discipline and of the most staunch and enlightened loyalty to the Party. They have engaged in large-scale activity in ideology and organization in order to strengthen and extend the Party's infrastructure, so that now the Party has a vigorous vanguard which, in collaboration with patriotic officers and soldiers, constitutes the Revolution's arm and its eyes watching over the country and the people's victories.[43]

The third change was to separate ideology from the military. Comprehensive party organization robbed officers of the opportunity to see themselves as surrogates and guardians of a national identity otherwise in jeopardy. In addition to the purges and reorganizations, the degree of Ba'thist social organization profoundly undermined the historic ratio-

41. Hirst, *The Guardian*, December 8, 1976, p. 2.
42. ABSP, *Political Report*, 103.
43. Ibid., 105.

nale that had led officers into Iraqi politics time and again since independence. The Military Academy was now restricted to Ba'th party members. Officers who were anything less than totally committed to the party were pensioned off. Any political activity not conducted through the ABSP was a capital offence. *'Afaq 'Arabiyya,* a theoretical Ba'thi journal published in Baghdad summed up the policy:

> The insistence on restricting political work in the armed forces solely to the ABSP . . . springs from the fact that only their loyalty to the ABSP by itself will guarantee the maintenance of the unity of the armed forces and the performance of their national and patriotic duty. In addition it will close the road in front of those elements opposed to the people. . . .
>
> For all these reasons the Revolution and its leadership is vigilant to prevent any political element, including those in the Progressive Front [in government with the Ba'th], from activity inside the armed forces. We say from the start: "There is no front in the armed forces." Legitimate political activity inside them is solely the province of the ABSP, and execution is the revolutionary and just punishment which will be brought down on all those inside the army who work politically and are not militants of the Leader Party, the ABSP.[44]

The mere fact of a soldier's membership in what might be construed as a political organization, irrespective of actual engagement in political activity, has been a capital offence for many years now. This may have been the grounds for the 1976 executions of soldiers accused of being in the ICP. The death penalty was also decreed for any member of the military or police establishment whose service terminated "after 17 July, 1968 if his relation or work [after termination] is proved for the account or interest of any party or political authority except the Ba'th Socialist Party."[45] Virtually any breach involving the army or the police, including not reporting back on time from leave, incurred the death penalty. Finally, to have ever been a member of another party (after 1968), while serving in what is after all the conscript army, is a capital offence—a law that had to have been broken all the time.

In 1971 Saddam Husain expressed the hope that "with our party methods, there is no chance for anyone who disagrees with us to jump on a couple of tanks and overthrow the government. These methods

---

44. See "Political Work in the Armed Forces," *'Afaq 'Arabiyya* 11 (July 1978): 6. This editorial was first published in the party daily, *Al-Thawra.* Later it was reprinted as a pamphlet and translated into English for international distribution by the Ministry of Information.

45. Resolution no. 884, published in the Official Gazette, *Alwaqai al-Iraqiyya* 36 (September 6, 1978): 7.

have gone."[46] In a rare 1982 interview granted to the West German journal *Stern,* he could take the new situation for granted:

STERN: It is known that your Excellency is not satisfied with the Iraqi military command. Is it true that in the recent period 300 high-ranking military officers have been executed?

HUSAIN: No. However, two divisional commanders and the commander of a mechanized unit were executed. This is something very normal in all wars.

STERN: For what reason?

HUSAIN: They did not undertake their responsibilities in the battle for Muhammara [Khorramshahr].[47]

The executions mentioned by the *Stern* reporter belong to a new generation of purges, motivated not by ideological or power-grabbing criteria but by the issue of efficiency. Before the fall of Muhammara/Khorramshahr, rumours spread among Iraqis of massive purges among officers involved in the first setbacks. One story concerns an officer who gave the order for a tactical retreat from some position because he could not stomach mowing down waves of fanatical teenage revolutionary guards. The man was hauled up before Saddam Husain who pulled out his revolver and shot him dead on the spot, in front of an audience of course. Whether true or not, the story is doubly suggestive: first, of a society's need to bedeck its officers with noble motives (it would not have done to say that the unit and its officer were simply defeated); and second, the officer, assuming he existed, was shot for a new reason that had nothing to do with earlier generations of purges—his failure on the battlefield. Even the manner of his death is suggestive of the new reality: an army metamorphosed into a creature of the Ba'th.

Many Iraqi exiles have spent the last decade waiting for news of a military coup that would rid them of the Ba'th. Illusions in the army are deeply rooted and fostered by all varieties of pan-Arabisms and the Left who have always celebrated the armed forces as the spearhead of national rejuvenation.[48] Historically, civil society in Iraq has relied on the

46. Quoted by David Hirst in his excellent article, "The Terror From Takrit," *The Guardian,* November 26, 1971.
47. Taken from an Arabic translation of the interview in *Al-Bidaya,* 1982, a publication of the Iraqi Students Society in Hanover, West Germany.
48. Consider for instance this August 1982 editorial of the ICP in *Tareeq al-Sha'ab* 46, no. 1, printed under the headline: Noble Military Men, Organize Your Ranks and Fuse with the Struggling People. "The Iraqi army has participated in many of our people's patriotic battles . . . its well known role in detonating the glorious 14th July 1958 revolution was a great militant feat. . . . The tyrannical clique [Ba'th] has inflicted the greatest catastrophe on the army since its foundation. . . . This reality places upon the honest sons of the army . . . the task of organizing their ranks for united struggle."

armed forces to bring a sense of its own identity into political focus (1936–41 and 1958–68). Now, however, the structure of power has changed in Iraq with the Baᶜthicization of the army. An unprecedented event like the Iraq-Iran war shows that Iraqi politics has been thrust into both turbulent and completely uncharted waters.

The Party Militia

"Armed struggle" has always been an idea subordinated to building the Baᶜth party and extending its mass influence. In 1951, George Habash approached Michel ᶜAflaq with a proposal to "give the Baᶜth teeth." The suggestion was to attach his secret paramilitary organization to the Baᶜth party. ᶜAflaq did not turn the proposal down, but when he insisted as a precondition that the new cadre individually become party members, negotiations broke down. Not only was this the first practical step taken by the party to organize an armed capability, but the story is suggestive of how political the orientation of the Baᶜth was in relation to a paramilitary organization, an orientation far removed from considerations of revenge or the venting of frustrations.[49]

In Iraq, ABSP paramilitary organization dates back to the founding of the *Haras al-Qawmi,* the National Guard, organized in the late 1950s under ᶜAbd al-Karim Nasrat (murdered in 1971). The units were first used to overthrow the Qassem regime in 1963. When the first attacks on the Ministry of Defence began "the signal to go ahead was given to the Baᶜthi militia, who for the first time donned their green . . . armlets, kept in readiness; at least two thousand men, many armed with submachine guns, poured out of Aᶜzamiyya [a nationalist quarter of Baghdad]."[50] Other squads were dispatched to assassinate key figures in the regime.

Between 1,500 and 5,000 people died in three days of street fighting. The *Haras al-Qawmi* fought civilian supporters of Qassem and the ICP (only 100 soldiers were killed defending Qassem in the Ministry of Defence). A house-to-house search for communists followed based on elaborate lists prepared beforehand. In the aftermath, sports clubs, movie theatres, an entire section of *Kifah* Street, and private houses

49. George Habash and Hani al-Hindi founded their paramilitary group right after the 1948 war. The account of the incident with the Baᶜth is by Basil al-Kubaysi, a leader of the Iraqi branch of the Arab Nationalist Movement, and later the Popular Front for the Liberation of Palestine. See *Harakat al-Qawmiyyun al-ᶜArab* (Beirut: Dar al-ᶜAwda, undated), 74–94.
50. Uriel Dann, *Iraq Under Qassem: A Political History, 1958–1963* (New York: Praeger, 1969), 367.

were requisitioned by the *Haras* as temporary prisons and local head-quarters. During the nine-month Baʿthi regime of 1963, 149 commu-nists were officially executed. But this is a gross underestimate. Hundreds of people died "unofficially," and ever so horribly, in *Haras* headquar-ters. In such centers, men like Nadhim Kzar learnt the less subtle me-chanics of interrogation. Basing his account on official government sources, Batatu writes:

> The Nationalist Guard's Bureau of Special Investigation had alone killed 104 persons, the bodies of 43 of whom were found in 1963–64 buried in aj-Jazirah and al-Haswah districts. . . . In the cellars of al-Nihayyah Palace, which the Bureau used as its headquarters, were found all sorts of loathsome instruments of torture, including electric wires with pincers, pointed iron stakes on which prisoners were made to sit, and a machine which still bore traces of chopped-off fingers. Small heaps of blooded clothing were scattered about, and there were pools on the floor and stains over the walls.[51]

The army, supported by its Baʿthist officers, turned against the civil-ian Baʿthi leadership and their *Haras* in November 1963. They were disbanded but not before yet another round of fierce citywide clashes. The declaration issued by the president, ʿAbd al-Salam ʿAref, gave this justification:

> The attacks on the people's freedoms carried out by the . . . bloodthirsty members of the National Guard, their violation of things sacred, their dis-regard of the law, the injuries they have done to the State and the people, and finally their armed rebellion on November 13, 1963, has led to an intolerable situation which is fraught with grave dangers to the future of this people which is an integral part of the Arab nation. We have endured all we could. . . . But as our patience increased the non-National Guard's acts of terrorism also increased. The Army has answered the call of the people to rid them of this terror.[52]

The next time an organized Baʿthi militia made an appearance was in the wake of the July 1968 coup that ushered in the second Baʿthi regime. It emerged from clandestinity as a subsection of the party, grouped in tightly organized cells that were isolated from one another. Saddam Husain had organized *Jihaz Haneen* from this same membership, and his carefully selected cadres played a role in the coup to become even-tually the nucleus of the *Mukhabarat*, the chief executive organ of Baʿthist policies. However, unlike 1963, the militia as a paramilitary

---

51. See Batatu's moving chapter "The Bitterest of Years," in *Social Classes*, 985–90.
52. Quoted in Majid Khadduri, *Republican Iraq: A Study in Iraqi Politics since the Revolution of 1958* (London: Oxford University Press, 1969), 216.

organization did not play an important role in the coup or in the new regime in its first years. Many of its duties were handled by the secret police. Harsh memories of 1963 still lingered among the officers.

Nonetheless, the existence of a party militia always remained an extremely important component of Baʿthist ideology because of their pedagogical value as a counterbalance to the army. The party never lost its own suspicions of the army, which also dated to November 1963, and were reinforced by the struggles inside the Syrian Baʿth in 1966 that led to the expulsion of ʿAflaq and the capture of that party by professional officers. In making a balance sheet of the 1963 overthrow of Qassem, the ABSP Political Report noted that "what was planned was a people's revolution, in which military units and armed civilians fought side by side under the Party's leadership to bring about revolutionary change." However, "the hazards besetting the Revolution unfortunately prevented it from carrying out this plan thoroughly and consistently." The "Revolution" was hijacked nine months later by a "rightist military aristocracy." After 1968, the Political Report says the party considered "disbanding the old army and replacing it with a new revolutionary one." But this course was rejected as impractical in favour of the policy of purges and appointments already discussed.[53]

The militia system never evolved into the army. But it was overhauled in 1974 following the Kzar affair (when some units showed confused loyalties) along with the whole policing system. The reorganized "popular militia" or "people's army" fell under the authority of the *Mukhabarat*. By the late 1970s, with the army no longer a political force, the militia began to take on a new character. The units became viewed as auxiliary to the army, and as vehicles for party recruitment and the promotion of Baʿthi values among youth. Membership, once confined to men of the party over eighteen years of age, was expanded to non-Baʿthists in 1975 and to women in 1976. Militia members undergo a two-month annual training period and come from all walks of life (factory workers, civil servants, students). Employers are reimbursed by the government for the absences of employees, and students are excused from their studies. Many members have been involved in the Lebanese civil war. Training takes place in the militia's own schools by graduates of those schools. It includes lectures on political vigilance and Baʿthist ideology as well as weapon and tactical training. From a few thousand in the early 1970s, the popular militia mushroomed with the war to

53. ABSP, *Political Report*, 102–4.

450,000 people (in 1982).[54] Today the militia system is an experience that millions of people have passed through. Current thinking regarding the militia was first set out in the 1974 Political Report:

> Revolutionary transformation in the next phase demands our utmost effort in propagating national and Pan-Arab values and those of courage, self-sacrifice, responsibility, and respect for communal work. . . .
> . . . The military training of the masses has a special place in this domain. It must be extended to embrace the largest number of citizens, particularly the organized groups and the young. The use of weapons should be an essential component of the new man and the new society. Morever, the military training of a large number of citizens ensures that the country has a reserve army, in addition to its national army, which can contribute actively in protecting the Revolution and the country and in undertaking Pan-Arab tasks.[55]

Numbers of Armed Men

The size of the Iraqi armed forces in 1984 was 607,000 men and is probably larger today. Additionally, the popular militia was 450,000 strong, a figure that has also grown since. But these are numbers that exhibit the distorting effects of the Iraq-Iran war.

A good benchmark year for assessing the evolution of the second Baʿthi regime is 1980. The decision to go to war was probably made in the spring of that year, and no reserves were called up until after the war had started. Iraqi Baʿthism was at the peak of its powers. From one point of view, the country's future never looked brighter; economically, financial reserves were at an all-time high and oil revenues seemed everlasting; politically, the opposition was decimated and Iraq was poised to host the nonaligned nations summit, with Husain taking over leadership from Fidel Castro. Nineteen eighty is, therefore, the conclusion of the "normal" course of development of Iraqi Baʿthism before the onset of war.

By armed men, I mean those people (overwhelmingly men) institutionally charged with the infliction of violence. Clearly they don't have to be carrying guns all the time. The criterion is satisfied by the fact that they draw a wage from the state for the purpose of "defending" the homeland, policing citizens, controlling movement, surveillance, catching offenders, and anything else the Baʿth might fit into the label of "national security." How many people can be included in 1980?

---

54. Christine Moss Helms, *Iraq: Eastern Flank of the Arab World* (Washington, D.C.: The Brookings Institution, 1984), 100.
55. ABSP, *Political Report*, 175.

THE PARTY MILITIA

In the mid-1970s the popular militia numbered some 50,000 men.[56] The American Foreign Area Studies book on Iraq says that by 1978 "its strength was estimated at 100,000 or above; Iraqi leaders had expressed a goal of its reaching 200,000 by 1980. It was hoped to have these numbers formed into armed militia units in every town and village, and some outside observers believed that this latter goal may already have been achieved in 1978."[57] As soon as the war started there was a massive and largely voluntary rush to the recruiting offices. In 1980–81 the force was put at 250,000 strong.[58] In 1980, before the wartime recruits entered, the militia was probably around 175,000 people.

THE ARMY

Many sources concur on 242,000 as the number of active military personnel on the eve of war. The lowest estimate given is 222,000.[59] Conscription provides the bulk of the soldiery; every year about 120,000 men reach the age of conscription and the number formally fit for service in 1978 was 1.5 million. After serving either as a conscript or as a short-term volunteer, the men are obliged to serve eighteen years in a reserve unit with periodic training. Reserves are frequently called up on short notice to return to temporary active duty. In 1978 the reserve force was estimated at 250,000 men. Although conscription is supposed to last for two years, release is entirely discretionary, and certain categories of people have been kept for up to five years.[60]

Table 1 suggests a change after 1968. Whereas manpower grew significantly under army rule (1936–41 and 1958–68), it tripled in absolute terms in the twelve years of Ba'thist rule. There is nothing unusual about military expansion in regimes run by the army (before 1968), and for those years Iraq fits a typical Third World pattern. However, by 1977 Iraq's army was two and a half times the size of Algeria's, a com-

56. Khadduri, *Socialist Iraq,* 44.
57. Richard Nyrop, ed., *Iraq: A Country Study,* (Washington, D.C.: Foreign Area Studies, The American University, 1979), 248.
58. Helms, *Eastern Flank,* 100.
59. Ibid., 172, for the lower estimate; the higher was quoted in *The Observer,* September 28, 1980, p. 13, and *The Guardian,* September 24, 1980, p. 13. The most detailed treatment of the Iraqi army and security forces is in Nyrop, *Iraq: A Country Study,* chap. 5. Nyrop claims that by 1978 active military personnel numbered 230,000 (p. 238), which suggests that the higher estimate for 1980 is more accurate.
60. Ibid., 239–44.

TABLE I: GROWTH OF MILITARY MANPOWER
             RELATIVE TO POPULATION

Year	Main Events	Absolute Number[a] (in '000s)	Population (in '000s)	Relative Number (per 1000 people)
1933	Just after Independence	12	3,300	4
1936	First military coup in Middle East	20	3,600	6
1941	Highpoint of pan-Arabism	46	4,100	11
1943	Breakup of army after war with Britain	30	4,400	7
1949		45	5,100	9
1963	Qassem's overthrow	50	7,500	7
1967	Arab-Israeli war	82	8,500	10
1972	Ba'th in power	102	10,000	10
1977	Party hegemony	188	12,000	16
1980	War begins in September	242	13,200	18
1982	War goes on	342	14,000	24
1984	War goes on	607	14,600	42

SOURCE: Figures for military manpower by year are: 1933 and 1936, Mohammad A. Tarbush, *The Role of the Military In Politics: A Case Study of Iraq to 1941* (London: Kegan Paul, 1982), 94; 1941, Batatu, *Social Classes,* 30; 1943, Gerald de Gaury, *Three Kings in Baghdad: 1921–1958* (London: Hutchinson, 1961), 146; 1949 and 1963, Manfred Halpern, *The Politics of Social Change in the Middle East and North Africa* (Princeton: Princeton University Press, 1963), 263; 1967, 1972, 1977, and 1982, Joe Stork and Jim Paul, "Arms Sales and the Militarization of the Middle East," *MERIP Reports* 112 (February 1983): 7; 1984, K. McLachlan and G. Joffe, *The Gulf War: A Survey of Political Issues and Economic Consequences,* The Economist Intelligence Unit Special Report no. 176 (London, 1984), 48. Population figures are taken from the *Annual Abstract of Statistics* (Baghdad: Ministry of Planning, 1978), and the *Statistical Pocket Book,* 1972, (Baghdad: Ministry of Planning, 1972); figures are rounded off and adjustments are made for years not given based on estimated rate of increase.
[a] Figures exclude the reserves, police, security services, and the Ba'th militia after 1968.

parable country in many ways. By 1980, among the Arab countries, the number of Iraqi military personnel was second only to that of Egypt.[61]

61. My focus is on social weight. Actual fighting capability is not directly related to numbers; not interesting politically in peacetime; and discussed in Chapter 8 in the context of the Iraq-Iran war. Comparisons are based on figures provided in J. Stork and J. Paul,

But the more important comparison is given by the figure of eighteen able-bodied fighting men for an average one thousand unarmed citizens. This index is about twice its equivalent for Iran under the Shah at the peak of his manic military buildup, twice that of Egypt throughout the 1970s, and about twelve times that of Brazil with the largest army in Latin America. This index establishes that an unprecedented proportion of the male population was experiencing the army by 1980, and if one factors in the tightening up of the previously liberal policies of exemption from service promulgated by the Baʿth and the growth in the size and significance of the reserve units in general, the extension of the social impact of the military is even more pronounced.

Table 1 shows three periods of expansion. The first follows independence in 1932 right up to the denouement of pan-Arabism in 1941 and the short war with Britain. The second, more moderate period of growth, spans the interval between the short-lived Baʿthi regime of 1963 and 1968, a period marked by a succession of pan-Arabist military governments. Qassem's reign (1958–63) was associated with greater expenditure on equipment and salaries, but there is no evidence that manpower grew significantly. The third expansion began with the second Baʿthi regime. An important observation, therefore, is that there is a historical correlation between the ascendancy of pan-Arabism in politics and the growth of the army.

However, the big surge in numbers of the third period did not begin in 1968; it began after the high command had been purged and the structure of authority Baʿthicized (Table 1, 1972, 1977, 1980). This growth clearly posed no new threat to Baʿthist hegemony; it presupposed it. All other considerations aside, coup-making ability diminishes above a certain size threshold; power within the officer corps becomes too dispersed. But this is not an explanation of the extraordinary surge in numbers. In the past, the army had ruled directly or functioned as a force for internal suppression. Both conditions explain military growth taken separately or together. But now, the military was growing most rapidly while it was becoming apolitical and its historically central function of internal suppression was being taken over by other institutions. This tendency shifts the emphasis onto Baʿthist intentions, or internal party dynamics, and greatly magnifies the contrast in overall repressive capability between Baʿthism and all previous regimes.

THE POLICE

Under the monarchy, the police force grew from 2,500 men in 1920, to 12,300 in 1941, to 23,400 in 1958. This last figure includes 8,368 officers and soldiers of the Mobile Force, which served as the chief repressive instrument of the monarchy.[62] Between 1958 and 1968, policing resources were largely an appendage to army rule.

Comparable figures for the second Baᶜthi regime cannot be constructed because of the complete transformation in the category itself. Under "police," one must today include a number of separate agencies; relations between them are not always clear, and all are independent of the army and the party militia. They include the *Mukhabarat;* the *Amn;* the *Estikhbarat;* the Border Guards; the Mobile Police Strike Force; the General Department of Nationality; the General Department of Police, which contains the more or less normal array of specialized departments for traffic, narcotics, technical investigations, customs, local governate police, political direction, railroad security, building installation security, the police training college, *shurtat al-najdah* (emergency), and so on. All these agencies, apart from the *Estikhbarat,* are subsumed under the Ministry of Interior. The *Mukhabarat,* while not subject to this ministry's jurisdiction, probably has most of its personnel counted within (its agents are also dispersed throughout the state and in the mass organizations). The Ministry of Interior is entirely devoted to matters of policing, national security, national identity, and social control; at any rate no other labour-intensive activity is performed under its auspices (separate ministries deal with public works, housing, communications, information, culture and arts, labor and social affairs, and the usual subdivisions on the economy and foreign affairs).[63]

An eighth intelligence-gathering agency is in the Presidential Affairs Department. People in this agency could be *Mukhabarat, Amn,* a mix-

---

62. Figures from Batatu, *Social Classes,* 33.

63. Most of these agencies are described in the chapter "Policies of the Interior" in the official *Encyclopaedia of Modern Iraq,* ed. K. al-ᶜAni (in Arabic) (Baghdad: Al-Dar al-ᶜArabiyya li al-Mawsuᶜat, 1977), 2:898–911. The introduction emphasizes the "advanced achievements" of the revolution in detecting enemies of the nation, "purifying the region from spying networks," "isolating suspect, treacherous, and enemy elements who oppose in principle every progressive and revolutionary advance," and so on. The conclusion, therefore, that policing agencies not mentioned in the chapter (*Mukhabarat,* and *Amn*) are counted in the official statistics under the personnel of the Ministry of the Interior, and that policing is the main function of this Ministry, can be inferred from what the editor chose to include in his chapter and how he organized his material.

ture of both, or, as seems most likely, a special autonomous security organization directly attached to the presidency. The department mushroomed in the late 1970s when Saddam Husain became president.

Only one source has ventured to estimate the size of two of these agencies. In the second half of the 1970s,

> the Border Guards and the Mobile Force, accounted for an estimated 50,000 additional men within the security apparatus. . . . the Border Guards were stationed principally in northern Iraq along the borders of Iran, Turkey, and Syria to guard against smuggling and infiltration. . . . The Mobile Force was a militarized police strike force used to support the regular police in the event of major internal disorders. It was armed with infantry weapons, artillery, and armored vehicles, and it contained commando units that were believed to have been used against Kurdish guerrillas.[64]

Both agencies are highly specialized, and not nearly as ubiquitous as the *Mukhabarat* or the *Amn*.

Because all numbers are highly speculative, I shall proceed on the assumption that the size and growth of the Ministry of Interior and the Presidential Affairs Department provide an approximate estimate of Iraq's whole policing capability. The *Estikhbarat* (military intelligence) would be excluded from this count on the assumption that this agency has already been counted as part of the army.

The Ministry of Interior is by far the largest branch of government. Between 1976 and 1978 the number of its employees grew from 102,422 to 151,301; the Presidential Affairs Department grew from 24,073 to 57,768.[65] These were among the highest rates of growth for all twenty-three government ministries. Furthermore, in 1979 the interior minister announced the need to continue with an unspecified expansion of the internal security forces "in order to carry out transactions with citizens with the greatest possible speed."[66] Assuming, therefore, the same rate of growth of these two bodies between 1978 and 1980 as took place between 1976 and 1978 (the figures for which are available), one can estimate a total of 346,000 people for 1980. For the sake of argument, let's say one-fourth of these people have nothing to do with national security, or policing people. That leaves 260,000 various types of police and security personnel along with the bureaucrats, technicians, and civil servants required to administer and service their activi-

---

64. Nyrop, *Iraq: A Country Study*, 249.
65. 1976 and 1978 *Annual Abstract of Statistics* (Baghdad: Ministry of Planning).
66. Quoted in the party daily *Al-Thawrah*. See *MERIP Reports* 97 (June 1981): 16.

TABLE 2:   ARMED MEN RELATIVE TO POPULATION

	Absolute Number	Relative Number (per 1000 civilians)
Party Militia	175,000	13
Army	242,000	18
Police	260,000	20
TOTAL	677,000	51

ties. Even if I am wrong by a factor of fifty percent (most unlikely), then the combined numbers of police and militia will still greatly exceed the size of the standing army, and be in absolute terms twice as large as anything experienced in Iran under the Shah.[67]

SUMMARY

The overall picture in 1980, a peak year in the fortunes of Ba'thism, is shown in Table 2. One-fifth of the economically active Iraqi labour force (about 3.4 million people) were institutionally charged during peacetime (1980) with one form or another of violence. This is an extraordinary relationship, completely out of proportion with any other country that I can think of. Beyond a certain point, such numbers begin to account for every important specificity of the polity. Opposition can no longer arise except in people's minds, and then it is not really an opposition at all. In addition, the criteria used to justify this "security" are themselves continuously redefined (and have to be for the system to be self-perpetuating). A political opposition that does not exist in reality has to be invented because of the way in which the polity is constructed. Once such numbers come into play, very few things about society matter any longer (such as its class structure, confessional allegiances, the

67. An accurate comparison between the two is impossible. But Fred Halliday, *Iran: Dictatorship and Development* (London: Penguin, 1979), 76–84, estimates the size of SAVAK at thirty to sixty thousand in the mid-1970s. He identifies other policing agencies functionally analogous to the people's militia. The Imperial Iranian Gendarmerie was seventy thousand strong by the late 1970s. However, SAVAK was by far the most pervasive security instrument of the Shah's regime, responsible for a range of activities not normally associated with intelligence; it managed prisons, judged political crimes, mediated in strikes, performed overseas operations, and generally concerned itself with whatever fell under the rubric of "national security." Moreover, Iranian exiles have suggested on the basis of new information released after the 1979 revolution that previous estimates of SAVAK's size were exaggerated.

preoccupations of its intelligentsia, income disparities, and other social or political injustices).

The fact that oil revenues have made this bizarre state of affairs possible in Iraq is beside the point. These revenues were also used for development and conspicuous consumption in the oil-producing countries. Windfall income levels do not explain the political choices Baʿthism made in Iraq; they merely serve to highlight those choices from the circumscribing exigencies of development in a backward setting. Insofar as these numbers of armed men are open to a fully "rational" chain of causation, then only something intrinsic to Baʿthism can serve to explain them.

Party and State

Repressive institutions grew in tandem with party membership and employment by the state. The party organization, with all its many forms of membership, could hardly have exceeded a few thousand people in 1968. By 1976 the ABSP and its "organized supporters" were estimated at half a million. Of these, a mere ten thousand at most were full members; the rest were supporters with all of the obligations and none of the rights of full members. To enter the highest grade of party membership, "inferior Baʿthists have to go through a course of training at *Madrasat-ul-Iʿdad-il-Hizbi*—the School for Party Preparation." Moreover, "within this class the old Baʿthists and the direct participants in the 1959 attempt on Qassem's life and in the coups of 1963 and 1968 have higher standing and greater opportunities than others."[68] These figures were updated by Saddam Husain in 1980, who said: "more than one million organized persons practice democracy inside the party on a wide and deep scale, discussing the affairs of the people and what is decided [by others] about their affairs."[69] Finally, a 1984 book sympathetic to the regime made the claim that an "estimated 1.5 million Iraqis, or 10.7 percent of the total population of 14 million, are supporters or sympathizers of the Baʿth; full party members number 25,000, or less than 0.2 percent."[70] These figures are internally consistent concerning their growth over time, and are probably reliable.

Not many parties undergo such accelerated expansion. The Bolshe-

68. Batatu, *Social Classes*, 1078.
69. Iskander, *Saddam Husain*, 343.
70. Helms, *Eastern Flank*, 87.

viks grew from 23,600 members on the eve of the February 1917 revolution to 115,000 members a year later. During the civil war the party membership reached 650,000 but, on Lenin's instigation, was reduced to 472,00 by 1924. On the whole this growth was voluntary, "from below." Through Stalin's famous "Lenin enrollment," the party grew to 1,078,182 members in the two years following Lenin's death, a growth achieved "from above" by drafting unpoliticized workers and peasants en-masse.[71] This latter kind of growth resembles what happened to the Baʿth party in the 1970s.

Unlike the expansion of the party and the repressive institutions, "statification" has been going on since the 1950s, boosted by the overthrow of the monarchy and growing dependency on oil revenues, as shown in Table 3. For reasons of history and geography, the Middle East has a tradition of large state apparatuses and high levels of urbanization. However, by the late 1970s, Iraq had become an aberration even against this norm. The Shah's government, for instance, employed 800,000 people in 1977. If one includes all employees of state-run economic enterprises and financial institutions, then "10 per-cent of all those in employment could be said to be government employees."[72] The Iraqi equivalent was at least 30 percent. By combining civilian state personnel in 1980 with the army and, for sake of argument, half of the militia forces (assuming the other half are already employed by the state in some other capacity), the total is just under 1.2 million people, about half the economically active urban labour force—this in a society that is 65 percent urbanized by the official count.

Closely related but different factors were at work in the growth of the repressive institutions, the party organization, and the state apparatus. The numbers are not commensurable. Not all members of the party are employees of the state; and, although at first all militia members were in the party, by the second half of the 1970s this was no longer the case. The men of the secret police are today government employees. Hence what used to be a party intelligence system, the *Mukhabarat*, is today a state organization. Nonetheless, whereas personnel of the party and of the state were two completely different sets of people in 1968, by 1980 the picture had reversed. One million party members were inside a state

71. See E. H. Carr, *History of Russia* (London: Penguin, 1970), vol. 1: *The Bolshevik Revolution 1917–1923*, 211–13; and vol. 2: *Socialism In One Country 1924–1926*, chapter 19 on "The Monolithic Party," p. 193.
72. Halliday, *Iran*, 15.

TABLE 3:   GROWTH OF STATE EXCLUDING THE ARMY

	Number of Employees	Population (in '000s)	Relative Number (per 1000 civilians)
1938	9,740	3.8	3
1958	20,031	6.5	3
1968	224,253	8.7	26
1972	385,978	10.0	39
1976	526,578	11.6	45
1977	580,132	12.0	48
1978	662,856	12.4	53
1980	835,000	13.2	63

SOURCE: Figures for 1938, 1958, 1968, and 1972 are taken from *MERIP Reports* 97 (June 1981): 15. Remainder from *Annual Abstract* (Baghdad: Ministry of Planning, 1978). The 1980 estimate was arrived at by assuming the same rate of growth for civilian state employees between 1978 and 1980 as prevailed between 1976 and 1978.

that had itself become so bloated that it was virtually a stand-in for society as a whole. Party, state, and even civil society were merging into a single, great, formless mass.

The view of the ABSP is outlined in its 1974 *Political Report:*

> The Party . . . faced a vast and delicate task [in 1968]. Before taking power, it did not have machinery to replace the state system, as did for example the Chinese Revolution. . . . Suddenly in charge of the state, the Revolution could not simply dismantle the existing system and build a new one, as, for instance, the Russian revolution had done. . . . To abolish the whole system or to introduce radical change at a stroke would have brought total chaos.[73]

Consequently, the party adopted a programme of rapid expansion, training new members in party methods and gradually inserting this new cadre into the army, secret police, and the civil bureaucracy. "It was by a long, complex and gradual process that the necessary changes were introduced throughout the state apparatus, as well as in legislation, the information media, culture and education."[74] Looking back from the finished result, it is astonishing how determined and level-headed the party leadership was about the undertaking, despite its

73. ABSP, *Political Report*, 110.
74. Ibid.

wrenching administrative implications. Although obstacles such as bu-
reaucratism concerned them (as it had done Lenin in his last years, albeit for different reasons),[75] the party saw no alternative:

> It was not only objective circumstances which obliged the Party to adopt
> a gradual programme of appointing Party members to important govern-
> mental posts; there was also the difficult problem of cadres to whom differ-
> ent responsibilities had been assigned before the Revolution. . . . At the same
> time there was a need for extra cadres for Party work, which . . . was ex-
> panding continuously and entering new fields of activity. . . . The February
> 1963 experiment could hardly be relied on for guidance. The struggle before
> the Revolution, bringing imprisonment, exile and starvation to many Party
> members, had not allowed more than a small number of them to acquire the
> modern administrative and technological skills required. . . .
>
> For a time there was some confusion between governmental and Party re-
> sponsibility. . . . As a result, many comrades considered themselves respon-
> sible for everything, large or small, in the work of the government. . . . Such
> mistaken notions caused many difficulties and strained relations between
> Ba'thist and non-Ba'thist officials. Many Party members supposed that the
> Party's authority depended on the number of Ba'thists employed by the state,
> and on this mistaken assumption they demanded the wholesale appointment
> of Ba'thists at every level from minister to messenger. . . .
>
> The speed with which the Party had to place its members in key posi-
> tions . . . led to some unfortunate results. On being promoted, some mem-
> bers lost their sense of proportion, committed serious mistakes and became
> arrogant. The Party was often forced to reconsider its decisions and reshuffle
> its appointments. Promotion also produced a sort of impermissible competi-
> tion among some Party members.[76]

The Ba'th have saddled Iraq with two kinds of tyranny: the despot
and his means of violence on the one hand, and his bureaucracy on the
other. Salim's experience showed that these two kinds of violence merge.
But the scope of the latter is obviously far wider than the former and at
least equally implicated in the character of the new regime.[77]

In a recent book Mustafa Hijazi drew attention to the psychology of
the relationships governing bureaucracies and citizens in the Third

75. "Behind the screen of 'objectivity' and 'common sense', [some comrades] behaved
like bureaucrats, losing the vision and fervour of revolutionaries. They settled into government departments, just as the civil servants of the old regime had done, with no attempt to
develop creatively as revolutionaries, to carry their colleagues with them, to win patriotic
elements to the Party and Revolution, or to infuse into them the enthusiasm and self-
abnegation needed to expedite revolutionary change." Ibid., 111.

76. Ibid., 41–42.

77. "The greater the bureaucratization of public life, the greater will be the attraction
of violence. In a fully developed bureaucracy there is nobody left with whom one can ar-

World and coined the phrase "identification in the violence of the oppressor."[78] He argues that political administration hangs together on the basis of each level in the hierarchy of authority demeaning the one directly below with the object of keeping it "in place." The whole apparatus of state is united in regarding the citizen as an outsider placed at the very bottom of the heap. All personnel, from the lowliest clerk to the most exalted minister, treat every transaction performed as gratuitous generosity on their part. The notion of a public service, a merit system of promotions, or a citizen's inviolable right to something has always been absent. Instead, relations of conflict, diminution, and overlordship permeate all levels of the bureaucracy in its dealings with the public. Hence arises the tendency to grovel before authority, or to seek a personal solution to problems—*wasta* as it is called in Iraq. Appearances become everything in such a world. Who one is, how one dresses, and, most important, how one handles oneself is more important than rights or entitlements in the abstract.

In a more political vein, Sadiq al-ʿAzm and Fouad ʿAjami have in different ways stressed the remoteness, hostility, and disconnectedness of the Arab state from its citizenry. "The latter wish only to be left alone, and they shelter themselves from the capricious will of the state. The state—as is the case in oriental despotisms—reigns, but does not rule."[79] Both men were thinking of the failures of the state after independence, so dramatically underlined by the debacle of the 1967 war. The state reigns insofar as it maintains a monopoly over the means of violence; it does not rule because the violence that Hijazi was thinking about undercuts any form of consent. In short, such a state has in principle no authority outside of itself, or no authority in the eyes of its subjects: "It is not to the state that Arabs owe loyalty, but to their families and clans."[80] The writ of a state modelled in this way would in principle extend only

---

gue, to whom one can present grievances, on whom the pressures of power can be exerted. Bureaucracy is the form of government in which everybody is deprived of political freedom, of the power to act; for the rule by Nobody is not no-rule, and where all are equally powerless we have a tyranny without a tyrant." Hannah Arendt, *On Violence* (London: Penguin, 1970), 81.

78. Mustafa Hijazi, *Al-Takhaluf al-Ijtimaʿi: Psychologiyat al-Insan al-Maqhoor* (Beirut: The Arab Development Institute, 1980), chap. 6, esp. pp. 134–35.

79. Fouad ʿAjami, *The Arab Predicament: Arab Political Thought and Practice Since 1967* (Cambridge: Cambridge University Press, 1981), 32–33. Sadiq al-ʿAzm published his seminal indictment of the Arab state system, *Al-Naqd al-Dhati Baʿd al-Hazima* (ʿAka: Dar al-Jalil, 1969) in 1969.

80. ʿAjami, *The Arab Predicament*, 33.

as far and as firmly as the reach of its repressive capability. The Lebanese civil war provides a tragic new confirmation of these insights into the politics of legitimacy and authority in the Arab world.

There are in fact two problems here: first, the problem of the state versus civil society conceived as society less all those citizens who are inside the state; and second, the problem of authority in a state system riddled with the presumption of violence. In very small states (Lebanon) or very large societies (Egypt, Iran), the first problem outweighs the second as the formative influence on the polity. But in the case of a middle-sized country like Iraq, ruled by a party seeking "statification," the priorities can get reversed to the extent that civil society is swallowed up by the state.[81]

Having inherited a system not unlike that described by 'Ajami and al-'Azm, the Ba'th devised a novel approach to the problem of hostility and alienation from the state: they turned the people into its employees. In its old form, authority was a problem because the social base of power was limited, facilitating cyclical political change through wars and coups d'etat. In its Ba'thist form this problem withered away to be replaced by one of managing and administering conflicts within the bloated state. The system is more stable because, despite the higher levels of violence in society generally, the party on behalf of the new polity has actually manufactured its own social base, quite irrespective of whether it had one to start with. From this viewpoint, the bedrock on which the regime in Iraq rested in 1980 was its full-blown apparatus of violence comprising some 677,000 people. But as other numbers show (835,000 state employees and 1 million party members in 1980), there were still other layers between this bedrock and thin air on which the regime placed a good deal of its weight.

Not only have the Ba'th changed the terms of the problem because of these macrosocial changes, but they have injected an immeasurably larger dose of violence into the details that make up all state-mediated relationships in Iraq. Hijazi was writing about this kind of violence in Iraq not because rights that once existed were taken away, but because many of the old countervailing forces were ruthlessly uprooted (there was something to be said for *wasta* as a way of getting out of military

81. It should be noted that if the 1967 war, the Lebanese civil war, and the 1979 Iranian revolution confirmed the inherent weaknesses of those state systems, one should expect the Iraq-Iran war to test out the degree to which the Ba'thist state is different. I take this up in the conclusion.

service, for example). Authority used to be the butt of popular jokes, anecdotes, and satirical poems, cultural safety valves that provided relief from the traditional oppressiveness of the state. But all that is gone now. No one dares ridicule authority any longer in Iraq because everyone is afraid. The tone of political culture has become Kafkaesque: saturated with a sense of the impersonality of sinister and impenetrable forces, operating on helpless individuals, who nonetheless intuit that they are being buffeted about by a bizarre, almost transcendental kind of rationality.

A World of Fear

Thursday, October 30, 1969

While crossing the main Al-Nidhale Street on my way back home, holding the two orange juice powder containers with one hand and my daughter's hand with the other, a big truck approaches carrying a huge black war tank. . . . At first I don't notice that the truck is going with speed. Once I do realize that, I try to run with my daughter to catch the other side of the street quickly. As luck would have it, the two glass phials fall from my hand in the middle of the pavement and break into tiny pieces, strewing about a square meter of ground with the golden powder. For a fraction of a second I think what to do, and decide to stop with my daughter just where we are, in the middle of the pavement, assuming that the truck driver may have seen what happened. If so, he may suspect something . . . which he may exploit as a pretext against a Jew.

The truck halts close to us with a crashing noise. The driver, a fat, imposing soldier of about forty, gets down from his seat and comes running to see "what I have done." Another younger soldier, seated next to him, also comes running, with a small grey submachine gun in hand. While the driver, turning cherry-red, keeps looking with suspicious, wide-open eyes at the gold-colored powder scattered on the ground, the other soldier looks at me with sharp, burning eyes, and pointing his submachine gun towards my daughter's head as he would do in a moment of confrontation. The soldier driver shouts at me nervously: "What sort of powder have you deliberately sprayed on my path?!" I try my best to convince him and his companion that it is nothing but orange juice powder, and that the whole matter is nothing but a small accident. No use. They would not believe it. So I take some of the powder from the ground and put it in my mouth to prove to them that it is simply fruit powder. Again no use. The driver demands to see my papers, and when I show him my identity card, he orders me to accompany him to the Rashid Army Camp for questioning. Daughter, hearing this, gets scared and starts to cry. I say nothing but look at the driver for a moment. What bothers me most is that the other soldier continues aiming his gun at my daughter's head. I feel highly unnerved.

Many people gather all around by now and begin to ask silly questions. The scene lasts for about a quarter of an hour, when someone among the crowd, a decent man, approaches and asks both soldiers to get to their truck and make away, as no harm has been done and nothing of importance has occurred. A woman brings a broom from a nearby shop and starts to clean the pavement in a hurry, pushing glass and powder aside. The driver, simply feeling ashamed of himself, his anger stilled, takes his companion up to the truck. Turning back to me, he shouts: "Hey, Jew, you were wise and lucky to stop just where you were and not move! That saved you!"[1]

Sawdayee did not appreciate his good fortune. He was dealing with an army man, not a party loyalist; and there were still people on the streets whose instincts were not held in check by the presence of others, or actively sublimated in the service of more exalted aims. In later years not only would they disappear, but also the crowds would not form, either to side with hapless victims of circumstance or to glower at them. When the trucks rolled up in Shiʿite neighborhoods several years later bundling whole families and their possessions for a one-way journey to the Iranian border, hardly any force was required and no one obstructed their passage. The transition from one condition to the other in Baʿthist Iraq was achieved by an unprecedented assault on the willingness to act in public, by the inculcation of an all-embracing atmosphere of fear. The story of the fear that suffused Sawdayee's whole being and that conditioned his every reflex on that Thursday afternoon barely fifteen months into the new regime is a microcosm of the whole Baʿthist experience for all sects and religions in Iraq.

The First Spectacle

The conjuncture around which Baʿthism took power was defined by the magnitude of the Arab defeat by Israel in June 1967. Political life was traumatized. To emerge from such a state of shock, answers had to be forthcoming: the Palestinian movement in the states bordering Israel

1. Max Sawdayee, *All Waiting to be Hanged: Iraq Post Six Day War Diary* (Tel Aviv: Levanda Press, 1974), 145–46. This book is a selection of entries from a diary kept by an Iraqi Jew until his escape with Kurdish assistance in 1970. Its publication was delayed until more of Sawdayee's relations had fled via the route he pioneered. It is a unique untapped source on the early years of Baʿthist terror. I have relied on it for details on the persecution of Iraqi Jewry and the January 1969 trials. But the real importance of this document lies in the more intangible atmosphere of insecurity and fear that it conveys of an ordinary family trying to maintain its sanity in a newly emerging, topsy-turvy world.

was one such answer. In far-off Iraq, the Ba'th felt the need to come up with something equally concrete that was uniquely associated with them. The anti-Semitism that they assiduously cultivated between 1967–70 had all the hallmarks of a deliberately instrumentalist policy designed to reverse the trauma of defeat by drawing into its explanation the largest number of people possible. Tragically for the tiny remnants of Iraq's once flourishing Jewish community, it worked at their expense.

The Ba'th first staked out their claim a year before coming to power in the large September 6, 1967, demonstration that they led against the 'Aref regime. They demanded action against local agents of Zionism and imperialism and injected back into the political arena something that had been absent for many years: the idea of a fifth column specifically responsible for the devastation of the June war. The official count of Iraq's casualties during the six days of fighting was ten soldiers killed and about thirty wounded.[2] In these modest numbers the awesome reach of a pan-Arabist reference system was powerfully displayed. The ghosts of tens of thousands of Egyptian, Syrian, Jordanian, and Palestinian casualties, to say nothing of the occupation of territories, the collapse of whole armies, and the destruction of equipment—all of this was summoned up in the fantasies of ordinary men and women as the responsibility of Iraq's tiny Jewish community, whose near-total withdrawal from all facets of public life dated back to the 1940s.

In the post-Independence, Arab-Israeli era of conflict, Iraqi Jewry became social pariahs. To understand why, one must have recourse to the growing ideological hegemony of pan-Arabism in a context of increasingly bitter interstate conflict. The two main outbreaks of anti-Semitism in modern Iraqi politics (1941, 1967–70) are both firmly associated with the ascendancy of pan-Arabism; attacks on the Jewish community have not come from the Communist party, Iraqi nationalist currents, or even the traditional confessional leaders.

The pressure that the Ba'th succeeded in putting on the 'Aref regime in its last remaining months gave rise to a half-hearted series of measures against Iraqi Jewry: property transactions and liquid assets were frozen; contracts, government scholarships, and new jobs were cancelled; and quotas and other restrictions were imposed on the number of Jews accepted in Iraqi universities. Between the 1967 war and the installation of the Ba'th regime in July 1968, some one hundred Jews were

---

2. See Hanna Batatu, *The Old Social Classes and the Revolutionary Movements of Iraq* (Princeton: Princeton University Press, 1978), 1065.

jailed, of whom about forty were intermittently released; no one, however, was tortured or killed.

Within days, the Ba'th demonstrated their mastery of the art of manipulating symbols to confer a ghoulish realism to their general ideological assertions. The offices of the Iraqi branch of the Coca-Cola Company were raided and the Muslim president-owner and his Muslim manager taken away. What symbolizes the ubiquity of imperialist presence better than its most widely known commodity? Some weeks later, the mutilated corpse of the president and an ex-general manager driven insane were returned to their families. What levels of meaning had now been instilled in each innocent sip taken from the soon-to-be nationalized bottle of Coke? While the country pondered the terrifying sweep of this kind of evocation, which bound up people's rationality to their deepest fears, Jews were being picked up in ones and twos, along with former ministers, other industrialists, army officers, intellectuals, some physicians, and countless members of the independent professions.

On October 9, 1968, the government announced that a major Zionist spy ring had been broken up in Basra. Seventeen Jews were flown to a military base in Baghdad, and taken from there to a party interrogation centre. Arrests mounted through November, and on the 25th of the month Iraqi artillery units stationed in Jordan opened up in their latest valiant contribution to the war of attrition against Israel. On December 4, 1968, an Israeli air attack resulted in sixteen dead and thirty wounded; rumour had it that these official figures were gross underestimates. The following day a large party-organized demonstration started out from Liberation Square towards the Presidential Palace. Coffins of soldiers were carried in a crowd of some forty thousand people headed by party and government officials and a sizeable contingent of Palestinian guerrillas. President Ahmad Hasan al-Bakr addressed the crowd in a two-hour harangue carried live on Iraqi television:

> At the same time that we face growing pressure and repeated attacks on our heroic army, we face treacherous movements of a rabble of fifth columnists and the new supporters of America and Israel. They are hiding behind fronts and slogans which the people have seen through and exposed. These suspected and suspicious movements are undertaking the duties assigned to them and executing their role in the American conspiracy. They aim to create malicious rumour and disturbances employing for this end killings, sabotage and undertaking operations behind the front lines of our heroic army . . . with the intention of keeping us preoccupied from the great battle with the Zionist enemy.

... We shall strike mercilessly with a fist of steel at those exploiters and
fifth columnists, the handmaidens of imperialism and Zionism.[3]

Every so often Bakr cried out to the crowd: "What do you want?"
The answer would thunder back: "Death to the spies, execution of the
spies, all the spies, without delay!"

On the evening of December 14, Iraqi television presented an interview between a high-ranking party official and two Muslim accomplices
in the alleged espionage activities. After admitting their guilt (for which
the public prosecutor asked the court to commute their death sentence
to one of life imprisonment), they told their story. The plot involved
three countries (Israel, Iran, and Lebanon), a former Lebanese president
(Camille Chamoun), another Christian Lebanese politician (Henry Fi-
roun), the transfer of weaponry across the Iraqi-Iranian border going
back several years, the blowing up of a bridge in Basra (which most
people thought had been hit by a truck) and plans for similar actions,
the training of Iraqi Jews in Iran by Israeli agents, and the transfer of
vast sums from Israel through Iran to Iraqi Kurds via Iraqi Jews with the
help of a Pakistani shipping company. Among those implicated was the
agent for the Ford Motor Company in Iraq.

Iraqi Jews figured as the central villains of the plot, notwithstanding
an appropriate sprinkling of Muslims and Christians in secondary roles.
The archvillain of the piece was a kitchen-utensils merchant, a Jew from
Basra by the name of Nadji Zilkha, who communicated with Israel
from a wireless set operated out of a church, of all places. When the
regime's first batch of "spies" were brought to trial on January 5, 1969,
thirteen out of seventeen were Jews. The trial can usefully be compared
with two others: the Mahdawi tribunal during the early Qassem years
(1958–60), and the trial of Fahd and other leaders of the ICP (1947–49).
A progressive degradation in the essential quality of each spectacle is
evident.

In 1947, under the monarchy, the defendants were able to ridicule
the prosecution and reach for the public's soul, turning the proceedings
full circle against the regime. Death sentences had to be commuted to
life imprisonment. For the next two years the ICP was led by Fahd from
the Kut prison, which was turned into a debating chamber housing 125

3. The speech was published as a pamphlet entitled: *Kul shay' min 'ajl al-ma'raka*
(Baghdad: Ministry of Education and Information, 1970), 6–7. In addition to words like
"exploiters," "rabble," "riffraff," and "fifth columnists," al-Bakr is fond of some untranslatable words like *al-mashbuheen* (the suspected and suspicious ones) and *al-mutala'ibeen*
(the ones who play around frivolously with the national interest).

communists. Following the massive demonstrations of 1948 against the Portsmouth Treaty with Britain, Fahd and two other party personalities were again sentenced to hang on charges of having led the ICP while in prison. Their bodies were strung up in the capital and left for several hours. Iraqi communism was henceforth "surrounded with the halo of martyrdom."[4]

Much has been written about the revolting tactics of the head of the People's Court, Colonel Fadhil Abbas al-Mahdawi. This time the crowd could not be won over by the defendants, and it cheered and jeered as Mahdawi heaped ridicule, scorn, and abuse upon the prisoners from the ancien régime. Nevertheless, it was still possible for a former minister of the interior, Saʿid Qazzaz, to stand up and answer back, saying that he looked forward to the hangman's noose for then the true worth of all those present in the courtroom would be established as they looked up in awe at his feet swinging from the scaffold. No Iraqi old enough to remember can forget that retort.

By contrast, in 1969 the counsel for the defence introduced himself at the trial's opening session by apologizing to the prosecution for having to defend spies and stating for the record that he "would not like to see the traitors go unpunished."[5] His clients, the defendants, were afforded what at first appeared to be a small scrap of dignity as they mumbled "not guilty" to each count on the indictment amidst peals of derisive laughter from the press benches. But the Baʿthist performance rose to its true heights during the following weeks as the defendants were confronted with an inexorable unfolding of the truth, which their own conscience could not permit to be held back. They began to confess, one by one, slowly.

In death Fahd acquired superhuman stature; even Saʿid Qazzaz had been able to command a measure of public respect. But under the 1968 Baʿthi regime Jewish "spies" were deployed like mannequins on the broader stage of Baʿthi rationality. Today no one even remembers their names. From now on the victims of Baʿthist violence would go out with even greater anonymity.

The very publicity of the spectacle in January 1969 masked the erasure of the public as a self-consciously independent entity. The media and the press went berserk. Mysterious initials of fifth columnists (no names) being asked to give themselves up were flashed intermittently

4. Batatu, *Social Classes,* 569.
5. Sawdayee, *All Waiting,* 84.

across radio broadcasts. Car bombs exploded in the streets of Baghdad, and occasionally, so alert was public vigilance, the bombings were announced in the papers before they actually occurred. More and more spies were rounded up.

At first the Iraqi public entered this new world of experiences with great gusto. Later, it grew more reserved as fear took an increasing hold. Estimates on the size of the crowds that came to view the dangling corpses spread seventy meters apart in Liberation Square—increasing the area of sensual contact between mutilated body and mass—vary from 150,000 to 500,000.[6] Peasants streamed in from the surrounding countryside to hear the speeches. The proceedings, along with the bodies, continued for twenty-four hours, during which the president, Ahmad Hasan al-Bakr, and a host of other luminaries gave speeches and orchestrated the carnival-like atmosphere. Salah ʿUmar al-ʿAli, minister of guidance and a member of the RCC, addressed the chanting, spitting, stone-throwing crowd in a voice hoarse with emotion:

> Great People of Iraq! The Iraq of today shall no more tolerate any traitor, spy, agent or fifth columnist! You foundling Israel, you imperialist Americans, and you Zionists, hear me! We will discover all your dirty tricks! We will punish your agents! We will hang all your spies, even if there are thousands of them! . . . Great Iraqi people! This is only the beginning! The great and immortal squares of Iraq shall be filled up with the corpses of traitors and spies! Just wait![7]

Al-ʿAli was right. This was only the beginning. Conspiracy and spy trials became the rage over the next few years. Bakr gave speech after speech proclaiming: "One hand lies behind all the crimes."[8] In 1969

6. The lower figure is Sawdayee's (*All Waiting*, p. 98) for 9:00 A.M. on January 27. The higher figure, based on Western news sources, is quoted in Lorenzo K. Kimball, *The Changing Pattern of Political Power in Iraq, 1958 to 1971*, (New York: Robert Speller & Sons, 1973), 148.

7. Sawdayee, *All Waiting*, 99. According to Kimball, Baghdad Radio summoned people to "come and enjoy the feast," and called the hangings "a courageous first step toward the liberation of Palestine." In a retort directed at the international condemnation that accompanied the hangings, Baghdad Radio said: "We hanged spies, but the Jews crucified Christ." Moscow Radio found the proceedings "fully justified," while de Gaulle saw the hangings as an "inexorable" part of the Arab-Israeli crisis. Thankfully the Egyptian daily, *al-Ahram*, was able to maintain some dignity: "The hanging of fourteen people in the public square is certainly not a heart-warming sight, nor is it the occasion for organizing a festival." Kimball, *The Changing Pattern*, p. 148. This was the only significant international outcry about atrocities in Iraq; the reason has less to do with the activities of a Zionist lobby as the Baʿth claimed, as much as it was the outcome of the deliberately public nature of the proceedings. Later the Baʿth learnt the art of sealing out the outside world.

8. See his speech of February 8, 1969 where he links together the ouster of the 1963 Baʿthi regime, the failure of some obscure unity attempt between Iraq and Syria, the ineffectiveness of the nationalizations of the mid-1960s, the Kurdish problem, and many other

alone, official executions of convicted spies (or announcements of such executions) took place at least on the following days: February 20, April 14, April 30, May 15, August 21, August 25, September 8, and November 26. The victims now were Muslim or Christian Iraqis with the occasional Jew thrown in for good measure. In a February press conference, Bakr went out of his way to emphasize that the forthcoming batch of spies were all Muslims. The reversal had a touch of dramatic artistry. However, the bigger the catch, the more probable it was that the bait would be laced with Jews. Thus, at the trial of former Prime Minister Bazzaz, two out of the thirteen people in the dock were Jews. Having been transformed from social pariahs into fifth columnists and agents of Zionism, the presence of one or two Jews among several dozens of accused was all it took to "prove" Bazzaz guilty on a charge of spying for Israel.

Bakr was capable of being disarmingly straightforward when appraising Baʿthist strategy regarding the unearthing of conspiracies. This is what he said in a July 1969 speech:

> The crushing of spy networks has a revolutionary class meaning because of the organic connection between the spies and the oppressive exploitative classes [a code word for bourgeois, liberal, pro-West, foreign, the private sector]. It also has a tactical meaning which is within the tasks of liberation. . . . Any plan to achieve victory over the enemy must consider from the start liquidating those pockets which guarantee that the enemy has information, and that play a role in generating destabilizing propaganda thereby weakening the spirits of the people and their resolve to win. This leads to a loss of self-confidence in preparation for defeat. . . . When we became determined to wage war against the spy networks, we were aware of all of this and we knew that hitting at these networks must necessarily be accompanied by an assault on the pockets of feudal and capitalist exploitation in order to purify the nation and its economy from imperialism and its control.[9]

On January 21, 1970, a new conspiracy was foiled.[10] Executions began hours after the first announcement on Baghdad radio. In less than a week forty-four people had been executed, unknown numbers arrested, and countless properties confiscated. The conspirators were accused of acting on behalf of Iran, which had supplied them with enormous sums

---

things to "the same hand that participated in making the catastrophe of the 5th of June [1967]." See *Min Khuteb al-Raʾis* (Baghdad: Ministry of Education and Information, 1969), 15–24.

9. See Ibid., vol. 2 (no date), 58.

10. Information on this conspiracy is taken from a special pro-Baʿthi, forty-eight-page pictorial supplement of the Arabic magazine *Al-Anwar*, Beirut (1970), entitled "The Failed Conspiracy on Iraq: How Did It Begin, and How Did It End?"

of money, various sophisticated transmitters, and 130 tons of arms, all of which was elaborately displayed in a central exhibition facility in Baghdad. Piles of guns, boxes of ammunition, shelves of tapes, and wads of bills, all enclosed behind glass partitions, were the sort of lurid proof the regime provided. From a certain point of view it was not all that unconvincing; no one could disprove the existence of a conspiracy. Large demonstrations and assemblies were duly organized to publicize the invincibility of the revolution and mourn the deaths of two soldiers who fell, it seems, in a struggle with the conspirators (a nice Baʿthist detail). Taped confessions and photographs of huge arsenals were widely circulated; handwritten letters giving code words and announcing unnecessary details were made available; and wives denounced their husbands. No conspirator came out of the affair looking like anything other than a monster and an imbecile to boot. (The conspirators had planned to flood Baghdad and Sammara in the event that they could not instantly kill off all Baʿthist leaders.) The Baʿth said they penetrated the plotters a full year before they were ready to act, and placed thirty agents in their ranks. In *Al-Anwar,* the story is too perfectly told of the RCC assembling before the plotters' zero hour to follow their every move. After being picked up in little groups, they were confronted with the unimpeachable evidence of a year of footwork, confessed without exception, and were instantly shot or hanged. Lists of future ministers and proposed occupants of other government posts were collected from conspirators' pockets, facilitating the generation of more names and more evidence. The whole thing was very elaborate and must have been a nightmare to work out. Saddam Husain in a dignified statement claimed that the plot was first hatched in the immediate aftermath of the 1958 revolution; it was designed to return Iraq to Anglo-American imperialist control, under a monarchy presumably; and its precise timing was dictated by the desire to weaken the struggle against Israel, and defeat all attempts at arriving at a peaceful solution of the Kurdish dispute.

Whereas in 1970 the details of plots and "proof" still had to be submitted to the public, by 1974 Baʿthist rigour could afford to slip. In that year some 160 prominent professionals, businessmen, academics, and intellectuals were arrested on charges of Freemasonry. The arrests were sparked by the discovery in a safe-deposit box, opened by the authorities after the expiry of a fifteen-year limit, of an invitation list to a party that had taken place in 1942 at the house of a Major Chadwick who left Iraq in 1958. The average age of those rounded up must have been in the seventies; some had been fellow travellers of the ICP in the first years of the Qassem regime. The oldest victim (ninety-two) and prime culprit had in fact joined a Masonic Lodge in Bombay in 1908, a full decade before the collapse of the Ottoman Empire.[11] Imputing insidious links to a foreign power had obviously degenerated into pure farce. The stories gradually lost all semblance of even internal intelligibility. Somehow it seemed the more the Ba'th laboured to eliminate their imagined opponents, the less credible they needed to become (even to themselves) to maintain their degree of efficacy.

The meaning of the four-month spectacle that inaugurated the new Ba'thist regime and culminated in the January 1969 hangings arises out of three of its essential characteristics.

First, it was the precursor of similar but politically more important killings, all of whose focus was a demonstration to "the masses" of the concreteness of imperialist and Zionist designs on the freedom-seeking Republic of Iraq. Neither Qassem nor the communists in 1963 had been eliminated for these reasons. In an article reflecting on the events, published in *al-Thawra* on July 17, 1972, RCC member Tariq 'Aziz said:

> To be frank, the people after their experience since the 1940s and up to the [1968] revolution, doubted the intention and capability of any regime to eradicate the espionage networks.
>
> They believed that any campaign of this kind would be a fiction which would end in a kind of compromise. They even suspected that the tentacles of these networks extended into the highest levels of any Iraqi government. So the revolution set out to eradicate the networks ruthlessly and it was decided to execute the condemned men in public. One should not think that the hundreds of thousands of people who enjoyed going out to look at the hanged bodies, are barbaric or primitive. This would be an injustice and also a false impression. That event was a monument of confidence staged by the revolution in the most important square in Baghdad to prove to the people that what had been impossible in the past was now a fact that could speak for itself.[12]

Second, the January 1969 episode was not directly linked to the uncovering of a coup attempt (real or imagined) or to the whittling down of alternative power centres in the state (purges of the army or party, for instance). Yet it was the most stage-managed of all the later conspiracy trials. In this isolated respect, the January 1969 trials stand alongside the Moscow trials of the 1930s as another of this century's dra-

---

11. See the report in *The Guardian*, December 15, 1974.
12. Taken from a collection of 'Aziz's speeches entitled, *The Revolution of the New Way*, ABSP pamphlet, March 1977.

matic showcases highlighting the power of fabricated confessions when handled intelligently by a determined leadership. The Moscow trials (1936–38) involved on the face of it only a few dozen of the Bolshevik old guard. But, of course, this was only the tip of a gargantuan iceberg of terror that claimed millions of people in the bureaucracy and urban society. The Ba'th's hidden victims are still unknown but certainly will not prove to be as numerous.

The third characteristic of the 1969 spectacle, however, sets it apart from its 1930s counterpart. The January hangings, involving only a few victims but permitting mass identification with the ritual, were crucial to the legitimation of Ba'thism in Iraq. Legitimacy was a big issue for a party that had not taken power through the type of revolution in which it believed. Mass participation was evident from the gory climax in Liberation Square and discernible from the concrete reactions of people on the street while the drama was unfolding. The Moscow trials, by contrast, involving a purge of what remained of the real makers of the 1917 Russian revolution, were less spontaneous and more clinically exacting in their construction. The bond that Stalin had been working with was one that tied his person to *the party* that had led the revolution, whereas that which the Ba'th were forging was one between their party and the mass of the population (their inner-party purges were yet to come). It was taken for granted that Iraqi Jews were social pariahs, and therefore the issue was not to prove this proposition but rather to translate it into a larger demonstration of how the Ba'th were acting "in the interests of the masses" and forever watching over their security.

For both Stalinism and Ba'thism, the world of appearances is but a mask for deeper historical truths—on imperialism, Zionism, and Arab unity, in the case of the Ba'th—that are set apart from what is "on the surface."[13] The degradation of this world in which one sees, hears, and feels reality, as opposed to analytically constructing it in the imagina-

---

13. Note how the distinction between appearance and truth arises in these words of Tariq 'Aziz on why not all party members are alike: "The struggler with an honourable record who may appear today to be in the wrong, is one thousand times more beneficial to the revolution, than the person without such a record, who appears before the people to be in the right. The struggler with a true revolutionary record, has within him the urge and instinct which moves him to be in the right. But to judge a person without such a record is something like guesswork. When falsehood appears, the revolutionist must obliterate it very firmly and must not be deceived by its appearance. To stand steadfast in the face of falsehood will reveal its fallacious covering and it can be rejected." Consider, while reading them, the utter contempt he has for what is given by the facts, keeping in mind that this "appearance" is in principle all that is knowable in the context. From *The Revolution of the New Way*, 70.

tion, is therefore already a part of its innermost nature, long before specific actors came along to make it even more so. Confessions and stage-managed trials simply confirmed truths that were given a priori.

The fervent sincerity with which such a system of beliefs was held by the Ba'th party membership was matched only by the breadth of the genuine social consensus on which it rested in the Iraq of the late 1960s. Only on the basis of such a consensus, whether in the party (the USSR) or in society as a whole (Iraq), could show trials of the sort described succeed in their ghastly work. The sincerity with which the party membership believed that during 1969 they lived with "guns at hand night and day, ready to defend the Party and the Revolution against possible conspiracy,"[14] was as deeply genuine as the Iraqi public's belief that a nest of spies had actually been uncovered by the state. After all, imperialism and Zionism, being what they were, had to have spies; and, if not all, certainly some Iraqi Jews must be guilty; and if not that convincingly by their own admissions, it was safe to assume that the course of justice would be served by the workings of the law of averages when coupled to that of historical necessity.

Anything that appeared to contradict this or that detail of the underlying analysis championed by the Ba'th regarding the guilt of the accused and the plausibility of their scenario was degraded at the outset. Truth was a fortress no longer assailable by the evidence of the senses. The January 1969 spectacle elicited no sympathy for its victims. This was not the outcome of deeply embedded anti-Semitic traditions in Iraqi society; on the contrary, such traditions never existed. Rather, it was an indication of how much that society was changing. Common sense was dying in Iraq along with civil society; and while the latter was finding its grave in the enormous growth of the Ba'th party and state, Ba'thist ideology was substituting itself for the former.

Notwithstanding the publicity at the time, the January 1969 spectacle hardly ever gets mentioned in the growing number of new books on modern Iraq appearing in the West. Certainly no one has ascribed to it this significant a role in the legitimation of post-1968 Ba'thi rule. However, when one chooses to look at the Ba'th through the prism of their violence, then the January 1969 spectacle acquires this unique status. My claim is that it made an original contribution to the creation of a new kind of fear—a Max Sawdayee fear—which is now deeply em-

14. *The 1968 Revolution in Iraq: Experience and Prospects* (London: Ithaca Press, 1979), 40. Henceforth, ABSP, *Political Report.*

bedded in the Baʿthist polity, a fear that continued to grow long after the issue of Iraqi Jewry evaporated from the public imagination.

A New Kind of Fear

The January show trials stood apart from what followed because of the participation of the masses. None of the later killings of this genre gave rise to the same levels of mass participation. In fact, a note of unease had already crept into the smaller demonstrations that accompanied the February 20th public hangings of six Muslims and two Christians. As the terror struck deeper into the population—and no longer solely at its margins—withdrawal, cynicism, suspicion, and eventually pervasive fear replaced participation as the predominant psychological profile of the masses.

But it was the complicity of the masses in the first instance that elevated fear to such prominence. If this were based solely on a few demonstrations and other indications of mass support in the years 1967–70, then it would be a weak and diminishing force. However, the original complicity manifested in the first spectacle was nurtured by the regime over the years, and institutionalized in the prodigious growth of the party and state apparatuses. The post-1968 statification of Iraqi society, unlike that of other Third World countries, evolved by compromising people in the violence of the Baʿth, by sucking them into the agencies of the secret police, army, and militia. The inordinate role of fear in Iraq can only be understood from this standpoint.

Once masses of people actively engaged themselves to absorb into their individual and collective view of the world not only a set of empty abstractions about what caused what—imperialism, Zionism, Arab reaction—but also a caricaturelike "appearance" of those abstractions in the form of unpitiable demons onto which they clutched, all ingrained distinctions between the truth or falsity of what they experienced and felt began to break down. Society's view of itself as a whole made up of separated parts surrendered to an outlook in which the very separateness of the pieces had become an original sin. Through this opening all-embracing fear stalked its prey.

Compare the January 1969 show trial with another spectacle organized by the first Baʿthi regime in 1963 and designed to counter the continuing popularity of the ousted president, ʿAbd al-Karim Qassem, among certain sectors of the Shiʿite population of Baghdad. In the first week of the coup, the citizens of al-Thawra, a suburb of Baghdad, had

fought the army and Baʿthist militia in some of the bloodiest street
battles in the history of the country. They refused to believe that Qassem had been overthrown. Stories were rife that he was in hiding and
would emerge like the awaited *Mahdi* to lead the people against the
counterrevolution.[15]

The Baʿth, then led by a faction considered on the extreme left of the
party, dealt with this emotive imagery by televising a lengthy film clip
displaying Qassem's bullet-ridden corpse. Night after night, they made
their gruesome point. The body was propped up on a chair in the studio. A soldier sauntered around, handling its parts. The camera would
cut to scenes of devastation at the Ministry of Defence where Qassem
had made his last stand. There, on location, it lingered on the mutilated
corpses of Qassem's entourage (al-Mahdawi, Wasfi Taher, and others).
Back to the studio, and close-ups now of the entry and exit points of
each bullet hole. The whole macabre sequence closes with a scene that
must forever remain etched on the memory of all those who saw it: the
soldier grabbed the lolling head by the hair, came right up close, and
spat full face into it.

The fear that the Baʿth were trying to instill in this and other in-
stances was brutally direct. The centuries-old message was simple: he is
dead, you had better believe it, we can do the same to you. The fact that
it was on television extended its reach, nothing more. This kind of fear
is a powerful political force and should never be underestimated; but if
it stops there, it is shallow and ultimately transitory. The Baʿth were cast
out of power after only nine months, largely because people were re-
volted at their excesses. The broad layers of support they attracted in
the last years of the Qassem regime had eroded in the course of their
short tenure.

The contrast with the first spectacle in 1969 could hardly be more
dramatic. The terror that, from a Baʿthist viewpoint, was premature and
badly handled in 1963, worked and was skillfully deployed the second
time around. The public had changed in the sense of its greater weariness and apathy in relation to politics as a whole; more important, however, its view of its own reality was transformed from that of the previous decade. The Baʿthist post-1968 success must be largely attributed to
this change.

When the crowds first erupted on the streets in 1958 to celebrate the

15. *Al-Mahdi* is the twelfth imam of Shiʿism whose reappearance will introduce
the millennium by delivering all true Muslims from evil shortly before the transfer to
paradise.

fall of the monarchy, they spontaneously raised the banner of Arab and Kurdish partnership in a common homeland. The streets of Baghdad were emblazoned with slogans and images that attested to such a vision. There was an instinctual celebration in the fact of diversity. The Kurds were not an issue in Iraqi politics at the time, and certainly they had not been an influence within the Free Officers' movement which, if anything, had a pan-Arabist bent (Qassem excluded). The Iraqi artist, Jewad Selim, captured this unselfconscious feel for the Iraqi social fabric in his design for the new republic's national emblem. In place of the deathly eagles and guns of later pan-Arabist imagery was an original mosaic of sparkling colors and abstracted symbols of the country's constituent elements: the sun and the earth accommodating agriculture and industry, and embracing equally Arab and Kurd.

All this was dissipated in the course of the following decade. No one should consider for a moment that the Baʿthist escalation of the war against the Kurds in 1968, and the new ferocity with which they pursued it, did not have the backing of the population. Not only were the Kurds no longer "partners" but they had become "mercenaries" and agents manipulated by the CIA, Israel, and Iran. Even the concessions made to the Kurds by the regime in March 1970 were resented as going too far; and were it not for the average citizen's instinctive understanding that the Baʿth had no intention of honoring the March autonomy agreement, the regime would have had a harder time pushing it through party and public, neither of which was then the malleable putty they became in the second half of the 1970s.

The point, in brief, is that between 1958 and 1968 the self-assurance of the masses gave way to a debilitating moral vacuum as they lost or at least questioned all instinctual knowledge of themselves accumulated over several decades of a slow political emergence. Their own "truth" could no longer be taken for granted, and was open to being managed or shaped into something else. Furthermore, this possibility might even be desirable in that at least it opened up new vistas that had been checked from every other direction. In such a setting, terror laced with culpability, the fear of death becomes an inordinately powerful and positive force for holding the body politic together. The Baʿth understood this bond, and vigorously fashioned it in Iraq. Over the years, they succeeded in placing this new kind of fear at the centre of the modern Iraqi condition, and to it must be credited the durability of their rule.

Whether such a regime exists can be judged from its ability to suppress storytelling. In a very important sense, the telling of stories by word of mouth or through print, journalism, and the media, is the only way political actions as such acquire meaning. Of course, everyone tells the story as they saw it, but without all the different stories that surround a public act, no remembrance attaches to it, and the event simply ceases to exist in the collective experience of a community. This is what differentiates politics—the domain of public actions—from say artistic or intellectual creation which has as its end artifacts or ideas imbued with a meaning in and of themselves that becomes detached from the private actions of their creator.

For every sphere of life, the world of Ba'thism substitutes "analysis" sprinkled with lies for the magnificent human impulse to tell a story. People outside this world frequently associate their contempt for such a conception of the public domain with the ingrained belief that it cannot be all that effective. Such self-deception is based on the inability of these outsiders to conceive of a situation in which the telling of stories about public affairs seizes up totally for no other reason than that people are afraid. But by the late 1970s in Ba'thist Iraq, political dialogue and gossip about public affairs, once the staple diet of all gatherings and conversation, had vanished. More sensitive minds who resisted the relentless pressure to join the party became positively repelled by the mere notion of engaging in political activity; it was deemed an intrinsically degrading and contemptible preoccupation. A polity whose self-definition is that "everything is political" today comprises one of the most apolitical populations around. This profound metamorphosis of attitude was carried through in a handful of years. The result is a very vulnerable populace, unable to "think" or accumulate experience in dealing with itself, and consequently more prey than ever to believing the most fantastic lies.

Storytelling can only be suppressed through broad and graduated informer networks whose main function is not to identify malefactors, but to embroil the largest number of people in the terror of the regime. Success is achieved by the degree to which society is prepared to police itself. Who is an informer? In Ba'thist Iraq the answer is anybody. To start with, the party membership along with its organized supporters amounted to half a million people in 1976, growing to about one million in 1980. Not casual cash-for-information informers, they are a mass under discipline, expected to inform on all acquaintances, including other party members.

All members of the National Union of Iraqi Students (NUIS) and all recipients of a government scholarship in the last ten years are informers of one sort or another (which means nearly everybody studying overseas, because privately financed education is forbidden, and accepting a scholarship from an unapproved foreign source carried a penalty of five to fifteen years of imprisonment). In Britain the National Union of Students (NUS) withdrew its recognition of the NUIS in May 1979 following the discovery of an internal directive from its executive asking many thousands of members to identify anti-Ba'th activists in British universities. The NUS then resolved to instruct its branches in the United Kingdom to adopt measures for the protection of Iraqi students not belonging to the NUIS; and to raise the problem of physical defence and protection with college administrations and the Foreign Office, and to urge the unions of other countries to do the same.[16]

Most people passing through a period of detention will routinely, even enthusiastically, inform; the act becomes a loyalty test to the state and affirms its capacity for generosity in granting the privilege of release even when it judges all charges to be unfounded. In the early 1970s, one faction of the ICP made it an absolute irrevocable condition to break off all ties and links with members, sympathizers, or contacts who passed through the hands of the security services.

Finally, there are the truly innocent. Consider this story: a child under ten in a party youth group meeting blurts out that his parents don't approve of something. The next day both parents are hauled off for "questioning." Then there is the case of a primary school teacher glancing through the newspaper at break time in the common room. She comments on the unsuitability of Saddam Husain's dress given his status as president. Along with her family, she disappears for two weeks without a trace. Upon returning, everything goes on as normal.[17]

The atmosphere created by masses of informers was described by a journalist during a visit to Baghdad:

> Diplomats are unanimous in declaring their inability to meet Iraqis. "Some leave here after three years without knowing a single Iraqi," said a representative of a neutral European country. Official business, diplomats said, is conducted in the minimum of time, with a minimum of preliminary chitchat and usually in the presence of more than one Iraqi functionary.
>
> The hotel lobbies are occupied day and night with idle men filling most available seats, playing with worry beads and keeping an eye on the guests, particularly when the guests meet what in most cases are their Iraqi business contacts. This enhances the claustrophobic feeling to which most foreign

16. See the report in the *Morning Star*, May 21, 1979.
17. Both stories were related to me by third parties.

residents confess. Their sense of isolation is not diminished by the fact that Iraq admits no foreign publications.

Whatever the degree of surveillance of aliens, it is far surpassed by the controls that the regime imposes on its own people, according to diplomats and other foreigners working here. "There is a feeling that at least three million Iraqis are watching the eleven million others," a European diplomat said.

. . . The security services permeate society to a degree that "no one ever knows who's who," said an Arab specialist in a Western embassy.[18]

The quasi-institution of the *taqrir* (report) is one device employed to inculcate this atmosphere. Writing various reports is an important activity of party members. The most coveted tell on friends and colleagues. Reports may be demanded, volunteered, or routinely administered. They get handed in to party organizers at all levels of membership. For the most part, they are routine gossip sheets tailored to what the next man up wants to read. Still, they form the essential backbone in a system designed to suppress storytelling through the elevation of lies, hypocrisy, innuendo, malicious slander, and betrayal. For the system to work the truth value of a report is irrelevant. The simple fact of its existence is enough to generate the appropriate atmosphere of suspicion and fear, and to implicate with impeccable proof broad layers of people in the violence of the regime.

Nothing fragments group solidarity and self-confidence like the gnawing suspicion of having an informer in your midst. Therefore, to the extent that the public polices itself—a function of the number of informers—it inevitably disintegrates as an entity in its own right, separated from those who rule over it. Informer networks invade privacy and choke off all willingness to act in public or reflect upon politics, replacing these urges with a now deeply instilled caution. In so doing they destroy the reality of the public domain, relegating what little remains to a dark and shadowy existence. In such a world the more well-known violence of state institutions—executions, "disappearances," murders, reprisals, torture—take on a new societal meaning. Nothing is as it seems and nothing can be taken for granted.

The numbers of victims are not as important as the psychological atmosphere constantly being invoked. When Amnesty International reported that in 1981 over 350 people were officially executed in Iraq, or when the Committee Against Repression in Iraq gives biographic par-

18. *New York Times*, April 3, 1984.

ticulars on 798 executions (along with 264 killings of unknown persons, and 428 biographies of unsentenced detainees and disappeared persons),[19] all of this is not a measure of the terror inside Iraq. Numbers do not capture the quality of death that remains the main issue for those still alive. In any case most victims meet a different fate. The pattern is for agents to pick someone up from work, or at night from his house. No explanations are proffered as there would be in an official killing. Unlike Central American "disappearances" in which the state denies complicity, the Baʿth give the event a macabre twist. What one assumes to be the corpse is brought back weeks or maybe months later and delivered to the head of the family in a sealed box. A death certificate is produced for signature to the effect that the person has died of fire, swimming, or other such accident. Someone is allowed to accompany police and box for a ceremony, but at no time is he or she permitted to see the corpse. The cost of the proceedings is demanded in advance, and the whole thing is over within hours of the first knock on the door.[20]

The gap between the formality and the reality of such a death can henceforth be acted out as a gigantic lie by all concerned, including the victim's family who are now able to announce the event and carry out the appropriate public mourning ceremony. The lie that lives has replaced the grisly truth buried in the casket. When the public world becomes a continuum of such lies, even opportunism—saying and doing one thing, while thinking and feeling another—gets confused. It is so permanent a condition of everyone's life, that fixed reference points around which clear judgements can form and strong opinions be held, cease to exist. An insipid formlessness and shallowness sets in on all thought and public interaction.

At the extremes, even straightforward self-serving institutional deception fades into an infinitely stranger, almost phantasmagoric underworld of human existence. Such is the case of the heavy-metal-poisoning stories that came out of Iraq in the late 1970s. Suspects, or relatives of escapees, were unsuspectingly administered long-term poisons (thallium and lead) in soft drinks offered during the course of otherwise ordinary

19. Amnesty International, *1982 Annual Report* (London: Amnesty International Publications, 1982), 329; and *Nahnu Nudeen* (Paris: French Committee Against Repression in Iraq, 1981).

20. The names, ages, and occupations of eighty-two people tortured, assassinated, executed, or poisoned in 1982 were detailed by CARDRI, *Iraqi Solidarity Voice*, London, no. 10 (Spring 1983): 8–9. Among these, many would have had their corpses delivered in the manner described. They came from all walks of life: building workers, secondary school students, civil servants, taxi drivers, tobacco workers, university students.

interrogations. Amnesty started receiving reports of this kind in May 1980, and in September of the same year they were sufficiently convinced to write to Saddam Husain urging a public inquiry. At least two people, one of whom died, have been confirmed by British doctors as suffering from thallium poisoning, and the biographies of fifteen Iraqis who died this way inside Iraq have been published abroad.[21]

The British journal *New Scientist* conducted its own investigation of the poisoning stories among Iraqi scientists:

> Shawkat A. Akrawi, a consulting industrial chemist who graduated from Leeds University, managed to "smuggle" a telephone call from a Baghdad hospital to a *New Scientist* contact. Speaking in Kurdish, he said: "The accident they arranged didn't kill me, so they gave me thallium in the hospital where I am being treated. Say good bye to everybody." The line was then cut off.[22]

Torture and bizarre practices in Iraqi interrogation centres have been going on systematically ever since 1968 with hardly a mention abroad. The activities of the Iranian SAVAK on the other hand, were covered by the international press notwithstanding the Shah's close ties to Western governments. This does not highlight the deviousness of Western intentions as much as it points to how much more closed, secretive, and terrorized society in Iraq is than its Iranian counterpart under the Shah ever was. Iraqis in exile in the 1970s, refused to go to organizations like Amnesty to publicize their plight because of almost paranoiac fear. It was not until April 1981 that Amnesty was able to document medically the mutilation of fifteen Iraqi volunteers who had escaped Iraq after being let back into the community, having been judged innocent by Ba'thist standards. Only two of these hapless victims of circumstance had ever been formally tried. According to their testimonies, the object of the torture was to probe their views, those of other people, and in some cases to press them to join the Ba'th party or sign statements denouncing alleged political affiliations.[23]

No one who has seen faces etched with the insecurity of it all can fail to understand the tragic depths of Iraqi self-withdrawal in the 1970s. This kind of fear reduces human beings to a bundle of reactive sensa-

21. Amnesty International, *1981 Annual Report* (London: Amnesty International Publications, 1981), 359; and *Nahnu Nudeen*, 148–51.

22. *New Scientist*, April 2, 1981, p. 4. This excellent report focusses on the repression of Iraqi scientists. It contains interviews with victims and describes individual cases.

23. All details from the special Amnesty Report, *Iraq: Evidence of Torture* (London: Amnesty International Publications, 1981).

tions, all keyed up for the next blow. With its emergence, civic values, comradeship, nationalism, any sense of community, and even the private capacity to reflect disappear. These sensibilities do not gently fade away; they are obliterated the instant fear of this nature takes grip of the psyche and irrespective of how highly cultivated they may once have been. Consider a situation in which ordinary apolitical students go about routine affairs at their embassy with friends posted on street corners to whom they make a periodic appearance in confirmation that they have not been kidnapped and bundled back to Iraq. Here is a state of mind teetering on the edge of rationality and originating in conditions of rampant institutional cruelty.

Cruelty and Power

Systematic institutional torture is not only a mechanism for the unearthing of "facts" relating to perceived deviancy (Iraqi criminals, for instance, are hardly ever tortured and may in fact enjoy comparatively civilized prison conditions), or for obtaining information rapidly, although this is one justification according to Latin American torturers.[24] For this reasoning does not explain the emergence of whole institutions that are crucial to what has become of politics itself. The investigatory institutions whose organizing principle is torture (whose criterion is not the number tortured, any more than the number of executions defines a system of capital punishment) usually emerge *after* all political opposition has been eliminated, and hence all immediate threats that might require "rapid" thwarting through torture. This was the case in Iraq where the enormous expansion of these agencies occurred after 1975, and not in the Ba'th's first years when the regime was still unstable.

The methods, instruments, and structures needed for effective torturing institutions in countries of the Third World normally get imported from the outside. Langguth has focussed on the role of the United States in providing technical assistance, advisors, training, and even ideological focus (a special type of Cold War mentality inculcated in the training centres) in three Latin American countries. In Iraq, this role was undertaken by the USSR and East Germany. In both cases, however, the local demand for investigatory and torturing expertise is logically prior to the availability of eager suppliers and the resources (for example oil revenues) that make the proliferation of such an "unproductive" activity possible.

Putting aside the banalities of the economistic or development school

24. A. Langguth, *Hidden Terrors* (New York: Pantheon, 1978).

theorists regarding modernity, one is compelled in the case of Iraq to consider the novel problem of the emergence of a new type of "aborted" modern individual. Unlike his Western counterpart of the eighteenth and nineteenth centuries, this individual is stamped by his or her presence in a polity that has put enormous resources into the systematic invasion of privacy, denial of individuality, and generation of fear. Torture is the apex of that system. From this standpoint the truly intractable problem of modernity in a country like Iraq is coming to terms with the emergence of a polity made up of citizens who positively expect to be tortured under certain circumstances.

The range of cruel institutional practices in contemporary Iraq— confession rituals, public hangings, corpse displays, executions, and finally torture—are designed to breed and sustain widespread fear. But these practices are also visible and invisible manifestations of power, extensions of, for example, the state's right to wage war on the nation's enemies. The first spectacle in January 1969 served a combined juridical and political function; it "punished" those who had offended the nation by supposedly betraying it to outsiders, and it reconstituted a sovereignty that had allegedly been injured from the outside by Zionism but had actually been internally shaky. The increased power of the reemerging sovereignty was visible in the splendour of the ceremony and confirmed by the numbers of people who came to participate in the occasion. Although not very different from the parades and displays of military might held every January 6 (Army Day) in Iraq, the 1969 hangings were a unique ritual, celebrating a new beginning and not the continuity or stability of power. Because of the visibility of the occasion, the display of cruelty was intentionally excessive. The point was not only to execute a judicial judgement, but to come down like a ton of bricks on the frailty of those convicted. In this very imbalance, which had to be seen and felt to be appreciated, power was affirmed.[25] The point therefore was to intensify and heighten the imbalance by being as cruel as possible.

But what about the later forms of violence, like torture and death in the shape of the sealed-box ritual? Here the intentionality is reversed. Everything is secret including the arrest, the charges, the interrogation, the extraction of the evidence, the trial, the judgement, the execution of the sentence, the kill, and finally the corpse which bears in its markings that last record of the whole affair. The punishment that was once so

25. Michel Foucault made this point in relation to eighteenth-century Europe in his book, *Discipline and Punish: The Birth of the Prison* (New York: Vintage Books, 1979), 48–49.

public and sensual, almost tactile, has become a total abstraction; it is
now the knowledge of the inevitability of a horrible and anonymous
death under certain conditions. The sovereignty that previously had to
be reconstituted is now a terrifyingly solid omniscient presence. A new
kind of fear has become the precondition for this consolidated power,
born and sustained through complicity.

Widespread corruption, or ostentatious display of wealth and status
such as flourishes in the Gulf countries (and toppled the Shah), also do
not fit in well with perfected and smoothly operating torturing institutions. Not only can fear not rule in such a context, but also the required
seriousness and singlemindedness of political intent is missing. Torture
loses its political credibility in an atmosphere of rampant corruption.
Here again the ideological austerity of Iraqi Ba'thism and its relentless
pursuit of all acts of "economic sabotage" stands in a class unto itself.

Law in the classical bourgeois sense cannot rule in a Ba'thist world
because there is no reciprocity in a fear-ridden environment. Moreover,
the law is at best gradualist in its workings, predicated on the idea of the
unchanging individual who remains responsible for his actions through
time (the underlying premise of prison). Ideal Ba'thi individuals tran-
scend the law because their identity and behaviour are totally fused with
their beliefs (see Chapter 6). The real modern Iraqi individual is always
caught up in the endless motion of becoming something else. The law is
secondary at best, and as citizens they cannot escape the logic of punishment as torture any more than they can escape the endless flurry of
edicts and commands that shower down upon their daily lives.

Under torture, the high and mighty are quite literally exposed as
being made of the same stuff as everyone else. The phenomenon of the
poor rural migrant making good in the secret police (say, Nadhim Kzar)
and then confronting a former prime minister over his bench and instruments (say, 'Abd al-Rahman al-Bazzaz) is a very powerful symbol of the
precariousness of privilege, influence, and power in this world of fear.
Perversely, torture is an egalitarian levelling operation, which in this
sense resembles the pure theory of a system based on law.

However, the object of torture is the erasure of difference; it is the
business of surgically intervening in the biological fact of irreducible individuality so as to "disprove" it in reality. The confession is proof of a
deviancy that was not thought to exist before. Victims who survive are
hardly ever the same as the persons who went in. No matter how well
the scars heal, the memory of the bodily invasion is permanent according to the testimonies of victims. This quality of searching for a pre-

supposed essence behind the appearance, of establishing it as the new reality, is at the heart of the truth that torture goes in search of. It explains why men can be torturers out of commitment and belief and not mere brutishness.

Torture is not merely about social control through the inculcation of fear any more than a prison sentence under bourgeois law is merely about vengeance. The idea must exist that power as a matter of principle and ideological necessity needs to be so pervasive that it takes over a reality capable of being perfected and hence no longer given as a constraint on power. At this juncture the more straightforward notion of social control shades into one of "making," "forming," and "molding" people. Torture is a corollary to these sorts of words in politics; its bourgeois analogue is "rehabilitation" of offensive behaviour. The objects of torture are not criminals but sick patients or morally incomplete individuals whose deviancy lies in the subjective realm, rather than in concrete transgressions. Torture goes about fashioning them anew, and if death is a frequent result, at least someone cared enough to try. When the Ba'th talk about the "new man" and the "new society" they wish to create in Iraq, these are not metaphors. They are the substantive issues of politics, present in every sphere of life: in school curricula, the media, social programs, and the disciplining of men in the army, militia, and party.

The transition from mobilizing masses for the sensual perception of power in the form of cruel spectacles, to one of personally experiencing power through fear as an abstract yet deeply entrenched and seemingly ubiquitous psychological trait, is a measure of Ba'thism's passage into modernity. The social consciousness implied by each is totally different. The later phenomenon implies a development in what might be called the literate imagination. More important, however, Ba'thism's aborted modernity derives from a new kind of entanglement with bureaucracy. Power is no longer an external force from which one can choose to withdraw into the security of home and family—by, for example, not showing up at the scene of the spectacle. Power is felt by everyone, including those who wield its instruments, because of a new kind of knowledge and experience of its inner workings. The anonymity of death in the case of the sealed-box ritual is an extension of a Kafkaesque world of experiences new to Iraq. Even the choice to treat death heroically, or as an expression of martyrdom, has been taken away from the public.

Without doubt the passage from one state to the next is associated with increasing social control. But the outcome is control of a different order from anything known in a premodern or early modern framework. From the bureaucratic party and state viewpoint, what is going on is a simple logical extension of censorship, the elimination of all freedoms, and indoctrination. The erasure of difference between individuals, or between what "belongs" to the state and what "belongs" to the individual, is passed over with the greatest of ease. From the victim's viewpoint, on the other hand, a qualitative threshold sets apart the temporary state of being afraid from the fully suffused psychological condition of being ruled through fear. During the first spectacle only a few thousand members of the Jewish community were ruled in this fashion. Ten years later definitive proof that this condition had become generalized surfaced in the shape of another spectacle.

The Penultimate Spectacle

A discussion that began with the terrorization of a tiny community of political outcasts is concluded with the sweeping 1979 purges of the top Baʿthi command. Unlike their 1968–69 bid for legitimacy with the masses, these events were party-centred and shrouded in secrecy. All that is known for certain is that Saddam Husain purged president Ahmad Hasan al-Bakr sometime in June, and took over the presidency. For a month he held hostage the families of one-third of the members of the RCC while these officials continued to sign papers and make appearances. In the meantime, he purged hundreds of their cronies, and finally executed the lot, including some of the families, following a dramatic extraordinary session of the ABSP leadership on July 20. Reports put the number of executions of high-ranking Baʿthists at around five hundred by August 1, 1979.[26] However, the full scale of killings and lesser degrees of terror at all levels of the party must be considered still unknown today.

Explanations of this purge have centred on political differences at the top levels of leadership. Issues like the assessment of the Iranian revolution, the degree of severity to employ against the Iraqi Shiʿite opposition, and differences over the union with Syria, then in full bloom, have been brought up as central ingredients in the search for "rational" motives behind the orgy of bloodletting.

The speculation suffers from a possible misjudgement of the relation-

26. Information on the purge is culled from: a confidential serialized report by a major European journal that does not permit references to itself; Al-Nahar al-ʿArabi al-Duwali, August 12, 1979; Al-Tayar, a pro-Shiʿite Iraqi opposition weekly published in London (the July 16–23, 1983, issue contains an article on fifty-seven prominent Baʿthi leaders killed in one fashion or another since 1968); personal sources. No two accounts match, but the general sense of the scale of the purge is more or less common.

ship between Saddam Husain and al-Bakr at that time. Through the first half of the 1970s, al-Bakr was more than a figurehead in Iraqi politics in the sense that his party seniority coupled with his high standing among officers was probably important in facilitating the repeated purges and growing hegemony of the civilian wing of the party over the army. His decade-long partnership in power with Saddam Husain was, to say the least, convenient for Saddam. But by the second half of the 1970s power had shifted away from the army and resided firmly inside the structures of the party. In fact, it was now pointless to distinguish between the two in that probably there was not a single officer in the country who was not also a party member, responsible to the party leadership in the first place, and watched over by party intelligence. Furthermore, if one looks closely at the background of some of the RCC members purged in July 1979, the idea that this was just another demonstration of the Ba'thist way of settling important political differences breaks down yet again. At least two of the victims, 'Adnan Husain and Ghanin Abdul Jalil, were close protégés of Saddam with no base in the party. Catapulted from minor clerical positions into the RCC at his instigation and attached to his personal office, they were already shadows of real people. Having them shot as coconspirators in a plot whose origins somehow reside in real political differences is tantamount to pulling the rug from under one's own feet.

Undoubtedly the purge marks a climactic moment in the personal emergence of Saddam Husain as "the Leader." It was also the last major publicly oriented cycle of terror prior to Saddam's launch of that spectacle of all spectacles, the Iraq-Iran war. It is fair to conclude that the 1979 purge was an important prologue to his 1980 crusade, Qadisiyyat Saddam, the term the regime reserved for this war at its start.

Whereas in January 1969 the masses both in and outside the party had been active participants, in July 1979 they were passive spectators. Consider the metaphor of a staged theatrical production being held the second time round, not for the benefit of the actors themselves, but a captive audience whose innermost fantasies were being indulged each time the curtain lifted onto a new scene. The 1979 purges were designed to transfer already existing bonds of complicity away from the party and firmly into the person of Saddam. This had become a powerful imperative of the system itself, once all political opposition had been eliminated and truly absolute power had emerged. Now even the appearance of shared power detracted from its absolutism; consequently, the party-state that the Ba'th created had to vomit out its Stalin, or its Hitler.

The production that Saddam managed had all the hallmarks of his personal style. The first to "confess" was RCC member Muhyi ʿAbd al-Husain Rashid whose whole family was held hostage. The confession was filmed and then, as one version of the story has it, shown to an all-party audience of several hundred leaders from the entire country.[27] A grief-stricken Saddam addressed the meeting with tears running down his cheeks. He filled in the gaps in Rashid's testimony and dramatically fingered his former colleagues. Guards dragged people out of the proceedings and then Saddam called upon the country's top ministers and party leaders to themselves form the actual firing squads. Neither Stalin nor Hitler would have thought up a detail like that. What Eichmann-like refuge in "orders from above" could these men dig up in the future if they were ever to marshal the courage to try and depose their Leader? Can anyone devise a more brilliant tactical move to implicate potential foes in their personal ascent to immortality, assuming brotherly love is put aside as a consideration? With this act, the party leadership was being forced to invest its future in Saddam, just as previously it had herded the whole populace into investing their future in the party. The complicity that marked the January 1969 hangings had worked its way up into the corridors of power. The terror had turned against its perpetrators as it is wont to do, but the circle of guilt and responsibility was also closing, and this does not as frequently happen.

27. The Baʿth have a weakness for making confidential video tapes of important spectacles, some of which are leaked, become impossible to suppress, and end up serving the opposite function from that originally intended. Others get described by voluble party men, and start to make the rounds. One such tape was made of Rashid's confession and the details given are from a viewer's account. I have not seen the tape myself.

CHAPTER 3

Baᶜthism and the Masses

Ideology and Organization

Experience shows that the framing of a future, in some indeterminate time, may, when it is done in a certain way, be very effective, and have very few inconveniences; this happens when the anticipations of the future take the form of those myths, which enclose with them all the strongest inclinations of a people or a party or of a class, inclinations which recur to the mind with the insistence of instincts in all the circumstances of life; and which give an aspect of complete reality to the hopes of immediate action by which, more easily than by any other method, men can reform their desires, passions, and mental activity.[1]

Napoleon called philosophers who did not approve of his imperial ambitions "ideologists," which was for him a way of dismissing them as useless intellectuals. Since Marx, more or less everyone in the Western tradition understands ideologies and their advocates as structurally related to the societies they sprout from. For Marx that structure was class-centred; for Durkheim or Lévi-Strauss it was something else. Ideologies were perceived as partial, and usually interest-biased systems of thought. For these reasons it cuts across the grain in the West to think of oneself as an ideologist, which can now be taken to imply a lack of objectivity and even irrationality in decision making.

By contrast in the Third World, since World War II, having one's own

---

1. Georges Sorel, *Reflections on Violence* (London: George Allen and Unwin Ltd., 1925), 133. Sorel was a turn-of-the-century anarchosyndicalist who glorified violence, and the idea of a permanent class war. In his argument, Sorel adopted the novel starting point of taking it for granted that he was dealing with a myth. His reasoning is an excellent formulation of what ideological thinking means to the Baᶜth.

homemade "ideology" has become a very positive thing. The search is no longer for universal "truths," as it was for Western thinkers from the time of the Enlightenment through to Marx (however Euro-centred those "truths" might have objectively been). It is for a nationally constrained set of motivating principles geared to political action, which are as true as anything else about the world, especially if they work. Third Worldism is the umbrella ideology under which all such local ideologies shelter. Almost by definition, it represents a way of looking at the whole world exclusively from the point of view and in the sole interests of the "Third World" part of it. Like all varieties of nationalism, some antiimperialisms, and nowadays Islamic fundamentalism, Third Worldism, which embraces them all, is totally uninterested in, if not actively hostile to, broader considerations on the human condition. Whatever else this may be, it no longer has the remotest connection with either Marx or Napoleon's philosophers.

The Ba'th carry this thinking to their usual extremes: everything is relative and in the process of becoming; nothing is legitimate that is not made by them; everything has a purpose derived solely from the exigencies of the movement and its goals. "Remember always," Saddam Husain once said to party militants, "the principles and experiences which are special to you are the only ones that represent final truth and which are able to respond to the task of building the new society for the Arab nation." Elsewhere in the speech he talked about cultivating within each militant an "external wall" to ward off bad influences that not only came from the outside, but manifested themselves in an unacceptable "deviant environment."[2] In another speech on the role of "flexibility" in revolutionary work, he harshly berated all those who saw flexibility as an end in itself in dealing with problems because of their failure to understand that the permanent condition "of the revolutionist in struggle is assault and confrontation," from which it was possible to depart for only the briefest of tactical manoeuvres.[3]

Ba'thist ideology, which can hardly be pinned down to a real social class in the absence of a singular Arab society, is about fabricating a parochial world view made up exclusively of social myths. These myths are culled from Arab and Islamic tradition, and organized intellectu-

2. The speech is "Recommendations to Militants." Excerpts are from Hasan Muhammed Tawalbeh, ed., *Muqtatafat Min Ahadith Saddam Husain* (Selections from Saddam Husain) (Beirut: Dar al-Tali'ah, 1979), 160 and 151 respectively. Earlier 'Aflaq had developed the same idea (see Chapter 6).
3. Ibid., 148.

ally with the help of a host of concepts borrowed from the Left. Arab unity, freedom, Arab socialism, and the struggle against imperialism and Zionism are some of the catchwords of the mythology. The combination of myths and organizing concepts like imperialism acts as a filter in relation to the outside and provides a model not for what Arab society is, or what it might realistically change into, but what it is willed into becoming.

The important thing about this ideological production is not the ideas themselves, or their correspondence to social reality, *but the initiative taken in making them real.* The myth is portrayed as a new beginning, rather than a pack of lies about the present or the past. From this standpoint the Ba'th, far from trying to insist that they are being "scientific" or "objective" as Stalinism once did, relish the act of fabrication:

> Those researchers and historians who call themselves objective might very well be presenting different viewpoints and possibilities to explain one event . . . leaving it to the reader to draw his or her own conclusions. . . . The Ba'thist must never deal with history and all other intellectual and social questions in this way. . . .
>
> . . . The writing of history must take on the same specificity as our Ba'thist way; in other words the writing of Arab history should be from our point of view with an emphasis on analysis and not realistic storytelling.
>
> When we discuss the unity of Arabs, for example, we must not occupy the young student with details about fragmentation, thereby entering into a discussion on whether or not we are one nation. It is sufficient to talk about Arabs as one nation, considering this an absolute truth, with a simplified summary on the role of imperialism in fragmenting the nation in order to weaken it and secure its control over it. . . . Also when we talk about the ABSP as the Leader party, this should be presented to the young as an accomplished fact. As to the details of how it became the Leader, this we explain by focussing on the party's accomplishments and its role in saving the Iraqi people through revolution, without worrying the student at such a stage with complex theoretical, philosophical or political analyses.[4]

Parochialism and mythmaking, the twin pillars of Ba'thist ideology, are inseparable, because both emanate from the unifying idea of a permanently hostile outside always directing its attention to Ba'thism. The world beyond reach is hostile simply because it exists, and is deemed responsible for what is not there; even the slightest corruption within

4. From a 1977 speech by Saddam Husain published in a volume containing his thoughts "on history" and how it should be taught, along with the adulatory commentaries of sixteen Iraqi professors with ever so many Ph.D.'s. Saddam Husain, *Hawla Kitabat al-Ta'rikh* (Baghdad: Dar al-Hurriyya, 1979), 25, 23, and 14.

the movement stems from it. The fullest realization of Baᶜthism, a united Arab Baᶜthist nation, is limited by the size of the Arab world. Consequently, the hostility is not overcome by merely eliminating all obstacles and achieving unity; it is in the nature of things as they are and will remain. Conversely, the only protection from the divisive assault of the outside is a perpetual motion towards greater degrees of unity or more levels of organization. The outside can only be warded off by a force derived in the first place from organization. It is not good enough to be convinced; it is necessary to be organized. The aggressive restlessness of Baᶜthism emanates from this compulsive drive.

For Baᶜthism, ideology is a framework for acting politically on the present. Although the ideology will eventually justify and legitimate everything, it is not in the first place meant to be a justification for actions the party or its Leader would have done anyway. That kind of separation between political actors and "thinkers" got left behind with Napoleon and his philosophers. The party organization and its world of myths are a single, completely inseparable entity. This unity also implies that only the myth taken as a whole is important, for the ideology is an all-or-nothing affair. But how did more and more organization make myths become real in Iraq?

THE IMPORTANCE OF BEING YOUNG

The true Baᶜthist mistrusts anyone whose intellectual formation preceded July 30, 1968. For although "it should be our ambition to make all Iraqis in this country Baᶜthists in membership and in belief," and "we aspire to make all our people in the Arab homeland Baᶜthists," the party must understand "that the young have a longer time to live. Therefore, they have a longer period of contribution to make to the constructive work of the future as required by the revolutionary transformation process." Furthermore, it is in the very nature "of the young to adapt themselves and develop in response to the new ideas and principles of the transformation process."[5]

The seriousness with which the Baᶜth treat their ideological assertions materializes in its most deadly form in their organization of youth. Primary school children are organized in the Pioneers; boys and girls between the ages of ten and fifteen in the Vanguards (*tala'iᶜa*); and

---

5. Speech by Saddam Husain delivered at a meeting of the General Federation of Iraqi Youth on February 15, 1976. Saddam Husain, *On Social and Foreign Affairs in Iraq* (London: Croom Helm, 1979), 57, 56.

youth between fifteen and twenty in the Youth Organization (*futuwwa*). These are not the boy scouts; they contribute to the revolution and the Ba'th party. The 1974 congress of the ABSP summed up the party's ambitions in this regard:

> What has so far been achieved in this domain represents only a beginning. It falls far short of the Party's ambitions and the needs of the new phase. . . . The Party itself must exert great and urgent efforts to promote the activities of youth organizations. They must come to embrace a majority of our young people, boys and girls, and contribute actively to cultivating Pan-Arab and socialist principles among them, inspiring them with the vision and educating them in the ways that will allow them fully to participate in revolutionary construction, national defence and Pan-Arab tasks.[6]

Within a few years of the eighth congress, most Iraqi youth were passing through the youth organizations. Members take oaths, wear uniforms, and are organized in a hierarchy that resembles that of the Ba'th party. The Vanguard, founded in 1973, is probably the most important among the three; it has national, regional, and local congresses that elect a "Central Office," which in turn elects a "Core Committee." None of these organizations, held together under the umbrella of the General Federation of Iraqi Youth, are formally party bodies. They belong to the state. The party has its own youth front organization called the Partisans. But as members gather in their weekly cell meetings held at school, they are instructed in party ways and general principles of "the transformation process" by the highest-ranking party members or sympathizers available. They are asked to write reports and provide other information. Although membership is not compulsory, the fear of nonconformism makes it so. Ten-year-olds on up have been organized in this way for many years now in Iraq. Their injection with Ba'thist ideas started many years before that, when they first entered school at the age of five or six.

Ba'thism's radicalism lies in its willingness to harness the power accumulated through this kind of organization to break down cherished boundaries taken for granted by society. Consider the chilling implications of these words by Saddam Husain on the private, hitherto inviolable world of the Arab family:

> To prevent the father and mother dominating the household with backwardness, we must make the small one radiate internally to expel it. Some

---

6. *The 1968 Revolution in Iraq: Experiences and Prospects* (London: Ithaca Press, 1979), 174. Henceforth, ABSP, *Political Report*.

fathers have slipped away from us for various reasons, but the small boy is still in our hands and we must transform him into an interactive radiating centre inside the family through all the hours that he spends with his parents to change their condition for the better. We must also keep him away from bad influences.

. . . The unity of the family must not be based on backward concepts, but on congruence with centralizing mores derived from the policies and traditions of the revolution in its construction of the new society. Whenever there is a conflict between the unity of the family and these mores, . . . it must be resolved in the favour of the new mores. . . .

You must surround adults [the word used is *tatwiq,* which has the sense of closing all avenues of escape] through their sons, in addition to other means. Teach the student to object to his parents if he hears them discussing state secrets and to alert them that this is not correct. Teach them to criticize their mothers and fathers respectfully if they hear them talking about organizational and party secrets. You must place in every corner a son of the revolution, with a trustworthy eye and a firm mind that receives its instructions from the responsible centre of the revolution. . . . Teach him to object, with respect, to either of his parents should he discover them wasting the state's wealth which he should let them know is dearer to him than his own; for he would not have personal property if the state did not have its wealth, and this property belongs to society. . . . Also teach the child at this stage to beware of the foreigner, for the latter is a pair of eyes for his country and some of them are saboteurs of the revolution. Therefore, accompanying foreigners and talking with them in the absence of known controls is forbidden. Plant in the child's soul a vigilance not to give the foreigner anything of state or party secrets. Also he must warn others, young and old alike, in a respectful way, that they also should not talk in front of foreigners. . . . The child in his relationship to the teacher is like a piece of raw marble in the hands of a sculptor who has the power to impart aesthetic form, or discard the piece to the ravages of time and the vagaries of nature.[7]

To dismiss these passages as the musings of a demented albeit powerful personality abstracts from the long history of a movement that has consistently laid stress on this conception of education. Michel 'Aflaq, Salah al-Din al-Bitar, Ahmad Hasan al-Bakr, and many other Ba'thi leaders were educators by profession. The thinking behind these words was incorporated in documents and speeches, over many decades of party building. However, because Saddam Husain was addressing a mass meeting of the employees of the Ministry of Education, chastising them for their shortcomings to date, the speech acquires a greater sharpness than might otherwise appear from old programs and other items of

7. Saddam Husain, *Al-Dimuqratiyya Masdar Quwwah li al-Fard wa al-Mujtama'* (Baghdad; al-Thawra publications, 1977), 14–15, 19–21.

propaganda. Behind the "will" of the party personified in Saddam, and behind the enormous organization of the Ministry of Education whose leading personnel were assembled before him, there lurked the power of the even more enormous secret police and its hosts of informers among educators in particular.

In a ceaseless drive for a "new order," each generation is to be sacrificed for the next. The very generation that had granted Ba'thism a power never dreamed possible in Iraq, and that had acquiesced while all its more independent souls were killed or driven into exile, was to be consumed on the altar of revolution. But this was to be so fiendishly organized as to transfer the burden of complicity into the psychological constitution of their children in the form of future guilt. All the other sins of Ba'thism, from its xenophobia to the mercilessness with which it liquidates both real and imagined opponents, pale into insignificance beside the magnitude of this crime. Childhood in Ba'thist Iraq is being invaded, not in some remote and general way to do with curriculum or the availability of schools, but right down in the innermost privacy of mind and personality formation.

Every family has its stories. I was told about a child barely eleven years old who blurted something out in school, got promptly questioned about it, and ended up with both parents disappearing for two months. Upon returning, daily routines were resumed as if nothing had happened. The damage done here must wreak a revenge in the form of recurrent guilt. Non-Ba'thist parents commonly put on a show of support for the regime in front of their children, or even compel them to join the youth organizations. Such conformity draws less attention and provides more security for their children.

The sense of urgency in Saddam's speech is present in the core of the analysis. Although there have been improvements, "our ambitions are greater than anything we can achieve." The speech refers to "failed experiments of the Third World," which got dissipated, "because the persons in the second ranks were either not changed or did not produce revolutionary transformations in others. They did not create firmly rooted and new revolutionary mores in society." For this reason, the responsibility of the primary-school teacher exceeds that of the secondary-school teacher, which in turn exceeds that of the university professor, who takes over morally formed students and cannot be expected to bring about "changes of essence."[8]

8. Ibid., 22, 8–9. See also p. 28.

The traditional hierarchy of status and authority in Iraq—the professor followed by secondary- and primary-school teachers—has not been inverted by Saddam Husain; it has been abolished. The primary-school teacher is merely closer to the raw material of the revolution. All educators are equally subject to police scrutiny. This equality before political authority he calls democracy. The fundamental idea is conveyed by the title of the speech, "Democracy: A Source of Strength for the Individual and Society." In a passage designed to reassure his audience, Saddam said:

> There is no contradiction between democracy and legitimate power. Let no one among you imagine that democracy weakens him, or robs him of his dignity and legitimate sphere of control. This is not true. According to the well-known balance between democracy and centralism, there is no contradiction between the practice of democracy and legitimate central control. Only those of poor understanding could imagine such a contradiction between guardianship [riʿaya] and comradely dealings, or between preservation of role and the position of leadership.[9]

The authority Saddam Husain wants to abolish is that represented in political thought by the image of the solid pyramid, in which the seat of power is the point at the apex, but real authority and lesser degrees of power are successively filtered down.[10] Each layer in the hierarchy possesses more authority than the layer below and less than the one above. This is the shape of authority in the patriarchal family and the bureaucracy of the post-independence Arab state. The traditional hierarchy of the pyramid still preserves a degree of real although diminishing freedom for each successive layer, commensurate with its "level" of authority. Saddam's scheme of things can be represented by a hollow sphere where all dots on the skinlike surface are the same and all are equally focussed on the singular point of absolute power situated in the vacuum at the centre. In this world, children are brought up to inform on their parents "with respect." The child, the least free member of the traditional Iraqi family, is put on an equal footing with his mother and father, and the latter are stripped of authority. In the "democracy" that ensues, "power springs forth in the form of a very high level of commitment to the execution of orders with precision and enormous enthusiasm. The power in this instance is not personal, it is a condition, and a

9. Ibid., 29–30.
10. See this idea in Hannah Arendt's essay "What is Authority?" in *Between Past and Future* (London: Penguin, 1970), 98.

primordial and objective force. . . . All other representations of power are false and connected to a specific time and place."[11]

Saddam urged his audience to instil in youth "a love of order." Extolled as "one of the secrets of our success in building the new society," this was the ultimate guarantee that the Ba'thist experiment would not fail like those of other Third World countries. But what is meant by order? The speech provides a partial list: valuing time and exercising economy in its use, sitting properly, table manners (half a page on the importance of eating with knife and fork as opposed to the Arab custom of using fingers), respect towards parents even as they are denounced to the state, respect for "socialist" property, and general hatred for all "bourgeois" habits (not further defined). Finally,

> the student who gets used to working through many details and types of orders, for this reason as well as others, will, when necessity calls, stand in the sun holding his weapon day and night without flinching. And when it is asked of him to confront an imperialist or an offensive assault in this volatile region, he will do it, because he became acclimatized from childhood in orderly ways of working.[12]

In the summer of 1983 a BBC television program presented interviews with teenage Iranian prisoners of war held in an Iraqi camp. In an inspired move the director injected film clips of uniformed *tala'i'a* children dressed in commando camouflage uniforms prancing about on a stage in an orderly way and chanting eulogies to Saddam and the Ba'th in front of a beaming audience of fat officers and party bosses. A dialogue of the deaf went on between a reporter and one thirteen-year-old Iranian boy; tattered, crippled, and with his head shaven, the boy projected a mesmerizing aura as he calmly looked right through his interviewer. Paraphrased, the exchange went like this:

Q: Were you not afraid while assaulting the army's position knowing that you and so many of your friends were going to die?

A: Those who died were fortunate. They honoured God and he took them into his arms. I did not fight hard enough. Maybe next time.

Q: Aren't your parents worrying for you? Wouldn't you like to be home with them, away from all this?

11. Saddam Husain, *Al-Dimuqratiyya*, 30. "Primordial" can also be translated as "principled," but in the context this word diminishes the force of Saddam's idea of the involuntary objectivity of political power when constituted according to the hollow-sphere image. The speech is underpinned by a certain conception of human nature that will triumph in a society governed by Ba'thi norms.
12. Ibid., 13.

A: Their hearts must be filled with sadness that I was not honoured by martyrdom for Islam.

Pristine faith was for this boy what order and unquestioning obedience was for his older Iraqi counterpart on the battlefield—poorly organized obscurantist fanaticism, matched against well-organized caricatures of real people. For each side the presence of both ideology and organization was essential. But in war the relative weight varied considerably reflecting the breadth and depth of the Iranian revolution. The Ba'th never built upon this kind of mass experience of revolution, and so they had to instil from above through institutions and organization that which came naturally to Khomeini "from below." But there is no reason to suppose that the parody of Ba'thism prancing on that stage was any less damaged than its Iranian counterpart; the two are simply made of different stuff.

Over 40 percent of the Iraqi population is under the age of twenty-five. Therefore, those whom Ba'thism hurled to their deaths in the Iraq-Iran war had a view of the world formed after July 30, 1968. The test of war points to a large degree of Ba'thist success in moulding the country's youth in their own image. On the other hand, if rumour is anything to go by, the rout of at least a few Iraqi units while on Iranian territory took place when the same kind of young men were ordered to mow down human waves of teenage volunteers careening down minefields in pursuit of martyrdom. It seems a few of Saddam Husain's "orderly" generation trained to "stand in the sun . . . day and night without flinching," did mercifully flinch. From this small measure of the humanity of our species, it is necessary to draw hope for the future.

THE EDUCATION OF MASSES

The fabrication of a citizenry prepared to sacrifice itself in a gruelling war entails a new mode of comprehension of an individual's place in the larger scheme of things. The religious community and traditional ethnic or kinship ties were given by birth; even the political community of pre-1958 Iraq was increasingly being accepted as a mosaic of separate parts whose integrity, although administrative, was nevertheless very real.[13] Once this umbrellalike notion of community got discarded a

13. Benedict Anderson, *Imagined Communities: Reflections on the Origin and Spread of Nationalism* (London: NLB Verso, 1983), chap. 4, has drawn attention to the importance of administrative organization in the establishment of new South American re-

problem arose as to how the population was going to identify with the Ba'thist vision. A peasant from the tribe of Albu Muhammad who lived in a village in the *Majarr* district of the province of *'Amarah* tilling the estate of Shaikh Muhammad al-'Araibi had his whole world given to him by these variables; his post-1958 urban and rural counterpart, by contrast, needed a less "organic" and more synthetic reference system. The Ba'thist appeal, resting as it always did on pan-Arabism, required permanent allegiances to be constructed differently. How were individual minds to be reached enabling some kind of bonding with the new regime to take effect in the midst of appalling backwardness?

Under the monarchy "realistic storytelling," which Saddam Husain wanted to banish, was probably the principal mechanism by which a broader sense of political community evolved in the overwhelmingly illiterate society of Iraq. Radio and television were others. Under the Ba'th, political dialogue, national political parties, spontaneous public activity, and even mundane gossip about public affairs have disappeared as an outcome of repression and the pervasiveness of fear in people's lives. Something had to fill the vacuum.

The stretched-out formation of national communities in western Europe dating back to the sixteenth century was the outcome of fresh "imaginings," to use Anderson's aptly chosen phrase. But the proliferation of printed matter and the emergence of a mass reading public, which was largely the vehicle that made the new consciousness of community possible, was at the same time deeply subversive of tradition, power, and authority; rampant storytelling in the hands of the public usually is. The irony of our times is that once it became technically feasible to suppress storytelling in a comprehensive way among huge agglomerations of people, then this very same proliferation became capable of serving entirely new ends. Stalin's obliteration of the person of Trotsky from the history of the Russian revolution despite (or is it because of?) the elimination of illiteracy is a salient example of what was now possible. If Trotsky is to be "remembered" at all at some point in the future of the Soviet Union, it will only be because his memory was kept alive in the West.

The Stalinist era is sharply separated from life in the Soviet Union

---

publics in the late eighteenth and early nineteenth centuries. Separate communities in the Spanish American empire began to "think" themselves nations, as he puts it, which accounts for the failure of a Spanish-American-wide nationalism to arise. The discussion is suggestive for the post-Ottoman Arab world.

today because the fear that choked off all storytelling in Stalin's time abated after his death, allowing an underground storytelling culture to arise. That was what Solidarity was all about—people able and intent on reclaiming, or creating anew, a public domain for themselves, making their own Gdansk heroes, and telling their little tales about the Polish bureaucracy.[14] Spain after Franco, Portugal after Salazar, and Argentina since the October 1983 elections either experienced or still are experiencing an explosion of storytelling and an exhilarating creation of a public world after many years of groping around in the dark.

In Iraq the mass consumption of printed matter and the fabrication from above of an imagined/imaginary world through party or state manipulation of all communications media has acquired the awesome power once wielded by the Soviet and Polish bureaucracies. In 1980 the Baʿth claim to have exported through their embassies, cultural centers, and party organization 9,750,000 copies of the two nationwide daily newspapers, *al-Thawra* and *al-Jumhuriyya*. In addition, they say they freighted 4,235,000 periodicals (various titles), and 18,000 copies of every pamphlet or book published by the Ministry of Education. For the internal distribution, the regime claims an annual output of 10,050,000 books and 176,400,000 magazines devoted exclusively to the welfare of its children.[15] Three million copies of nineteen speeches by Saddam Husain were distributed during 1978.[16]

By contrast in 1947–48, when the ICP was at the height of its nationwide influence and popularity, it distributed 3000 copies of its banned monthly *al-Qaʿida*. "Few of the legal papers or periodicals of Iraq could claim a bigger circulation" at the time.[17] Moreover, the massive output of two ideologically identical Baʿthist dailies in 1980 should be contrasted with the following: in 1908–1909 there were 18 different news-

14. Even after the repression of Solidarity, a vast underground counterculture continued to function in Poland, which the authorities were unable to uproot without reintroducing a regime of widespread fear. Through publishing houses, weekly news sheets, scholarly journals, lectures delivered in churches, "flying universities," actors performing in apartments, and tape cassettes, Poles kept alive some form of a public life after the crackdown. This life cannot be eliminated with cycles of arrests and releases involving a few hundred people; mass arrests, abuse, torture, and killings on a large scale, all culminating in hopelessness and knowledge of the certainty of death, are preconditions that the Polish bureaucracy may no longer be capable of.

15. See the semiofficial pamphlet by Latif Nasif Jasim, *Al-ʾIʿlam Wa al-Maʿrakah* (Baghdad: Dar al-Hurriyya, 1981), 14, 12. Even though the figures are probably exaggerated, a formidable increase over previous years is undeniable.

16. Tawalbeh, *Muqtatafat*, 6.

17. Hanna Batatu, *The Old Social Classes and Revolutionary Movements of Iraq* (Princeton: Princeton University Press), 607. Actual readership was larger than the figures suggest.

papers being put out in Arabic, Turkish, and Persian (not to mention books printed locally in at least six languages, including Hebrew, Syriac, and Chaldean); in 1917 there were 69 local newspapers whose circulation rarely exceeded 500 copies per issue, only 3 of which were government controlled; in the half century preceding the 1958 revolution there were over 350 different dailies and magazines; and finally between 1958 and 1963, 33 new dailies appeared including some for the first time in Kurdish.[18]

What explains the changes evident by 1980? First, total censorship and sheer bulk were used to uproot and swamp the variegated texture of all forms of public dialogue, at least insofar as this was reflected in a variety of independent newspapers and journals. Second, the Ba'th broke down the traditional exclusivity of reach of printed matter by enforcing compulsory education laws and promulgating repeated and sustained campaigns to eradicate illiteracy.

Although compulsory education laws had been passed after 1958, not until the 1970s were all Iraqi children attending school. The content of education was changed with the same vigour.

> The next five years must be devoted to building an educational system compatible with the principles and aims of the Party and the Revolution. . . .
>
> In the next phase there can be no question of putting up with the slow development of this domain in the last period. Time is not on the side of the Revolution. . . .
>
> New syllabuses must at once be prepared for every level from nursery school to university, inspired by the principles of the party and the Revolution. . . . Reactionary bourgeois and liberal ideas and trends in the syllabus and the educational institutions must be rooted out. The new generation must be immunized against ideologies and cultures conflicting with our Arab nation's basic aspirations and its aim for unity, liberty and socialism.[19]

From an illiteracy rate of 99.5 percent in the last years of the Ottoman rule, to 81.7 percent in 1957, the rate for the early 1980s can be in-

---

18. All figures from a supplement to *The Baghdad Observer*, June 15, 1969, issue entitled "The Beginning of Printing Presses and Journalism in Iraq," pp. 3, 12, 13, 15. The main article, written by Dr. Abdul Wahab Abbas al-Qaysi, is based on his study, "The Impact of Modernization on Iraqi Society During the Ottoman Era" (Ph.D. thesis, University of Michigan 1958). The large number of newspapers is attributable in part to the short life a newspaper had, and the fact that it would quickly start again under a new name once it had been banned. There was in addition a strong "personality" attached to many of them. *Habazbooz*, for example, was a satirical weekly that managed to put out 303 issues between 1931 and 1938, before being shut down. It was published by an official in his spare time who enjoyed ridiculing the very job from which he eventually resigned. The significance of this story lies in its sheer inconceivability today.

19. ABSP, *Political Report*, 171–72.

ferred at significantly less than 50 percent. This turnaround was largely
due to measures taken after 1968, which coincided with underlying demographic trends.[20] Among illiterate adults, however, Ba'thist resolve
was also very striking. In May 1978 the "Comprehensive National
Campaign for Compulsory Eradication of Illiteracy" was promulgated
by the RCC. The Minister of Education and representatives from the
Ministry of Defence, internal security forces, the ABSP, and the mass
organizations formed a Supreme Council, which was replicated at the
governate and local council levels. This method of organizing the campaign was linked to party resolutions dating back to 1963 and also to
the "historical decisions" taken at the eighth regional congress of the
ABSP in 1974,[21] which specified the involvement of the army and the
internal security forces in the campaign.

All illiterates between the ages of fifteen and forty-five had to attend
assigned adult education classes. A time limit of twenty-one months (reduced from thirty-six) was set for the eradication of illiteracy in this category—technically unfeasible and an operational nightmare, but typically
Ba'thist. Laws stipulated that those who failed to attend would become
ineligible for employment in the public and private sectors, for any government licenses, and for all bank loans. They also faced imprisonment
and a fine. By 1981 around 2 million people had passed through a designated programme either in one of the 1,779 Anti-Illiteracy Centres or
in one of the 21,853 People's Schools established throughout the country.[22] In 1965 there had been a mere 368 adult literacy centres in Iraq.
By 1979, UNESCO was giving the Supreme Council an award for having
"harnessed in a remarkable way the country's full energies in promoting
a far-reaching literacy campaign."[23]

For a while the country was gripped by a feverish campaign. Hundreds of thousands of people were enrolled using various public build-

20. See Alya Sousa, "The Eradication of Illiteracy in Iraq" in *Iraq: The Contemporary State*, ed. Tim Niblock (London: Croom Helm, 1982), 101. The figure for the early 1980s was extrapolated on the basis of other figures in the article. Official figures for 1977 put the illiteracy rate at 53.0 percent; however, the really intensive campaigns were only just starting and their effects would not have shown up yet. See *Annual Abstract of Statistics* (Baghdad: Ministry of Planning, 1978). During the 1950s and 1960s, Iraq's population was growing very rapidly and although the absolute number of literates was increasing, Sousa notes, the illiteracy rate probably did not decrease significantly; this confirms the extent of the Ba'thist achievement.

21. See law no. 92 of 1978 and its Statement of Grounds. *Alwaqai al-Iraqiyya* 41 (October 10, 1979): 2–10.

22. Numbers given in *Iraq* 22 (October 27, 1981), a weekly bulletin put out by the Iraqi embassy in the United Kingdom.

23. See Sousa, "Illiteracy," in Niblock, *Iraq*, 108 and 101.

ings, "floating schools" in the southern marshes region, and "travelling schools" in remote villages and nomadic areas. The mass media, trade unions, and state organizations were all mobilized. Special programmes were broadcast on radio and television. Daily literacy lessons were televised. Prisoners were informed that educational achievement under incarceration would be taken into account in the remission of sentences. Significantly, the majority of those enrolled in the literacy programs were Shi'ites because of the higher rates of illiteracy known to prevail in the south.[24] Needless to say, education at all levels and of all categories was free. This 1974 exemption from costs applied to books and all other educational material.

A later administrative regulation issued by the president's office attempted to sort out the responsibilities and lines of authority of the various officials who were by now falling over each other trying to get the campaign to meet its stated objectives. It listed the registers that each centre must keep, and the files that had to be opened on each student. Article 12 imposed the criterion on all teachers in the campaign that they "be bound by the principles of the ABSP" in the execution of their duties.[25]

The 1978 legislation combatting illiteracy defined an illiterate as a person who could not read and write and as someone who "did not reach the civilized level." One reached this level "provided" that these skills "enable him to undertake the duties and rights of citizenship." The knowledge gained "should be continuous and developing" and bound up "with the movement of society and aims of the Arab nation in Unity, Freedom and Socialism."[26]

These and other measures created a new audience held in thrall to Ba'thist ideological productions whose chief characteristic was that it had never existed before. Terror campaigns to weed out that "old generation" of intellectuals associated with another world's inbuilt elitism (if by no means ever advocates of it) were thus combined from the outset with laying down the groundwork for a society made up of mass consumers of ideological artifacts.

24. The government daily *al-Jumhuriyya* reported in its August 30, 1980, issue on the entry of a new batch of 40,000 recruits to the adult literacy programme. All came from the Shi'ite province of Basrah. They were allocated to 762 people's schools, 315 of which were for men, 416 for women, and 31 were mixed.

25. See articles 11 and 12 of Regulation no. 2 of the National Campaign promulgated in January 1979, published in *Alwaqai* 14 (April 4, 1979).

26. See article 1 of law no. 92 of 1978, *Alwaqai* 41 (October 10, 1979). For more on the impact of the literacy campaign, see *Middle East Economic Digest* 23, no. 38 (September 21, 1979): 8.

This was genuinely a "new society" (a constantly invoked Baʿthist formulation) from the standpoint of those who made it up. Its rationale henceforth was to be found in the sameness of each individual's allegiance to the total mass; or rather in his or her being held in check by the same kind of personal loyalty, however constructed (conviction, complicity, self-interest, fear). Accidents of birth, territoriality, religion, and even class would no longer determine identity. For these "accidents" in the past had given rise to a multitude of allegiances, a diversity that Baʿthism could not tolerate.

Just as it is in the essential nature of pan-Arabism to abstract from the factuality of Arab fragmentation, so too was each individual now being taught to rise above personal circumstance into that rarified world of Baʿthist make-believe. The object was to forge a new mass man and woman, as repeatedly emphasized by the party and all its media. The literacy gained was for the express purpose of "translating the education gained into social conduct."[27]

THE STATUS OF WOMEN

In 1965, 12 percent of adult literacy centres were for women, although female illiterates outnumbered males by more than two to one. A national breakdown for 1980 is not available. However, *al-Jumhuriyya* reported that out of one batch of 762 people's schools, 416 were for women and 31 were mixed. By the fourth grade the proportion of women increased, presumably because the men were dropping out faster (the illiteracy centres and people's schools that follow on from them have their own grading system). Moreover, nursery and childcare facilities were available in many of the new centres.

The entry of women into the educational system as a whole is another noteworthy Baʿthist accomplishment. In 1970–71, there were 318,524 girls in primary school, 88,595 at the secondary level, and 9,212 at the university level. For the 1979–80 school year the absolute numbers were respectively as follows: 1,165,856, 278,485, and 28,647.[28]

By 1980 women accounted for 46 percent of all teachers, 29 percent of physicians, 46 percent of dentists, 70 percent of pharmacists, 15 percent of accountants, 14 percent of factory workers, and 16 percent of

27. The purpose of the campaigns as given in the *al-Jumhuriyya* article of August 30, 1980.

28. All figures are from an article by Amal al-Sharqi, "The Emancipation of Iraqi Women," in Niblock, *Iraq*, 80–81.

civil servants. It has even been claimed that in the Ministry of Oil in 1980, 37 percent of the design staff and 30 percent of the construction supervisors were women. The State Organization of Buildings is another government department technically staffed by many women. Women's participation in senior management, however, was 4 percent overall in 1980 and showed no sign of rising. Generally the total participation of women in the nonagricultural labour force rose from 7 percent in 1968 to 19 percent in 1980.[29]

The labour and civil service laws promulgated to bring about these trends include equal pay and opportunity measures, preferential hiring regulations in government departments, paid maternity leave, childcare facilities at the workplace, and a reduced retirement age for working women.

As in the case of youth, women are organized in a General Federation for Iraqi Women. It has 18 branches, 1 in each province of Iraq, 265 subsections based on major towns, 755 centres that incorporate villages with more than 200 families or quarters of cities with more than 6,000 people, and an additional 1,612 liaison committees that extend to all remaining villages and quarters.[30] Conferences and elections determine a General Council out of which a Central Council of thirty-eight members is elected and an Executive Bureau chosen. In short women were not only learning to read, entering higher education, and forging ahead in the labour force, they were, like everyone else, being thoroughly organized.

These important changes in the social role of women ought to be considered alongside the 1978 amendments to the Code of Personal Status introduced by the Baʿth. The preamble states that the new code is based on "the principles of the Islamic shariʿa [Islamic law], but only those that are suited to the spirit of today."[31] The break with tradition as it affected women occurred in two important areas: first, authority was given to a state-appointed judge to overrule the wishes of the father in the case of early marriages; second, the new legislation nullified forced marriages and severely curtailed the traditional panoply of rights held over women by the men of the larger kinship group (uncles, cousins,

29. Ibid., 83–85. If these figures are exaggerated, they nevertheless point to a trend that every visitor to an Iraqi government department can attest to.
30. Taken from a book by Christine Moss Helms, *Iraq: Eastern Flank of the Arab World* (Washington, D.C.: The Brookings Institution, 1984), 99. The information in the book was collected through extensive interviews and statistical information provided to the author inside Iraq.
31. Taken from Amal Rassam's excellent article, "Revolution within the Revolution? Women and the State in Iraq," in Niblock, *Iraq*, 94.

and so on). The intent of the legislation as a whole was to diminish the power of the patriarchal family, and separate out the nuclear family from the larger kinship group whose hold over the lives of women was considerably weakened.

A Baʿthist innovation was the insertion of one or more "popular committees" in each *shariʿa* court to deal with the Personal Status Law. These committees of five people were to be formed from the mass organizations, and the law regulating their establishment stipulated that at least two members must be women. The mass organizations were listed in the legislation, headed by the General Federation of Iraqi Women. They were instructed to observe a political criterion in the choice of members (specifically knowledge of the 1974 political report of the ABSP).[32] The committees focus on disputes involving child custody in the event of separation or divorce and issue written recommendations to a state-appointed judge after undertaking "direct research" (interviews, questioning neighbours, and so on). Members are held accountable for their decisions, even though the judge makes the final decision.

In general, wherever women were clearly being involved in new areas of decision making, these were explicitly formulated as pertaining somehow to their sex (not their individual personhood) and simultaneously "politicized" to a remarkably unnecessary extent. The only way in which the "popular committees" could function is as pressuring agencies, forcing couples to conform to whatever outcome the party line deemed suitable. The facts of the case, the letter of the law, and the "rights" of everyone concerned are shunted aside in such arrangements. In addition whenever traditional male rights over women were weakened or abolished, the state adopted this role, acting "on behalf of" the female sex, not upgrading the status of women *as individuals* who were being discriminated against because of their sex.

In the 1977 law regulating women's entry into the armed forces, no mention was made of any military functions. However, enrolled women were considered completely subject to all military regulations, with the exception of "what does not conform with her nature." The law stipulated that a woman may be appointed as an officer if she carried a university degree in a health-related field (medicine, dentistry, pharmacy). Her rank descended from a low-set level on a scale carefully correlating health-related qualifications to military title (for example, a nursing

---

32. See Article 4, "Tasks and Role of the Popular Committees," *Alwaqai* 43 (October 25, 1978).

qualification of not less than two years' study attracts the rank of sergeant second-grade).[33] Clearly the army was absorbing women because of their dominant position in the health services. Much the same story applies to women's entry into the popular militia forces, which started in 1976. By 1982 some 40,000 women had been enrolled.[34]

These nonetheless bold legislative steps must be set against the surprising mildness of the reforms in those areas that most directly affected women as individuals: polygamy, divorce, and inheritance. Here male dominance in the spirit of Islamic law held sway, albeit with some reforms to the letter of the *shari'a* in the case of adultery (no longer called *zina* in the new code, but *khiyana zawjiyya*—marital treachery). The Ba'thist measures in this truly personal domain are considerably less radical than the 1956 Tunisian Code for example, or the Shah's family reforms, to say nothing of Attaturk's radical break with Islamic family law in 1926.

The important thing about all the legislation on women was precisely where it chose to make the break with tradition. Islamic law has always been clear regarding its view of the subordinate status of women in relation to men as a direct consequence of their sex. The focus is not on the virtues of the extended family, or the sanctity of paternal authority. If these can find modern substitutes in the shape of the nuclear family, state bureaucrats, or "popular committees," then, although a deeply rooted Arab sociological tradition was being undermined (one common to non-Islamic societies), *ideologically* Islamic *values* were still intact. Moreover, there is nothing in the very sincere and far-reaching efforts of the Ba'th to involve women in the labour force or to mobilize them that is un-Islamic, although it certainly represents a radical break with traditional society and deeply cherished values. One need only mention the masses of veiled women mobilized by the Islamic movement in Iran, not only against the Shah, but to break up some of the early feminist demonstrations against Khomeini's edict on the veil.

A fundamental distinction exists between an ideological core that is in some way based on traditional mores and the powerful radicalism of Ba'thism, which can ruthlessly uproot social barriers and prejudices that have lasted for centuries. The worst way to interpret the milder side of the reforms on personal status is to suggest the Ba'th feared the reac-

33. See Law no. 131, "For Women Service in the Army," in *Alwaqai* 52 (December 28, 1977).
34. Helms, *Eastern Flank,* 100.

tion of a conservative religious establishment. There is not a shred of evidence to support such an argument. And it contradicts their radicalism on other aspects concerning the social position of women. Moreover, the more radical amendments of the 1978 legislation do not display a tendency for increasing autonomy of the individual woman in Iraqi society that might lead in the long run to conflict with a wider Arab-Islamic cultural ethos and eventually place the Baʿth in a "dilemma" as Rassam thinks. Why are they radical in one place and not another? This is the important question.

The Baʿthi measures must not be exaggerated. No social group, least of all Iraqi women, was exerting pressure on them. But by choosing a particular "style" of legislating on this issue, they reveal how they think when *not* being boxed into a corner by the "contradictory demands of modernization and development and those of 'cultural authenticity.'"[35] The dilemma is attenuated when one takes seriously what the Baʿth themselves have to say. For they are remarkably consistent in trying to put into practice their own view of modernity and Islam. Their pan-Arabism is doctrinally linked to the Islamic experience in a way that will be discussed in Chapter 6. In Iraqi conditions, this very particular Baʿthist vision must always be kept in focus, and not our own preconceived opinions about what modernization may or may not entail.

Baʿthist ideals, tied up as they are with the Baʿthist view of the Islamic experience, provide the ultimate source of authority and the final test for what is justified. Even the power of the Leader is derivative from these ideals, and all sources of authority outside them threaten the Baʿth. It rankles to have fathers, brothers, uncles, and cousins, all lined up to exert varying degrees of real power and control over half of the Iraqi population. Thus, if a new loyalty to the Leader, the party, and the state is to form, women must be "freed" from the loyalties that traditionally bound them to their husbands and male kin. This was the essential purpose of the 1978 legislation on Personal Status, which diminished the power of the patriarchal family. Therefore, women (like children, as we have seen) gain somewhat in status in relation to these particular groups of men, only what they must lose in freedom to the Baʿth. Politically, the appropriate imagery is once again that provided by Saddam Husain of the child informer. Even in the traditional male-dominated Arab family group, the woman has a degree of personal freedom that is taken away under Baʿthism (in relation to her children, for example).

35. Rassam, "Women," in Niblock, *Iraq,* 97.

Male domination has not been done away with; it has found a substitute in the all-male RCC, the higher army command, and the ever-so-male person of Saddam Husain who is surely more awesome than most fathers. The locus of legitimacy and allegiance was being changed in Iraq; and the motivation for making the change on the part of the individual woman is a mixture of traditional obedience to the dictates of men, and the much newer drive of fear. This is the direction in which the legislative measures were heading, however gradually, and with whatever eventual social effect. Pressure "from below" might have blown the Ba'th off course; but in relation to women, this pressure was not and never has been the issue in Iraq.

DEVELOPMENT VERSUS FREEDOM

There is a characteristically Ba'thist relationship between the forced mobilization of large numbers of people to better themselves and the breakthrough in the ability to produce millions of publications, vastly increase the number of schools, and involve large numbers of women in the labour force. The latter constitute no mean organizational feat. Society was being convincingly shown that its own experience in overcoming backwardness was causally linked to the diminution of its political freedoms; new literacy skills and a censored content were indissolubly given by the same experience. If literacy and printing facilities were all that was at stake, then the growing faith in such a causality would be weak; however, this causality appears in most of the socioeconomic indices that matter for a developing country, as shown by the changes in the social role of women. A regime of terror actually presided over an across-the-board increase in the standard of living in Iraq, and it significantly improved the lot of the most destitute layers, furthering the levelling of income differentials that began after 1958.[36] The changes are impressive: the prices of most basic necessities were stabilized by state subsidy; the minimum daily wage greatly increased over the rate of inflation, which was kept low; new labour laws provided complete job security; the state became an employer of last resort for all graduates; free

36. There are no carefully done econometric studies of the changes in the standard of living under the Ba'th up to the start of the war. However, all recent and critical writers are agreed that a substantial real increase over the previous decade must have occurred. See for example Batatu, *Social Classes*, 1095; and Joe Stork, "State Power and Economic Structure: Class Determination and State Formation in Contemporary Iraq," in Niblock, *Iraq*, 42.

education and health care was provided; and per-capita national income increased from 195 ID in 1970 to 7,564 ID in 1979.[37]

Whether this improvement is attributable to oil revenues or to intelligent economic management may be important in the long run, but is quite beside the political point at hand. The mass campaigns that broke the back of illiteracy in Iraq take on their political dimension quite independently of how they were paid for; and the same could be said of the enormous expansion of medical services, the electrification of villages, the vast network of new roads that crisscross the country, forward-looking social legislation, the development of transport systems, telecommunications, industrialization, and massive housing projects.[38]

All of this development highlights a dilemma whose underpinnings in our century arise within the communist tradition. The Russian experience has deeply affected all thinking on the relationship of political freedoms to development in backward countries irrespective of political persuasion. The contradictions were most paradigmatically expressed in the thought of Leon Trotsky. In his trenchant attack on Stalinism, *The Revolution Betrayed,* Trotsky sought an explanation of the Stalinist phenomenon taken from outside its own peculiar distinctness and history of development. He wrote of the despotism of the new state as being an outcome of "the iron necessity to give birth to and support a privileged minority" in conditions of backwardness and how "the power of the democratic Soviets proved cramping, even unendurable, when the task of the day was to accommodate those privileged groups whose existence was necessary for defense, for industry, for technique and science."[39] The sense is of a transcendent causality maybe beyond the capacities of human intervention, through which today's freedoms have to be sacrificed in the interests of progress. This did not come from an economist, academician, or armchair revolutionary; it came from a leading intellect and political actor of the Russian revolution who had himself been cast aside by the "iron necessity" of the course it later took.

37. Per capita national income figures are from the Central Statistical Organization, quoted in Niblock, *Iraq,* 79.

38. For infrastructure and development spending in Iraq in the late 1970s, see the following articles in *Middle East Economic Digest:* vol. 21, no. 49 (December 9, 1977); vol. 21, no. 51 (December 22, 1977); vol. 22, no. 12 (March 24, 1978); vol. 23, no. 44 (November 2, 1979); vol. 24, no. 19 (May 9, 1980); vol. 24, no. 35 (August 29, 1980). On the growth of state-led industrialization, and the extent of the transformations wrought by the Ba'thist experiment on the economic structure, see Makram Sader, *Le développement industriel de l'Irak* (Beirut: Centre D'études et de Recherches sur le Moyen-Orient Contemporain, 1983), particularly section 2.2, "La période 1970–1980: vers une industrialisation accélérée et étatisée," 43–57.

39. Leon Trotsky, *The Revolution Betrayed* (New York: Merit, 1965), 55, 59.

What was for Trotsky a wrenching universal and personal dilemma, which he could only resolve by holding fervently onto the idea of world revolution, was transformed in the nationalist withdrawal and accelerating parochialism of all subsequent revolutions into an immutable law of the historical process, one that had been proved by the Stalinist experience. Invariably the ideology that captures this quality of imperial economic necessity in the Third World is the carping on about the "falsity" of bourgeois freedoms and the universal tendency to dislocate the realm of "true" freedom from the political to the social and economic domains. All later revolutions of this century (China, Vietnam, Cuba, Algeria) and all post–World War II nationalisms (Nasserism, Peronism, Baʿthism) have reaffirmed to one degree or another the apparently stringent objectivity of the choice: development or freedom?

ʿAli Baddour, a Syrian lawyer and literary critic of pan-Arabist persuasion, wrote openly about the freedoms that existed under the multiparty system in pre-1952 Egypt. In two influential 1957 essays he argued the Egyptian revolution of 1952 could only solve the economy's problems after it had firmly abolished Egypt's main inheritance of the colonial era: the multiparty system. The splits and quarrels of this system had cast "supply lines" to imperialism. He called for major surgery on this "leadership disease" throughout the Arab world and the establishment of "planned dictatorships" to bring about Arab unity and economic progress:

> Our belief in the value of dictatorship is not theoretical . . . it springs from our need for [Arab] unity . . . [and] for a system which can under no circumstances be a fluid, democratic one. . . . Liberty is not necessarily identical with democracy. . . . Liberty is synonymous with sufficiency of food, clothes, housing, hygiene; of cultural consciousness and emotional participation in the nation's problems. I do not know whether the Egyptian citizen of today is not getting a greater measure of freedom than he had in the days of the monarchy, political parties, of the Constitution, and the freedom of the Press; when everything was permitted, but everything had its price.[40]

In Iraq, the ICP conceded politically to the ABSP (see Chapter 7) because it believed them to be acting out this historical imperative formulated by Baddour. The intelligentsia with only a few exceptions was being won over from around 1958, and where an ingrained temperamental resistance to the starker formulation of the choice still persisted, it was temporarily resolved by idealizing Stalinism, Maoism, or what-

---

40. Taken from an article "Arab Nationalism" by N. Rejwan in *The Middle East in Transition*, ed. Walter Z. Laqueur (New York: Praeger, 1958), 145–65.

ever was the latest fashionable insurgent model of change. Among the masses the same preference prevailed with none of the prevarications of the cultural elite. The extent of the societal consensus was manifest long before the Baʿth came to power in the ease with which the institution of parliament was abandoned after 1958. The rapid succession of coups in the 1958–68 decade reaffirmed the underlying presumption of the public at large that it hankered less for political democracy than for a stabilization of arbitrary shifts in power, which would permit *economic* stability.[41] The significance of this presumption is that once the Baʿth had taken power and introduced policies, with the help of oil revenues and an unconstrained willingness to use violence, "progress" appeared as a self-fulfilling prophecy; it was not merely Baʿthist propaganda that was being confirmed, but society's own understanding of the nature of its condition arrived at long before the Baʿth came along.

Thus were forged bonds between Baʿthism and the public whose efficacy and power enormously surpassed anything possible through simple indoctrination. These were ties stemming from a shared experience that bound together Baʿthism's world of myths with broader societal assumptions, equally ideological, on progress versus freedom. The irony is that on the face of it political action pure and simple had ended up legitimating itself by creating a situation perceived to be not entirely of its own making. The reality Baʿthism appeared to confirm in the 1970s was one of the masses' own making in the shape of the myths they had adhered to from the 1950s and 1960s, on pan-Arabism, "unity, freedom and socialism" and "forces" or "laws" of progress and development.

BACKWARDNESS AS JUSTIFICATION

Even if the conditions for freedom have not yet emerged in Iraq, why *so much* violence? Or, what historical function did all this *extra* violence serve? Let us examine a reference frame widely believed to provide an adequate outline of an answer.

Isaac Deutscher, whose work on Stalinism is probably the most thoughtful contribution from within Marxism, wrote:

> It is now very nearly a commonplace that Stalinism was the product of a post revolutionary, isolated, underdeveloped, largely pre-industrial society

---

41. Khair al-Din Haseeb, the architect of the comprehensive nationalizations of 1964, has said that between 1964 and 1968 there were eight ministers of industry and transport, seven ministers of public works, six ministers of agrarian reform, and six minis-

engaged in "primitive socialist accumulation," that is, in a process of rapid industrialization and modernization carried out under the aegis of the state, on the basis of public ownership of the means of production. As a system of government and an ideology, Stalinism represented both the backwardness of its national environment and the progressive transformation of that environment. Hence the duality in the character of Stalinism and its Janus-like appearance. Hence its crude violence and primitive isolationist, ideological outlook on the one hand, and on the other, its historic élan and determination in replacing Russia's archaic mode of production and way of life by a modern planned economy and extensive mass education. Admittedly, the whole phenomenon of Stalinism cannot be explained by these factors alone, but they do account for its most essential features.[42]

Ironically, so "commonplace" is this assessment that replacing the word Baᶜthism for Stalinism does not affect the argument. Deutscher has situated Stalinism in terms that are shared by most countries conscious of their backwardness and striving to overcome it. In effect, Deutscher was providing a historical summation for Trotsky's "iron necessity" formulation, possible because time had passed, the Stalinist terror of the 1930s had abated, and something new was happening in the Soviet Union.

From within his frame, however, Stalinism as forged in the reign of terror of the 1930s and late 1940s, right through to Stalin's death and the ouster of Beria by the bureaucracy, must be considered the generic model for understanding Baᶜthism. Stalinism is the "original" Third Worldism that Baᶜthism as well as other post–World War II nationalisms sought to emulate. By putting aside all considerations regarding modes of production, and focussing on each, like Deutscher, as "a system of government and an ideology," the conclusion is inescapable: somehow, two phenomena utterly alien to each other by origin have acquired a structural correspondence.

Even if the reasons behind Stalin's violence were completely different from those of the Baᶜth, violence still produced very similar forms of government. A wondrous and uplifting historical design for one and not the other would not diminish this correspondence. Here is a very disconcerting result, regardless of how different the later evolution of the two regimes might turn out to be once the terror recedes in Iraq. The

---

ters of planning. See J. F. Penrose, *Iraq: International Relations and National Development* (London: Ernest Benn, 1978), 467.

42. Isaac Deutscher, "Ideological Trends in the USSR," in *Marxism in Our Time* (San Francisco: Ramparts Press, 1973), 210.

fact is that Baʿthism modelled itself self-consciously, as a movement and in power, on Stalinist norms. Moreover, it "won over" the masses to the detriment of the ICP, legitimizing its rule on that basis (as discussed in Chapters 6 and 7).

Unfortunately, the exercise of switching labels on the quotation renders Deutscher less and not more profound. There are explanations that explain too much. The question is: Granted there is no freedom, why *so much* violence? Deutscher and Trotsky merely confirmed the general proposition that scarcity creates the conditions for violence. However, backwardness can in principle resolve itself in many different ways. Even if Russian backwardness implied that privilege in the postrevolutionary society could not be eliminated in the short term, the issue of consciously engineered purges that wiped out millions of more or less randomly selected victims, and the type of government this resulted in, was not being addressed.

The idea that Stalinism's "most essential features" can be summed up without a single specifically political characteristic of the phenomenon is very disturbing. Is the extreme distinctiveness of Stalinism conceived "as a system of government" derivative only from a series of relationships between it and the mode of production? Its essence remains a mystery even after all the essential features have been identified. There is a glaring omission in the characterization: the realm of deliberative action, judgement, ideology, errors, and random happenings, of the unforeseen and unforeseeable—in short, the realm of politics—is totally absent. In addition, the realm of necessity—economy and labour—is termed "primitive socialist accumulation." Deutscher places the concept in quotation marks because he knows that primitive accumulation is always primitive (never socialist by Marx's own standards), and the millions of Russian peasants who starved to death attest to the fact that Stalin's version was no more civilized than his capitalist predecessors'.

Such considerations raise the issue of backwardness as a justification for violence, a view in no way associated with Deutscher but with those half-baked Marxists and "progressive" nationalists like the Baʿth who have raised high the banner of parochialism, cultural relativism, and Third Worldism. If Stalinist violence were "compensated for" by the emergence of the Soviet Union as a superpower, then Baʿthism could find its justification by way of precedent. Such a justification is bound to have much greater weight than Stalin's own abuse of Marxism had in Russia. He after all had to look into a crystal ball. All that a later generation of apologists for Third Worldism have to do is look backwards, and in this they usually excel. In short, in Iraq the real historical experience of the Soviet Union was ideologized by the Ba'th to serve the political purpose of unleashing a regime of terror.

The Degradation of Thought

How do barrages of myths coming from every direction—newspapers, the media, workplace, street, and family—affect people after twenty years, especially those once illiterate? What does the administration of lies from the cradle to the grave do to a people's judgement, especially when they are afraid? No one knows. From the outside one can reach in and scratch at the surface. From within the world is black, and having the courage to want to understand is about groping around trying to get a sense of what cannot be seen. This is the cold world of analysis in which all stories are forbidden.

A society like Iraq has choked off all the avenues by which anything other than mediocrity can flourish. Its share of good and caring minds belong now to a different world. Those who did not sell out are either dead, or locked into the Sisyphus-like labours of exile politics. The problem is superficially one of language by which I do not mean the rules and inherited structures of a society's mode of communication, but the really fundamental conceptual categories through which all thought and dialogue outside the daily routines of living must be carried on.

The exiled opposition recently presented a serialized directory of key concepts in politics and philosophy. The "precise scientific meaning" of al-sha'ab (the people), we are told, is the sum of all classes in society who "by virtue of their position in the class and political map" are able "within a given historical period" to bring about progress and development. In primitive societies apparently there is "no essential difference between residents and al-sha'ab," but as class society evolved the two concepts bifurcated. In other words some long-term residents are excluded from "the people" of Iraq either on objective socioeconomic criteria, or by virtue of what they think.[43] Culture is defined not as "the spiritual outgrowth of an elite." Rather, "the scientific outlook understands that the material production of needs is the basis and origin of all spiritual culture, which in other words means that it is the product of the activity of the masses."[44]

43. *Wahdat al-Talabah,* Journal of the Iraqi Students Society in the United Kingdom, issue no. 1–2 (April 1983): 33.
44. Ibid.

The Iraqi Students Society is an influential organization trying hard to fight Baʿthism but completely trapped in its categories. They naively think that the problem is reducible to drawing attention to what Marx really said in this or that book written over a century ago. The argument over words may or may not be won, but the original *meaning* deriving from the reasons for the degradation is bound to remain triumphantly Baʿthist. The battle is lost before it has even begun.

Curiously, concepts originally conceived as aids to the comprehension of reality have taken on their own life, becoming agents of action in a world they were originally intended merely to explain. Thus, "imperialism" taken from Leninism and integrated into a Baʿthist world view can be reappropriated by Muslim clerics along with the Iraqi opposition as the overarching explanation for Baʿthism's war against the Islamic state in Iran. And the same applies to words like "socialism," "freedom," "left," "right," "reactionary," "liberal," "bourgeois," and phrases like "the interests of the masses," and "the world capitalist system."

When the Red Cross released a statement condemning both sides in the Iraq-Iran war for their treatment of prisoners, one reaction was: Why did they put it out now? Which great power had most to benefit from such a declaration? What sort of new conspiracy was unfolding behind the scenes? The information that the Red Cross put forward was not even considered at face value, it being self-evident that all countries brutalize and kill off their prisoners. What is the difference between such an outlook coming from a casual encounter with a group of anti-Baʿthi Iraqis, and for example Tariq ʿAziz (a member of the RCC) attributing the Watergate affair to the Zionist lobby out to get Nixon for his allegedly pro-Arab stance? In fact, I know an educated anti-Baʿthist Iraqi who does not think this "analysis" unreasonable, and might only balk at stating it as an absolute fact because it was enunciated by a Baʿthi.

Conspiratorial thinking has broad roots in the extreme fatalism and hostility to individualism that may be a characteristic of Islamic culture generally. The idea of submission to the will of God is the passive counterpart of the quest for martyrdom in His Cause. Both undermine the modern notion of people as actors, makers of their own history, manipulators of nature, responsible ultimately only to themselves. Pan-Arabism enriches this legacy by setting up a yawning chasm between its ultimate goals and existing realities. The chasm grows with time creating an even more conducive atmosphere for "thinking" conspiracies. By the late 1960s, the Baʿth had become veritable masters of the craft.

An adjunct of conspiratorial thinking is the espousal of political ideas at such a level of abstraction that only by vague inference can their relevance to local conditions be adduced. This device allows radical rhetoric to reach a high pitch without ever threatening real interests or entrenched values. Radicalism of this sort is the antithesis of, for example, the Enlightenment thought of the eighteenth century located at a roughly analogous historical conjuncture for western Europe in terms of the rupture with tradition. Thus, when espousing socialism, "the interests of the masses," or even the ideas of Marx, many Arab thinkers, largely aided by a world of pan-Arabist and conspiratorial categories, do not have the devastating penetrability and moral universalism of say a Voltaire. Political thought outside the management of affairs of state, increasingly became a very surreal affair in the Arab world.

The real experience of politics in a country like Iraq over the last quarter century has so degraded the language of public discourse that the whole population, including those in opposition, lack the barest rudiments of a conceptual apparatus with which to comprehend their reality (to say nothing of formulating a happier alternative to it).

Part of the post-1967 radical rejection of "the progressive" regimes of Nasser and the Ba'th was their association with the demagoguery of Hasaneyn Heikal (the editor of al-Ahram), the bombast of Ahmad al-Shuqairi (the Palestinian leader discredited by 1967), and the flowery utterances of 'Aflaq.[45] The journal Mawaqif launched by a group of Arab radicals in 1968 made some bold contributions; its writers questioned the linguistic heritage itself, finding in it a tendency towards entertainment as opposed to critical thought. The Lebanese writer Adonis wrote scathingly of the Arab poetical tradition for elevating pronunciation at the expense of meaning, and he called for "the formation of a new writing."[46] Others launched the first attempts to criticize religious thought and traditional social mores in relation to the 1967 defeat.[47] But this creative spasm petered out, quite apart from finding little resonance even at the time in more distant Arab countries like Iraq.

The post-1967 assault on tradition and the rhetoric of Nasserism and

45. For an excellent discussion of this, see Fouad 'Ajami, The Arab Predicament: Arab Political Thought and Practice Since 1967 (Cambridge: Cambridge University Press, 1981), 25–30.

46. The title of an important article he wrote in Mawaqif, Beirut, No. 16 (July–August 1971).

47. The writings of one person loom large in these areas. Sadiq Jalal al-'Azm's critique of the Arab regime's conduct of the 1967 debacle was especially influential: Al-Naqd al-Dhati Ba'd al-Hazima (Self-Criticism after the Defeat) ('Aka: Dar al-Jalil, 1968). Other important books he published are: Naqd al-Fikr al-Dini (Critique of Religious Thought) (Beirut: Dar al-Tali'ah, 1969); and Dirasah Naqdiyah li-Fikr al-Muqawamah al-Filistiniyyah (A Critical Study in the Thought of the Palestinian Resistance) (Beirut: Dar al-Tali'ah,1973).

the Ba'th, although very important, remained hemmed in by a "them" versus "us" framework: "How were they able to defeat us so devastatingly?" This, for instance, is the theme underlying *Al-Asfour*, the important film by Youssef Chahine, which depicts how the 1967 war was lost from within. Maybe at the time this was the only way of phrasing the question. But today it is grotesquely inadequate. The focus then was on an outside world bringing itself to bear on the inside, and the assault on backwardness was blunted at the outset by the underlying premise of unity at some stage in the face of outside aggression. The heroes of the hour—Fanon, Guevara, Ho Chi Minh, Debray—were symbols that cut in two directions, but in the Arab context they were primarily about combatting the outside rather than the rot within. In the end, like all Third Worldism, there was no human message, just the same old suffocating parochialism. To challenge the language and categories of the Ba'th on a terrain so well trodden by them was bound to be futile.

Since the Lebanese civil war, and alongside the rise of religious fundamentalism, it has become easier to identify an actual experience of degradation in Arab politics and culture. The phenomenon, as most thoughtful Arab intellectuals will privately admit, is of awesome breadth and depth. Even in moderately free Arab countries where state censorship has been loosened (for example, Egypt), a conformist "self-censorship" has arisen. The writer Louis Awad committed the sin of asserting that al-Afghani was born in Iran; for a year no one published his articles, and critics questioned his right as a Christian Copt to comment on Islamic affairs.[48]

Characteristically, this degradation does not take the form of a confrontation between what are perceived to be two hostile but *indigenous* currents. In place of such a more creative clash of ideas and values, the once ascendant Marxist, radical-nationalist, and left currents have proceeded to purge themselves of whatever "outsider" values they might have inadvertently retained since their rise in the late 1960s. In this they are following in the footsteps of an earlier (much smaller) generation of Arab liberals and social democrats who conceded to the radical nationalists and the Left in the same way. The Iranian Islamic revolution, for example, was at first embraced by intellectuals like Anwar 'Abd al-Malik, Adonis, Clovis Maqsoud, Mahmood Amin al-'Alim, and Edward Said. The most articulate elements in the Iraqi Marxist opposition to

---

48. For this and other stories, see the report by Judith Miller, "The Embattled Arab Intellectual," *New York Times Magazine*, June 9, 1985, pp. 56, 61, 64, 67–68, 72–74.

Ba'thism have also evolved in this way, as can be seen from the editorial line of the journal, *al-Ghad*.[49] The rising tide of fundamentalism in turn absorbed useful leftist and nationalist formulations like imperialism, socialism, and mass struggles against hoary capitalist exploiters whose physical existence never bore any relation to their imagined omnipotence. Both sides found confirmation of themselves in the other. The union of the two in this manner is manifest in the shifting allegiances and language of the Muslim, pan-Arab, and Left alignment in the Lebanese civil war, and in the stigmatization of Lebanon's Christians as surrogates for Israel or the West in their own country.

The severe manifestation of this intellectual degradation in a country like Iraq, as opposed to say Egypt or parts of North Africa, is attributable to the ideological hegemony achieved by pan-Arabism and its assimilation of communism, the hitherto main language of protest and opposition. The difference between the more benign populist version, Nasserism, and Ba'thism lies in the latter's compulsive drive to organize. Therefore, along with the experience of politics in the Arab world as a whole, one must consider the additional effect of Ba'thist measures to "organize" how people are going to think in Iraq.

In 1978 the RCC decreed that all personnel of the "armed forces, internal security forces and Presidency of Public Intelligence shall be admitted in all universities, colleges, institutes and schools." The resolution excluded as criteria age, academic achievement, period of enrollment, and attendance. "The Ministries of Defence, Interior and Presidency of Public Intelligence shall organize in proper time lists of names of nominees of their personnel for admission to be submitted to the institutions."[50] Within seven months three thousand were enrolled as students. If one includes the thousands of ABSP members entered on the same basis in that year, the total makes for one-fifth of all admissions for 1978–79[51] (the same proportion of "armed men" in society at large). Additional supporters and party members could enroll in the normal way.

By itself, ideology as mythmaking is powerless to fashion reality in its own image; married to this kind of organization, however, it acquires that capability by squeezing out of the social organism remaining vestiges of an irreverent and nonideological mode of thought. Even when

49. *Al-Ghad* (The Future), published in London, provides a forum for the exiled Iraqi left opposition.
50. Resolution no. 25, *Alwaqai* 13 (March 29, 1978): 5.
51. I am relying for this calculation on an "Open Letter" issued by the Iraqi Students Society in the United Kingdom, dated February 16, 1979.

its control over people is far from completed, the magic that has been injected between experience and reality on the one hand and concepts and discourse on the other remains operative. This hallmark of Ba'thism in power greatly accentuates the general degradation of Arab thought in politics and culture previously mentioned.

Building Defences

When fear, violence, and conformity become the norm, individuals desperately need to fight back—not to overthrow the surrounding tyranny but to retain a degree of psychological balance simply to go on with the routine business of living. When every dimension of daily life is under threat, and nothing is in principle private, then a deep existential crisis is generated.

The first act of self-defence is to conceal and calculate with respect to all thoughts and emotions, to pretend things are other than what they really are. Appearances become even more important than in other "normal" backward societies.[52] More unhealthy is the compulsive Iraqi concern with being publicly inconspicuous in contrast with the ostentatious and yet less inhuman preoccupation with social standing and conspicuous consumption that afflicts societies in the Gulf. In the Iraqi setting it is essential that things not be called what they are; violence, for example, is thought by the average citizen to be at a "normal" level. To think otherwise is to let down one's defences in the face of its onslaught. The obsession with putting a mask on oneself in the workplace, in dealings with officials, in relations to neighbours and even within the family is so pervasive today in Iraq that inevitably the distinction implicit in the original act of deception gets blurred; the mask fits so completely, so tightly, that it can no longer be readily discarded. Like a snail sealed in its shell, personality and character shrivel up.

One means of self defence in a Ba'thist world is to identify wholly with the powers that be; join in party activities, become a Ba'thist, make contributions, believe in the righteousness of what one is doing. Even when the first gesture is calculated to be a deception, complicity makes

---

52. See Mustafa Hijazi, Al-Takhaluf al-Ijtima'i: Psychologiyat al-Insan al-Maqhoor (Beirut: Ma'had al-'inma' al-'Arabi, 1970), 136–41. I am indebted to this book for some of the ideas presented here, particularly his part 2 on "Defence Mechanisms" and chap. 6 on "Identification with the Aggressor." Hijazi's concerns broadly originate in his observations and experience of the Lebanese civil war. At no time does he apply them concretely to Ba'thism. All distinctions between the Iraqi experience and that of the broad majority of backward countries with whom Hijazi is concerned are my own.

the final act one of wanton abandonment. Stepping back, and pretending one does not know what is going on (as people did in Argentina under the terror in the late 1970s), is not enough. Citizens find themselves psychologically driven to become totally immersed so as to liquidate their personality and selves into the oppressor "group" and its values. This source of Ba'thism's social base can be measured by party size (1.5 million in 1984). It is an ephemeral base in the sense that it can disappear overnight as the experience of Nazi Germany in 1945 showed; but in order to evaporate, the crisis of the regime must be complete, and its defeat a foregone conclusion. The Iraq-Iran war has not yet produced this kind of crisis for Ba'thism.

The either-or quality of this allegiance provides a much stronger base of support than mere opportunism that combines outward subservience with an inner critical distance. Most Third World regimes rest on one variant or another of hypocritical allegiance, the Shah's regime being a perfect example. The manner of the Shah's overthrow clearly demonstrated that his rule rested on a thin and parasitic layer of Iranian society that never had roots in the populace. Khomeiniism on the other hand sprouted precisely because a "critical distance" existed, not only within each individual but in society at large. In the end all the talk about the ubiquity of SAVAK and the Shah's "police state" proved to be considerably exaggerated as many Iranian exiles today who have tasted the lash of both SAVAK and the Islamic Republic will privately attest. By contrast the support that Ba'thism literally made for itself is rooted in a deep personal internalization of extraordinarily high levels of institutional violence. This must warp the psychological constitution of individuals, a phenomenon that bears no relation to run-of-the-mill opportunism.

There exist, however, other important means of self-defence in Iraqi society. No matter how completely Ba'thism succeeds in destroying all alternatives to itself in the public domain—in politics, the workplace, and culture—it is much harder for it to be as thorough in the private and social domain of family, kinship relations, and religious group affiliation. This would be true for all human societies and cultures insofar as they all separate social networks from the political sphere, however broadly defined. The well-known traditional strengths of the extended Arab family and religious group affiliation provide an even more formidable obstacle to Ba'thist penetration.

Historically in the Middle East, "the social" has been very broadly and communally defined (religiously and ethnically). The Ottoman Empire called it the millet system. The sense of nationality that arose out of the millet always had a tribal-religious air about it, with no equivalent in the experience of western Europe. The establishment of modern states in the twentieth century pushed back the former all-encompassing boundaries of "society"—legally, economically, and socially. But there was never a head-on *political* confrontation with the rigidity and dominance over individuals present in social networks and the traditional moral order. In other words, for all the socioeconomic changes, there was no "enlightenment" or revolution in values. Sometimes this gave rise to an Alice-in-Wonderland quality to radical Middle East politics, which theoretically presumes such a transformation in values but has always tended to shy away from the kind of critique of traditionalism that calls into question its credentials with the masses. Such a deeply rooted biworldism does not give in easily to political action from above, no matter how determined.

Khomeiniism's union of these two alienated worlds—the public and the private, politics and society—in the name of resurgent Islam makes the movement so revolutionary. Strands in Muslim thought lend themselves to such a project; but it is their masterful manipulation in the service of twentieth-century political ends that will prove to be Khomeini's legacy in this part of the world. By contrast, the Baʿth are amateurs.

Thus in Iraq a degree of personal refuge from the onslaught of Baʿthism is still possible by a sort of "reverse dissolution," back into the arms of an original social group, whether family or confessional. Phenomenologically (although not politically) a more intense version of this withdrawal is being expressed by more independent or financially able individuals when they patiently scheme to get out of the country, sometimes taking years. Several thousand Iraqis have escaped this way to Kuwait, or the United Arab Emirates, and many eventually made it to Europe by various hair-raising stratagems. But the predominant form of withdrawal for those who are locked in is still religious identification and the family group, which is why sectarianism and a new preoccupation with family trivia and gossip has mushroomed in recent years. This has created a climate favourable to the emergence of fundamentalist political thinking, whose appearance in Baʿthist Iraq is remarkable given the amount of repression.

Such trends are common to both the Sunni and Shiʿite Arab communities of Iraq, although *political* Islamic fundamentalism (as opposed to religious sectarianism, which is not necessarily political) has grown more rapidly among Shiʿites. Sunni fundamentalism is being held in check by the close connection between the pan-Arabism of the Baʿth and the Sunni Islamic tradition. Shiʿi fundamentalism, however, is not an import from Islamic Iran as the Baʿth claim, although there is some Iranian influence.

Generally, religious sectarianism is a mechanism that provides frightened and atomized individuals with a closed group in which to submerge their individuality further, while gaining some degree of identity in relation to the "new society" in which they would otherwise be terrifyingly alone. Alienation from the state is not necessary, except for those who plot to leave or who become Islamic fundamentalists. The greater part of religious sectarianism in Iraq is expressed in the form of a growing hostility to Sunnis as Sunnis, or Shiʿites as Shiʿites. Features include avoiding unnecessary interaction, conformist pressure on youth, retrenchment and intransigence, and a growing sectarianism in casual conversation, jokes, and gossip; none are explicitly political.

The underground political organizations of Shiʿism—the largest of which, *al-Daʿwah al-Islamiyyah* (the Islamic Call), was formed before the Baʿth came to power—have been largely crushed, and their major leaders and families executed. In May 1983 ninety members of the al-Hakim family ranging from nine to seventy-six years of age were arrested because one member, Mohammed Baqir al-Hakim, leads an Iraqi opposition group from exile in Tehran. The Baʿth laid down an ultimatum that he cease broadcasting. He did not, and on May 20 six leading members were executed in front of other relatives. Of the remaining eighty-four, only five elders were eventually released.[53] The Shiʿite village of Dujayl, known for its political militancy and as a stronghold of the Islamic fundamentalist underground, was destroyed after an attempt on Saddam's life only to be promptly rebuilt by the regime. Both the destruction and the reconstruction established how completely the Baʿth were in charge.

Such political acts of defiance and rebellion are the exception rather than the rule, as reflected in the statements of support for the regime and its war effort by several prominent Najafi dignitaries such as Shaykhs ʿAli Kashif al-Ghitaʾ and ʿAli al-Saghir.[54] Moreover, there has historically been some tension between Iranian and Arab Shiʿite clerics. Among the eight acknowledged highest authorities of Shiʿism (*marjiʿ*), Mohammed Baqir al-Sadr was the only Arab. When the Baʿth executed al-Sadr

---

53. See Liz Thurgood's report in *The Guardian* of June 28, 1983; and the personal account by the al-Hakim family in the May 21, 1983, issue of *The Guardian*.

54. See Hanna Batatu, "Iraq's Underground Shiʿa Movements: Characteristics, Causes and Prospects," *The Middle East Journal* 35 (Autumn 1981): 592.

and his family in 1980, Iraqi Shi'ism gained a martyr to be sure but lost the only personality who might have taken on the mantle of a Khomeini. Ever since, the Iraqi movement has been in a state of fragmentation. Not only has it lost its Khomeini, but also it never had the organizational network independent of the state with which to fuel its activities. There were 180,000 clerics and religious students in pre-1979 Iran who formed the organizing cadre of the revolution. By contrast there were less than 2,000 registered theology students in Najaf in 1958, the overwhelming majority of whom were Iranians.[55] Barring an Iranian victory in the Iraq-Iran war, the Shi'i underground has to be discounted as a force in Iraqi politics for the time being.

A religious-sectarian view of the world and Iraqi Ba'thism, however, share very important assumptions which facilitate their coexistence inside Ba'thi Iraq. Sunni and Shi'i Iraqi Arabs share a deeply rooted political sensibility regarding what it takes to rule Iraq (see Chapter 4). And the fundamentalists on either side find themselves in agreement with Ba'thi ideologues in that all view themselves as the authentic "spirit" of the people rising in hostility to an outside construed as "materialist," "imperialist," or simply morally and culturally decadent. For a Sunni Arab, Islam and Arab nationalism find a synthesis in Ba'thism that can hardly be improved upon. Even the Iraqi Shi'ite, while struggling with his national identity, has a hard time demonstrating that the Ba'th are not good Muslims. All he can say with assurance is that they rely on Sunnis at the top. Moreover, all varieties of "popular Islam," recently reinterpreted to represent a genuinely democratic tradition of revolt by Iraqi Marxists,[56] find an ideal populist counterpart in Ba'thism on this score also. Neither can direct their wrath at the destruction of all civil liberties or for freedoms that apply irrespective of belief, only at injustices perpetrated against them. Finally, Shi'ism in particular has an undiluted hero-worship; take away its object of veneration, or replace it with another, and you have transformed the relationship of the creed to those who wield power from one of rebellion to one of allegiance. Ironically, these same commonalities that facilitate coexistence under a single authoritarian polity also lead Shi'ism and Ba'thism to irreconcilable hostility in separated political settings. Nothing explains the irrational streak in the Iraq-Iran war better than some of these structural identities between the two protagonists.

55. Ibid., 586.
56. See "al-Islam wa al-Dimuqratiyyah," in *al-Ghad* 11 (July 1981): 5–15, and 12 (March–May 1982): 5–31.

To conclude, indirectly Ba'thism heightens religious sectarianism in the social and private domain as a direct consequence of its total control over the public realm. Up to a point, it can live with this, just as it can live with the loss of all "brotherly love" on the part of individual citizens who have become informers. The fear that is the binding cement of its edifice has a counterpart in growing confessionalism, so long of course as neither spills out onto the streets in the form of incidents of personal revenge, or bloody communal clashes in the name of religion. On the other hand, fundamentalism in the service of expressly political ends can never be tolerated, and will always be ruthlessly eradicated by the Ba'th. Ba'thism, however, is not a religious or confessional view of the world. Its long-term rationale must be to undermine all communal bonds and forms of group affiliation not wholly determined by itself. This is a polity whose ideal is the transformation of everybody into an informer; there is therefore in the long run no place for even the temporary haven of hate-filled religious sectarianism.

CHAPTER 4

Authority

The Leader Syndrome

Portraits of leaders signify power in the Middle East. But these are rarely as big and varied as in Baʿthist Iraq. A large painted cutout figure of Saddam Husain towers over the entrance of every Iraqi village; often at night it emits a lurid fluorescent glow. A thirty-foot high version can be seen near Baghdad city center. Photographs adorn every shop, school, police station, army barracks, and public building, and can be seen in people's offices and living rooms and overhanging the streets from the parapets of houses. No official will appear before a camera without a picture of the president in the background, and his name is evoked in every public address.

Saddam is president of the republic, chairman of the Council of Ministers, commander in chief of the armed forces, chairman of the RCC, general secretary of the Regional Command of the ABSP, chairman of the Supreme Planning Council, chairman of the Committee on Agreements, chairman of the Supreme Agricultural Council, and chairman of the Supreme Council for the Compulsory Eradication of Illiteracy, among other things. In addition to these party and state functions, an impressive array of honorific titles and forms of address include the leader-president, the leader-struggler, the standard bearer, the Arab leader, the knight of the Arab nation, the hero of national liberation, the father leader (previously held by al-Bakr), and the daring and aggressive knight (*al-faris al-mighwar*).

On radio, in a typical political broadcast, his name is mentioned thirty to fifty times an hour, along with reams of titles suited to the occasion.[1] News broadcasts shower him with congratulatory telegrams

---

1. This count was done by A. Hottinger, "Personality Cult and Party in Iraq," *Swiss Review of World Affairs* (June 1984): 12.

and grovelling speeches. The streets of Baghdad grind to a halt whenever he leaves the presidential palace; sirens go off, soldiers line the route, and busy people rush to the public squares to see him pass. School children memorize verses in his honour, praising his qualities. Slogans attributed to him are visible everywhere. School notebooks carry his portrait on the front and his latest sayings on the back. Iraqi teenagers wear Saddam Husain T-shirts, and the real enthusiast can buy a gold wristwatch with Saddam Husain peering through the dials.[2]

Following a coup in the Middle East, the pictures disappear as instantly as the reality behind the shift in power. By the late 1970s this could no longer be said of Ba'thist Iraq, where the imagery is so much more orchestrated. The concern now is with making a completely different statement about power. When Ahmad Hasan al-Bakr was purged in 1979, his photographs were slowly phased out, while Saddam's were gradually built up. Al-Bakr's photographs in a handful of standard poses used to appear by themselves in the first years of the second Ba'thi regime; around the mid-1970s they hung alongside those of Saddam Husain. By the summer of 1982 they were withdrawn completely from circulation. No painted thirty-foot cutouts were ever made of al-Bakr, much less a statue in every village. When Iraqis saw the pictures of al-Bakr after 1979, and heard that he was still being referred to as "a father to Saddam Husain," they knew the son had been true to his 1977 speech; he had informed on his "father" but with all the proper deference and respect.[3]

In this way Iraqis learned to become more afraid of Saddam Husain as they looked at the picture of Ahmad Hasan al-Bakr and reflected on their loss of authority over their children. The political reality behind all the photographs and appearances is the power of fear. Very soon the same people were "choosing" to surround themselves with pictures of Saddam Husain in their homes and offices, hoping in this way to "ward off evil." This is how it looks at first sight, on the surface. Once people stop saying things in front of their children, and even encourage them in their spoon-fed enthusiasm for the Great Leader, things become less clear. Raw power lording it over civil society has been turned into a new kind of authority, one that rules inside each soul. No longer merely sig-

---

2. On T-shirts, see *Christian Science Monitor*, July 20, 1984. A blow-up of a Saddam wristwatch is displayed in the pictorial, "The New Face of Baghdad," *National Geographic* 167, no. 1 (January 1985).

3. Saddam Husain maintained that Ahmad Hasan al-Bakr was like a father to him. In the summer of 1981, RCC member Taha Yasin Ramadhan was still referring to Saddam as being a son to Bakr. See the interview with Christine Moss Helms, *Iraq: Eastern Flank of the Arab World* (Washington, D.C.: The Brookings Institution, 1984), 95.

nified, this authority is expressed as so omniscient and absolute that it intended the humiliation of everyone: making them do, say, and begin to believe things are other than what they really are.

The new Leader heaps contempt and disdain even upon those who surround him. In conferences and public assemblies attended by Saddam Husain, the most powerful men of the country can usually be seen with folded hands, peering down at the ground, or applauding him harder than anyone else. Ministers do not turn their backs on Saddam when leaving the room; they shuffle out sideways, inconspicuously. In a party-political videotape, made after the start of the Iraq-Iran war, a scene is shown of Saddam Husain humiliating a group of sheepish-looking ministers and party bureaucrats. They are being hauled over the coals for not having enthusiastically volunteered for the front trenches, an omission they hastily proceeded to rectify. The tape was given a limited release to pep up party loyalists on Baʿthi egalitarianism in warfare. But it had to be quickly withdrawn after it began circulating in the Gulf and the Baʿth realized they had made a terrible mistake. The mistake is as revealing as the tape, because the moral is that in the fictional world of Baʿthism, an emperor who has no clothes can forget his condition when he ventures outside.

All the pictures, big cutouts, and film clips work for a reason; when not present, ridicule takes over from fear. The problem is to understand this reason. Ideology as mythmaking exists at the heart of Baʿthism, both as a movement and in power. Fictional goals and ideals about the future are axiomatic in the present and self-defining to every militant. Normally these are screened by rituals of membership and a hierarchy of degrees of commitment through sympathizers to the mass organizations and finally to the remains of a less organized population within whom can be found degrees of subservience, neutrality, and opposition to Baʿthism. In such a mediated and graduated environment, the inner sanctum of total fiction is rarely perceived as such, being buffered by layers of people whose location in the hierarchy generates confidence in the layers below and provides a small window on reality to those above. Baʿthism grew in this way as an opposition movement and set out to organize society along the same lines once it took power.[4]

Larger-than-life leadership originates in sweeping social control administered by the party political organization. The party is only super-

---

4. Hannah Arendt has analysed this phenomenon with striking brilliance in *The Origins of Totalitarianism* (New York: Harcourt Brace and Jovanovich, 1973), 364–88.

ficially at variance with its Leader for having been supplanted in its vanguard role. As soon as the party ceases to compete in the political arena
because all opposition has been consumed by it (the outcome of how
sweeping its social control really is), the two functions previously housed
within—generation of ideology and the organization of members—tend
towards separate identities. The whole of society is in principle being
routinely organized by the party; the vision that led an individual into
the party when competing world views were at stake has its charisma
threatened by routinism, drudgery, administration patronage, and personal incompetence.

The tendency for the original vision to become the substance of politics is matched, therefore, by a countervailing tendency for it to preserve
itself by receding away from the mass of party members in the direction
of ever more removed and secretive bodies. The mark of the emerging
separation is that the original vision, along with its interpretation (politics), is now the domain of the secret police. That most dreaded of all
institutions judges everybody and everything in relation to this vision
and, in the absence of opposition, administers and monitors the masses'
conformity with it. The relationship of the secret police to the person of
the Leader is absolutely crucial to a regime like the Baʿth; not only do
these agencies always report directly to him, but his rise invariably originates in them.

The Leader at this point appears to be taking over from the party
political organization; in fact, a new division of labour is emerging between them, which artificially replicates the distinction between civil society and the state. The vision whose original purity was bound to be
tainted by the spread of the party's elephantine organization is now
swaddled up in the terrifying aura of omniscient "presence" associated
with the secret police. The separation reinforces the social weight of the
party and its overall bureaucratic efficiency, making it more "rational."
All political charisma can now be located in the person of the Leader.
One's colleague or boss can be criticized for insufficient loyalty to the
party when he shows up late for work because such criticism (like all
public forms of "self"-criticism) no longer introduces wrinkles into the
world of the party line, and what the Leader said or did not say. Before
the separation it was harder to ask such questions because these instantly took on a "political" character, threatening the fictional core of
the party and jeopardizing the organization.

To be such a Leader, the part must be well acted out. Authority is not
in the form of "pure" Weberian charisma, rooted in personal attributes

like extraordinary heroism or revelatory powers; it is rehearsed, staged, and elaborately organized. Charisma is indissolubly bound up with bureaucratic organization. The Leader's image must be at least as ubiquitous as his secret police, but in contrast to the hidden presence of agents and informers, it must be visible, solid, and overpowering.

In October 1983 new images of Saddam Husain disappeared from the media. Sources within the Iraqi government confirmed that an attempted coup had taken place, led by the head of Intelligence, Saddam's half-brother, Barazan al-Takriti. Months later Arab diplomats dismissed the initial reports, claiming there had been a family quarrel between the two men over Saddam's daughter's choice of fiancé. The president himself appeared to confirm this new interpretation in a news interview around the same time when he said his ousted half-brother was "not a plotter" and "no conspirator."[5] What was going on?

No one apart from Saddam Husain himself knew in 1983, or knows today, what if anything actually happened. More important, no one could find out even if they were foolish enough to try. This precondition makes the affair serve Saddam's absolutism, as opposed to undermining it. The signal to the masses that something was going on, or that they were supposed to start thinking that something was going on, was the disappearance of fresh images of the Leader from the news media. This was all the "proof" needed for whatever story Saddam Husain wished to concoct. Earlier conspiracies, the reader will remember, required a considerably larger dosage of "proofs" to achieve the same politically stabilizing effect. By 1983 Iraqis had become more gullible—that is, less political—than they were in 1969–70. It is quite wrong to think that "all of this can have happened only under pressure from high-ranking military officers."[6] Even perceptive and highly critical commentators fail to appreciate just how bizarre is the form of government that has arisen in Iraq.

Saddam's appearances on television lasting several hours a day in various guises are masterpieces of calculated duplicity. Only when we impose the criteria of the outside do we fail to see the deadening impact on the mind of this continuous flow of images. The propaganda is so "bad" that even some Iraqis will pretend to dismiss it; yet they bring their children up to applaud it. Imagine endlessly varied film clips of

---

5. For the first interpretation that a coup attempt had been foiled, see the report in *The Times*, October 27, 1983. For the new interpretation of a year later, see the *Christian Science Monitor*, July 20, 1984.

6. This is Hottinger's interpretation of the incident ("Personality Cult," 15).

Saddam Husain in local Arab attire one day and Kurdish dress the next. Picture him crouching around trenches in camouflage fatigues, standing erect in full parade uniform, embracing foreign dignitaries at the airport in the latest Pierre Cardin suit, handling machinery, reading the Qur'an, meeting Shi'ite religious notables, opening new buildings, giving lectures on architecture and the environment, looking grim, smiling, berating officials, sucking Cuban cigars, fondling babies, dropping in on "unsuspecting" citizens for breakfast, as a family man, and reviewing the latest captured military hardware. Saddam Husain had his family tree issued to the public; it traced his roots to 'Ali, the fourth caliph and patron imam of Shi'ism.[7] 'Ali was related to the prophet of course, but the tree does not make this last link in order to underline the political point of the whole exercise, and leave a little something to the imagination. This gesture was not made in weakness, or as an attempt by Saddam to ingratiate himself with Shi'is at a time of their regional activism. On the contrary it signified total contempt for the populace, large numbers of whom he knew would accept this proof of ancestry, largely because there was no longer a soul in the length and breadth of the country who could be heard if they were prepared to deny it.

Subjection to Ba'thist propaganda and organization over an extended period left the populace as cynical as it had become gullible. Politics in a country like Iraq is invariably associated with cheating and lying. This union of cynicism and gullibility begins to appear everywhere in society. No one has expressed it better than Arendt:

> In an ever-changing, incomprehensible world the masses had reached the point where they would, at the same time, believe everything and nothing, think that everything was possible and that nothing was true. . . . Mass propaganda discovered that its audience was ready at all times to believe the worst, no matter how absurd, and did not particularly object to being deceived because it held every statement to be a lie anyhow. The totalitarian mass leaders based their propaganda on the correct psychological assumption that, under such conditions, one could make people believe the most fantastic statements one day, and trust that if the next day they were given irrefutable proof of their falsehood, they would take refuge in cynicism; instead of deserting the leaders who had lied to them, they would protest that they had known all along that the statement was a lie and would admire the leaders for their superior tactical cleverness.[8]

7. The tree is reproduced in his semiofficial biography. See Amir Iskander, *Saddam Husain: Munadhilan, wa Mufakiran wa Insanan* (Paris: Hachette, 1981), 21.

8. Arendt, *The Origins*, 382.

Like infallibility, which is continually tested and reaffirmed through the pervasive recycling of lies, the Leader's omnipotence is acted out dramatically, as though performed on a stage. Favours are bestowed on people in such a way as to break the very rules the Leader's state enforces; he opens a hot line to the citizens at a fixed hour in order to listen to complaints, and follows this up by releasing someone's husband or son from a life sentence that his police had originally imposed; he hands out television sets and wads of freshly minted notes while touring villages in the south; and he drops in on apparently unsuspecting humble citizens to have breakfast and listen to their complaints. In all of this his freedom to act, even to break his own rules, is intentionally pitted against everyone else's profound unfreedom. The effect, however, is not to highlight the latter, but to confound it with the former.

The combination of all-pervasive organization and a closed ideological system, in which reasons for everything "float" magically in relation to the objectivity of the world, produces not only a stable polity (while the Leader is alive) but also citizens who feel extremely fragile. Doomed to teeter on the edge of a precipice, they are possessed by the need for a safety line of some sort. Hero worship of the Great Leader variety presents itself as such a safeguard. The heroes that do not exist in reality have to be clutched at in the imagination. This has now become possible (even necessary) because an individual's freedom has become so totally fused with the nation's sovereignty, which is only real because of the Leader's absolute freedom. Just as sovereignty is indivisible and singular, so too must personal freedom conform to the nation's dictate and adopt these attributes. The notion of freedom as a political condition that only exists because of the capacity of human beings to be different, to be in a minority, and not have to think the same deathly "free" thoughts is absent in Iraqi society. When it arose in the modern era, it was snuffed out, first by the growing ideological hegemony of pan-Arabism and later by the social organization of the second Baᶜthi regime. The absence not only of freedom, but also of the very *idea* of this kind of freedom, makes Saddam Husain's role-playing so effective.

The separation between organization and the generation of ideology taking place in the emergence of the Leader corresponds to a growing loss of identity on the part of the public. The original distinction in reality and definitionally between any public and those who rule over it was being erased in Iraq. Pervasive fear and insecurity resulted in a collapse of self-confidence. To the extent that society was successfully organized along Baᶜthist lines (and only to that extent), this fundamental boundary between ruler and ruled was torn down, and the Iraqi public lost its most important safeguard against the vagaries of authority. The masses' need for a leader correspondingly intensified as it took the form of a longing for that which they had allowed to be taken away from them.

The outcome can actually be seen in the physical appearance of a large number of Iraqi men, in their mannerisms, dress, mustache styles, and even some of their acquired character traits. The greater the pervasiveness of this manufactured aura of leadership, the more it is surrounded by fear and awe and the more it gets identified with the original vision of the party, not as this manifests itself in party platforms, but as the vision is now crystallized in the dreams of one man. Saddam Husain can now say anything with impunity. He can expostulate on the virtues of ʿAli, pray like a Shiʿite, and even espouse a new-found Iraqi patriotism. Unlike outsiders, the mass of Iraqis have not been duped into this stance; they have arrived at it by coming to believe in their own utter political worthlessness after having also experienced the same. Now the very phenomenon of Saddam Husain has about it the air of an "iron necessity" if the fragmentation and backwardness of the past is to be overcome.

As constitutions, laws, government departments, and routine procedures come and go, and as edicts continuously shower down from those on high with the most improbable and unpredictable implications on daily and personal affairs, the reality of the political edifice continuously slips out of the public's reach. Even in dealing with government departments or one's colleagues, things are never what they seem; the janitor may command more real power than the boss. A new directive does not have to have reasons for existing in the public mind, and reflecting on what they might be, even to oneself, would only distract from accepting the directive for what it is: an emanation of the will of the Leader, that one irreducible and solid fact from which the ephemerality of all the rest can be organized in the imagination. From all of this springs the oneness of identity between the public and its Leader created by *total* organization and the impossibility of achieving the same through populism or mere military dictatorship, no matter how brutal.

Even the most popular Third World leaders never commanded such a death-grip on their image and status as leaders. Thus, whereas Nasser's leadership was greatly tarnished by the magnitude of the 1967 defeat, the Egyptian public remained intact, demonstrating this to itself and to those who had defeated it by tossing back into office this ghost of the hero that once had been. Soon, this same self-assured public made the impossible—a peace treaty with Israel—possible, and even desirable as shown by the hundreds of thousands that came to greet Sadat upon his return from Jerusalem. It is simply unimaginable that an Iraqi defeat in the Iraq-Iran war would have remotely comparable consequences.

Unlike Nasser, the phenomenon of Saddam Husain does not arise from personal accomplishments; it originates in his relation to the party. Saddam emerged as Leader while lacking some of Nasser's greatest assets: his personal magnetism, powers of oratory, sense of diplomacy and political timing, and most important "his" Suez.[9] Nonetheless, it takes a very special kind of person to become Saddam Husain's kind of Leader.

Ironically, the Suez watershed in Arab politics first brought the young Saddam into the Iraqi branch of the Baʿth party while still a teenage secondary-school student. Shortly after joining, Saddam ("the one who confronts") made his mark by assassinating a prominent Qassem supporter in his hometown of Takrit. The party leadership subsequently selected him as a member of the hit team that tried to assassinate Qassem in 1959. The myth and the man merge in this episode. His biography—and Iraqi television, which stages the story ad nauseam—tells of his familiarity with guns from the age of ten; his fearlessness and loyalty to the party during the 1959 operation; his bravery in saving his comrades by commandeering a car at gunpoint; the bullet that was gouged out of his flesh under his direction in hiding; the iron discipline that led him to draw a gun on weaker comrades who would have dropped off a seriously wounded member of the hit team at a hospital; the calculating shrewdness that helped him save himself minutes before the police broke in leaving his wounded comrades behind; and finally the long trek of a wounded man from house to house, from city to town, across the desert to refuge in Syria.[10]

Saddam Husain, the quintessential professional militant, had no per-

9. Saddam Husain understood that his relation to the party was the basis of the differences between himself and Nasser. In December 1978 he had this conversation with Castro:

> *Castro:* Time works in favor of Iraq, because you are developing the country as a whole, you are mobilizing the masses. This was not done in Egypt.
> *Saddam:* There was no revolutionary party in Egypt; there was only ʿAbd al-Nasir. He was a revolutionary, but his conditions differed from yours [i.e., Cuba's]. You created revolutionaries before you came to power; this ʿAbd al-Nasir did not do. In Iraq, we created revolutionaries before taking power . . . the party gave sacrifices and martyrs and suffered imprisonment and torture. All of this was indispensable in order to forge revolutionaries who know how to hold on to the revolution."   From Iskander, *Saddam Husain,* 214.

10. The lurid details are in ibid., chap. 3–7.

sonal or working life outside the party. Even his years in secondary school and college were immersed in political activity. His lack of military training sets him apart from so many other militant youth of his generation (although his political vocabulary is permeated with military metaphors). The pent-up violence in the man's personal makeup was always controlled and directed by a political sense of judgement. The Ba'thi traditions in which he was immersed were originally applied to the new problems of consolidation, elimination of opponents, and organization of a new Iraqi social order. Saddam Husain, unlike Idi Amin or Papa Doc, is marked by this calculated, disciplined, and above all effortless resort to violence genuinely conceived to be in the service of more exalted aims. His language is therefore a reflection of his personality—as opposed to professional training—in which violence and vision, through party organization, got distilled into a volatile mixture.

Such men are feared, not loved; above all they command enormous respect in a populace to whom strength of character is invariably associated with the ability to both sustain and inflict pain. The madness inherent in the elevation of raw violence to such a status in the affairs of human beings appears as such only from the outside; from within respect, no matter how grudgingly bestowed, eventually gives way to awe. Promoted by the organizational omnipotence of the party and the preeminence of fear in people's daily lives, such awe accentuates individual feelings of utter helplessness and worthlessness. The size of the gap between awe and worthlessness is a measure of the Leader's infallibility in the eyes of his followers, a perception that follows from their loss of identity and defencelessness brought on by the dissolution of all moral norms that are not those of the Ba'th. The public's ability to judge what is right or wrong about its affairs, what is real as opposed to mere illusion, has broken down completely.

The rise of Saddam Husain signifies the fulfillment of a logic in Ba'thism that had almost been choked off by the party's long-standing love-hate relationship with the military. Ideologically the Ba'th were inimically hostile to military rule, but the founding leaders had toyed with using the military to gain power. In view of the attraction that pan-Arabism has always exerted among officer elites, the combination (which overwhelmed the Syrian branch) had on several occasions threatened the entire existence of the party in its original form. The legacy of Saddam Husain is that he kept alive that original purist content in Ba'thism by realizing it in one country. He held the military at bay while cutting away at their power base, and eventually he transformed them into creatures of the party that had nurtured him and that had been the obsession of his entire mature life.

This rise took place at the expense of other leaders in the RCC. The July 1979 purge was a blow against the political authority of the party only in the sense that it completed the transfer of its ideology-generating, politics-making, and charismatic functions into his person; the rest of the party's organizing function remained intact. It therefore clarified an ambiguity that existed in the formal status of the RCC as the highest decision-making authority in the land, despite the fact that Saddam Husain had actually been in control of all real power for many years now. This ambiguity tainted Baʿthism as much as the party's organization of society tended to do, because just as no two people can tell a lie or keep a secret as well as one, so too no plurality of men can ever be as good an embodiment of a fictional essence—or a sovereign "general will"—as one man. With this last impediment out of the way, the stage was set for the will of the Leader to be ipso facto that of the party leadership, the party organization, and society as a whole. The freedom of all was now completely coincident with the absolutely unfettered freedom of Saddam Husain. At this crucial point it became possible for Baʿthi violence, hitherto contained within Iraqi confines, to spill over into a great war with the least chance of a split in the party's own ranks and hence in the loyalties of the masses.

Saddam Husain as a phenomenon goes beyond the Baʿth party and the extent of its organization of Iraqi society. He has become the personification of what that same public perceives to be its own "Iraqi" character. There is no paradox in the fact that the Leader of an intensely pan-Arabist party combines qualities that reinforce his imagery and status in Iraqi society in particular. A distinction must be maintained between an Iraqi national "character" and Iraqi nationalism.

Iraqi nationalism understood as a sense of identity with a territorial entity known as Iraq does not exist. The mosaic of communities and sects that make up the country have never been prepared to sink their differences into a broader sense of community, as happened, for example, in Egypt. This state of affairs was a factor in the stabilization of Baʿth rule and the form of legitimacy on which it became based.

On the other hand, an Iraqi national "character" is a complex centuries-old ensemble of perceptions and sensibilities affecting myriads of phenomena in culture and society. I will focus on that small part of it that deals with the Iraqi perception of "what it takes to rule in Iraq." Sunni and Shiʿi Iraqi Arabs have always thought of themselves as having to be ruled in a certain way. Frequently in casual conversation they will contrast themselves with Egyptians or Indians for whom being subjugated, as many Iraqis would put it, is "part of their nature." Such prejudices have deep and far-flung roots in Mesopotamia. But the most persistent ideas of rulership can be traced to events decisive to the rupture between ancient and Arab-Islamic Iraq: the Muslim conquest, the emergence of Iraqi Shi'ism, the martyrdom of Husain in A.D. 680, the shift in control of the province of Iraq from Persia to a Damascus-based Umayyad dynasty, and eventually the breakup of this last purely Arab-centred caliphate coincident with the rise of a still Arab but now Persian-tainted Abbasid dynasty based in the new city of Baghdad. Iraqi Shi'ism and Sunnism are still rooted in the emotionally charged mythologies surrounding these events (see Chapter 6).

A key figure in this centuries-long transition was the fascinating personality of al-Hadjadj ibn Yusuf al-Thaqafi. Appointed governor of the province in A.D. 694 after serving with distinction as head of the police force of 'Abd al-Malik, the Damascus-based Caliph, al-Hadjadj brought stability and economic growth to turbulent Iraq. Historians believe he laid the foundations for the flowering of culture under the Abbasids. Long before oil revenues made life so much easier for despots, al-Hadjadj built cities, struck the first Arab coins, and revolutionized agricultural productivity. He took drastic measures to stop migration into towns (as did Saddam Husain) and forced newly converted Muslims to return to lands they had abandoned and continue paying the *kharadj* (a tax on non-Muslims that stimulated conversions, resulting in a fiscal crisis for the Caliphate that Hadjadj is largely credited with resolving). Under his tutelage, the first uniform edition of the Qur'an was produced. To end the quarrels of the theologians, Hadjadj then decreed it the authoritative text, enforcing his decision by draconian rule—or what has gone down in popular folklore as such.[11]

The analogy between al-Hadjadj and Saddam Husain is very striking. The Sunni–Shi'i schism was making its first appearance in the form of Damascene Arab hegemony over what had been a province of the Iranian Sassanian Empire. Remarkably, Iraqi Ba'thism has succeeded in reassembling highly charged emotive ingredients plucked out of Iraqi

---

11. Marshall Hodgson describes al-Hadjadj's reign as one of "frank terror" in *The Venture of Islam* (Chicago: University of Chicago Press, 1974), 223. The *Encyclopaedia of Islam*, 2d ed., is more cautious, contending that the mythology surrounding his reign has exaggerated the issue of violence. Either way makes no difference from the standpoint of the relevance of the analogy.

history in such a manner as to embody no longer only the Sunni claim to the Islamic and political heritage but also the whole splendiferous drama of Iraq's rise to preeminence under the Abbasids, the preconditions for which were laid down by al-Hadjadj's visionary ruthlessness.

Thus, for instance, Saddam Husain's new-found emphasis on Iraqism in the 1980s (after the start of the Iraq-Iran war) entailed an enormous ideological buildup on the superiority of the homegrown Abbasid heritage as contrasted to other epochs in the classical Islamic period. The emphasis shifted towards pan-Arab socialism passing through the success of the Baʿthi revolution in Iraq. "The glory of the Arabs stems from the glory of Iraq," Saddam Husain said in a hyperbolic speech delivered in 1979 in a southern Shiʿi province. "Throughout history, whenever Iraq became mighty and flourished, so did the Arab nation. This is why we are striving to make Iraq mighty, formidable, able and developed, and why we shall spare nothing to improve welfare and to brighten the glory of Iraqis." [12] The lion's share of ideological attention could now be placed on the Iraqi people and "their" party-state, which nonetheless remained uncomfortably housed within the artificial confines of the Iraqi borders.

Saddam Husain was not calling upon Iraqis to rally around their state in the name of some sense of territorial identity that he thought they shared regarding the borders of Iraq. Of all people, he was most acutely aware that Iraqi nationalism, to the extent that it existed in modern times, was entirely a product of the hated ancien régime between 1941 and 1958. At the same time, Saddam Husain was expressing his party's belated realism about the receding likelihood of Arab unity as originally envisioned in the ideology. Many Baʿthists now wanted to put aside the "Arab revolution" as a permanent or simultaneous happening. "Socialism in one country" was the slogan of the late 1970s. To use these kinds of post-1979 statements from Saddam Husain—or the elaborations of his army of propagandists, artists, historians, teachers, and archaeologists who started searching for an authentically Mesopotamian Islamic identity—as "proof" of some kind of genuine Iraqi nationalism—is to make a false extrapolation from the experiences of other countries (Great Russian nationalism during World War II is the classic example—Stalin did not invent it, he simply chose to fan it). Regardless of whether Saddam wished to rely on Iraqi nation-

---

12. Quoted in A. Baram's article, "Qawmiyya and Wataniyya in Baʿthi Iraq: The Search for a New Balance," *Middle Eastern Studies* 19, no. 2 (April 1983): 194.

alism during the Iraq-Iran war, his regime actually ended up stressing the Arab versus Persian theme.

By contrast, the analogy with al-Hadjadj is deep rooted and to the point. Unlike Iraqi nationalism, it can be construed as a threat to the Ba'th. In 1975 'Abd al-Sattar Nasser published in Beirut a satire *Sayyiduna al-Khalifa* (Our Lord the Caliph) that captured the essential quality of Ba'thi rule: "Sorrow is absolutely prohibited, as noted by the Caliph in the margins of file number 105B, which is an appendix to the decree of al-Hadjadj ibn Yusif that states: laugh a lot so that we can show you off to the world." 'Abd al-Sattar Nasser committed the mortal sin of scorning the Ba'th. Shortly after publication, he was arrested, charged with spying for an unnamed country, and tortured.[13]

In the end Iraqi nationalism in Ba'thist hands is, to paraphrase 'Abd al-Sattar, merely a device designed to force Iraqis to "laugh a lot" so that they can be shown off to the world, thereby fooling all the instant experts who think it has something to do with how the Ba'th are surviving a gruelling war they cannot hope to win.[14] The powerful bonds that have kept army and society intact during the war have more to do with the very specific type of polity created by the Iraqi Ba'th than with Iraqi nationalism.

The ideas of rulership that Saddam Husain has come to epitomize in the public imagination were vividly spelled out many centuries ago by al-Hadjadj. Upon assuming his governorship, he is said to have promptly executed a number of dissidents whose heads were placed on public display. The occasion was used to give an address to the assembled populace. It contained these immortal lines, which every Iraqi school child knows, and which are popularly felt to be a truism on the exercise of political power in Iraq:

> I see heads before me that are ripe and ready for the plucking, and I am the one to pluck them, and I see blood glistening between the turbans and the beards.

13. The story first appeared in *Al-Mawqif al-Adabi*, Beirut, no. 9 (January 1975). It was reprinted in *Free Kurdistan*, London, no. 6 (December 1975). In 1975 the journal *Mawaqif*, nos. 30–31, noted the facts of the arrest along with a commentary.

14. C. M. Helms is such an expert. The publication of her book coincided with the reopening of the Iraqi embassy in Washington, closed since 1967; it so warmed the hearts of Ba'thist authority that they took to distributing free copies. Helms thinks that Saddam Husain the pragmatist is really an Iraqist at heart, who "publicly discarded with absolute clarity the notion of a single Arab state." Moreover, the Iraqi Ba'th's tough line on Israel stems from a purely "idealized conception of unity." The Ba'th therefore have two completely contradictory positions; an "idealistic" one that she wants readers to discount, and a pragmatic one that she wants the American State Department to take seriously. See *Eastern Flank*, 110 and 114.

By God, O people of Iraq, people of discord and dissembling and evil
character! I cannot be squeezed like a fig or scared like a camel with old
water skins. . . . The Commander of the Faithful [the caliph] emptied his
quiver and bit his arrows and found me the bitterest and hardest of them all.
Therefore he aimed me at you. For a long time now you have been swift to
sedition; you have lain in the lairs of error and have made a rule of transgres-
sion. By God, I shall strip you like bark, I shall truss you like a bundle of
twigs, I shall beat you like stray camels. . . . By God, what I promise, I fulfill;
what I purpose, I accomplish; what I measure, I cut off. Enough of these
gatherings and this gossip. . . . I swear by God that you will keep strictly to
the true path, or I shall punish every man of you in his body.[15]

The Authority of the Ba'th

Analogies always break down; the one between al-Hadjadj and Saddam Husain does so in one very interesting way. Al-Hadjadj's Kufa
speech was a declaration of war against the very people he had come to
govern. One simply cannot imagine Saddam Husain using such speech
by the late 1970s. His problem with al-Hadjadj's words would not arise
from a more refined cultural background, or an aversion for forth-
rightness. The discerning observer must look elsewhere: at the completely different perceptions of each ruler emanating from below.

Not all power is legitimate; political authority, unlike raw power, is
power delegated through a process of legitimation. Al-Hadjadj's power
was not yet a genuine authority, because the populace in Kufa would
not give him their allegiance and had other ideas about who should rule.
Damascus sent al-Hadjadj to deal with the situation. In such circumstances the war analogy holds, up to a point. Al-Hadjadj was out to defeat the authority that was imbued with legitimacy in the minds of
Kufans, but not to the point of killing every last one of his future subjects.

On the other hand, Saddam Husain already exercised genuine authority. The partnership between social organization channelled through
the Ba'th party bureaucracy and political leadership now focussed on a
manufactured personal charisma presumes a legitimacy to the conditions surrounding the exercise of political power. In other words, the
Leader syndrome in Iraqi Ba'thist conditions entailed the rise of a shared
conception of legitimate authority within the polity. This was a new conception of authority for modern Iraq uniquely associated with the Ba'thi
experience.

15. Bernard Lewis, ed., *Islam: From the Prophet Muhammad to the Capture of Con-
stantinople,* vol. 1: *Politics and War* (New York: Harper and Row, 1974), 23–24 (an an-
notated English-language collection of historical documents).

If power had not undergone such legitimation, authority could not be absolutely vested in a Leader. It might remain, for instance, vested in the party and more than one leader. In single-party regimes this is a recipe for conflict, factionalism, *and* a modicum of real political life, however spurious some of us may find this kind of politics. A powerful leader who has not focussed onto his person all political authority, and wanted to do so, would necessarily conflict with his party and remain "fallible" in the eyes of his public—the outcome of the necessarily public nature of such a conflict. If the Leader emerged triumphant, absolutism and infallibility would become once again (or for the first time) attributes of a leadership vested with authority.

Whereas the history of the second Baʿthi regime is littered with such conflicts between 1968 and the middle 1970s, there is no evidence that they played a significant role after that. Despite seven gruelling years of warfare, a string of costly miscalculations, about a million mobilized men, possibly two to three hundred thousand dead, many times that number of casualties, to say nothing of all the economic and infrastructural destruction, the leadership of Saddam Husain remains unchallenged. Of course party–leader or party–state conflicts *do exist,* in some incipient psychological or even barely detectable behavioural form (absolutism and infallibility are unattainable ideals to which the kind of Leader we are discussing aspires, but in practice life becomes intolerable relatively soon in the long march). But this is not relevant. In politics, a conflict only exists in public; otherwise it is merely a potential for conflict, which we can never be certain exists or will materialize.

An even prior assumption (or condition) for this kind of leadership is the forfeiture of authority by "the people" to the party organization. The same line of reasoning applies to this depoliticization of society as did to the party organization. To the extent that such a forfeiture is not accomplished (for example, because of the actions of small fundamentalist groups like *al-Daʿwah*), the party organization remains political, and leadership is that much less absolute, and fallible.

Saddam Husain's authority can be thought of as having been acquired across three stages of transference. First, authority was merely posited to exist in the party by an act of will. The party was the originator/author of that which it wanted others to carry out. Second, compliance with this act of authorship was acquired gradually by means of the numerical and qualitative growth of the party and the front organizations it created. The power of large numbers of people was becoming an attribute of the party. Now through growth the authority of the party was on its way to becoming *real,* as opposed to being merely posited.

The party organization was substituting itself for a civil society, which was ceasing to exist. Third, as a consequence of this metamorphosis, the authorship of political ideas became jeopardized; the "author" was in danger of being lost in the bodily morass. Hence the Leader syndrome as the substitute for all politics. However, the party that conceded its political authority to the Leader as it replaced civil society remained the power base of the new authority.

Logically the second stage of transference was the crucial moment. What motivated people to enter the party? While many complex reasons probably exist, I believe that fear was, and still is, the socially dominant motivation in Ba'thist Iraq. Fear lies at one extreme of a continuum, the other end of which is autonomous consent based on active belief. Normally, the latter is viewed as a binding motivation on individuals that gives rise to a truly legitimate authority. Fraudulent elections, for example, delegitimize power, as demonstrated by the dramatic fall of Marcos, the former president of the Philippines. If it can be shown that deep-rooted fear also legitimates power, albeit of a very unusual kind, then surely it would follow that a genuine authority had become vested in Saddam Husain. Herein resides the most fundamental specificity of the Ba'thi regime in Iraq.

Four centuries ago, during the English civil war, when life was "nasty, brutish and short," Thomas Hobbes integrated fear into an analysis of legitimate power. He was the first, and certainly the greatest, political thinker to do so. The world from which he made his deductions was made up of equal but separate individuals whose arithmetic sum constituted "society." Separateness arose from the absence of any obligations or sense of responsibility between individuals. In this "state of nature," the war of each against all was the governing condition of existence.

Individuals, Hobbes argued, were driven by their reason and their passions. Reason led them to realize that to further their own interests they would have to give up their natural rights "even to one another's body," not by wishing these rights away, which was fanciful, but by ceding their quotum of power in perpetuity, each separately, to some entity authorized to use the aggregated power thus assembled to maintain the peace. His point was to argue that the mere existence of state power implied a covenant of this nature binding men to each other.[16] The cove-

16. "This done, the Multitude so united in one Person, is called a COMMON-WEALTH, in latine CIVITAS. This is the Generation of that great LEVIATHAN, or rather (to speak more reverently) of that *Mortall God*, to which wee owe under the *Immortal God*, our peace and defence. For by this Authoritie, given him by every particular man in

nant only worked because each person did not have to rely on the other's virtue, but on the simultaneity of all persons having ceded their little bit of power to a third party entrusted to intervene as it saw fit. Whereas notions of justice, obligation, and morality were meaningless in a "state of nature," in the new state the unfettered will of the ruler was justice, and a system of moral obligations towards him was incumbent on citizens being in the nature of the contract made to ward off insecurity. No wondrous and uplifting virtues had been presupposed. "Reason" dictated that an underlying consensus existed in the polity, and nothing was in principle inviolable to the ruler's will. The elegant nub of Hobbes's argument is this derivation of a theory of political obligation from a world he so insistently defined as utterly amoral.

The passions that drive individuals, however, are even "more potent" than their reason. Foremost among the "Passions that incline men to Peace" is "Feare of Death." Whether state power was originally acquired by consent of the multitude or by force, its legitimacy derived from this fear "which is to be noted by them, that hold all such Covenants, as proceed from fear of death, or violence, voyd."[17] The liberty enjoyed in the new polity is consistent with fear, and arises from the refusal to do violence to one's own person. Of secondary importance is that domain in which the sovereign chooses not to legislate, and in which, as a consequence, citizens are free to pursue their own desires.

Hobbes maintained at the centre of his analysis the fundamental insight that state power always rested on a monopoly of the means of violence. However, he placed the emphasis on an underlying *consensus* for which a monopoly of violence by some third party was intrinsic. The system of obligations and responsibilities, which he did not presuppose on the grounds of some prepolitical (frequently religious) conception of human nature, was constituted politically by the very construction of his kind of state power.

To grant Hobbes his assumptions is to concede the argument. Clearly, he had no place for society as a category set apart from the political realm. Civil society, however, presents itself factually as a complex en-

---

the Common-Wealth, he hath the use of so much Power and Strength conferred on him, that by terror thereof, he is inabled to forme the wills of them all, to Peace at home. . . . And in him consisteth the Essence of the Common-Wealth; which . . . is *One Person, of whose Acts a great Multitude, by mutuall Covenants one with another, have made themselves every one the Author, to the end he may use the strength and means of them all, as he shall think expedient.*" Thomas Hobbes, *Leviathan* (London: Penguin, 1982), 227–28.

17. Ibid., 188 and 252, respectively.

tity with many acquired and inherited stratifications, divisions, and associations of individuals. These "groups," whether arising from birth, belief, division of labour, or the relationship to the means of production, render transfers of power an enormously more complicated affair than Hobbes's agglomeration of Robinson Crusoes suggests.[18] Furthermore, the Hobbesian schema assumes that the source of all obligations in human affairs must be rational. Contrary to Hobbes's philosophically untenable logic, nineteenth-century capitalism and bourgeois democracy evolved in tandem in the form of the liberal state and on the basis of an intensely disputed, yet real, broadening of the democratic franchise.

However, Hobbes's "errors" look different when viewed through the prism of Iraqi Ba'thism. The Ba'th can be thought of as having aimed at the manufacture of a Hobbesian world. Their project was to destruct the social reality they inherited into a new set of equally weighted constituent elements—frightened, rootless individuals, alienated from their traditional groups (kin, tribe, sect, class)—and then to reassemble these fragments within a new state-centralized network of relationships. The undifferentiated Leviathan-like mass that emerged was in principle either hostile to or sealed off from any other "partial," non-Ba'thist sense of belonging.

The only sense in which one can speak of the Ba'th as bourgeois lies in their trenchant insistence on the creation of a genuinely mass society in which individuals have been uprooted and alienated from their past. The individualism of the masses is a very radical project, and to go about administering such surgery on a backward society is bound to be a nasty business. Moreover, the individual "made" in this fashion is different from the one who has so to speak "made himself" through acting upon the world in a struggle to expand personal space and degrees of freedom. The ideally formed Ba'thist individual lacks the civilizing attributes of bourgeois society and consequently is left suspended in a no-man's land, one that is both characteristically modern and terrifyingly primitive—a Hobbesian "state of nature" if you will.

For this imaginative leap, Ba'thism needed to expunge from reality that which in Hobbes's model had not even existed—civil society. They could only do this by instilling the kind of fear that he had merely posited. Therefore, they needed the institutions of violence described in Chapter 1. Of course, Hobbes's concern was quite the reverse: to rid

---

18. C. B. Macpherson has convincingly shown this flaw in Hobbes's reasoning. See his introduction to the Penguin edition, esp. pp. 55–56.

individuals of the "feare of death" that haunted them in their naturally "free" state. The establishment of order through the absolute power of the sovereign would banish that fear by taking away the individual freedom to act autonomously; the Ba'th take away the same thing by instilling a fear that did not originally exist.

Both thus end up—the Ba'th in political reality (to the extent that they have succeeded), and Hobbes in abstract theory—having conferred upon the sovereign power by "the consent of the people" the fundamentally devastating attribute that "every particular man is Author of all the Soveraigne doth; and consequently he that complaineth of injury from his Soveraigne complaineth of that whereof he himself is Author; and therefore ought not to accuse any man but himselfe."[19]

AUTHORITY AND MORALITY

Tyrannies and dictatorships resort to violence when their authority is placed in jeopardy. But for the Ba'th, violence is no longer merely the ultimate sanction used periodically against a genuine opposition. The Ba'th invent their enemies; violence—not the threat of it—is institutionalized, forever reproducing and intensifying that all-pervasive climate of suspicion, fear, and complicity so characteristic of their polity. Violence generates the fear that creates the complicity that constitutes the power, which first passed to the party and then to Saddam Husain in the form of his authority. Fear, which under other conditions can tear authority asunder (for instance, soldiers refusing to fight, or the dramatic collapse of central power in some civil war situations), drove authority in Iraq to collapse inwards, into the bottomless black hole of absolutist leadership.

The larger the number of armed men and informers, and the better organized by comparison with what the opposition can muster, the greater the power behind the authority. Authority is singular, but power exists in numbers and is the outcome of people acting in concert. So defined, power is distinct from violence, which is instrumental and in need of a human agency willing to act for the sake of justifiable ends.[20] Even in Ba'thist Iraq violence itself can never be the main issue. The problem has already been transferred onto other levels. Why were there 1 million

19. Hobbes, *Leviathan*, 232.
20. Hannah Arendt's essay "On Violence" draws out the distinctions between power, violence, and terror employed in this argument. They are, however, also implicit in Hobbes. See *Crises of the Republic* (New York: Harcourt Brace and Jovanovich, 1972).

party members, or 677,000 armed men by 1980? Who "forced" them to enter? Once inside, did complicity take over, or were they still able to make "choices"? Were their families coerced? What about informers, followers-of-orders, careerists, the meek, victims of circumstances, and members of labour, student, women's and children's groups organized en masse by the party? These are murky waters indeed. We can only navigate through them with a view of politics rooted in people's behaviour, not in the ineffable realm of human psychology.

Before the Ba'th came along, the experience of fascism and Stalinism taught the lesson that legitimate authority involved compliance or assent, irrespective of whether these were given voluntarily or not. The Nazi concentration camps, the Gulag, and Stalin's purges were legally justifiable actions of regimes endowed with legitimacy. By acquiescing in the abolition of an important bourgeois distinction between law and morality, society had become implicated in anything political authority might do in the name of either.

The difference between law and morality never resided in *what* they prohibited or commanded, only in *how* they went about shaping behaviour. Law is a coercive order that attaches the state's monopoly of the means of violence to its sanctions; the moral order does not have these means. The political issue in Germany in the 1930s was not the morality of the German people; it was acceptance of the idea that state violence could be used to purify the German race, promote a "racial conscience," or develop a "healthy national sentiment," all in the service of a morality that, however obnoxious it might have been, was novel only in that it would and could use the state to eradicate all others. Large numbers of Germans chose at that moment in their history to look to the Nazis to carry through this fusion of the legal and moral orders. Moreover, bourgeois Germany had the wherewithal to achieve this formidable task, something no premodern state ever possessed. Procedural law gave way to administrative decree signifying that the state, harbinger of a new intolerance, was now able to get on with its business. If one does not uphold the preposterous notion that Hitler perpetrated an enormous lie on the German people, then the legality of the gas ovens originated in the acceptance of this particular transformation of the German polity. Whether we like it or not, learning from the moral conundrums posed by such experiences necessitates putting aside the infantile notion that people treat all rulers who coerce them as illegitimate.

On a smaller scale, the experience of the Iraqi Ba'th establishes yet again the radical separation of the question of legitimacy from that of autonomous consent. The Baʿth turned fear into the precondition for their legitimacy. In various societies and historical situations, people have been deemed not responsible for actions committed under duress; a confession extracted under torture is today inadmissible as evidence all over the world (in principle, not in practice of course). But it was not always so; Roman law and later on the practices of the Inquisition prized the "truth" dug out through bodily disfigurement above all other evidence. By presupposing, for instance, that torture is immoral, later generations of Iraqis will certainly try to untie the Gordian knot of Baʿthist legitimacy. In the meantime, Iraqis must live with the consequences of their actions regardless of legal niceties and despite postulated "rights," which at this point in time have no real currency within the culture. The world of political facts is less kind than that of human rights. For even if an authority rooted in fear and complicity is deemed to differ in quality from that generated by say free elections, Iraqis are bound to be haunted in the future, as Argentines were in the wake of the collapse of their military junta, by the knowledge that however different the new circumstances, the outcome was nonetheless authoritative.[21]

The Source of Authority

If the form that the authority of the Baʿth eventually adopted was that of the Leviathan, or the Leader syndrome, it still had to have a content made up of principles peculiar to Baʿthism. These principles would have had to become broadly accepted to be used by the Leader with impunity to justify all his actions, including the fear that lay at the roots of his authority. These principles are the Baʿthist analogue for a Hobbesian social contract; they underpin the system of political and ultimately moral obligations that originate in the Hobbesian construction of

21. Argentine political life since the 1983 elections has been transfixed by the memory of the years of terror under the military. Newspapers, magazines, books, and films keep on exposing new atrocities and probing into the memory of victims and perpetrators, asking how could it all have happened and why did so many Argentines keep quiet. It is impossible to exaggerate the impact of the issue of responsibility asked by Argentines of themselves, particularly during the eight-month public trial of former military rulers. Nor have the guilty verdicts passed down in those trials ended two years of moral introspection recently highlighted by two compelling new Argentine films, *The Official Story* and *The Kiss of the Spiderwoman*. A riveting account of the new atmosphere in Argentina was given by a former torture victim of the military junta, Jacobo Timerman. See his article "Return to Argentina," in the *New York Times Magazine*, March 11, 1984, pp. 36–99.

authority. Aryanism, anti-Semitism, and state-worship, among other things, fulfilled such a role in Europe during the interwar period. What is the Ba'thist equivalent in Iraq today?

> Authority is not exercised for itself or in itself by man for the sake of man. Thus the exercise of Authority must be carried out with the people's consent and only then can it be legitimate. Therefore the people are the source of the legitimacy of authority.
>
> But if the people is "the source of authority and its legitimacy," as is stated by the Iraqi Constitution (Art. 2), then it is the definition of the concept of people on which the definition of the kind of democracy depends. This . . . will determine the kind or nature of the political system, i.e. the way of exercising authority in the society. . . .
>
> The people as interpreted by the Revolution and the Leading Party, the Arab Ba'th Socialist Party, is all the members of the Society who enjoy equal rights and equal duties. But in exercising democracy . . . it is inevitable to exclude all persons who take a political, economical or intellectual attitude hostile to the Revolution and its programme. The status of these people shall be defined . . . by the laws and measures taken by the authorities concerned. Revolutionary political consciousness shall play a decisive role in immunizing public opinion towards them. This being an exceptional case created by the necessity of transforming society.[22]

The criterion for membership in a polity is the starting point for politics. The Legal Reform Law, a forty-three-page document promulgated by the RCC in 1977 after a stable political situation was emerging for the first time since 1958, was intended to set guidelines for the complete overhaul of the Iraqi legal system. The preamble states that the new law "has depended in defining the goals, concepts and purports of legal reform on the ideological bases and notions contained in the Political Report of the Eighth Regional Conference" of the ABSP. In other words the law was designed for internal purposes, taken very seriously, and conceived as a follow-up to a document that itself represented an ideological benchmark in assessing the party's experience in power. We are considering, therefore, a true statement of the Iraqi Ba'thi conception of this criterion.

The idea at issue is the necessity to define "the people." For some reason, this category cannot be taken for granted by the Ba'th as it was for so many other movements and revolutions. Nor does it fall in place "naturally" from considerations of birth and residence, adherence to a certain religion (Israel), or by virtue of racist ideologies that make a bio-

---

22. Law no. 35 of 1977, Legal System Reform, *Alwaqai al-Iraqiyya* 20, no. 37 (September 14, 1977): 21.

logical (Nazism) or racial claim (South Africa and the United States before the Civil War). Because the people are the source of authority, their definition is a serious issue.

The most striking thing about the definition is the absence of even pseudoobjective criteria. The Baʿth do not place the emphasis on birthplace, domicile, place and duration of residence, skin color, racial origin, or ancestry. Even Arabic and Islam, the formal language and religion of the state according to the 1968 constitution, are secondary to this original act of faith in the principles of the Revolution and its leading party, which the individual is asked to make in advance of citizenship.

The same point was made by Saddam Husain in a 1973 speech on the Kurdish question in Iraq. The ABSP, he said, "does not regard itself . . . as the Arabs' authority alone. In fact it regards itself as the authority representing the will of both the Arabs and Kurds alike, or the will of the whole Iraqi people with its Arabs, Kurds and other minorities. On this basis, the concept that the national authority is a party to a dispute in which our Kurdish people are the other party is unacceptable."[23] We should keep in mind that a civil war was on the verge of breaking out whose chief characteristic was going to be the unprecedented degree to which the Iraqi Kurds would rally around their Kurdish leadership. The vehemence with which Saddam rejects *the very idea* that a national authority could be in conflict with a section of *its own* people is important. From such a standpoint all Kurds had to become mercenaries and foreign agents during the 1974–75 war unless they were fighting with the government. And this was the only way Kurds were ever referred to in Baʿthist literature of the time. Simply by rallying to *another* leadership they were no longer included in the definition of the people to which the ABSP subscribed. Because they were resident on Iraqi territory, they became outsiders of an insidious sort. Saddam's view that a people divided on itself simply cannot exist is a long-standing and deeply rooted Baʿthist doctrine to which I shall return in Chapter 6.

Formulating the question like this is not the same as making the claim that a part of the people no longer understands what is in its own best interest, or have been misled by false leaders. When Reza Shah and Attaturk subdued rebellious nationalities in Iran and Turkey, they did so on the grounds that the hundreds of thousands of people they killed

23. Saddam Husain, *On Current Affairs* (Baghdad: al-Thawra Publications, 1974), 12.

were already Iranians and Turks. To think otherwise would have robbed their nation-building wars of their legitimacy. To this day in Turkey, a Kurd can only be referred to as a "Mountain Turk." On the other hand, when the Young Turks resolved in 1915 to settle the Armenian question by way of exterminating some 1.5 million Armenians, they did so because their pan-Turkic racism *excluded the idea* that an Armenian could ever become a Turk. This also is not what Saddam Husain said about Iraqi Kurds in 1973.

In principle, for the Ba'th, the exercise of power is not associated with membership of a particular ethnic or religious group. However unlikely it might be that a Kurd would ever amount to anything inside a party that is after all indubitably Arab, the Ba'th cannot formalize the exclusion of all Kurds on the grounds of their Kurdishness. Allegiance to their party is strictly ideological, almost to the point of incoherence:

> The constitution of the Party does not restrict membership of the organization of the Party on the basis of race. All those who believe in the future of the Arabs and struggle for the Arab nation can join the Arab Ba'th Socialist Party and consider themselves, as a consequence of their leading responsibility in the state, leaders not only of the Arabs but of the entire state, which is responsible for all citizens, Arabs, Kurds, and minorities.[24]

People can of course be excluded in various ways. Saddam Husain's generosity originates in the extreme subjectivity of both his criteria for party membership and the Ba'thist notion of what it means to be an Arab. The quality of being an Arab is itself an entirely subjective act resting on faith in the message of Arabism. The moment one begins to "believe in the future of the Arabs and struggle for the Arab nation," a metamorphosis into Arabhood takes place. In fact, the onus is on the Kurd to deny his or her Kurdishness.

The Legal Reform Law treats people "hostile to the Revolution and its programme" like an infection against which public opinion needs to be immunized. The wholly different noncitizen status of these people is reinforced in the Reform Law in a section providing guidelines on criminal legislation. When punishing a citizen for a nonpolitical offence, "it is necessary to protect the convicted from the harshness of punishment . . . and rehabilitate him as an active member in his society." The judiciary is instructed to show leniency and take into account the "social and private circumstances" behind the crime to ensure a fair ver-

---

24. Saddam Husain, *On Current Events in Iraq* (London: Longman, 1977), 35–36.

dict. But crimes are ranked in accordance with the extent to which they conflict with society's interests. Hence, "those who committed crimes affecting the security of the State, the people's rights, or the honour of loyalty to the homeland" are specifically excluded from these humane considerations. The punishment of a "hostile" person is different in principle from that of a citizen in good standing.[25]

The Ba'th seem obsessed with this problem of who is "in" or "out" of their polity. In 1968, 1975, and 1976, laws and resolutions decreeing the execution of nonexistent categories of enemies—Freemasons and Zionists—were either reiterated, amended, or promulgated.[26] Sweeping pardons or exemptions from prison sentences, a regular Ba'thist device, invariably exclude "those who are sentenced for cases of espionage, masonry, Bahaiyah and sabotage."[27] Separate laws are usually passed for anything to do with "hostile elements." Both types of laws reinforce the ephemerality of all legal procedure, and the centrality of loyalty as the criterion for everything.

This mindset has plumbed some bizarre depths. Consider the case of the deportations of about two hundred thousand so-called Iranian fifth columnists from the late 1970s. Every Iraqi in the modern period has been issued a document called *Shahadat al-Jinsiyyah*, witness of citizenship. It recorded the origins of each person as one of two alternatives: *taba'iyya Uthmaniyya* or *taba'iyya Iraniyya*, meaning either Ottoman or Iranian origin. Every Shi'i deportee who held the Iraqi nationality was a *taba'iyya Iraniyya*. The phrase is frequently found in the book written by al-Barak, the head of the *Mukhabarat*, where it is associated with people "who are linked historically, psychologically, socially, politically and economically with their Iranian homeland."[28] Clearly this category is at risk (many Arabic-speaking, Iraqi-passport holders have escaped the country fearing deportation merely because they were *taba'iyya Iraniyya*). How did the distinction come about?

People old enough to remember say that in the very early censuses, taken shortly after the collapse of the Ottoman Empire, the inhabitants

---

25. See Legal Reform law no. 35, *Alwaqai* 20, no. 37 (September 14, 1977): 29–30.

26. Finally the law reads: "whoever promotes or incites Zionist principles, including Freemasonry, or belongs to any one of its institutions, or helps them materially or morally, or works in any form for achieving its purposes shall be executed." From N. Safwat, *Freemasonry in the Arab World* (London: Arab Research Centre, 1980), 21.

27. See Resolution no. 958, *Alwaqai* 42 (October 18, 1978): 7. See also resolution in *Alwaqai* 46 (November 15, 1978).

28. Fadhil al-Barak, *Al-Madaris al-Yahudiyya wa al-Iraniyya fi al-'Iraq* (Baghdad, 1984), 145.

of the mandated territory of Iraq were asked to state their "origin." Many Arab Shi'is from the southern provinces chose "Iranian" in the mistaken belief that this would get them out of military conscription and maybe other state obligations. The category survived the passage of generations without incident, until the Ba'th came along.

According to an ex-employee of one of the ministries, ABSP calculations on the number of Iraqis implicated by this administrative reasoning total two million people. If this estimate has any value, it may explain the decision to scale down the deportations. Maybe the thought was that a country of fourteen million people cannot afford the kind of "surplus population" levels of, say, Nazi Germany. However, in a discussion on how dangerously lenient all Iraqi nationality laws remained until 1963 when the first Ba'thi regime came along and added "great services to the country" as a new condition of citizenship, Barak has estimated that some twenty-five thousand Iranians proper still resided in Iraq.[29] Clearly, all Iraqis with a *taba'iyya Iraniyya* on their police records must always be suspect. Nevertheless, the regime has not yet produced an edict defining every *taba'iyya Iraniyya* as an actual fifth columnist (and if they number two million, it is unlikely they ever will). But who are these people? Sooner or later every person with a *taba'iyya Iraniyya* on their certificate of nationality must internalize this question until they themselves no longer know who they are.

Unfortunately, books on modern Iraq published overseas after the deportations of Shi'is began refer only to Iranians or people of "Iranian origin," often lumping the deportations in the "rough justice" of wartime conditions in spite of the fact that they began before the fighting. After all, even the United States incarcerated Americans of Japanese origin in camps during World War II, and the Ba'th make no claims about "human rights." Khomeini says he wants these deportees repatriated as a condition for ending the war. Thus, another problem of "stateless persons" promises to keep many people very busy in the coming years.

The strange feature of Ba'thist criminality is that it implicates everyone, even their harshest critics. In order to write the above paragraphs, I had to try to establish the meaning of *taba'iyya Iraniyya*. I also caught myself in the act of thinking whether at least some of these people might not have mixed loyalties, or even have been agents at some time, thereby providing the Ba'th with some sort of pretext. Then I asked myself whether there was any independent way of falsifying Barak's assertions

---

29. Ibid., 142.

(based on secret police records). There isn't. Previous writers have not engaged in such a mental exercise before; more important, it was rightfully never deemed necessary to do so. The deportations do not rest on any precedent relating to the presence of Iranians in Iraq. Common sense said that I was dealing with a monstrous lie. But two hundred thousand people were actually deported; the chief of secret police wrote the only book on the subject utilizing information no one even knew existed before; he alleged that all sorts of crimes had been committed over the decades although they had never found their way into any court; those Iraqis who may know something to the contrary are not willing to talk about it; perfectly intelligent critical individuals have accepted some version of the official story because, I suppose, they can see no reason not to; and finally I keep on rummaging around in the refuse of it all trying to find out what is "behind" the affair. Why do I think these thoughts? Reasonable human beings find it difficult to live with the fact that it is all pure invention. In the end, this ability to implicate all of us is the measure of gross criminality.

Statelessness is merely the outer limit of the everyday quality of citizenship in Ba'thist Iraq. In a world of nation-states, even the privileged few who travel abroad are perpetually reminded of the existence of this wasteland into which they can be dumped. All Iraqis are a hostage to their passports in a way rarely found in other states. A perfectly valid document can be withdrawn from any individual without warning. Travel is restricted to an extraordinary extent and is regulated arbitrarily. Bans can last for months or even years for certain categories of people; or they can apply absolutely, or be flicked on and off. Secondary-school students in their last two years before graduation are not allowed to travel; the state forbids them not only passports, but also official grade transcripts (working on the correct assumption that these are just as important once outside). In any case a valid passport is not enough to travel on; Iraqis also need an exit visa. When a traveller has "unauthorized" intentions, like staying abroad indefinitely to work or study, then the real problems begin. There is a veritable industry in forged renewals, the purchase of the passports of strange and far-away places, and arranged marriages of a decidedly nontraditional variety. But even tourists who want or have to return find themselves taping their passports to their bodies or forever feeling inside their jackets and peering into handbags; no Iraqi will ever leave impossible-to-get official papers in a hotel room. By contrast, exiles and political refugees from repressive regimes, like the Islamic Republic and the Shah's Iran, take their documents for granted unless they have a specific reason to know otherwise. In no other Arab state is a passport so coveted as it is inside Iraq, and such a millstone around a person's neck the moment he or she is abroad.

All such hopes and fears spring from the criterion for membership in the Iraqi polity being such that neither ruler nor ruled can ever take it for granted. However much we may hate the injustices of those who rule over us, or however apolitical in our daily lives we may prefer to remain, belonging to a polity is a basic datum of civilized existence. Any state, even that of the Iraqi Ba'th, is preferable to none at all. This is what all gradations of the shattering personal experience of statelessness and reversible citizenship brandished by the Ba'th as a weapon in their dealings with all Iraqis eventually proves.

THE FUTURE AS AN AUTHORITATIVE SOURCE

The idea that political authority should reside in that agency that best embodies the "national will" ties in with another notion in the Reform Law, that authority is always unitary, never fractured, mediated, or conditioned. Because "authority in the State is one, this means the negation of the idea of 'Multiplicity of Powers,' Legislative, Executive and Judicial."[30] The size of the agency acting on behalf of the "national will" does not matter. By definition this agency has already established that the people have objectives corresponding to its own. Nonetheless, the conclusion that formulates the legitimacy to rule is stunning:

> Every party, including the ABSP constitutes a minority in proportion to the population. . . . But when it represents, by its will and daily conduct, the people's will, when its acts correspond to the people's objectives, in present and future calculations, then it constitutes a majority.[31]

The "people's will," also referred to as "the interests of the masses," involves a calculation with respect to future developments. The party cannot be judged solely on the basis of its actions today, or people's current circumstances; future actions, and later unfolding implications on welfare of the party's current and future policies, must be taken into account. In short, political authority never stems from the objectivity of a people as given in a society, even when this people meets the Ba'thist criterion of admission to the fold.

---

30. Legal Reform law, *Alwaqai* 20, no. 37 (September 14, 1977): 20.
31. Husain, *On Current Affairs*, 47–48.

Power is not exercised for its own sake but for achieving objectives. . . . the method of practising the power which is defined by the constitution, is itself influenced by the economic, social and political reality of the country over which power is exercised. Owing to the importance that these . . . foundations enjoy, they have to be stressed and declared in the constitutional document. . . . Yet, the social, economic and political principles included . . . may not be in part data but an objective or aim to be realized. Therefore, in this meaning, the "Constitution" shall also be a guide of action for the Political Leadership and a programme for a future policy the political leadership intends to realize through exercising the power.[32]

The constitution is not conceived as a fixed set of rules governing the relations between institutions, much less some kind of a check on the exercise of power. A constitution is conceptually no different than a party political programme; it is a blueprint for the future, along with guidelines for how to get there. Hence, it is completely irrelevant to how politics is conducted. Having a measure of fixity about the polity makes no sense when starting from the idea that it "is not possible for the Revolution to deliver its message in constructing and realizing the new society without renewal of the individual's values, their concepts, and conduct."[33]

TOWARDS A NEW ARAB INDIVIDUAL

In formulating the Legal Reform Law quoted previously, why did the Ba'th not start, like so many nationalisms have done since the French Revolution, with the last sentence: "the people are the source of . . . authority"? From here, they could still proceed to qualify "people" in the way that they do.

The reason involves the priority in their own minds of the first sentence: "authority is not exercised . . . for the sake of man." The operative notion here is "man" considered independently of the ends he possesses or chooses. The Ba'th want to reject the idea of an antecedently individuated bourgeois self, endowed with "natural rights" that precede in some moral sense the fact of community and political allegiance.[34] This pivotal conquest of modernity is excluded along with the notion that authority is transcendental in origin (mediated only by those who speak on God's behalf). In their concept of "man," individuals cannot

32. Legal Reform Law, *Alwaqai* 20, no. 37 (September 14, 1977): 28.
33. Ibid., 43.
34. 'Aflaq's early ideological writings corroborate this interpretation of "man" as I will show in Chapter 6.

have a meaningful moral existence unless swaddled in the concreteness of a society morally and self-consciously fixated on itself. Belief is constitutive of identity; like an obsession, it "possesses" the self (the other way around invokes the idea of choice among alternative beliefs). The polity precedes individuals, not the reverse, because it forges their morality, a theme suggested not only by my reading of Hobbes, but also by the Arab-Islamic experience.

The Ba'th emphasize collective values and solidarizing sentiments in counterposition to all aspects of individuality. For instance, the Reform Law says that the foundation of all law in the area of personal rights is the necessity "to give priority to the interest of the society, represented by the State, over the interest of individuals, represented by the principle of rule of the will . . . and, consequently, to reduce those differences between the relations of the public Law and those of the private Law which find their foundation in the liberal and capitalist thought."[35]

The 1974 ABSP Political Report promoted a society purged of the "noxious attitudes" that had prevailed in all previous regimes—lack of patriotism, and indifference and irresponsibility towards the community. In their place must come "national sentiment, patriotic duty in face of the dangers and challenges facing the Arab nation, and—an indispensable concept for building the new society—respect for collective work done voluntarily and with enthusiasm." The only other words one finds on the attributes of citizens are intransigent pan-Arabism, courage, sacrifice, and selflessness, "which have constituted the moral basis of the Party's conduct throughout its long struggle."[36] Noxious or hostile attitudes arise when the polity is corrupted from the outside, or when the individual is alienated from the community in the realm of ideas, or through physical separation over a prolonged period. Saddam Husain identifies the crucial element:

> Regardless of what we say concerning the external forces conspiring directly against our revolution and, more generally, against the Arab peoples and the peoples of the area, our main protection remains subjective immunity.[37]

Everything about the source of authority under the Ba'th is deemed by them "an exceptional case created by the necessity of transforming

35. Legal Reform Law, *Alwaqai* 20, no. 37 (September 14, 1977): 15.
36. "New Values and Attitudes of the Revolutionary Society," in *The 1968 Revolution in Iraq,* Report of the Eighth Congress (London: Ithaca Press, 1979), 118–20.
37. Saddam Husain, *One Common Trench? Or Two Opposite Ones?* (Baghdad: ABSP pamphlet, 1977), 13.

society." So many years of exceptionalism and still the end is nowhere in sight. Because opposition may always develop, immunity requires prognosis of all possible pathways of disease before the actual onset of infection. The appropriate protective measures can then be taken. Hence, the executors of political authority, the secret police, still promise to find new fifth columnists, foreign agents, and saboteurs. Though no longer engaged in detection and surgical excision of real disease, their prognostic functions never end. Politically their new function is to render the body politic "subjectively immune." But is subjective immunity in the new society maintained through consistent alignment with the views of the majority? For a good Baʿthist this is an inverted way of posing the question. Their programme is not to win over the masses, but to change them.

To transform in accordance with a vision of "that which cannot be seen" is inherent in human nature, said Saddam Husain. Individuals are not satisfied "merely because they belong to the earth and can take what is available from its surface." Historically men have searched for "the spirit" of that which is between their hands. A long time ago, they took stones, sculpted them, and read "spirits" into the forms they created. The need to do this is the driving force for change towards greatness. Moreover,

> the greater one's control and knowledge over that which can be seen, the greater the pleasure extracted from it—exceeding the point at which all material needs are fulfilled—the more do human beings start to choke and feel an emptiness inside as a result of all of this material fulfillment. . . . In this way we find that the human being looks always for the horizon, and even higher up, going beyond that which can be seen, precisely when he has reached the highest summits.[38]

Saddam Husain's biographer rightly observed that Baʿthist revolutionism "is a permanent dream for change. . . . Once achieved, this dream freezes into a reality which must once again be overcome with new dreams and new struggles."[39] Saddam wishes to translate into politics his belief that reality has no fixity because of the human faculty of imagination. Politics is a "struggle" because it is such uphill work against a permanently obnoxious reality. We saw these ideas at work in the refusal to accept the reality of what "the people" think, even when this

---

38. From a dialogue between Husain and his biographer on "The Problematic of Rootedness and Alienation." Reprinted in "Thus Spoke Saddam Husain." Iskander, *Saddam Husain*, 320.
39. Ibid., 220.

people is constituted according to Ba'thist criteria. Now this quality of the individual psyche, fused to the spirit it has discovered in the nation, keeps everything in perpetual motion. Thus, a harmonious end state, or total "subjective immunity," never arrives *because of human nature* and not merely because of the hostility of the outside. This impulse renders exceptionalism the norm inside Iraq.

Saddam Husain was talking about himself and modern Iraq. We should keep in mind that as he talked, "the people" were cradled in his arms, just like the stone idol in the hands of its maker. Probably "the spirit" that he desires to read into his handiwork will never move mountains. Nonetheless, the force of the imagination that he holds so dear is behind all great art, thought, and creativity. The rub is in the thorny unwieldiness of real people—the fact that they are not things. Something about their variegated and unpredictable reality positively disgusts the Ba'th who can never accept "the people" for what they are. Instead of withdrawing from the world, as misanthropists choose to do, Ba'thists engage with it politically, intent on expunging from it everything that does not fit their ideals. Meanwhile, their fertile imagination makes contact with ordinary people only by way of their tremendous capacity for hate.

PARTY AND STATE RECONSIDERED

However indispensable, the Ba'thi state is simply a means for arriving at the new society, and a revamped Arab individual as regards values, concepts, and conduct. These distant ideals underline the party's deep-seated conception of itself as the vehicle for something more uplifting than a mere tawdry exercise of authority "for itself or in itself." Party objectives are separate from the state, unlike the Italian fascist model of authority that placed absolute value and an overpowering spiritual force in the State. For Mussolini, individuals and groups were only "'thinkable' in so far as they are within the State."[40] Such an idea is anathema to the Ba'th who are closer in spirit to the Nazi idea of political authority being the instrument for the rise of the pure racial nation, with the proviso that the Ba'thi nation is based on faith not race. Faith in the "eternal message" of pan-Arabism leading to faith in the party is the key to realizing the uncorrupted Arab nation.

40. Benito Mussolini, "The Doctrine of Fascism," in *The Social and Political Doctrines of Contemporary Europe*, ed. M. Oakeshott (Cambridge: Cambridge University Press, 1941), 176.

The Reform Law wants "a reconsideration of the apparatus of the state . . . so as to enable it to reflect exactly the orders of the Political Leadership."[41] Throughout the document, the Baʿthist state tends towards a technical, administrative, and expressly nonpolitical "organ" of society, which only carries out previously formulated intentions of political authority. Presidential power does not originate in the totality of the state, but only in a part of it, the secret police, which is ruled by the party intelligence network. The *Mukhabarat* is the most political of all state institutions, and it executes the cherished long-term policies of the party. Other matters like collecting the garbage and running construction projects can be left to state personnel, who still have to be carefully watched.

The separation in theory between party and state does not belittle the strategic influence of state power in the achievement of Baʿthist goals. But it does permit, for example, Kurdish or communist ministers in government (as happened in the early years), because their unambiguous brief is to implement the orders of the all-Baʿthi RCC. Even a certain type of "self-criticism" directed at administration, or the inefficiencies of government, is now possible. Because such self-criticism is the most apolitical form of criticism, it is invariably associated with reprehensible regimes that see a threat in politics, other parties, minorities, and the natural diversity of human groups and individuals.

Because the state is merely an instrument in the service of perpetual change, experimentation can affect the constitution, administrative-geographical divisions of Iraqi territory, and the number, names and functions of ministries, departments, and state organizations. No institution and no routine is sacrosanct. This continuous effervescence takes the form of a flood of directives and edicts from the RCC dealing with every subject imaginable: work and money regulations, travel restrictions, state appointments at what seem like randomly chosen levels of authority, street names, new construction projects, international agreements, promulgation of the death penalty for writing slogans on walls, changes in pension schemes for state bodies, the listing of people decreed to have passed the secondary-school baccalaureate, their placement in universities with all academic requirements waived, weight limits for officers of the armed forces, and so on.

A key effect of all of these edicts originating from the Leader is the destabilization of state authority, with the consequence that all genuine

41. Legal Reform Law, *Alwaqai* 20, no. 37 (September 14, 1977): 22.

hierarchy within institutions based on procedure, law, or merit is destroyed. The same thing that happened to a once-political army (Chapter 1) is now carried through into the most trivial matters. The natural tendency for the state to become a power base for individuals or cliques is therefore vitiated. The Leader, through the party, is in control, but at a useful distance.

The separation of party and state allows a duly immunized citizenry to enjoy a new "type of democracy required in the Revolutionary society." This People's Democracy needless to say "differs radically from liberal democracy which is the form of domination of the bourgeois class."[42] Ba'thists have the right to express opinions through the mass organizations and through People's Councils, first developed in the 1974 Political Report. Although the Reform Law attempted to give the idea formal structure, these councils have not been implemented yet, but the thinking behind them is the genuine expression of what Ba'thism in its most expansive mood hopes to achieve in Iraq.

Councils "strengthen the relationship between the State Bodies and the masses by drawing increasing . . . numbers to participate in the administration of the State and linking the local requirements with the general tasks of the State." Thus, "the People's Councils carry out economic, social, cultural tasks or activities bearing local character and participate in performing the economic plan and the budget of the administrative unit within the National Economic Plan and the State Budget."[43] Councils do not make political choices (spelled out elsewhere as being the exclusive province of a separate "Political leadership"). Other provisions in the Reform Law give the political leadership powers to supervise and direct Council elections and their daily operations, and to issue directives for immediate implementation by the Councils. These powers include instant repeal of Council decisions and suspension of the head or any other member of a council or suspension of the whole Council, for "not conforming with the general line." In short the People's Councils are yet another mass organization managed by the party. This addition to a long list of more specialized front organizations (for labour, youth, and women) is specifically charged with mobilizing the whole people into state activities—a function not catered for thus far in Ba'thi Iraq.

The separation between party and state is impossible to maintain in

42. Ibid., 21.
43. Ibid., 26.

practice. The tendency is for continuous and increasing merger of personnel and institutions. Such a merger followed the reorganization of the secret police system in 1973; the *Mukhabarat* became much more tightly woven into a combined party–state security system. The Ba'thicization of the army also meant that it could now share in a division of labour with the secret police, erasing what used to be competing boundaries between the two. However, the ultimate merger between party and state took the form of Saddam Husain's 1979 purge of the RCC and self-appointment as president. The Leader syndrome, we have argued, was necessarily associated with the emergence of a separation between the ideology-generating (politics-making) functions of the party—now consolidated in the infallible Leader—and its social-organizing function, still maintained by the party organization. The party had become some 10 percent of the population; it represented slightly under half of all residents on Iraqi territory (multiply each member by four or five dependents). Therefore, its posited identity with the people (at one time merely a bizarre idea) had taken on a real semblance. In reality, the authority of the regime now derived from "the people" organized by the party. The very identity of civil society was passing insensibly into that of the party organization. By way of transference from the mass organizations to the party and the RCC, this originally posited authority legitimately crystallized into the person of a real leader. Saddam's presidency was in effect a formal takeover of the state by the party. The 1968 military coup had finally acquired the legitimacy that can only be imparted through numbers of people. The apparatus of the state was not being taken over (that was done in 1968); rather, the pre-1968 legitimacy of the Iraqi state was given the coup-de-grace. Its abolition signified that the Reform Law promulgated in 1977 was in effect enacted in the 1979 purge. In other countries the same sort of thing is usually achieved through elections or revolutions.

CONCLUSION

Why did the RCC bother passing a public law in 1977 enabling it to pass secret laws?[44] Because the Ba'th take themselves very seriously indeed. They rarely indulge in middling thoughts of a cynical or hypo-

---

44. See law no. 78 of 1977, *Alwaqai* 27 (July 6, 1977): 14. The issue is *not* the universal tendency of all bureaucratic bodies to want to keep as many of their decisions secret as they can get away with; it is the idea of a secret *law*. This it seems to me can only arise from a Ba'thist type of mentality.

critical kind. Their moral universe, like that of revealed religion, is re-stricted to the extremes: the infinitely good (pan-Arabism, socialism, struggle), and the infinitely bad (imperialism, foreign agents, Zionism, reaction). Unlike revealed religion, however, the source of Baᶜthist au-thority is not in heaven; it is after a fashion present in "the people." This they need to explain. The issue at stake is internal party rationale—the perfectly understandable Baᶜthist compulsion to justify their actions to themselves, from their own ground rules and political traditions.

Unfortunately, the conditions of power in Iraq presume that Baᶜthist justifications are no longer contentious to a majority of Iraqis today. The party that takes itself so seriously is in turn taken seriously by those who are the object of its attentions. The reading public and intelli-gentsia take most, if not all, of these Baᶜthist ideas on "the people" as self-evident. Without a public life it is hard to be sure of such an asser-tion; but then the absence of dialogue sets in motion a self-fulfilling prophecy that in practice places the seal of acceptance on the principles of the Reform Law. One could argue that dialogue itself necessarily un-dermines the acceptability of such reprehensible principles. However, even this argument would not alter the fact that today the Iraqi opposi-tion itself does not choose to express its aversion to Baᶜthism by denying the validity of these principles.

In what traditions did these principles originate? Why did so many people come around to accepting them? How did they become the source of Baᶜthist legitimacy in Iraq? These are historical questions, and, unlike the enquiry into what the principles are, this next enquiry is not open to definitive resolution. I can only make analogies and point to some of the ingredients that might be involved.

PART TWO

The Legitimation of Baᶜthism

CHAPTER 5

Pan-Arabism and Iraq

The essential core of Baʿthism is pan-Arabism, a doctrine that posits the existence of a single Arab nation and demands the establishment of one Arab state. All pan-Arabists agree on this, however much they may disagree over how to define the quality of being an Arab, the territorial extent of the proposed entity, and the means to be adopted for realizing their goals. The doctrine enjoyed widespread public support after World War II, falling into disfavour following the Israeli victory in the June 1967 war. Of the multiplicity of parties, politicians, organizations, and movements that once espoused pan-Arabism, today only the Baʿth remain. Despite coming to power in the immediate aftermath of defeat, the movement created stable and durable polities in two of the most coup-ridden countries of the Middle East. From the standpoint of the peoples of Iraq and Syria, the post-1967 period is set off from the rest of their modern history by this fundamental fact. Iraqi Baʿthism in particular has translated its stability and durability into legitimacy, the principles underlying which arose out of Baʿthist doctrine and the tradition of pan-Arabism as experienced twice in the history of modern Iraq: 1918–41, and 1958–68.

Ottoman rule over the Arabs ended symbolically on October 3, 1918, when the Bedouin army of Faisal, the son of Sharif Husain of Hijaz, and leader of the Arab revolt, entered Damascus amidst scenes of unparalleled emotionalism. In four years of war, a quarter of the Syrian-Lebanese population of four million people had died, most from famine and disease.[1] During those years, Turkish rule had been harsh, brutally crushing the Syrian movement; Faisal appeared by default as the liberator of the heartland of Arabism and the embodiment of aspirations for a better future. In fact, of course, the British army had done the lion's share of liberating, but in line with British policy, General Allenby avoided entering the Syrian cities that were falling one after the other. An Arab administration of sorts was set up with Damascus as its center.

French designs on Syria, which the British were not prepared to overrule, led to the battle of Maysalun in 1920 and the rout of Faisal's ill-equipped and still Bedouin army by French forces. The British then installed Faisal as monarch in Iraq intending to negotiate some sort of independent status for this grouping of ex-Ottoman provinces that would preserve British interests.

The different positions that Iraq and Syria found themselves in by the 1930s resulted largely from the widely divergent colonial policies that Britain and France adopted over their respective mandates. The center of Arab aspirations as personified by Faisal and his entourage, notwithstanding his humiliation by the French, had moved from the Hijaz, where the revolt of all the Arabs had been proclaimed, to Damascus, where Arabism had been prematurely crowned, to Baghdad, where it was to run its course for the next two decades. In a culture that valued the representation of things as much as the things themselves, this parody of the succession in the Classical Age of Islam was not without meaning.

Faisal never abandoned his pan-Arabism. His early experiences, however, made him more cautious and explicitly gradualist.[2] In the end Faisal's achievements during his twelve years in Iraq stemmed not from this "foreign" policy orientation but from his personal role in consolidating the institutions of a modern state out of a patchwork of conflicting tribes, sects, and ethnic and religious groups. His major accomplishment, and the central preoccupation of his reign, was the abrogation of the British mandate and the recognition by the League of Nations of the independent state of Iraq in 1932.[3] By contrast Syria and Palestine re-

---

1. George Antonius, *The Arab Awakening* (New York: Capricorn Books, 1965), 241.
2. See the article by A. Shikara, "Faisal's Ambitions of Leadership in the Fertile Crescent: Aspirations and Constraints," in *The Integration of Modern Iraq*, ed. A. Kelidar (London: Croom Helm, 1979).
3. The Anglo-Iraqi treaty also came into effect in 1932. It preserved specific British interests in Iraq, notably British control of the airfields at Habbaniyya and Shuʿayba. The treaty was a bone of contention in the politics of that period, between Iraqi nationalists, who generally supported it, and the pan-Arabists who denounced it.

mained under direct rule by France and Britain. Since the French never even contemplated independence during this period, the nationalist movement remained locked in a bitter conflict with France over this issue until the 1940s.

Following independence a new set of issues came to the fore in Iraq. The army emerged as a political actor; radical reformers jostled with an emerging landowning class; the ICP was formed; pan-Arabism took on a party political form and attracted the new officer elite; and in 1936 the Arab world had its first military coup of the modern era. These happenings were passed on to the rest of the Arab world by many active Syrian and Palestinian exiles resident in Baghdad, including Haj Amin al-Husayni, the Mufti of Jerusalem exiled by the British for his nationalist activities, and the Syrian nationalist leaders Shukri al-Quwatli and Jamil Mardam. Many of the leading lights of pan-Arabism of those years were Iraqi parliamentarians and politicians, including Rashid ʿAli who was to confront British forces in the name of a resurgent Arabism in 1941. The short-lived affair bearing his name has entered the annals of Baʿthist historiography as the "first revolution for Arab liberation."[4] A Syrian Committee set up in Damascus to aid Iraq during this period, organized by Michel ʿAflaq and Salah al-Din al-Bitar, was effectively the direct precursor to the founding of the Baʿth movement.[5] Finally, and perhaps most important, Faisal installed in the fledgling Iraqi civil service leading pan-Arabist ideologues like the Syrian Satiaʿ al-Husri who arrived in 1921, served as an advisor, became director general of education, and then became dean of the Law College through which many of Iraq's first generation of politicians passed. Husri brought in scores of Syrian and Palestinian teachers and fundamentally shaped the Iraqi educational system for a whole historical period. In 1941 he was deported and stripped of his Iraqi nationality in the aftermath of the Rashid ʿAli affair.

Iraq, therefore, occupied a very special place in the history of pan-Arabism in the 1920s and 1930s. The country was a test case for pan-Arabism as it confronted for the first time the social realities about which it had such a firm view. All the actors—state institutions, parties, social forces—that were to figure so prominently in the nationalist struggles after World War II were being formed in the hurly-burly of local events and internal tensions that in Iraq at least had little to do

4. See *Nidhal al-Baʿth*, 4th ed. (Beirut: Dar al-Taliʿah, 1976), 4:5. This eleven-volume collection of Baʿth party statements and documents is used throughout. All translations by the author.

5. Mentioned in the Third National Congress Report, October 1959; ibid., 48.

with outside interference. Events in Iraq illustrated the ability of pan-Arabism to take root in a society whose communal mix on the surface did not lend itself to such a project. Hence, this period came to fore-shadow the kind of solutions and political themes that resurfaced more virulently in the second Ba‘thi regime. The period 1920–41 highlighted the struggles of a populace at a time when the social question was still in abeyance, modern social classes virtually nonexistent, and the central question of politics was not "Who should rule?" but "Who are we?"

Husri and the New Morality

The interwar years were a time of intellectual ferment in Arab politics, during which the concept of *al-qawmiyya al-‘arabiyya,* pan-Arabism, was explicitly forged. The consciousness of being an Arab was ide-ologized for the first time. To a large extent the real issues had never been examined before. Now that the last truly comprehensive Islamic polity had been dismembered, the existential dilemma facing the Arabic-speaking Muslim masses—to which the nineteenth-century secular Arabism pioneered by Lebanon's Christian minority had never ad-dressed itself—could at least be intellectually confronted. Satia‘ al-Husri, the founder of modern pan-Arabist thought, undertook in the 1930s and 1940s an ambitious project of ideological reconstruction. In-fluenced by a careful study of Fichte and the German Romantics, Husri came to believe that nations were organic and natural divisions of the human species, existing as objective entities independent of their mem-bers' feelings. This quality was first imparted to a nation by its lan-guage, combined with a deliberately selective reading into its own his-tory. The nation was therefore logically prior to statehood, geography, and even the religious community. Islam, though not incompatible with Arabism, was relegated to a secondary place.

But Husri was important both as a theorist and senior civil servant. In fact his more polished theoretical works after 1941 were all based on the articles, lectures, letters, and practices of his years in Iraq, now pre-served in his splendid autobiography. This document is not a compen-dium on the origins of grand theories, but a record of the real stuff of politics in the 1920s and 1930s, told in the form of myriads of little stories. Here is Husri at his best: chronicler of events and opinions, faithful to his adversary's point of view, and a true modern in that long-term abstract goals governed his every action as a civil servant. These qualities stood out in the fractious and tribal state of Iraqi politics and loyalties at the time.

In one revealing incident, Husri tells of a confrontation in the 1920s between him and the Shiʿite poet Muhammad Mahdi al-Jawahiri, generally considered one of Iraq's great twentieth-century literary figures, and a long-standing supporter of the ICP until the mid-1970s when he, like so many others, finally made his peace with the Baʿth.

Ordered by his minister to appoint Jawahiri as an Arabic language teacher in a Baghdad primary school, a reluctant Husri interviewed the young poet:

> I told him: First, I want to know your nationality.
> He replied without hesitation: I am an Iranian.
> I said: In that case we cannot appoint you.
> He said: Why? Don't we have Syrian and Lebanese teachers?[6]

The exchange went on with Jawahiri wanting to know in detail all the material benefits he would enjoy by becoming an Iraqi citizen. Husri departed in a big huff, reaffirming his initial recommendation that the appointment not be made because Jawahiri did not have the proper respectful attitude towards nationality. He was overruled, and the minister rushed through both an Iraqi passport and the job. A few days later the poet published a sarcastic ode in the very free press of those years, that sang the praise of Persia's natural beauties. In one line he said: "I have in Iraq a gang / without whom Iraq would not be beloved by me."

Husri was furious. There followed lengthy exchanges of bitter and recriminatory official correspondence between him and his minister analyzing every nuance and turn of phrase in Jawahiri's poem. The poem was even checked out with another great Iraqi poet, the Sunni Maʿruf al-Rusafi, who confirmed according to Husri that the item in question was "*shuʿubi,* in every meaning of the word."[7]

Salman Rushdie says in *Shame* that there are words whose very untranslatability unlocks a society's innermost secrets. *Shuʿubi* is such a word. Crudely put it means anti-Arab, or better still someone who has chosen to reject his *ʿurubah,* his Arabism. In this sense it is akin to the idea of a "self-hating Jew" in the hands of Zionist ideologues; but unlike

---

6. Satiaʿ al-Husri, *Mudhakarati fi al-ʿIraq: 1921–1941* (Beirut: Dar al-Taliʿah, 1967), 1:588–89.

7. Ibid., 1:590. The correspondence between Husri and his minister is also appended (pp. 591–602).

this epithet shuʿubism carries the implication of having chosen to leave the community of all Arabs. However despised, a self-hating Jew, from the point of view of their community, cannot shed his or her Jewishness; it would be like trying to step out of one's own skin. Shuʿubism's meaning dates back to Abbasid times to a literary movement in Iraq called *al-shuʿubiyya* that championed the cultural merits of the non-Arab Muslim peoples at the expense of the Arab literary tradition, deemed by these critics as uncivilized and lacking in good taste. Ironically, the critique was conducted in the Arabic language on lands that were later to be identified as Arab and at a time when the Arab military aristocracy was being demoted from its hitherto dominant position in the Islamic polity. It is precisely this nexus that has given the term such a powerful and emotive content within Arabic culture.

Today, nothing can be worse for an Arab than to be called a *shuʿubi*, because the term combines the attributes of a racist invective (most frequently used against non-Muslim minorities and Shiʿites) and the imputation of a treasonous act analogous to betraying state secrets in a Western context (used in this context against communists). The Baʿth have used the word in this sense since the 1940s. The specifically racist connotation was probably not present when Husri and Rusafi discussed Jawahiri's poem. Language after all was the key to Husri's whole conception of Arab identity (even though he was brought up with Turkish as his first language and had to struggle to perfect his spoken and written Arabic). However, the title of the chapter in which the story is recounted ("Iranian Teachers Who Caused Us Big Problems") suggests an ambiguity was already creeping into Husri's meaning. Was Jawahiri Iranian, or a *shuʿubi* Arab? Nevertheless, only when this "objective" linguistic criterion of identity gives way to the intensity of one's faith in Arabism as the measure of identity, can a fully blown racist content be invested in the term. Incidentally, Husri's criterion was so objective that it would surely have disqualified him, certainly not Jawahiri, from Arabhood. But it is the privilege of ideologists not to notice such inconsistencies.

In his own mind Husri was merely combatting foreign influences amongst the Arabs. He was struggling against centripetal forces that existed among those he had defined as Arabs, and he considered the primacy of these loyalties in the lives of individuals to be the hallmarks of communal and tribal primitivism. Jawahiri's loyalties, whatever else they may have been, were in Husri's eyes expressions of a petty, self-serving outlook, which had no "higher" aims rooted in a broader historical conception of the national interest. In this very precise sense, Jawahiri, like the Iraqi Arabs generally, was "backward" and exhibited, to a man like Husri, the effects of centuries of national decline.

Pan-Arabism takes itself very seriously; it is literally unable to comprehend sarcasm, irony, or laughter directed at itself from within. It dreads them to the point that it no longer understands them for what they are. Hence, no matter how great a linguist Jawahiri might have been, his wit appeared as a rejection of Arabism, quite unsuited for the edification of impressionable children. One can already feel the logic of a world view unravel in the face of human reality. What a typical irony of the Middle East! A Syrian Arab brought up as a Turk creates a theory of identity based on the Arabic tongue, and yet feels compelled to exclude one of this century's great linguists.

Another story is as revealing of the deep-rooted pluralism of Iraqi society in the 1920s, and the limits to which Arabism could be pressed. Husri tells of a campaign he waged against a school in a Shi'ite neighbourhood whose headmaster was an ex-Ottoman officer who "placed his hatred of the Arabs in the service of the Iranian state." Among other things, he did this by choosing a school uniform that included a "Pahlavi hat." Husri chose to combat the influence of this school in the only way open to him at the time: by setting up another school in the same neighbourhood managed by Shi'ites and splendiferously equipped with the latest in "maps, panels and illustrations." Within a few months, he tells us, he had started to win over the students. The headmaster reacted by establishing evening adult education classes. For this he needed the permission of Husri's department, which, needless to say, was refused (on administrative grounds). Taking advantage of Husri's absence, the indefatigable headmaster pulled a few strings of his own and got a junior official to ratify the permission. "Saddened" by what had transpired, Husri nevertheless accepted it and once again rushed through his own adult education program, which he succeeded in starting up "first."[8]

For Husri, education was the means to a new kind of morality, which the family and tradition were incapable of instilling in the individual. The teacher, like the institution of the school, was a moral agent through whom children were made aware, often for the first time, of their Arab identity and its implications. As early as 1922, Husri introduced into the primary school curriculum "Information on Moral and Civil Duties," significant in that it was offered as a subject separate from reli-

8. Ibid., 1:401–4.

gion, and "Group Singing," an uplifting experience that could also serve nationalism by careful choice of the song content. The study of history in the formative years was devoted to the nation's past and the inculcation of Arab national feeling. For the sixth year of primary school he finally relented, letting in the history of Italian and German unification.[9]

In the 1920s Iraqis were placing all moral authority over their lives onto their sects, tribes, and families. Individuals were not self-directing or autonomous, but acted in accordance with the mores of these traditional groups. The state stood apart from individuals in a way that these other groups did not. Here was an authority stemming from the traditional group into which one was born, and manifesting itself within each person as a positive willingness to conform. The ultimate sanction was exclusion, maybe even death (for example, "honor crimes") but the principal *fear* was not of dying; it was the danger of being released into the terrifying wasteland between groups.

In this world, there was no question of "self-discipline" in the modern sense of persons struggling with their conscience to arrive at a set of individually imposed moral norms. Such a "bourgeois" morality had taken many centuries to evolve. Satiaᶜ al-Husri understood this; he was not of that later generation of nationalists, celebrators of the culture of backwardness, who were going to lump this characteristic of modernity into catchall phrases like "alienation" or "Westernization."

In the interwar years a new notion of politics was inserted into the moral no-man's land between the communal and sectarian boundaries in Iraq, although it was not yet a force within communities. A new kind of freedom emerged for the first time in Iraq championed by the state. The new post-Ottoman state chafed at the communal logjam and probed its way around the boundaries, while accepting these for what they were. It provided an arena for excluded individuals (or minorities), becoming in effect a magnet for the drawing out of individualism and a measure of political freedom from the communal morass. In the Iraq of the 1920s and 1930s the debate raged over the issue of the intelligentsia and college graduates: Why did they always end up as functionaries, and not as entrepreneurs? Could it be that becoming a functionary in those days had something to do with this new-found sphere of freedom? In later years peasants would rush to the cities for such reasons (among others), so why not individuals lured out of their communities by the only power capable of standing outside the communal group?

9. Ibid., 1:211–19.

What was the function of education for Husri? Whatever else it might have been, it did not start as one of unscrambling these relationships. His writings on the individual and society suggest that he saw the structure of moral authority within each "group" in the abstract, as an ideal type, which if anything was marred because Arabs in his opinion were still too individualistic. The new problem for state-led education was how to order these fractured loyalties into a new hierarchy whose apex was a newly created tier—the Arab nation. The process was one of gradually moving the whole mass towards a new collective ideal in which the moral order was the same as before, except that the authority, into which individuality was submerged, was first the nation, then the religious and family group. Individualism in the modern sense was not the issue for Husri, and his point was never to make the cardinal error of turning it into one.

Among intellectuals and some politicians one can sense something like modern individualism struggling to break through the encrusted trappings of tradition. The atmosphere of untrammelled freedom in between communities in the 1920s facilitated this by giving public expression to so many shades of opinion. But when Husri lamented the presence of a strong "individualist spirit . . . in contrast to the social spirit which is still weak in our souls,"[10] he was not referring to this, but to the particularist loyalties and communal attachments that still took precedence in people's minds, obstructing the state's efforts to instil through education the new morality of an Arab order. The irony is that to the extent that Husri made inroads by politicizing the moral no-man's land of Iraqi society, he generated far more free space than Arabist aspirations were eventually able to live with.

Husri polemicized against the idea that education should form self-sufficient individuals who judged their own behaviour irrespective of someone else's blueprint on their future.[11] At the same time he rejected the use of education to preserve the existing social order. The two ideas were logically related in his thought. He was also aware that the new moral authority he sought to constitute within the new generation had no already constituted society to back it up; there was not yet a united Arab nation. However, an Iraqi state was at hand, and its institutions were slowly firming up. In fact, Iraqi loyalties were also rapidly emerg-

10. Ibid., 2:313.
11. Ibid., 2:277–80, for his views on education and social change. "What the Arab needs before anything else is 'social education', which strengthens and develops within his self the spirit of solidarity, obedience and sacrifice." Ibid., 2:280.

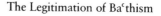

ing. Husri's memoirs are littered with stories of conflicts between him and the "Iraqists," generally from the non-Muslim minorities, the Kurds, or the Shiᶜites.

Finally, Husri knew that the morality he was preaching was not present even among the country's notables or wealthier elite. There was no nobility or aristocracy with aspirations that went further than the ends of their noses. This awareness is conveyed in his comments on the purpose of education. For Husri the highest duty of the entire educational system was "the cultivation of the enlightened [and ruling] class on the one hand, and the attempt to spread education among all the nation's classes on the other, in the knowledge that the latter could not be achieved before the former." Hence the eradication of illiteracy was secondary and "without large benefit" unless it was used to provide pamphlets and publications addressed to the "commoners." [12]

When leftist nationalists claim that Husri was used "to serve the vital political and social interests of a specific social class, namely the notables," they disregard social realities and assume the existence of a class that could rule in and for itself. [13] The presence of abysmal poverty and degrees of wealth (still not all that sharply differentiated) does not make self-conscious classes. Certainly Husri was Faisal's ideologue; but the whole point is that Faisal, his Sharifian entourage, and their allies among the landed tribal shaikhs (still being created by the effects of British land policy) did not yet constitute a cohesive class prepared to rule or even be "dominant" in a meaningful political sense.

The Faisal–Husri vision, although it understood and was immersed in the social reality of its time, did not accept it, but chose to work within its confines towards broader national ideals. At the purely intellectual level, one cannot but admire both their grasp of the real problems, and their choice to solve them politically. Both men had received an Ottoman court education. However, Faisal's time spent defending Arab causes in the Turkish parliament seems to have implanted in him a dedication for a political resolution of conflict such as the Arab world has rarely known in its leaders. The epigones of later generations would go about things very differently with much talk about the "true" interests of society, the venom of its exploitative classes, and the heroism of its toiling masses. But even with the best of intentions the intellectual

12. Ibid., 2:340–41.
13. See Walid Kazziha, "Another Reading into al-Husri's Concept of Arab Nationalism," in *Intellectual Life in the Arab East: 1890–1939*, ed. Marwan R. Buheiry (Beirut: Center for Arab and Middle Eastern Studies, American University of Beirut, 1981), 159.

penetration of these radical nationalist thinkers was shallow, marked by a fixation on abstractions that concealed more than they revealed (anti-imperialism, Arab socialism, petit bourgeois, economic freedom). Modern Iraqi politics is a case study in the growing ascendancy of both intellectual vacuity and violence. Faisal and Husri were devoted to reshaping civil society by the admittedly poor instruments of state that they had at their disposal, yet it never entered their minds to violate that organism in any way. For all its numbing backwardness, society had to be coaxed, cajoled, admonished, even deceived, but never forced. By the time the Ba'th came to power, things would be handled very differently.

Lionel Smith, a British advisor to the Ministry of Education (1920–31), wrote an unusual memorandum on the occasion of his departure from Iraq. In it he bitterly criticized the British hands-off and let's-do-everything-cheaply policy during the Mandate years: the British would have been better off not to have become involved in the first place, or else to have seen it through in the proper colonial way. His memorandum sets out an interesting view of the structural problems that plagued the British experiment in Iraq:

1. The smallness of the governing class. "I do not suppose there is in the whole of history another example of a state with a representative government of a modern type, in which the only people who count are two or three hundred at the most."

2. The "complete absence of any true patriotism."

3. The laxity of even religious morality (much less civic or national values) amongst educated Muslims in particular. The moral "incompleteness" that arose placed "a premium on mental dishonesty. This may be only a phase, but while it lasts I do not see how it can fail to produce a state of what Plato called 'the lie in the soul,' which makes truthful and straightforward dealings very difficult."[14]

Despite their views on independence, Smith and Husri worked together against most of their superiors and appear to have had consider-

---

14. The memorandum is reprinted in *Middle Eastern Studies* 19, no. 2 (April 1983); quotations from pp. 254–55. In it Smith expresses these racist feelings: "This country has been decked out in a few years with all the trimmings of modern civilization, while remaining essentially uncivilized. Those who think that a savage is civilized by being dressed in a tail coat will judge of the civilization of Iraq by the appearance of New Street. . . . I feel certain that this rapid progress in the mechanism of civilization, as opposed to the moral side, has had a disturbing influence especially on the youth." Replacing "savage" with "Arab," and "civilization" with "modernization," one has in effect the position of Satia' al-Husri during the Mandate years.

able professional respect for each other. Smith, for example, refers to Husri as "the only man in the country who combined administrative experience with a knowledge of and in fact a passion for education. He did much for efficiency, though I consider that on broader questions of policy several of his views were wrong."[15]

Whatever their differences, Husri and Smith shared an intellectual assessment of the relation between social, political, and moral structures in Iraq: public education could instil one or another kind of morality in the future elite; and an embedded social pluralism, not compensated for by any unifying network of values, could only be overcome by the inculcation of a new collective morality, which they associated with modernity. The freedom that had emerged in the moral no-man's land of Iraqi society was not good enough for either man. Deep down each sensed it to be uncontrollable, irresponsible, and unconnected to long-term goals that would make behaviour more self-disciplined and predictable, more in fact like Husri and Smith themselves. But Iraqis were not like them in the 1920s and 1930s; their unpredictability incensed both men.

Lionel Smith admitted defeat around the mid-1920s, but continued in his job in a grudging and embittered mood. Faisal died in virtually total despair brought on in part by the Assyrian tragedy of 1933 but also, one can surmise, by the realization that measured against his own aspirations he had failed. In a confidential memorandum on the eve of his death, Faisal wrote:

> There is still—and I say this with a heart full of sorrow—no Iraqi people but unimaginable masses of human beings, devoid of any patriotic idea, imbued with religious traditions and absurdities, connected by no common tie, giving ear to evil, prone to anarchy, and perpetually ready to rise against any government whatever. Out of these masses we want to fashion a people which we would train, educate, and refine. . . . The circumstances being what they are, the immenseness of the efforts needed for this can be imagined.[16]

The Road to Discipline

Unlike Faisal and Smith, Husri matured into new times. He may have stumbled upon the conclusion that pedagogy alone could not give rise to

---

15. Ibid., 259. Smith went on to complain of Husri's departure from the ministry in 1927, because "we have lost his efficiency and energy, while his views, especially his wrong views, are more firmly rooted than ever."

16. Quoted by Hanna Batatu, *The Old Social Classes and the Revolutionary Movements of Iraq* (Princeton: Princeton University Press, 1978), 25–26.

a new moral order, or maybe he thought all along that modernism was in essence a form of discipline engendered by institutional authorities exerting themselves upon the individual in a new way. Leading European theorists were writing in this vein, and Husri was an avid follower of developments in the educational field.[17] The purpose of entering into a relation with a disciplining authority was never the exercise of immediate control through the threat of punishment, but was always the imposition of "remote" or "self" control, driven by the inculcation of more abstract goals that were not self-serving in the narrow sense. Disciplining meant actually fabricating a "new man," not merely substituting one set of norms for another; it meant, for example, inculcating new habits, order, obedience, and attention to detail in every thought and bodily gesture, and as part of a new economy of time and spatial organization without precedent in traditional society.

This kind of discipline was already present in the new state school system, taken over from the British by men like Husri and his successor Sami Shawkat. Classrooms ranked, compartmentalized, and examined children and the subjects they were learning differently from anything experienced under the Ottoman empire. In practice, however, the disciplining force of education by itself was not enough, particularly when a man like Husri had to rely on teachers like Jawahiri and schools run by unrepentant "Pahlavi" headmasters. Husri concluded that, in the absence of a real Arab society, pan-Arabism needed more than just schools to take root.

Iraq never had until recently analogues for Europe's centuries-old disciplining institutions—monasteries that inculcated in the interstices of European feudalism a new work ethic and a preoccupation with the self, or manufactories or even schools that drilled people into becoming modern subjects.[18] The decline of population in Iraq was only arrested in the last quarter of the nineteenth century. A third of Iraqis were

---

17. For example, Emile Durkheim lectured in 1902–3 to future lycee teachers on a secular alternative to clericalism: "An inability to restrict one's self within determinate limits is a sign of disease. . . . Discipline is in itself a factor, *sui generis*, of education. There are certain essential elements of moral character that can be attributed only to discipline. Through it and by means of it alone are we able to teach the child to rein in his desires, to set limits to his appetites of all kinds, to limit and, through limitation, to define the goals of his activity. This limitation is the condition of happiness and moral health." The lectures were published in the 1920s; quotations are from the English translation, *Moral Education: A Study in the Theory and Application of the Sociology of Behavior* (New York: The Free Press, 1973), 38, 42, 43.

18. Michel Foucault, following on from Durkheim and Weber, developed these ideas for Europe in *Discipline and Punish*, part 3 (New York: Random House, 1979).

nomads for most of the nineteenth century. The public health networks, schools, hospitals, prisons, and asylums that defined and operated on the mass of citizens in the West only made a tentative appearance in Iraq towards the end of the first half of the twentieth century. Before civil society had any chance to constitute or define itself in these and other ways, modernity suddenly appeared in the form of a parliament and an army.

Parliaments evolved in western Europe over centuries. Common nationalist wisdom has it that a parliament was insidiously grafted onto Iraq to further British interests under the Mandate. The truth in the allegation has been taken as proof of the inherent inability of a parliament to serve any genuine democratic function in a country like Iraq. When the monarchy was overthrown in 1958, the parliament was discarded effortlessly, without a whisper of protest. Under the Bacth, democracy was redefined in a more suitably "participatory" way through People's Councils. In the end, truths and nationalist myths mingle in the inadequately analysed history of the parliamentary experience in Iraq.

Any system of representation—as opposed to participation—implies rules, and hence "self-discipline" in observing them. The most important rules establish the group identities that are to be represented. Identities, structured corporatively (as in some European cities, districts, orders, and classes), by voluntary self-interest (classes, lobbyists, interest groups), or through political parties act on human volition as a disciplining or filtering mechanism.

The British set up a parliament in Iraq "representing" a territory that had never been so defined, and presided over by a non-Iraqi monarch who did not believe in the legitimacy of the borders he was saddled with. For his overwhelmingly Muslim subjects, the very notion of formal representation in groups was problematic. Islam had historically distinguished itself from Christianity by opting for "participation," not "representation." Moreover, Islamic jurisprudence never evolved the notion of a corporate legal personality. No impersonal corporate "authority" is interjected between the Muslim and God. On the other hand Islam legislates for the behaviour of the community as a whole as well as in the personal and private domain. Thus, a built-in denial of individuality is combined with a participatory celebration of religiosity that finds its perfect synthesis in, for example, the ritual of the *hajj* or the *jihad* (holy war). When this cultural distance from representation is combined with nonexistent or unselfconscious social classes, organized under an irrational set of specific rules imposed by Christian outsiders, the artificial character of the Iraqi parliamentary system can be readily acknowledged.

Yet, despite such burdens, in practice the Iraqi parliament before 1941 was astonishingly vibrant as a mechanism for drawing out individuals from their communities. It was, moreover, the only institution responsible for inculcating and symbolizing the true breadth of societal freedom—typified by a completely open press—in which every shade and current of opinion, however bizarre, resonated.[19] Because of this freedom, much of what happened after 1958 was foreshadowed in some way in the interwar years. Put differently, the "freedom" of the 1920s and 1930s stood in the same relation to state and society as the absolute nonfreedom that took such firm root in 1970s Iraq. Both threatened traditional society, and emerged in part as radical instruments for dealing with its excruciating backwardness.

Later generations of Iraqi intellectuals looked back in anger at those years:

> In the mandatory period the exclusive interest in politics had transgressed the limits within which it was wise and advisable . . . unduly obscuring the social aspects of the national problem. There were some people—unfortunately they were in the minority—who viewed this general preoccupation with politics with a certain concern. One of them was ʿAli al-Sharqi [a poet]. He said that it seemed, on the face of it, as though the whole nation consisted of nothing but political groups. Mosques, bedrooms, cafes, shops, streets, schools, law offices and army barracks—all of them without exception felt irresistibly attracted by the magnet of political activity.[20]

Izzidien waxes eloquent on the "foreign yoke" that imposed upon Iraq so much freedom. To the pan-Arabist imagination, the Iraqi parliament symbolized everything that was wrong with the kind of freedom that Izzidien found objectionable.

But for the Iraqi public at large, the frequent parliamentary failures were caused by parliamentarians who did not have the necessary *personal* attributes. Much of the extreme personalization of politics in those years belonged to that shadowy psychopolitical realm in which dress, habits, figures of speech, and behaviour generally were all shifting alongside people's identities and self-perceptions. The public was drawn to a mythologized image of what it perceived to be the source of the British Empire's greatness: the emotionally cold, scrupulously fair, self-

19. Consider the career of Maʿruf al-Rusafi. He was a member of the Iraqi parliament, and its most bitter critic; certainly he was the most eloquent. His Arabism and visceral hatred of the British was undoubtedly religiously conditioned. Typically his poetry, which every Iraqi is taught today, is scathing on all the institutions of the emerging Iraqi state, except the army.

20. Yousif Izzidien, *Modern Iraqi Poetry: Social and Political Influences* (Cairo: The Cultural Press, 1971), 187.

disciplined, and rational Englishman. An Iraqi of the 1920s probably felt a Briton was free because he was so disciplined, whereas his fellow Iraqis were too hot-blooded to argue things out in a parliament. People joked about their uneasiness with this kind of imagery, created with more than a little assistance from the mandatory power. But the jokes and the sarcasm concealed a quite understandable obsession that somehow modernity was associated with such qualities. However much the British Mandate might have been resented in Iraq, it fascinated the public imagination. The "antiimperialism" of later years was bound up with this fascination, and the two feelings could go hand in hand in the same individual. This was a world that had been catapulted across the centuries, with dizzying results. Latching onto "appearances" in this way was a clumsy but understandable way of coming to grips with the issues. Individuals were on display for the first time in Iraqi politics, which was entertainment as much as it was the stuff of real politics.

The rise of pan-Arabism changed things. All the "fun" and lightness in political behaviour began to evaporate from the 1930s on, along with the Iraqi sense of humor. Pan-Arabists in particular became obsessed with the "falsity" of what they saw around them. "Appearance" became the guise for manipulative hidden forces, the trappings of a corrupting imperialist/Western influence. Still, this constant pan-Arabist theme of the 1930s, unlike its later Baʿthist counterpart, was often couched in irony, satire, and a multitude of creative literary forms.[21]

In the formally new but deeply traditional world of post-Ottoman Iraq, now encroached upon by so much invigorating freedom, the army was the only institution that was truly modern and not alien. Standing armies were the basis of all politics, cities were founded in their wake, and landed property was a fragile extension of central military power. By working its way through military organization in the Middle East, modernity simply took the path of least resistance. Faisal had embarked on the Arab revolt of 1916 with ex-Ottoman officers, not propagandists and educators.

The significance of the adoption of the army as a vanguard of modernization in Iraq (unlike the experience in Europe or even in Egypt under Muhammad ʿAli) resides in the extreme isolation of this mechanism of modernization. In Iraq, in 1921, officers and particularly the veterans of the Arab revolt were by far the most educated, experienced,

---

21. Musa al-Shabandar was an anti-British journalist who eventually served as Foreign Affairs Minister under the Rashid ʿAli government in 1941. His early satirical articles, published as a collection under the title *Shararat* (Baghdad, 1967), capture this denigration of "appearance" in a very original way.

and worldly layer of the population. Nine of fourteen prime ministers between 1922 and 1932 were ex-Ottoman officers who shed their uniforms for politics and personal gain.[22]

The debate over forced military conscription broke out in the mid-1920s, long before formal independence. Conscription was opposed by the Kurds, Muslim Shiʿites, and the British. The weight of opinion in the first two communities kept Faisal from pushing it through right away. Husri, however, saw conscription and military service as the logical complement to a compulsory public education: the army was an institutional "factory" for the production of modern men and the overcoming of sectarian and communal divisiveness. In his writings, school and barracks have an identical social and *moral* function, distinguished in principle only by age and the amount of discipline that could be brought to bear.

> In military service the soldier lives outside his original sphere of work, away from his self-interested life, to the point that he lives apart from his own kin. . . . He leaves everything that belongs to him or his family to live with other sons of his country in barracks filled with people from other towns, from different families, classes, faiths and occupations. He lives with all of these people subjected to a generalized comprehensive system. He works for a purpose that is not personal, family related or even connected to region. It is loftier than all that. . . .
>
> . . . Military barracks are like social schools. They free the individual from selfishness and make him feel the presence of others—the country and nation. It teaches him true sacrifice in all its forms. . . .
>
> Certainly the human being is civic-minded by nature. . . . He cannot live in isolation, but must always mix in with a group of his kind. The degree of this "socialization" and social consciousness is not, however, the same among all individuals: it might be strong in some and weak in others, and a socialized education is aimed at strengthening the socialized spirit and social labour. From this standpoint we can say that military life which groups the youth by their forced service to the flag, is one of the most important means for the spread of such an education and the unification of its direction.[23]

With no coherent ruling class, and education being a feeble means of creating it, the army was a way out of a genuine morass. In the emerging public perception, the army was also a symbol of what it meant to have a modern identity. To be modern, and to be somebody, was to have an army and be inside it if possible. Masses turned to the army because they had to become modern. Modernity and the disciplining of men in the art of killing each other were becoming one and the same thing in

22. See P. J. Hemphill's excellent article, "The Formation of the Iraqi Army, 1921–33," in Kelidar, *Modern Iraq*, 91.

23. Husri, *Mudhakarati*, 2:309–10. See the whole discussion, pp. 306–13.

Iraq. Unlike those countries of the Third World that rested on a century or so of statehood, corresponding roughly to twentieth-century boundaries (for example, Egypt and much of Latin America), in Iraq everything was very "new," having had no time to evolve. The army at least rested on a tradition that bound together officers and modernization; besides, it was the only thing that "worked." This was not a case of competing institutions (bureaucracies, parties, unions, armies), or even a matter of the army's proximity to power and control of the instruments of violence (the British were holding this in check). The army was not yet a saviour of the "nation" or an instrument of sovereignty; it was all that Iraqi society had going for it in the way of real modernization in precisely the sense that Husri had understood the word.

As the educational system shuffled along, as new ideas filtered in, as the dialogue of parliamentarians looked more like bickering and posturing, as patronage and self-interest shaded into corruption of public duty (so natural in a communal world), a young generation of army officers emerged, formed under the British. To these men coming out of the Military College in the late 1920s, the older Ottoman-formed generation had been compromised. Satiaʿ al-Husri made sense. So in the tradition of their older colleagues and inspired by Husri, they adopted the mantle of progress.

Reactions to the army question varied. The Shiʿites were justifiably wary of Sunni dominance. However, Sunnis like Husri were also justified in seeing a tribalist reaction to modernization in the Shiʿite opposition to conscription. Ultimately the Shiʿite position crumbled because in holding out against conscription they were holding back the same thing they were eagerly seeking in other areas (for example, in education). However, for this initial hostility to crumble, there had to be a galvanizing issue other then conscription, some concrete evidence of the army's vanguard role in modernization. This came in the summer of 1933, around what has euphemistically come to be known as the Assyrian affair.

The Army and the Assyrians

The Assyrians[24] were a mountain people of Semitic origin in northern Iraq who claimed descent from the ancient Assyrian Empire based in

---

24. Information on the Assyrians, the Iraqi army, and the events of the summer of 1933 is taken from R. S. Stafford, *The Tragedy of the Assyrians* (London: Allen & Unwin Ltd., 1935); Khaldun S. Husri, "The Assyrian Affair," *International Journal of the Middle East Studies 5* (1974): 161–76, 344–60; Hemphill, "The Formation of the Iraqi Army."

Nineveh (3000–600 B.C.), the ruins of which are just outside Mosul. They spoke Syriac, which is directly derived from Aramaic, the language they still use for liturgical purposes, and the language of the whole Fertile Crescent before Arabic. They adopted Nestorian Christianity and were officially recognized as a millet by the Ottomans in 1845. In 1915 the Turks terrorized the community and drove around fifty thousand of them further south into Iraq. They ended up in refugee camps, managed and financed by the British. In 1920 Assyrians were used effectively in combat and as scouts in the suppression of the large-scale anti-British uprising. In 1922 they were recruited into military units paid and officered by the British, called the Iraq Levies. These were organized to offset the costs to Britain of the administration of Mesopotamia. A proportion of the community (those expelled by the Turks) remained rootless, in search of a "homeland." Like the Kurds in those years they did not consider themselves Arabs and retained a strong Assyrian sense of identity. Their grievances and demands as a community passed through their spiritual Leader, the Mar Sham'un, who dealt with the British High Commissioner directly, pointedly refusing to deal with the Iraqi authorities. He only finally took up Iraqi citizenship in 1932.

The crisis of 1933 originated in the feelings of the Assyrians that they had been betrayed by Britain, which had failed to ensure their future after the termination of the Iraqi Mandate. In 1931, the Mar Sham'un presented to the League of Nations a demand for the establishment of a separate enclave in Iraq, then a petition proposing the settlement of all Assyrians in Europe or, failing that, Syria. Despite the failure of these measures, they placed much pressure upon the Iraqi government; eventually Iraq's entry to the League was made conditional upon formal guarantees for the protection of the country's many minorities.

In July 1933, the Mar Sham'un proposed that the Assyrians be recognized as a millet inside Iraq, and not merely as a religious community; that a national home in the Amadiya, Zakho, and Dohuk districts of Iraq (populated by their traditional enemies, the Kurds) should be open to Assyrians from all over the world; that the former Assyrian units of the disbanded Iraq Levies be formed as a separate regiment inside the Iraqi army; that the districts ceded to the Turks in 1925 should be annexed into this national home by the Iraqi government; and finally that the Mar Sham'un should be officially recognized by the League of Nations as Patriarch of the Assyrian community and paid an annual subsidy. Who paid did not matter much. Faisal negotiated with endless patience, but firmly rejected the first three demands.

The upshot of all of this was a pogrom engineered in Faisal's absence by the army with the connivance of Hikmat Suleyman (minister of interior, destined to become a member of the left-wing al-Ahali group) and Rashid 'Ali (prime minister, an ardent pan-Arabist who was destined to become the leader of the 1941 "revolution" against the British). General Bakr Sidqi who instigated the idea and directed the grisly operation, was going to lead the Arab world's first military coup of the modern age in 1936.

The tiny Assyrian community never represented a genuine threat to the state. A party of several hundred Assyrians had crossed the border into Syria in search of their "homeland" but were turned back by the French; an incident at the border cost a dozen or so lives. The army, the government, and later the Arab nationalist historian Khaldun al-Husri (son of Satia' al-Husri), dubbed this a "revolt." But not even K. Husri's apology for the army's actions denied the broad outlines of what followed. Kurdish tribes were armed and instigated; Assyrians were rounded up and shot on sight; villages were looted wholesale by Kurdish, Arab, and Yazidi tribes; civil officials who protested were terrorized by the army. In short it was open season on Assyrians in Iraq in the summer of 1933. K. Husri estimated that six hundred were killed in this way, but the Assyrians claimed upwards of three thousand victims.

Refugees poured into Mosul and the larger more secure Assyrian villages. On August 11, a motorized machine-gun unit of the Iraqi army, on the orders of General Bakr Sidqi, entered Sumayl and disarmed all the men, who had put up no resistance:

> Suddenly and without the least warning the troops opened fire upon the defenceless Assyrians. Many fell, including some women and children, and the rest ran into the houses to take cover. . . .
> This took some time. Not that there was any hurry, for the troops had the whole day ahead of them. Their opponents were helpless and there was no chance of any interference from any quarter whatsoever. Machine gunners set up their guns outside the windows of the houses in which the Assyrians had taken refuge, and having trained them on the terror-stricken wretches in the crowded rooms, fired among them until not a man was left standing in the shambles. In some other instances the blood lust of the troops took a slightly more active form and men were dragged out and shot or bludgeoned to death and their bodies thrown on a pile of dead.[25]

The historical importance of what happened in Iraq that summer lies not in the events themselves but in how they were interpreted by the population. All accounts are unanimous in describing the overwhelming

25. Stafford, *The Tragedy of the Assyrians*, 174–75.

popular enthusiasm for the army's actions. In the city of Mosul, tri-
umphal arches were set up, "decorated with melons stained with blood
and with daggers stuck into them. This delicate representation of the
heads of the slain Assyrians was in keeping with the prevailing sentiment."[26] K. Husri, then a young boy, was an eyewitness to the army's
reception in Baghdad:

> On 26 August practically the entire city turned out to welcome the army
> units returning after completion of their operations against the Assyrians.
> Thousands upon thousands of men, women, and children filled the streets,
> the squares, and rooftops of the city, bringing everything to a standstill for
> hours. The immense crowds cheered deliriously as the troops marched
> through the capital. Men, women, and children showered flowers and rose
> water on them from the roof-tops. The writer well remembers that on that
> day he and his sister were allowed to pick all the roses and flowers of their
> garden . . . scattering their contents on the heads of the marching troops
> from the balcony of a doctor's clinic overlooking Rashid street. Planes of the
> Iraqi air force flew over the city, raining coloured leaflets that carried the fol-
> lowing words written by a welcoming committee: "Welcome, Protectors of
> the Fatherland! . . . Stand up to Your Enemies the Tools and Creatures of
> Imperialism!" The army and Crown Prince Ghazi, whose openly displayed
> approval of the campaign against the Assyrians had made him the darling of
> the masses, were cheered to the heavens. But few cheers were lifted for
> Faysal. . . . The same thing happened five days later when almost all Bagh-
> dad turned out again to greet Ghazi, Bakr Sidqi, and Rashid 'Ali, on their
> return to the capital from a ceremonial parade of the army at Mosul. When
> Faysal left Baghdad on 2 September there were hardly more than fifty people
> to see him off in the airport; two days earlier there had been a crowd of
> 50,000 men in the same airport greeting Ghazi on his return from Mosul.
>   The writer met Bakr Sidqi for the first time a few days after his return
> from Mosul. When he patted me on the shoulder and asked me what I
> wanted to be when I finished school, I said: an army officer.[27]

Under the Mandate there were three armies in Iraq: the British air
and ground forces; the Iraqi army founded in 1921; and the Iraq Levies,
which started as an all-Arab force recruited from a Shi'ite province in
the lower Euphrates. In the 1920 uprising, the Levies, though still an
Arab force, "rendered excellent service" during these operations, displaying "steadfast loyalty to their British officers."[28] In 1922, when
Assyrians as a group were recruited into the Levies, the community initially showed considerable reluctance. However, the force became en-

26. Ibid., 201.
27. K. Husri, "The Assyrian Affair," 352.
28. Stafford, *The Tragedy of the Assyrians,* 63–65.

tirely Assyrian in 1928. Some four thousand Assyrians passed through the organization and in 1933 eight hundred Assyrians were left.

British prevarication in giving way to Faisal's urgings for a strong army facilitated the emergence of an assertive officer corps that by independence was chafing at the bit for having been put into "swaddling clothes" by the British.[29] Faisal wanted an army of 15,000 to 20,000 men. The army actually grew from 3,500 in 1922 to 7,000 in 1927, reaching 11,500 by 1932. Between independence and 1936 the army doubled in size, largely a result of the rush on recruiting officers in the wake of the Assyrian massacres. Moreover, an acute inferiority complex inside the officer corps towards the British and what is described in the literature as a strong "fear" of the Assyrians was engendered by the Iraqi army's failures to suppress Kurdish and other rebellious tribes. Repeatedly the Arab army had to be bailed out by the British, and in particular the Assyrians. Like the Kurds and unlike the Arabs of the plains, the Assyrians were excellent guerrilla fighters and knew the mountain terrain. These feelings of resentment and fear were coupled with the rising mythology of Iraq as the Arab Prussia of the Middle East (largely a consequence of Husri's pedagogy and the sense that the Iraqi state was the center of pan-Arabism).[30]

The Assyrian pogrom was the first genuine expression of national independence in a former Arab province of the Ottoman Empire. Popular enthusiasm was clearly fixated upon only the armed forces, pointedly turning away from Faisal and his way of handling the problem. In this choice, the masses of Iraq were making a positive political statement about what "independent modernization" meant to them. Moreover, it is impossible to separate the new intensity of anti-Assyrian feeling among the Arabs and Kurds (as opposed to traditional hostilities of a religious, tribal, and ethnic nature) from the fact of this community's service in the Levies. Iraqis were celebrating one modern institution, the army, and one way of dealing with problems, force, over all others, and calling

29. The words were used by the British High Commissioner Dobbs in recommending the restrictions he felt should be placed on the growth of the Iraqi army pending the withdrawal of British forces. Dobbs declared in 1925 that "9,000 good ground troops would keep internal order." See Hemphill, "The Formation of the Iraqi Army," 95, 97.

30. "Our souls were filled with pride for our history and its glories, compelling us towards the achievement of miracles in our homeland. Captivated by the dream [of Arab unity] we awakened to see in the Iraqi army, the Arab Prussia, the force able to realize our dreams of establishing a great Arab state which would restore to the Arab nation its past glories and forgotten civilization." Mahmud Durra, an Iraqi officer commissioned in 1930, recalling his early formation, is quoted in Hemphill, "The Formation of the Iraqi Army," 101.

that choice "national," as opposed to, for example, "problems of minorities" (the British way of posing the issue). During the crisis, many perceived this latter formulation as a foreign invention designed to undermine the country's capacity for nationhood.[31] In this the Iraqis were not being traditional, or "backward" (at least in one sense of the word), for the mere act of identifying with "their" army was a new experience; and by implication "its" project for genuine national independence was a progressive measure.

Bakr Sidqi, in his Mosul speech, virtually predicted his own coup in 1936 on the basis of his accomplishment in massacring the Assyrians, offering it as a "pledge of what the army is about to perform in the future, in accomplishment of the great duty which the Army has felt and is still feeling that it must be prepared to perform. Therefore let us, with Army and Nation, await that day."[32] These words were enthusiastically received. Killing Assyrians, however nonexistent their threat might have been, was perceived as enhancing the prospects of Iraqi unity. Modernism, in the shape of the Iraqi army, had given focus to what was fast becoming a seamless web of religious, tribal, ethnic, nationalist, and militarist sentiments. The Assyrian affair crystallized these traditional and modern sentiments into a new kind of hysteria and confessional politics, under the respectable title of "antiimperialism." "Independence" from the British defenders of the Assyrians had been expressed more effectively than all the solemn declarations and formal ceremonies of the previous year, the date Iraq first became a sovereign state.

A moment of glory was achieved at the expense of the Assyrians and dressed up as a struggle against the British, who became more unpopular than at any time during the Mandate period in spite of the fact that the official British position on the Assyrian question staunchly favoured the Iraqi government. Moreover, it was British officials, according to K. Husri, who "urged" the government to recall the Mar Sham'un to Baghdad and, if necessary, detain him there (which the government did

---

31. K. Husri raised this as an issue. In a parliamentary debate, "Sir Samuel Hoare described every and each Iraqi minority he spoke of as 'interesting'. The Kurds had some of the characteristics of the Highlanders of Scotland. The Assyrians represented 'one of the oldest and purest forms of Christianity', while: 'It would be a great loss, not only to Iraq but to the world at large, if this very interesting little community [of Yezidis] were in any way blotted out'. Such romantic British preoccupation with the minorities was highly suspect to the Iraqis. They could not understand that some Englishmen were Kurdophiles and Assyriophiles by the very same romantic token that others were Arabophiles. The Arabophile himself, in any case, was politically suspect in their eyes." "The Assyrian Affair," 163.

32. From Stafford, The Tragedy of the Assyrians, 204.

against Faisal's wishes as cabled from his sickbed in Geneva). Again, the British first recommended moving concentrations of the army up to positions in the north, presumably to apply pressure on the Assyrians. Yet, incredible though it may seem, the British became even more unpopular than they had been during the days of the great anti-British revolt of 1920, when the British army was actively engaged in fighting Iraqis. One of the most popular chants was "Ghazi shook London and made it cry."[33] The press alluded to plots by British colonizers employing Christian mercenaries to enslave the same Iraq to which they had just granted independence. The word spread that Faisal's old crony, T. E. Lawrence, was organizing here, and spying there; in fact like the Scarlet Pimpernel, he was everywhere. Several people accused of being British agents were murdered, and Bakr Sidqi openly executed all Iraqi "agents" of British intelligence caught by his army.[34]

A powerful political formula was invented in Iraq in the summer of 1933—its first recorded use on a significant scale in the Arab East. In its origins, it is closely associated with the innermost meaning of "national independence" in this century. The same formula was still at work under the second Baʿthi regime, during the January 1969 hangings, associated again with acquiring an ostensibly greater amount of "national independence." The story of Iraqi Jewry, it seems, was a repeat of the story of the Assyrians. The Islamic revolution in Iran and the American hostage crisis, among other things, demonstrate that this formula is by no means restricted to Iraq, nor has it spent its formidable force. After World War II and decolonization, nationalists and leftists of every variety labelled this formula "antiimperialism," the phrase also used to describe genuine wars of aggression, for example, against the peoples of Vietnam and Algeria. The advantages of this choice of words did not escape attention in Iraq as early as the summer of 1933. However, in the Iraqi case (unlike Vietnam or Algeria), the important thing about the formula is that it must be distinguished from all forms of opposition to the British for things they actually said or did. The formula was not employed in the 1920 anti-British uprising which was, on the face of it, exactly what it set out to be: a struggle against the British. In principle, therefore, the formula is not reducible to all forms of anti-British feelings.

Antiimperialism in Iraq, as manifested in the Assyrian events, should properly be understood as a representation or metaphor—an iconic sign in the language of semiotics. There is no simple cause-and-effect

33. K. Husri, "The Assyrian Affair," 353.
34. See ibid., 357.

relationship between the object of hatred—the British and their role in Iraq—and the intensity of the antiimperialist sentiment among the masses; the relationship is one of appearance and similarity, not causality. By way of illustration, consider the case of a psychiatric hysterical seizure, which to an observer looks exactly like an epileptic seizure; in fact the latter bears a definite organic relation to the body, whereas the former only conveys a message about one's confused state of mind. Hysteria is an indirect form of communication, a sign as opposed to a genuine manifestation of a bodily disorder. The feelings are of course almost always perfectly genuine, whether in the case of hysteria or this kind of antiimperialism. But in their role as symbols, icons of a dislocated consciousness, they must not be confused with the object they purport to represent, and in particular with the reality of the object's actions.[35]

But what is "antiimperialism" an icon of? What was an "antiimperialist" consciousness in Iraq in the summer of 1933? Could antiimperialism be a label for the impression left on the sensibilities of the population by a decade or so of abrupt modernization? This is suggested by the role of the army as the bearer of that consciousness, and by the rallying of a deeply divided population around what was perceived to be the army's test of fire. People realized that they had to have "progress," yet they did not consider that they had to change in themselves; an outside agency that "belonged" to them would be the agent. The British were aliens and Christians. Their freedoms threatened too much about the past, and at too fast a rate. Conformism, shame, and a religious moral code still determined people's daily lives, even as they accepted some notion of modernity. "Antiimperialism" set comforting limits on modernization: it drew the line at a certain amount and a certain kind of it; it did not ask for much and it offered the same protection from the assault of the outside as did religion and tradition.

Nationalists have a vested interest in the notion that the feelings expressed as "antiimperialism" are causally linked only to the oppressive reality of the objects they purport to be about. In much of the Third World, the Left and the secular intelligentsia have followed suit. This has led to a wholesale abandonment of critical thinking in relation to the behaviour of masses of people just emerging from appalling condi-

---

35. An incident in 1924, when a group of Assyrian Levies went berserk, killing some fifty people in the marketplace of Kirkuk, suggests they exhibited the same kind of disorientation. See Stafford, *The Tragedy of the Assyrians*, 70, who also notes how the racism of some British officers influenced the Assyrians. But the Assyrians' loss of contact with political reality was most profoundly expressed in their "refugee mentality" and unswerving loyalty to the Mar Shamʿun who seems never to have understood that some things changed after World War I.

tions of backwardness. The British Mandate, and the institutions it gave rise to in Iraq, were the agents of a modernization that did not arise gradually or indigenously as the outcome of a population's own resourcefulness and engagement with the world. The British in Iraq were modernizers more than colonizers, despite acting out of self-interest. On the other hand the Iraqi army, as much a British creation as the Levies, had ties to the past coupled with firm roots in modernization. It also had a sense of purpose. Satia' al-Husri had seen to that; his morality, while still unable to constitute the whole of Arab society in its image, had found its disciplinary agent at the expense of the Assyrians.

Khaldun al-Husri undertook to rewrite the history that his father helped to make. The son begins with the observation that whereas history was usually the propaganda of the victor, "alas," in Iraq, on the Assyrian question, "history has been decidedly the propaganda of the victims."[36] His concern, therefore, is to establish that the Assyrians were a threat to the Iraqi state; that they attacked "first" with premeditation; that Bakr Sidqi and the Higher Army Command only responded to a genuine threat; that they did not plan a pogrom; that in fact it was Faisal all along who instigated the tribes. He agrees that the official Iraqi version of events is a "barefaced and clumsy lie." His main concern is not to deny the facts, but to whitewash the army and lay the blame on Faisal, along with of course everything he stood for in politics.

Stafford's account was the target of K. Husri's rewrite. Unlike K. Husri, Stafford was there as administrative inspector based in Mosul charged with negotiating with the parties. In his book he distributes the blame, not sparing British policy (although he is not hard enough on the British who bear responsibility towards the Assyrians for what happened). Stafford was firmly against the Assyrian demands, and for Iraqi unity. By contrast, K. Husri's evidence is largely the opinion of other higher ranking British officers who were not on the scene. These were men concerned with buttressing their role as chief advisors to an army they wanted to think of as a professional force. General Headlam, of the British military mission in Baghdad, called Sidqi a "leader of determination, energy and foresight," and said "the government and people have good reason to be thankful to Colonel Bakr Sidqi and his force."[37] Yet, according to K. Husri, these advisors "were boycotted by the Iraqis."[38]

36. K. Husri, "The Assyrian Affair," 161.
37. Hemphill, "The Formation of the Iraqi Army," 107.
38. K. Husri, "The Assyrian Affair," 357.

Alas, K. Husri is also wrong about the history of these events being the propaganda of its victims. With a little help from intellectuals like himself, Iraqis stopped reading "imperialist" sources a long time ago. Important new books like Tarbush's study of the Iraqi army uncritically adopt his claims.[39] And by the time one arrives at the *Encyclopedia of Modern Iraq* produced under Ba'thist auspices, K. Husri is left far, far behind. No longer is there any mention of massacres or state involvement, only the history of a centrally organized "revolt" with surprise attacks by large units of Assyrians against the unsuspecting Iraqi army.

We conclude with a postscript that defies commentary. Apparently the Mar Sham'un went to the United States decades ago only to return to Iraq on April 24, 1970, just two weeks before the "historic" Kurdish autonomy accords were signed. He did this, we are told in the *Encyclopedia,* in the wake of an RCC resolution that forgave him and restored his citizenship. Upon arriving, "he expressed his gratitude to the leadership of the revolution, and his hopes for world peace. After seeing how the Assyrians now enjoyed stability, well-being, security, and equal rights, he said: 'The Arabs have helped to serve humanity, and from Baghdad the rays of civilization illuminated the whole world at a time when Europe still lived in the Dark Ages.'"[40]

The Denouement: 1936–41

Unlike Faisal, Bakr Sidqi was the forerunner of a new political world. The 1936 coup followed in the wake of the pogrom that had elevated its author into a national hero. On the day of the coup, demonstrations of support swept the streets of Iraq, just as they were going to do on July 14, 1958. These were largely the efforts of the important leftist-reformist group Ahali, which then occupied the position on the political spectrum that the ICP would fill from the 1940s. Some of those who would become the ICP's leaders were then still in Ahali. Moreover, unlike the ICP, Ahali was implicated in the coup through the person of Hikmat Suleyman, minister of the interior during the Assyrian affair, now appointed prime minister by Bakr Sidqi.

Ahali was formed in 1931 by a group of young liberal democrats who espoused the ideals of the French Revolution. The group never con-

39. Mohammed Tarbush, *The Role of the Military in Politics: A Case Study of Iraq to 1941,* (London: Kegan Paul, 1982).
40. *Encyclopedia of Modern Iraq,* ed. Khaled A. M. al-Ani (Baghdad: Al-Dar al-'Arabiyya li al-Mawsu'at, 1977), 2:995.

ceived of itself as a party, but their journal commanded enormous influence. It toyed with socialism in 1934, preferring to call it *sha'biyya*, populism. The titular head in the mid-1930s was Ja'far Abu al-Timman, an old Shi'ite Iraqi nationalist who had moved to the left out of disillusionment with politicians. Ahali's manifesto called for Iraqi patriotism instead of nationalism, whose history "is full of blood, tyranny and hypocrisy."[41] Long after its demise, leading members would serve in Abdul Karim Qassem's governments and be a major personal influence. In 1936, Ahali exerted influence on Sidqi through Suleyman. Ahali leaders, along with army officers, took the lion's share of seats in the new government, becoming the intellectual force behind a promise for large-scale socioeconomic reforms. Arab writers and correspondents flocked to Baghdad, and articles and pamphlets celebrating the new regime circulated widely.

Hikmat Suleyman wanted the army to establish a Kemalist regime in Iraq. Until 1935, he had been a member of Rashid 'Ali's National Brotherhood party formed in 1930 to oppose the Anglo-Iraqi treaty. This party spawned most of Iraq's nonmilitary pan-Arabists of this period. The attack on Suleyman's first cabinet, led by a coalition of landlords and his former pan-Arab colleagues, centred on whether the new government's proposed reforms were "communist" or "nationalist." Eventually Suleyman's hand was forced by Sidqi, and he dropped the reformists.

Ahali's departure was followed by the establishment of a pan-Arab government, even more subservient to the army, that lasted until Sidqi's assassination. The "popular front" episode lasted nine months. Its outcome was a considerable weakening of Ahali because of its collusion with an increasingly unpopular Sidqi, and Ahali's inability to push through its reforms. The newly formed ICP fared better.

Inside the army, two conflicting nationalisms were separating out: Iraqi and pan-Arab. Bakr Sidqi, a Kurd, aspired to build a strong Iraqi state modelled after Attaturk's Turkey and Reza Shah's Iran, both run by officers. Sidqi's role in the Assyrian affair and his brutal measures against Shi'i tribesmen had won him a following among officers arising out of his reputation as Iraq's most capable officer. He was assassinated by pan-Arabist officers in whose favour the pendulum now swung decisively. Abdul al-Karim Qassem, also a Kurd on his mother's side, was

41. From Majid Khadduri, *Independent Iraq: A Study in Iraqi Politics from 1932 to 1958*, 2d ed. (London: Oxford University Press, 1960), 71, also 69–74. For Ahali's links with the military and role in planning the coup, see pp. 81–82.

again an Iraqist and of course enjoyed exactly the same fate as Sidqi a quarter of a century later at the hands of the Ba'th.

Civilian pan-Arabists had been in power before, notably in the summer of 1933. The repressive measures of their last government had contributed to its downfall, and a period of exile for its most ardent members, including Rashid 'Ali. But a new and more militant pan-Arabism was advancing—still not a threat to this Faisal-reared generation of Arab nationalists but a sign of things to come.

Sami Shawkat, director general of education after his mentor Satia' al-Husri, captured the flavour of this new pan-Arabism in a speech *sina'at al-mawt* (The Manufacture of Death), delivered in 1933 and circulated in public schools throughout Iraq. It dealt with the need for a society like Iraq "to perfect the manufacture of death" in order to realize Arab unity and recapture "the spirit of Harun al-Rashid . . . which demands of Iraq to have quickly half a million soldiers and hundreds of planes. Is there a coward who would not meet this call?" The capability for death was in Shawkat's view far more important than the acquisition of wealth and learning, because it "shields the honour of nations and prevents their enslavement." Egypt and India may be rich and culturally sophisticated, but they were colonized and did not have the wherewithal to "smash the chains of humiliation." However, Afghanistan, "which still lives in the fourteenth century," and Saudi Arabia "whose populace feeds on camel milk," are independent. These states understood that "force is the soil which sprouts the seeds of truth. The nation that has no force is doomed to humiliation and enslavement." He went on:

> If Mussolini did not have tens of thousands of Black-Shirts who had excelled in the profession of death, he would not have been able to place the crown of the Roman Emperors upon Victor Emmanuel.[42]

Shawkat urged young boys to follow the doctrine of the "rugged life" and emulate the lifestyle of Arabs in the early Islamic period. He also seems to have gone so far as to declare that those history books that discredited the Arabs were to be burned, not excepting the greatest work on the philosophy of history by Ibn Khaldun.[43]

In 1935 the Muthanna Club was founded with Shawkat as a promi-

42. All quotes are from a collection of Sami Shawkat's writings and speeches entitled *Hadhihi Ahdafuna* (Baghdad: Wazarat al-Ma'arif, 1939), 1–3. Significantly, the full title translates as "These Are Our Aims: He Who Has Faith in Them, Is One of Us."
43. From Majid Khadduri, *Independent Iraq: A Study in Iraqi Politics from 1932 to 1958*, 2d ed. (Oxford: Oxford University Press, 1960), 167.

nent member. Named after the Arab Muslim commander who conquered Iraq in the seventh century, it organized influential lectures to
promote Arabism. The pan-Arab government also sponsored the Futuwwa Youth organization, modelled after the Hitler Youth movement.
Shawkat's popularity as leader of this organization eventually brought
him into government. As if presaging the Baʿthist militias, the "national
guard," and the militarized youth organizations of the 1960s and 1970s,
Shawkat, through the Futuwwa, made it a requirement for all school
boys and their teachers to wear military uniforms, be trained in arms,
and be disciplined as soldiers. Shawkat defined nationhood to an audience of schoolboys in a way that would have warmed the heart of the
Iraqi Baʿth half a century later:

> The foreigner, according to the values of the Futuwwa of Iraq, is not he
> who does not hold a certificate of nationality; rather, in our doctrine, the
> foreigner is he who does not feel as we do . . . even though he carries ninety
> such certificates and our cemeteries were sinking with the bones of his an-
> cestors from thousands of years. The foreigner for us is he who intrigues
> against Arab unity; and he is not only a foreigner in doctrine, faith and spirit,
> but he is also our bitterest enemy.
>   Musaylama the liar was an Arab Yemenite, but he was a traitor and so the
> Arabs despised and killed him. . . . Salman al-Farisi, God praise him, was a
> Persian who joined Islam, Arabized and remained true to these beliefs. For
> this the Arabs raised him high and venerated him. The Iraqi Futuwwa views
> the truly Arabized Salman who served the Arab nation, as a part of itself;
> whereas it repudiates Musaylama and those of his ilk.[44]

The 1936 coup eliminated that set of nationalist politicians reared
under Faisal who sought to blend pan-Arabism with a new kind of loyalty to the Iraqi state. Politicians moved in and out of pan-Arab, Iraqist,
and social-reformist parties. One knew the formal positions of institutions, individuals, and groups (which were fluid and open to change)
because politics was institutionalized and an intensely public activity.
Moreover, after 1933 everyone had "dirty" hands, because Bakr Sidqi
had been everyone's hero, particularly the Left's. His "Iraqism" came to
the fore in 1936, and he was eliminated because of it, not for his failure
to deliver on social reform. Henceforward, pan-Arabism would peel off
decisively from Iraqi patriotism, and the counterposition of the two is
personified in the ensuing conflict between Rashid ʿAli and Nuri al-
Saʿid. The army, now the power broker in post-Ottoman politics, cast

---

44. Shawkat, *Hadhihi Ahdafuna*, 5–6.

into office first the one pole, and then the other, in the next six coups straddling the 1936–41 period.

Pan-Arabism grew in leaps and bounds after the assassination of Sidqi. Arab exiles in Baghdad played a crucial role in generalizing pan-Arabism beyond the local Iraqi scene, exacerbating divisions in the Iraqi body politic. The former Grand Mufti of Jerusalem set up an "Arab Committee" with Rashid ʿAli to probe avenues of Arab–Nazi collaboration. Iraqi nationalists reacted by gravitating firmly towards Britain and the Allied Powers. The Muthanna Club, along with its affiliate the Palestine Defence League and the Futuwwa organization, all merged with the Arab Committee and the officer pan-Arabists in myriads of ways. Sami Shawkat's brother, Naji, a member of the secret inner circle of the Arab Committee, was dispatched on a secret mission to discuss collaboration with von Papen,[45] while Nuri al-Saʿid, a cabinet colleague of Naji, was doing exactly the same thing with the British.

The intrigue culminated in the proclamation of a state of emergency by four pan-Arabist generals, three of them members of the Arab Committee, on April 1, 1941. The Committee became the policy-making body under the new regime. The Regent, ʿAbd al-Illah, along with Nuri al-Saʿid and other pro-British politicians, fled Iraq aboard the proverbial British gunboat. A government of "National Defence" headed by Rashid ʿAli and the four generals was immediately supported by the Axis powers and the Soviet Union, Hitler having not invaded Russia yet. A month later British forces landed at Basra. Fighting broke out on May 2. The Mufti emerged publicly in a rousing speech against Britain that called for a holy war against "the greatest foe of Islam."[46] On May 12 German planes based in Syria attacked a British air base in Iraq, which retaliated with bombing sorties into Syria. Despite support from German aircraft, Iraqi troops were routed at Falluja on May 19 by a much smaller British force. The soldiers simply did not have the stomach for a fight. This poor military performance, along with the repression that followed, had much to do with the disappearance of the army as a political force in Iraq for the next seventeen years. Even the British were

45. Shawkat carried a letter from the Mufti to von Papen congratulating Hitler and referring to the struggle against "the democracies and international Jewry." It concluded the Arabs "confidently expect that the result of your final victory will be their independence and complete liberation, as well as the creation of their unity, when they will be linked to your country by a treaty of friendship and collaboration." See Khadduri, *Independent Iraq*, 179.

46. Ibid., 224.

taken aback at their success.[47] The road to Baghdad was open. Rashid 'Ali, the Mufti, and all the generals escaped to Tehran on May 29.

This chapter in the history of independent Iraq closes as it had opened, with a pogrom.

Iraqi Jewry dates to the sixth century B.C. Substantial conversions, rural-urban migrations, and assimilation of Jews and Muslims took place over the centuries, resulting in their concentration in Baghdad where they constituted up to a third of the population in the 1920s. By the late 1940s, the total Arabic-speaking Jewish population of Iraq numbered some 120,000, the largest concentration in the Arab East.[48]

Anti-Semitism gathered momentum in the late 1930s, coincident with the growth of pan-Arabism. Demonstrations and bomb-throwing incidents were directed at Jewish quarters in August 1938, and Jews were blamed for a massive fire at Suq al-'Attariyah in 1939. The Arab Committee's communications with Germany are littered with anti-Semitic comments reflecting the atmosphere that prevailed in organizations like the Futuwwa and the Muthanna Club. The situation worsened dramatically with the advent of the Rashid 'Ali regime. The ICP, in a letter to the prime minister aimed at qualifying its previously unconditional support, referred to the "violation of liberties, the intrusion into homes, the plundering of possessions, the beating and even murder of people."[49] The climax came two days after Rashid 'Ali's escape. Rioting and looting was initially organized by junior officers and Futuwwa youth who apparently thought they could lead a counterrevolution against the return of 'Abd al-Illah and the British. The next day tribesmen entered the city and joined in. The police sided with the rioters, and in the end hundreds of Jews were killed.

Two new and lasting myths were born out of the Rashid 'Ali affair. The first was that pan-Arabism had waged an actual struggle against British imperialism; the second was that the "revolution" failed because

47. The British historian, S. H. Longrigg, wrote that the Rashid 'Ali movement "could scarcely have failed" had there been just a little bit more coordination with the Germans. See *Iraq, 1900 to 1950: A Political, Social and Economic History* (London: Oxford University Press, 1953), 297.

48. See R. I. Lawless, "Iraq: Changing Population Patterns," in *Populations of the Middle East and North Africa: A Geographical Approach,* ed. J. I. Clarke and W. B. Fisher (London: University of London Press, 1972), 107–8. Gerald de Gaury in his book *Three Kings in Baghdad: 1921–1958* (London: Hutchinson, 1961), 17, puts the concentration of Jews in Baghdad at one-third of the population. In the mid-1930s the population of Baghdad was around 250,000 people; therefore, the high proportion of Jews is plausible given their concentration in the capital.

49. See text in Batatu, *Social Classes,* 454.

its vanguard the "military opposition . . . did not have faith in the importance of an active and precisely organized role for the anti-imperialist masses."[50] Dr. al-Barak, who became the head of the Ba'th party intelligence network in 1982, set out in his Ph.D. dissertation to "rewrite history in accordance with a new program." He concludes his published dissertation on the Government of National Defence in 1941 by comparing it to the 1871 Paris Commune. We learn that the Rashid 'Ali government was "truly" the "'commune' of the Arab National and Socialist revolution of modern times."[51] I will not insult the reader's intelligence by attempting to discuss his reasoning. However, not all lies are the same; some are capable of being "proved" true by events. Al-Barak's history, broadly speaking, is the version on which a whole generation of Iraqis have been raised; moreover, it was already "true" in the minds of the generation responsible for stabilizing the second Ba'thi regime. To find a different version, we invariably must turn to "imperialist" sources, or to independent Arab writers who have themselves relied on such sources and do not for the most part publish in Arabic.

The Ba'th turned lies into a new kind of truth. Before Dr. al-Barak, the party had already transformed the years 1933 and 1936–41 into a dress rehearsal for its own emergence between 1958 and 1968. Qassem was a stand-in for Sidqi, the ICP for Ahali, and they of course stood in for Rashid 'Ali. The degree of formal correspondence in terms of actors and sequence of events is uncanny. What is the meaning of this correspondence? Does it suggest a return to the unresolved question of identity that haunted the 1930s? Why is sovereignty in Iraq asserted through pogroms (1933) or public hangings (1969)?

By their very nature such questions are not open to definitive answers. In any case, my analogies should not be pushed too far. At least three fundamental differences between these widely separated periods come to mind. First, far greater numbers of people participated in politics after 1958. Second, politics itself began to mean something new in 1958 as parliament was abolished with the monarchy as though it were its logical counterpart. Politics was now about masses in motion and their fickle allegiances to inflexible parties and a new generation of coup makers. By contrast, in 1936, the parliamentary system had held on,

50. From Dr. Fadhil al-Barak's book, *Dawr al-Jaysh al-'Iraqi Fi Hukumat al-Difa'a al-Watani wa al-Harb ma' Baritaniyya Sanat 1941* (Baghdad: Al-Dar al-Arabiyya, 1979), 242. Al-Barak is typical of a whole generation of Arabist Iraqi intellectuals in his beliefs about 1941. For more on Barak, see Chapter 1.
51. Ibid., 261.

battered but still intact. Third, the outcome was not the same. And here of course is the rub. The Baʿth rewrote this part of the script. They had faith in organized mass action and in the antiimperialism and anti-Zionism of the masses. They took power on this basis, and it was this faith that allowed them to "rewrite history in accordance with a new program." This is how the Baʿth turned lies into a truth for which we have all become responsible.

CHAPTER 6

Formation of the Baʿth

In 1941, the Iraqi experiment with pan-Arabism that began with Faisal was terminated. The generation that pioneered a more militant pan-Arabism in the 1930s disappeared from the scene. Political repression and the outcome of World War II account for some of this withdrawal; the rise of Iraqi communism accounts for the rest. Pan-Arabism returned to Iraq in the late 1940s in the form of tiny student circles initiated by Syrian Baʿthis in a handful of colleges. From a Sunni quarter of Baghdad, their influence spread very slowly and almost exclusively among students. The Iraqi Baʿth party was formally founded in 1952 as a branch of the Syrian party. It had around one hundred members, most of whom had been recruited in the previous year. In 1955 some 10 percent of the membership were still non-Iraqi Arabs, and on the eve of the 1958 overthrow of the monarchy, the organization barely exceeded three hundred people.[1] Because organized pan-Arabism was virtually absent between 1941 and 1958, attention must be directed at the Baʿth's origins during the 1940s in Syria, the new, more "natural" center of pan-Arabism in the Middle East.

Founding Personalities
and Formative Events

The recognized founders of the Baʿth, Michel ʿAflaq and Salah al-Din al-Bitar,[2] were born in the al-Maydan quarter of Damascus, an area

1. Hanna Batatu, *The Old Social Classes and the Revolutionary Movements of Iraq* (Princeton: Princeton University Press, 1978), table 38–2, p. 743.
2. Personal information on ʿAflaq, Bitar, Zaki al-Arsuzi, and Akram al-Hurani, unless otherwise mentioned, is drawn from ibid., chap. 38; Majid Khadduri, *Arab Contempo-*

known for its militant hostility to the French during the uprising of 1925–26. 'Aflaq came from a Christian, Greek Orthodox background; Bitar, a Sunni Muslim, traced his descent to a long line of religious notables. Both had confessionally administered educations and went to university in Paris where they first met in 1929.

In the four years they spent in Paris, they formed a close political relationship, founding an Arab Students Union which brought them into contact with students from many Arab countries. The radicalizing climate of opinion sweeping European universities in the wake of the great recession carried them along in its wake. They read Marx, Nietzsche, and Lenin very enthusiastically by all accounts, and works by Mazzini, André Gide, Dostoevsky, Tolstoy, and Romain Rolland. 'Aflaq may have been attracted to the vitalistic philosophy of Bergson, the inspiration behind Sorel's celebration of the creative function of mass violence. But no proper biography exists, and no one really knows how he was formed intellectually. Unlike other Arab nationalists of an earlier generation, 'Aflaq never acknowledged the influence of Western thinkers. He even claimed in an interview with Eric Rouleau to have stopped following Western currents of thought from the beginning of World War II.[3]

Upon their return to Damascus they contributed regularly to a weekly communist magazine, al-Tali'ah, which Bitar claims they founded.[4] Whether 'Aflaq or Bitar ever joined the Syrian Communist Party is unresolved, although the odds are against it.[5] 'Aflaq hotly rejected any such association.[6] However, 'Aflaq never denied his admiration for communist militancy and organization. The beginning of his disillusionment with communist politics came with the election of the Popular Front government in 1936 and the emergence of the Syrian Communist Party from clandestinity.

---

raries: The Role of Personalities in Politics (Baltimore: Johns Hopkins Press, 1973), chap. 12; John Devlin, The Ba'th Party: A History From Its Origins to 1966 (Stanford: Hoover Institution Press, 1976), chap. 2.

3. Eric Rouleau, "The Syrian Enigma: What Is the Ba'th?" New Left Review 45 (September–October 1967): 56.

4. See Bitar's interview with Marie C. Aulas in 1980, reprinted in MERIP Reports 110 (November–December 1982).

5. Both Laquer and Halpren make this claim. See W. Z. Laquer, Communism and Nationalism in the Middle East (London: Routledge and Kegan Paul, 1956), 330, n. 15; and M. Halpren, The Politics of Social Change in the Middle East and North Africa (Princeton: Princeton University Press, 1963), 240. However, the dates both authors give for 'Aflaq's departure from the Syrian Communist Party are certainly wrong.

6. See his 1964 interview with Kamel S. Abu Jaber, author of The Arab Ba'th Socialist Party: History, Ideology and Organization (Syracuse: Syracuse University Press, 1966), 187.

What had the greatest impact on the two men in 1936—events in France, or France's intentions regarding the province of Alexandretta— is not clear. At any rate they turned on the Syrian communists accusing them of becoming agents for French communists and the French government. A period of introspection and intellectual soul-searching followed. On the eve of World War II, students began to collect around them:

> Everyone sensed that there was a vacuum, that the old leadership had gone bankrupt, . . . that a new movement had to be set on foot.[7]

The nucleus of what was to become the Arab Ba'th party was set up only after the defeat of France in September 1940, and the first leaflets against the French were circulated in February 1941. Therefore, like Iraqi pan-Arabism in the 1920s and 1930s, the Ba'th appeared after Syrian independence on some sort of terms had become a foregone conclusion.

The Ba'th claim that the party emerged in the 1940s out of a "struggle" against the French. Yet 'Aflaq was arrested once in 1939, but at least four times by postindependence Syrian regimes. He became a national figure only after his term of imprisonment in 1954, and his real test of fire as a politician had nothing to do with the French who were preoccupied with a Nazi occupation. Certainly both men were fined by a Syrian minister of education for objecting in their classroom to educational programmes "slanted by the imperialists."[8] On the strength of this, they resigned in October 1942 and devoted themselves to politics. In the meantime, 'Aflaq and Bitar had set up a Syrian Committee to Aid Iraq during the Rashid 'Ali affair, an organizational precursor to the Ba'th party proper.

According to a semiofficial party account, the Ba'th were conceived as a reaction to "three principal deviations," all of which had been in opposition in the 1930s and, unlike the Ba'th, were engaged in a struggle against the French.[9] By far the most important deviation was the Syrian Communist Party; the others were the Syrian National Party, which aspired to a secular union of Greater Syria, and the Muslim Brotherhood. The central idea that set the Ba'th apart from all three was pan-Arabism.

Both men ran unsuccessfully for the Syrian Parliament three times (1943, 1947, and 1949) after which 'Aflaq vowed never to run again.

---

7. 'Aflaq in an interview with Batatu. See *Social Classes*, p. 726.
8. 'Aflaq as quoted by Abu Jaber, *The Arab Ba'th*, 12.
9. See the historical introduction in *Nidhal al-Ba'th*, 4th ed. (Beirut: Dar al-Tali'ah, 1976), 1:14.

Bitar got elected in 1954 as a deputy for Damascus, and subsequently occupied several ministerial positions. He was very much the party tactician and down-to-earth organizer in the 1940s and 1950s.

ʿAflaq has held only one ministerial position, for three months. His party role, however, was considerably more important than Bitar's. He was the ideologue, the party political philosopher standing above the fray and avoiding administrative posts while retaining great influence with the party faithful. ʿAflaq was an intense and ascetic person, utterly devoted to his cause as acknowledged even by his detractors. He lived simply, had no interest in financial gain, and was able to inspire those already interested in his ideas. Student converts from the ten years he and Bitar had spent as secondary-school teachers in Damascus (1933–42) would go on to university and professional life (frequently also as teachers). Thus, party influence grew in the early years backed up by ʿAflaq's writings in various Syrian journals and newspapers. Through the first and formative decade of its existence the Baʿth was truly "Michel ʿAflaq writ large," as Batatu has aptly put it.[10]

In addition to the events in Iraq (1936–41), the concession by France to Turkey of Alexandretta with its ʿAlawi, Armenian, Sunni, and Turkish population had a crucial importance on the early formation of the Baʿth. The action was undertaken in 1939 as part of a deal in return for which Turkey would join the Allies in the war. Since 1936, agitation over the issue had been led by another schoolteacher and graduate of the Sorbonne, Zaki al-Arsuzi. The 30-year-old Arsuzi, an ʿAlawi, led a campaign marked by intense racism combined with Arab self-assertion. Local Turks were the object of his attacks. Nevertheless, Armenians and Sunnis, whom he called "Turkified Arabs," were also vilified. Commenting on French treatment of the Arabs versus the minorities, Arsuzi notes "the foreigner was afraid for his interests from Arabs, and used Jews to ward off this threat. It is only natural that the dregs of the earth should be preferred to us past masters of the world."[11] This confessionalism in the service of Arabism found expression in the typically ʿAlawite mysticism with which he cast all his pan-Arab formulations.[12]

10. Batatu, *Social Classes*, 730.

11. From Arsuzi's account of the 1936–39 events in Alexandretta; see *Mashakiluna al-Qawmiyyah Wa Mawquf al-ʾAhzab Minha* (Damascus: Dar al-Yaqdha, 1958), 96. The account is interesting for its extraordinary focus on virtues that also feature in ʿAflaq's writings (sacrifice, hardship, leader worship, faith, idealism). These appear in the stories and characters Arsuzi writes about, including his depiction of himself as an object of adoration for the downtrodden masses.

12. ʿAlawis are an obscurantist Shiʿite sect incorporating pagan elements, initiation ceremonies, and backward proscriptions on women, who are deemed to have no soul.

Following Arsuzi's expulsion from the district in 1939, he formed a group that had one condition for membership: the writing or translation of a book contributing to the renaissance (*ba'th*) of Arab heritage. The cultural section of the group was apparently called "The Arab Ba'th," the first usage of the term in an organized political context.

In 1944 the group fused with 'Aflaq and Bitar's tiny circle based in Damascus. Arsuzi did not join because of an intense hostility between him and 'Aflaq. Moreover, Arsuzi sometimes referred to himself as the "prophet" and "fate" of Arabism.[13] 'Aflaq never put things in such personal terms, and, though less charismatic, his writings were more coherent. Strangely enough, the content of both men's Arabism was identical. The Sunni Iraqi Ba'th now extol 'Aflaq as their "spiritual father," while their 'Alawi counterparts in Syria denounce him as a usurper and award the privilege to Arsuzi.

In developing the Ba'th party, Arsuzi's followers injected experience in mass politics and a feverish militantism into what was a glorified discussion group around 'Aflaq and Bitar. They had left Arsuzi under the leadership of Wahib al-Ghanim; his brother and other 'Alawis from Alexandretta organized the first embryonic Ba'thi circles in Baghdad in 1949. The Alexandrettans brought no new "theory" into the Ba'th, only organizational energy and a feel for the kind of politics belonging to the family of "struggles against imperialism" that we discussed in the 1933 Assyrian affair.

In the 1940s, the Ba'th was composed of students, teachers, lawyers, doctors, and other intelligentsia from the poorer strata. July 1943, when a group of less than ten people released a programmatic statement,[14] is the date most writers have fixed as the starting point of the party proper. In April 1947, when the first congress was held after the merger with the Alexandrettans, the total membership was a few hundreds. A five-man executive was established headed by 'Aflaq.

Sunnis dominated the leadership in the 1940s, but probably not the

---

They venerate 'Ali before Muhammad and see themselves as an elite among Muslims to whom has been revealed the hidden meaning of the original revelation. Similarly, Arsuzi interprets the nation as the unfolding of its creative *ma'na* (meaning). Arsuzi was greatly taken by Bergson's philosophy. In 1928, he recalled, he had a "metaphysical" experience. "I was at the entrance to the Sorbonne, plunged in thought . . . when I was suddenly invaded by a feeling of ecstasy. My soul was metamorphosed and my way of seeing the world completely transformed." This is how he arrived at his pan-Arabist convictions according to an interview with Rouleau, "The Syrian Enigma," 56.

13. See Arsuzi, *Mashakiluna*, 102, 103.

14. This is the number given by 'Aflaq in his opening speech to the first National Congress of the Ba'th in 1947. See *Nidhal*, 1:21.

membership after the 1945 merger. Despite the 'Alawi influx, only one 'Alawi was in the leadership. After a merger with Akram al-Hurani and his large Sunni peasant and officer following in 1952, however, the party's confessional distribution fell in line with that of Syria at large. By the late 1960s 'Alawis began to dominate the leadership of the Syrian branch through their penetration of the Syrian officer corps, and the civilian wing lost influence. The nonmilitary "tradition" of Ba'thism, however, continued in Iraq, as symbolized by the Iraqi Ba'th's choice of 'Aflaq as their founding father.

Hurani's group, though large, never properly integrated into the party. Hurani had gained a reputation as an Arab nationalist after supporting Rashid 'Ali in 1941 and leading irregulars in Palestine in 1948. He was elected in 1943 as Hama's deputy, and remained a member of parliament until 1958. Hurani founded the Arab Socialist Party in 1950 on the same program as that adopted by the Ba'th in their first congress in 1947. It "counted no fewer than 10,000 members and was able to attract as many as 40,000 people from the countryside when in the same year it convoked at Aleppo the first peasant congress in Syria's history."[15]

On the eve of the merger with Hurani, the Ba'th had grown into an organization of around 4,500 active members, with branches in Iraq, Jordan, and Lebanon. Although very significant in Syrian terms, the party still lacked a mass base. With the 1952 union, the newly named ABSP congealed into its more or less final shape. Through the 1950s and early 1960s it became a mass party in Syria, acted as the driving force behind the formation of the United Arab Republic in 1958, and had its first taste of power in Iraq in 1963.

In short, the personalities and formative events of the first decade bring to the Ba'th divergent experiences, an educated, urban, and lower middle-class leadership, confessional variety, and a territorial spread. Through Hurani the party acquired a rural base and a foothold in the Syrian officer corps, adding immeasurably to its middle class presence in Damascus, the hometown of 'Aflaq and Bitar. The coming together of a Christian ('Aflaq), two Sunni Muslims (Bitar and Hurani), and the 'Alawi followers of Arsuzi, palpably presented itself to the Syrian masses as a new kind of organization, apparently capable of bridging traditional barriers. Hitherto, only the Syrian Communist Party had an appeal across the confessional divide; but it was saddled with an alien

15. Batatu, *Social Classes*, 729.

mark, that historical tie with the Russian revolution that could never quite be severed. By cultivating an awareness of Arab identity implanted in an exclusively Arab historical experience, the Baʿth were able to bridge and take for granted the confessional mosaic of Syrian society. They were never perceived as posing a threat to traditionalism, and in fact spoke its language and used its categories. This was shown by the Alexandrettan affair, and the absorption of the party's first significant social base from the ranks of an uprooted and embittered community, who had waged a racialist campaign against the Turkish minority in Alexandretta. Yet the Baʿth represented something new in Arab politics. This combination of a constrained universalism and sectarianism in practice is a hallmark of the Baʿthi brand of pan-Arabism.

The Pan-Arabism of the Baʿth

The pan-Arabism of the Baʿth arose as a reaction to other currents within Arab nationalist thought for which the West was in some ways still a model. Intellectuals like Satiaʿ al-Husri and Constantin Zurayq did not hesitate to point to inherent obstacles to the growth of national consciousness. Theirs was not yet the purely technical or economistic view of modernity, which became popular in the postwar age.

In a seminal book published in 1939 Zurayq identified "factors of weakness in the contemporary Arab personality." He extolled not only the technological achievements of the West, but its "way of thought and manner of analysis . . . that constant search for the truth and alertness to doubt all that which does not correspond to reason. . . . It seems to me that between us [Arabs] and these true scientific qualities, there are many steps to be taken, and distant stages. It is better that we approach this science of the West with humble hearts and thirsty spirits." [16] Husri never went so far. But he was forever drawing on Western examples and emphasizing "theory" based on clearly formulated assumptions, which led to his view of the scientific objectivity of national existence.

In a critique of this generation of Arab intellectuals, ʿAflaq wrote in 1940:

> I fear that nationalism will be reduced in us to mental knowledge and verbal investigations, losing by this the force of nerve and the heat of emotion. . . .

16. Constantin Zurayq, *Al-Waʿy al-Qawmi*, new ed. (Beirut: Dar al-Makshouf, 1940), 43, 48–49.

It is as if they [other intellectuals] pinned their faith in nationalism on the degree of accuracy and power of their definitions, whereas, it is faith which precedes all knowledge and mocks definition; it is faith on the contrary that illuminates knowledge.

The nationalism we are calling for is love before anything else. . . .

He who loves does not ask for reasons. And if he were to ask, he would not find them. He who cannot love except for a clear reason, has already had this love wither away in himself and die.

How can some young people ask for reasons that would convince them that the love of their Arab nation must defeat their love for the Russians for example [a reference to Arab communists], superseding any tendency in them towards a particular confession, tribe or region? How can they question whether the Arabs have qualities that deserve such love? . . .

Love . . . comes first and definition [of nationhood] follows later.[17]

In 1941 'Aflaq went on to say, "Nationalism is not a science; it is . . . a living remembrance." The very attempt to deconstruct this feeling, and then reconstitute it through a mental process "drawn from books, abstract thought and the example of foreign nations" has to be rejected. The great danger as he saw it was the Western inclination to pursue abstraction to the point that it desensualized reality, thereby deluding the analyst as to its nature. All those whose nationalism came from Europe were afflicted with "abstract thought," which "strips things of their flesh and blood, and robs them of colour and taste."[18]

The very idea of a dialogue over premises such as the primacy of language and history is cast aside on the grounds that such an analytic/rationalistic way of posing the question is in itself fallacious. Debate is meaningless because it concedes there may be a problem. 'Aflaq is resting on an important new insight: the presumption of a profoundly emotional basis for a true nationalist experience. From a nationalist standpoint, if nationalism were overwhelming love, then 'Aflaq would have a point: the act of intellectualization cannot but rob the sentiment of some of its vitality; and it can be assumed that when intellectuals engage in analysing it, for whatever motive, they are doing so because they have been put on the defensive.

Consider the novelty for a Muslim society of 'Aflaq's theme: nationalism is love before anything else. It is not simply a matter of Christian

---

17. Michel 'Aflaq, *Fi Sabil al-Ba'th* (Beirut: Dar al-Tali'ah, 1959), 29–30. The article is entitled "Nationalism Is Love Before Anything Else." This book is the fundamental canonical text of Ba'thism. It is a collection of 'Aflaq's writings between 1935 and the 1950s. Unless otherwise specified, I shall be quoting from the first 1959 edition.

18. Ibid., 28 and 26.

overtones; it is more like a New Testament challenging the Old, a demand that the burdensome Jewish God of Law and fixed norms give way to the "love of God" as the main criterion of Christian identity.

For ʿAflaq *the attitude towards belief,* and hence the profundity of the individual inner experience of it, was becoming all-important. Conformism and mere acceptance were no longer enough in relation to an Arab's sense of identity, even though the masses were not lining up at the time to become pan-Arabists. He was raising the stakes. An experience of inward transformation was required: "love" was merely an unfortunate initial choice of words on ʿAflaq's part to express it. The words soon changed, but the fundamental intuitive idea never did.

To conceive nationalism as though it were a religious experience, is obviously separable from Christian doctrine, which I have used only for purposes of analogy. ʿAflaq was not known for a predisposition to any specific religious doctrine. His pan-Arabism was in the first place an answer to a question formulated by an-international order made up of nation-states which imposed itself forcefully on the Arab world in the interwar years. ʿAflaq was constructing his answer in religious categories, which is something no "secular" Arab intellectual had done before.

THE JULY 1943 STATEMENT

On July 24, 1943, the Arab Baʿth movement issued its first programmatic statement. The document was written by ʿAflaq for the Syrian elections of 1943, arranged under the auspices of the mandatory power to establish a Syrian National Assembly and government with which France could negotiate some sort of independence. ʿAflaq was a thirty-three-year-old candidate on behalf of the Orthodox Christian community of Damascus. I shall consider in detail the five banner headlines of this document in the order in which they appear.[19]

1. *"We represent the Arab Spirit against materialist Communism."* "Arab Spirit," *al-ruh al-ʿarabiyya,* is the phrase ʿAflaq now uses in place of "love" whose negative connotations he must have realized. Aside from its Christian overtones, overwhelming love of the nation is constricting because it does not obviously incorporate, for example, hatred of the nation's enemies. The force or inner drive behind that Spirit previously conveyed by the action of loving is henceforth *al-iman,* a pure

19. Taken from *Nidhal,* 1:27.

faith completely detached from any specific emotion. In an article devoted to *al-iman,* written in either 1941 or 1943, 'Aflaq stressed the
"eternal foundation of our work, the basis that will not change and can
never be replaced, which is faith."[20] Moreover, "the profound truth of
our times is that faith precedes clear knowledge."[21] The irreconcilable
hostility between Ba'thism and Western post-Enlightenment values begins here. 'Aflaq went on to argue:

> Were they [the imperialists] to give us the earth, or were they to give us an
> Arab state in which the goals of the Ba'th—unity, freedom, socialism—were
> all realized, but they said faith will be absent from people's lives in this ideal
> state, then we would say that we prefer to remain a divided nation, a colo-
> nized and exploited one, oppressed and enslaved, until, through pain and
> through the struggle between us and our fate, between us and ourselves, we
> rediscovered our true humanity.[22]

The Spirit understood as an objective historical force is a most elusive Hegelian construct. But whereas for Hegel this force resided in
the state, for 'Aflaq it resided in the nation (following in this possibly
Herder). Thus the spirit is independent of political vicissitude, which it
never was for Hegel; it is the "eternal message," *risala khalida,* of the
nation, timeless, and yet in a perpetual state of becoming. "Arabs do not
become nationalists by their adoption of the idea of nationalism, for nationalism is not an idea," 'Aflaq wrote. To treat it as one "adds to the
sects of the Arabs one more sect, and adds to the Arab self yet another
layer upon all those that already conceal it. . . . Arabs do not need to
learn anything new to become nationalists; rather they need to forget
what they have learned so that they can return to a direct relationship
with their pure, original nature."[23] The Arab Spirit is not an idea "imported from the West," but it is this irreducible essence accessible to the
members of the nation only through faith.

2. *"We represent living Arab History against dead reaction and artificial progressivism."* The negative condition of not having an "Arab
Spirit," or having it in a weakened or distorted form, is revealing. In
1943 'Aflaq wrote that the loss of the Spirit led to a loss of personality
and a "deformed" and "abstract" formation. For example, Arab intellectuals of the communist movement and generally Arabs formed by

20. 'Aflaq, *Fi Sabil,* 39.
21. From a 1946 article "On The Arab Message," which hearkens back in its phraseol-
ogy to his striking article of 1940 on "Nationalism Is Love," ibid., 76.
22. Ibid., 39.
23. Ibid., 28.

Western culture, products of an "artificial and false progressivism," "live with us in their bodies, but in their thoughts and in their spirit, they are with the European countries; and yet in spite of this they allocate to themselves the right to give an opinion on our problems, on our past, and even to influence and direct our work."[24]

> The philosophies and teachings that come from the West, invade the Arab mind and steal his loyalty *before* they rob him of his land and skies [emphasis added]. We want a unified nationalist programme of education that derives its roots from the particularities of the Arab nation, the spirit of its past, and the needs of its future. It should preserve loyalty to the Arab homeland and the Arab cause without sharing in this venture any other homeland or cause.[25]

If "artificial progressivism" is the condition brought about by the loss of the Arab Spirit, then "living Arab history" is the agency for reconquering it. And the imputation of a life-giving force to history must be understood through the "Arab Spirit," which expressed itself in great deeds in the past, and can continue to do so in the present.

The West is rejected wholesale, not for occupying armies and territorial designs. The emphasis is not on political or economic domination, but on a *culture* whose "philosophies" and "teachings" are deemed to threaten Arabic-speaking humanity. Ba'thi pan-Arabism elevates the backwardness of the Arab world into the status of an overriding principle in the name of national self-assertion. No concessions are made to the moral advances of Western civilization despite the fact that their nationalism suffered less at Western hands by comparison, say, with Indian nationalism in the 1940s. The insularism extends to education and history, which we are told have to be virtually sealed off to prevent contamination from the outside. Progress, and the ideas that give rise to it, is not seen as belonging to a common human species. In general, there is a remarkable similarity of tone between 'Aflaq's rejection of the West and that of Khomeini in Iran. Each, however, is embedded in a different world view: Khomeiniism works by rejecting the corrupting influence of everything outside of Islam, including all forms of nationalism. 'Aflaq, on the other hand, builds on the uniqueness of nations, which like different species, occupy a jungle without common norms.[26]

---

24. Ibid., 66.
25. The July 1943 statement, *Nidhal*, 1:28.
26. In a 1967 speech 'Aflaq talked about the party's original outlook from which it "never retreated which was to consider the Arab nation in a state of war. This . . . means that the party has not ignored the reality of the dangers which surround the nation, and the gravity of the diseases which rack it." He went on to talk of the necessity to educate

3. *"We represent the whole nationalism expressive of the personality against verbal nationalism, which is in conflict with the totality of conduct."* "Whole nationalism" is imbued with the "Arab Spirit" and emerges through the "totality of conduct." The "totality of conduct," a *measure* of the intensity of faith in the Arab Spirit, is the only permissible norm for the formation of judgements about the quality of an individual's Arabism. An individual's behaviour, just like his nationalism, cannot be judged by deconstructing it into its constituent actions. Behaviour and each individual action is judged across time and from the standpoint of its intentionality as expressed in the all-important faith that does or does not motivate it. The same point was nicely put by RCC member Tariq 'Aziz in his speech on why all members of the Iraqi Ba'th party are not alike (see Chapter 2, n. 14).

4. *"We represent the message of Arabism against the craft of politics."* The Ba'th saw themselves as "strugglers," harbingers of a new kind of militancy. "Our task is to cut the path, not to pave it . . . to plant the immortal seeds, not harvest the fruit. We therefore will not enter government quickly, and on the front of struggle we shall remain a long time."[27] Politics was a pejorative term, with politicians rarely well intentioned. The public arena was a battlefield. In their policy statements, the early Ba'th never addressed those on the opposite trenches; they talked past them, as though all they were engaged in was exhortation of their own troops.

"This is the age of heroism," 'Aflaq said in an early article, "and one might almost say of innocence, for the generation that is preparing itself to enter the battle has the honesty and candidness of children; it does not understand what they call politics." Our heroes do not seek to please people; rather they with to "infuriate all those they believe to be wrong and corrupt."[28]

Alternative viewpoints are always collapsed into degeneracy and corruption. Even when opponent politicians are "brilliant and intelligent," their "tricks" do not mitigate the effects of the "diseases that eat away at the nation, and the pain that wracks its body."[29] 'Aflaq was infatuated

---

everyone in this spirit. War, it should be noted, derives both from the hostility of the outside and the rot within. See Michel 'Aflaq, *Nuqtat al-Bidaya* (Beirut: al-Mu'assasah al-'Arabiyya, 1971), 60–62.

27. *Nidhal,* 1 : 28.

28. 'Aflaq, *Fi Sabil,* 18. In a 1955 talk 'Aflaq called politics a means to Ba'thist ends and a useful testing ground for Ba'thist idealism; ibid., 42 (1974 edition).

29. *Nidhal,* 1 : 28.

with the bodily metaphor. Sickness was the deep-rooted condition of
the Arab nation conceived as a "living being" that had lost its "Spirit."
The "craft of politics" as practised by the Arabs themselves contributed
to this debilitating condition. The notion of a degenerate society whose
demons the Baᶜth had come to exorcise was axiomatic, and it was the
principal reason for their revolutionism.[30]

5. "We represent the new Arab generation."   The "new generation," the carrier of the "message of Arabism," is the living embodiment
of the Arab Spirit in that its behaviour is guided by the right notion of the
ideal society. The new generation grows "out of a certain kind of youth,"
in whom is also necessarily "to be found a certain conception of education and a certain kind of intellectual." Yet the young can be bitter enemies of the new generation.

> Real society threatens the young with the greatest of dangers, because on
> the one hand it puts them forward as candidates for heroic tasks, and on the
> other it accepts from them the most minimal of deeds. There is no alternative
> therefore, but to disregard and elevate oneself above realistic standards and
> to absorb the eternal standards of the historical mission. Eternity is not the
> passage of the present into the future, it is the implantation of the future in
> the present.[31]

"Eternity," another keyword that links up with "living history," has
in ᶜAflaq's writings the idea of endless existence, not endless time. Something that was, is, and always will be. However, ᶜAflaq is fond of con-
verting this implicitly passive state into an activist one by inverting the
meaning: something that will be, always "lives." Thus the nation only
exists insofar as the new generation has come into being. From the
standpoint of all of ᶜAflaq's categories, and the relation of one meaning
to the other, this is the only consistent way he can achieve a definition of
nationhood:

> The nation is not a numerical sum, but an "Idea" [read Spirit] embodied
> either in the total or in part of it. Nations are not destroyed by a reduction in

30. The condition of degeneracy appears in article 6 of the 1947 party constitution as
the only reason why an all-embracing internal social revolution is required (the struggle
against imperialism and for unity are cited as reasons for the revolutionary character of
the party). Ibid., 4:26. A cursory survey of the first half of the 1974 edition of Fi Sabil,
reveals that social degeneracy is mentioned, or elaborated upon, on the following pages:
13, 29, 35, 57–60, 62–63, 68, 73, 79, 81, 90–91, 94, 134, 154–56, 161, 163–64, 166.
31. From a 1944 article entitled "The New Arab Generation," quotations from Fi
Sabil, 61 and 63. In later years the word "vanguard" would replace "The New Generation" with no change in meaning. However, the move towards a communist vocabulary is
significant and will be taken up later.

the number of their members, but by the constriction of the "Idea" amongst them. The numerical total is not a holy thing in and of itself, but only insofar as it is an embodiment of the "Idea" of the nation, or, insofar as it has a potential to embody it in the future. . . . The Leader, in times of weakness of the "Idea" and its constriction, is not one to appeal to a majority or to a consensus, but to opposition and enmity; he is not one to substitute numbers for the "Idea," but to translate numbers into the "Idea"; he is not the in-gatherer, but the unifier. In other words he is the master of the singular "Idea" from which he separates and casts aside all those who contradict it.[32]

These chilling words speak for themselves without ambiguity. The "new generation" is "the nation"; and elevated conditions like the "message of Arabism," "whole nationalism," "living Arab history," the "Arab Spirit," pure "faith" have wafted down into the mundane world of simple arithmetic. The nation is the sum of those who have the right kind of faith. The objectivity of the nation is constituted entirely subjectively, albeit in the "feelings" of only one man: the Leader.

The concept of nation as a sociological category that emerges from, for example, Satia' al-Husri's conception of pan-Arabism was very different. In a theoretical world, Husri would have had to learn to live with the idea of a self-hating Arab (an Arab like al-Jawahiri who did not believe in pan-Arabism). 'Aflaq, however, had elaborated the idea that when "love," "Spirit," or the "Idea" was not present, society itself was not constituted. The existence of the social order had become inseparable from the absoluteness of its moral order. Husri had been content with education and later with the army as agents for his morality. For the Ba'th these agencies were not enough. Faith was required as a precondition, not as a goal. This is the most fundamental and distinctive doctrine of Ba'thism.

'Aflaq had precursors in the Iraq of the late 1930s. Sami Shawkat, a protege of Husri's (later disowned by him), had defined nationhood in a theoretically identical way (see Chapter 5) but with a different emphasis, being more preoccupied with criteria for excluding people from the community of Arabs:

> Our nation, like all nations, has enemies. The enemy of the nation, like the enemy of the family, is of two types: internal and external. Usually the internal enemy is more destructive than the external one. No nation has had a real renaissance without first of all defeating and totally uprooting this in-

---

32. Ibid., 64. 'Aflaq is frequently inconsistent terminologically: "Spirit" has reverted to "Idea," a term he explicitly rejected in 1940. However, it is clear from the context what he is talking about. This kind of inconsistency does not imply incoherence.

ternal enemy from its foundations. The internal enemy consists of those individuals or groups who, led by values absorbed from school and community, come to see themselves as strangers in the midst of the majesty and loftiness of the state which they view as harmful to their interests and humiliating to their position. As their strength is not sufficient to allow them to stand up against their state and declare their enmity openly, they strive in secret, stretching their hands in darkness to the external enemy, conspiring to become his spy, while all along their heart is full of envy, anger, and vengeance. Thus is the pact struck between the two types of enemies.[33]

Shawkat's focus introduces practicality and clarity, which are missing in ʿAflaq's emphasis on the inestimable virtues of an elusive Arab Spirit. For Shawkat too, nationalism is love before anything else. In politics, one may not get as far by expressing love in this particular manner. On the other hand, ʿAflaq's convoluted doctrinal reasoning turned the raw basics of Shawkat's words into a full-fledged respectable doctrine. This is ʿAflaq's great legacy in Arab politics.

The Baʿth party formally ratified this conception of national identity. The constitution, adopted at the founding conference of the party in 1947, asserts as a matter of fundamental principle the belief that "all existing differences between the members of the nation are superficial and false, and will be dissipated with the awakening of the Arab soul." An Arab is one "who has faith in his membership to the Arab nation" (article 10). "Whoever has called for, or joined a racist anti-Arab grouping, and all those who immigrated to the Arab homeland for colonial purposes" are excluded (article 11). Political rights are restricted to those "who have been faithful to the Arab homeland, and have separated from any sectarian grouping" (article 20). Finally, the state is responsible for all intellectual work and all freedoms (article 41). These activities and all forms of organization are to be constrained "within the limits of the pan-Arab idea." Therefore, in a whole series of concrete ways, this document confirmed the fundamental intuitive idea of ʿAflaq with which we started—namely, that nationalism is faith before anything else.[34]

NATIONAL IDENTITY AND ISLAM

Confessional differences have distanced an important section of the Arabs from the Spirit of their country and its traditions. . . . We wish that a full

33. Sami Shawkat, *Hadhihi Ahdafuna* (Baghdad: Wazarat al-Maʿarif, 1939), 36.
34. *Nidhal*, 4:24–30. Unfortunately some writers on the Baʿth have gone through this same document and chosen to stress articles extolling democracy, freedom of speech,

awakening in Arab Christians of their nationalism takes place, so that they can see in Islam a nationalist education for themselves, which they must cherish and fill themselves of because it is part of their nature and history, and because it is the arena in which the Arabs have proved their ability in thought, moral force, and spiritual ascendancy.[35]

In this nationalist electoral appeal to a Christian community against confessionalism in the name of Islam, ʿAflaq was not trying hypocritically to broaden the Baʿthist appeal; he was formulating a genuine component of early Baʿthist thought, which evolved alongside the party's pan-Arabism long before the party had any mass resonance. The 1943 statement shared phrases with a long article "In Memory of the Arab Prophet," setting out the distinctive Baʿthist view on Islam:

> The abstracted nationalist idea of the West is logical in its separation of nationalism from religion. Religion entered Europe from [the Middle East], and is therefore foreign to its nature and history. . . . Islam for the Arabs on the other hand is not merely a belief for the end of time, nor is it abstract moralisms; it is the highest expression of their universalist feelings and outlook on life. It is the strongest expression of the total unity of their personality, in which expression mixes in with feeling and thought, reflection with labour, and the self with fate. Islam is the most brilliant picture of their language and literature, and the grandest part of their national history. . . . The relation of Islam with Arabism, therefore, is not the same as that of any other religion in relation to any other nationality.[36]

Arabism is a body "whose Spirit is Islam." ʿAflaq repeatedly draws attention to the exceptionalism of the Arabs, which stemmed from the fact that "their national awakening was bound up with a religious message." The Arabs never expanded for territorial, racial, or economic reasons, but in order to perform a spiritual obligation. Islam was a revolutionary Arab movement whose meaning was the renewal of Arabism. The West, which feared the former, knows that "the force of Islam" has reemerged "with a new appearance: which is Arab nationalism."

ʿAflaq castigated the idea of looking at Muhammad as an object of veneration and worship, and argued that every Arab should be trying to relive the meaning of his life. He wants every Arab to be Muhammad "since he belongs to the nation that gave birth to a Muhammad; or rather, because this Arab individual is a member of the community

---

and the need for reciprocity between nations, forgetting that it is the qualifications and exclusions, not the platitudes, that count.
35. The July 1943 statement, ibid., 1:28.
36. ʿAflaq, *Fi Sabil*, 49.

which Muhammad put all his efforts into creating. . . . Muhammad was all the Arabs; let us today make all the Arabs Muhammad." Muhammad was a Leader who emerged through relentless struggle against other Arabs, and not out of a conflict with the outside non-Arab world. Arabs were chosen by God to test out this message that Muhammad was carrying, and even the faults that he came to eradicate "were Arab faults on their way to extinction. The Muslim in those days was nothing other than the Arab, but it was the new Arab [generation], whole and more developed." [37]

In the person of Muhammad, all Muslim Arabs are confronted with a member of their ethnic group and the prophet of their religion acting out the role of political leader. The will of God and Caesar was manifest in one real person, who was both the founder of the religion and the head of its first state. For better or for worse, Christ died on the cross and political power in a Christian world remained at arm's length from religious morality. However, the fundamental import of early Arab memories cannot be set aside from politics with such ease.

Islamic civilization knitted together the most disparate collection of peoples in a way that the Roman Empire, or medieval Christendom, never did. Although ethnic groups exercised political dominance over vast Islamic domains (never as exclusively as the Romans), in civilizational terms, and especially at the level of "high" culture (the arts, philosophy, science, theological studies), Islam's originality was born out of a degree of cross-cultural fertilization hitherto unknown in human affairs. The novelty of pan-Arabism as it emerged in the interwar years originated in the search to recreate that same integration of a profoundly pluralist part of the world achieved by Islam, but on the basis of an awakening ethnic sentiment that was inherently exclusionary. Unlike even nineteenth-century "Eastern" Europe, which sought always to define itself in relation to models borrowed from its "Western" self, Arabism's most basic model always resided in its own past.

The consciousness of Arab identity that was ideologized into pan-Arabism originated almost exclusively from the fact that Arabic-speaking peoples were once a politically united "historic" people, who still retained in their majority religion the remembrance of that unity, despite the millennium or so of history they cannot call their own. The exclusively Arab moment of glory was in fact very brief. As Arab ethnic hegemony was terminated under the Abbasids, Arabic culture very

37. Ibid. Quotations from pp. 47, 49, 45, 46 in that order.

quickly metamorphosed into a wider Islamic civilization with the peoples of the Fertile Crescent—Persians, Turks, Berbers, and Spaniards as well as Jews and Christians—making their own contributions that soon obliterated the Gordian knot that had originally bound Arabism to Islam. However, the assimilation of Arabs from the peninsula and other ethnic groups into a dynamic new cultural paradigm presented itself in retrospect to the Arabist imagination as the "winning over" of "foreigners" to an "Arab" enterprise. Islam appeared as the greatest creation of timeless Arabism, when in one sense the exact opposite was true: the Arabic-speaking regions of the Fertile Crescent and North Africa were themselves a creation of Islamic civilization. As if by the stroke of a pen, Arabism acquired for itself a rich historical tradition which was to become the source of much of its attractive power in later years.

Arab nationalists have in one way or another always acknowledged the link with Islam. Like ʿAflaq, Zurayq, the most secular pan-Arabist of his generation, gave one of these speeches "In memory of the Arab prophet," but with far less conviction and psychological insight.[38] Maybe such speeches were a necessary ritual for Christian pan-Arabists. In Husri's commentaries on the subject of Islam and Arabism, one finds a more casual and refreshingly pragmatic approach.[39] Both men, while building bridges and protecting their flanks, were aware that pan-Arabism was compelled to acknowledge a debt to Islam, such as no other nationalism had to do. ʿAflaq, however, was intent on constructing a new obsessively inward-looking kind of pan-Arabism based on a pseudomystical reading of the Islamic experience. ʿAflaq alone among the pan-Arabist thinkers and ideologues of his generation perfected the notion of a modern community deriving not from descent, domicile, or language, but from the fundamental underlying premise of the Islamic experience: the reliance on faith.

Batatu saw a contradiction in ʿAflaq between his notions of national and religious identity. At times Arabness appears as if it precedes Islam, and at others the reverse. But, Batatu notes, what matters "is not ʿAflaq's disregard of logic, but the very practical aim that lies behind his romantic rhetoric: the harnessing of the emotions called forth by Islam in the service of the Arab national movement or, to be specific, of the Baʿth party."[40]

38. See Zurayq, Al-Waʿy al-Qawmi, 123–33.
39. See his 1939 article on Islamic versus Arab unity: Satiaʿ al-Husri, Araʾ wa Ahadith Fi al-Wataniyya wa al-Qawmiyya (Beirut, 1984), 56–67.
40. Batatu, Social Classes, 733.

While agreeing on what matters, I take issue with an implication of this argument. The contradiction, if it exists, is *within* his ideological style of reasoning. But here the whole issue must be posed on ʿAflaq's own terms, namely that religion represents the Arab genius and "conforms to its nature." Arab nationalism cannot possibly clash with religion, or be separated from it in any temporal sense, because fundamentally both "spring from the heart and are issued by the will of God."[41] The transcendental origin of both religiosity and pan-Arabism implies no priority in the relations of things that are unknowable because one cannot be more unknowable than the other. ʿAflaq might respond to Batatu the way he once did to the Husris and Zurayqs of his generation: Nationalism is faith before anything else, and that is all there is to the matter; don't go looking for anything else. In so doing he would be totally consistent with himself, and the majority of Arabs whose emotions were being harnessed in this way would understand what he was so sincerely saying to them whereas they would find Batatu's enquiry strange.

THE COHERENCE OF THE BAʿTH

ʿAflaq is prone to flowery phrases and a proselytizing messianic tone. According to Fouad ʿAjami:

> To read ʿAflaq's main contribution to the post-1967 debate, . . . is to perceive fully the bankruptcy and incoherence of the politics of the Baʿth. Nearly three hundred pages of text yield no insight, on his part, into what went wrong and what needed to be done; there is only the visible infatuation with words and ʿAflaq's summons to the party to renounce power and go back to its "pure essence."[42]

However, ʿAflaq as we have seen has never been interested in analysing the past objectively, or in looking at the future realistically. He espouses a world view and sees his personal role as one of exhortation to action. For ʿAflaq, reality is confined to the inner world of the party. On this he has been consistent, and for these purposes his prose is well suited. His thought may or may not correspond to immediate political reality, any more than the Bible did in its own time, or, more appropri-

---

41. ʿAflaq, *Fi Sabil*, 30.
42. Fouad ʿAjami, *The Arab Predicament: Arab Political Thought and Practice Since 1967* (Cambridge: Cambridge University Press, 1982), 27. See also his commentary on the evolution of the pan-Arabism of the Baʿth, pp. 40–50.

ately, the multitude of millenarian sects and movements that flourished in western Europe on the basis of Biblical eschatology in the late Middle Ages. The issue is only in the most abstract way connected with whether or not one became a Baᶜthist in the 1940s, or why masses of people were convinced by their "analysis" of the causes of the 1967 war (as evidenced by the reaction of Iraqis during the January 1969 hangings). For the most part concrete analyses of proposed actions are only present in the form of post-factum justifications. The important questions are: How coherent and original was this view from the standpoint of the postindependence, modernizing Arab condition? To what needs and aspirations did its myths and symbols address themselves? What was the fit between the broad parameters of Baᶜthist behaviour and the tendency of the ideology towards both phantasy and demonization?

Let us cast the problem that ᶜAjami is alluding to somewhat differently. Consider these questions: Is the Baᶜthist conception of national identity rational? If not, then what is the source of its coherence? A community may exist merely because it *thinks* itself to be in existence. One of the oldest insights of political philosophy is that such a minimal consensus, which is also a moral consensus, is the starting point of political society. But ᶜAflaq does not begin from a consensus, or from the "natural" drive to arrive at one; in fact, he posits a fractured, unselfconscious society that has been corrupted. The "given" datum is that society has *no shared morality* and, on the face of it, not even the chance to arrive at one by some "rational" process based on self-interest (Hobbes), the public good (Locke and Rousseau), or the workings of the economy (Marx). Material well-being and socioeconomic integrity are without motivating power in ᶜAflaq's scheme of things.

Quite apart from the appeal to faith, ᶜAflaq is the author of a view of the world that consistently, and quite remarkably, denies the logical distinction between that which *is,* and that which *ought* to be. His way of *thinking* obliterates this flaw in the way the world is actually constructed; his thought is ideological for this reason, and not merely because it rests on faith in pan-Arabism. The nation that *ought* to be united, incorrupt, and imbued with the Arab Spirit, actually *is* right now made up only of those who have faith in what it ought to be in the future; the "eternal message" of Arabism is "not the passage of the present [that which *is*] into the future [that which *ought* to be]; it is the implantation of the future in the present [their identity one with the other]." The idea of "living Arab history" embodied in a new generation guided by nothing other than its faith in the future is quintessential ʿAflaq; all three tenses are rolled up into one simultaneous happening. There are no causal connections in the relation of people to each other, either in the present or through time. The evils in society only have causes in the shape of self-evident demons (imperialism, communism, *shuʿubism,* and a host of other hopelessly corrupted groups). The millennium is here on earth in the shape of the party and its vision of the unknowable but fated future.[43]

The answer to the first question then is that Baʿthism, sealed off from everything outside itself, is totally irrational when viewed critically from this outside. ʿAflaq himself might admit to this critique. More to the point, however, it would not bother him, because from within Baʿthism, if faith is pursued with sufficient vigour, the whole stance acquires a perverse self-fulfilling rationality in direct proportion to the number of its proponents and the amount of their enthusiasm. What then is the source of the party's coherence?

The militancy and consistency of ʿAflaq and his cohorts kept them from appearing ridiculous to large numbers of Syrian Arabs in the 1940s. The Baʿth appealed first to the poorer strata of the urban intelligentsia, and then to the unorganized amorphous mass of the urban population, attracting people especially when communal or confessional feelings ran high. They did not address interest groups as such (workers, peasants, landlords). They appealed largely to atomized and disrupted individuals, or to those who felt threatened by the rootlessness brought on by population growth, urbanization, modernization, and the assault of large-scale demographic changes on a traditional way of life. In such a setting, frustration did not focus on specific and limited objectives; it was boundless and directly attached to the unknowability of the values that were its "mission." But what attracted people to the Baʿthi conception of pan-Arabism in the first place?

In the end, Baʿthist doctrine, irrational as it may be, conveys a nor-

---

43. "We do not tell the Arabs that you will arrive at a united, free, socialist existence—in a word at Baʿthism—sometime in the future when the Arab Baʿth is realized; rather we tell them this is its picture right now. . . . The future comes to us, and grows inside us; it is no longer something separate and apart from us." *Fi Sabil,* 158. ʿAflaq thought of fate as "choosing" the Baʿth to fulfill the imperative of the nation on condition that they forever strive in the direction of the standards it sets. This reasoning, ridiculous as it may sound, operates on the traditional passive fatalism of this part of the world by turning it into an active and highly charged doctrine. See also p. 43 of the 1974 edition for a 1955 article on "Our Living Conception of the Party." For a rejection of traditional fatalism that links up with ʿAflaq's notion of freedom, see the 1950 article "On Revolution, Fate and Freedom," 151–55 (1959 edition).

mative coherence such as can be found in the moral order of all the great
religions in the Middle East. An unambiguous and familiar moral imperative lies at the heart of ʿAflaq's pan-Arabism. "Were they to give us
the earth," but excluded faith, we have seen him say, "then . . . we prefer to remain a divided nation." This statement of self-abnegation elevates the moral attitude to conduct into the driving force of early Baʿthism. In a 1950 article ʿAflaq defined it:

> So long as a normal and honourable life is forbidden for the immense ma-
> jority of the people because of the corrupt conditions, then those who have
> faith in the justice of the people do not accept to participate in a life that they
> consider to be currently illegitimate and oppressive. Therefore they choose in
> its place the life of principle.
> Struggle and the law of life which cannot be denied, does not allow the
> achievement of large goals, formidable advance, and a fundamental revolu-
> tion without a large price in return. This price is sacrifice.[44]

ʿAflaq directed the politics of pan-Arabism away from concessions
and compromise, which is what Faisal had understood it to be; and he
drove it away from what would have been a corrosive preoccupation
with real Arab society, or concrete political questions. He directed pan-
Arabism towards an ideal standard of excellence into which all morality
was conflated. Thus everything about real society in the 1940s appeared
corrupt to him. The perfectionism of his ideal Arab (personified by
Muhammad) made him recoil with horror from the real Arabs all around
him. Here were ordinary people, who, like the rest of us, had their
foibles, prejudices, and simple wants and desires. These filled ʿAflaq
with contempt, a condition bordering on hate.

Many people conduct their daily lives with contempt for the behaviour of others, and this contempt as ʿAflaq noted is invariably associated
with a conflict over values. But what is special about the Baʿth is the
way in which their contempt got translated into politics. From the start
ʿAflaq's contempt was combined with an inner vision of a transformed
Arabic-speaking humanity. The combination was very powerful.

Unfortunately, commentators have insisted on seeing a contradiction
between ʿAflaq's emphasis on the individual and his nationalism. Such
problems can usually be resolved by turning to what ʿAflaq said and,
moreover, by starting from the presumption that he was sincere. In a
1950 article, ʿAflaq introduced a fundamental distinction:

44. ʿAflaq, *Fi Sabil*, 114.

I have always believed that our philosophy must never deify the human being [al-insan]. There is a difference between the individual [al-fard] and the human being. We must place the greatest value on the former and not the latter, because to deify [ta'lih] the human being is paganism [wathaniyya], or in other words, loss of faith. It is not possible for one human being to have faith in the other because the result will be a dissipation and a collapse of morality and the higher ideals. As for the importance of the individual, this conforms with spiritual philosophy which is based on conscience and moral reason, and not on the herd or the mass. The Spirit is found in the independently constituted individual motivated by his conscience who is the foundation. We do not tell him to fulfill the conditions of his nation and to make sacrifices as a human being, but as an individual. We do not tell him that he is the end of this life, rather, he—the individual—is its holy means.[45]

Phrases like "whole nationalism" and the "totality of conduct" in the first Ba'thi statement in 1943 implied an attack on the notion that a particular belief or an individual action could be treated in isolation, on its own merit. Such notions suggested that "individuals" were in some moral sense inviolable, that standards of excellence might vary, and that such variety is built into the human condition in some way. 'Aflaq wanted to reject this by constructing the distinction between "individuals" to whom a singular standard of excellence could be applied, and "human beings" whose very existence denied that possibility. The distinction fits in perfectly with his whole ideological system, and its creation is a stroke of intellectual brilliance.[46]

For whatever complicated historical reason connected with the consciousness underlying the phrase al-qawmiyya al-'arabiyya, 'Aflaq succeeded in linking the shock of modernity and the rootlessness it threatened with fasad, corruption of the present. The solution was to adopt an ideal standard of excellence in the shape of an absolute belief in Arabism and its moral worth. This now acted as a basic norm, or organizing principle, for other derivative and dependent norms that governed Ba'thist behaviour. The source of their appeal did not reside in local ob-

45. Ibid., 154. This passage was deleted in later editions.
46. 'Aflaq criticized the contemptible motivation of Arabs who indulged in thinking about "humanism", ibid., 67–69. He concluded: "The greatest service the Arabs can give to humankind is to uplift their own nationalism . . . and to forget somewhat humanistic thinking. . . . It is both a comedy and a disgrace that Arabs who are poor, and whose country is occupied by others, should be thinking of humanism and supporting other nations; humanism demands of us that we forget it, until we are up to its level [sic]." Moreover, the humanism of Western intellectuals, while not as pernicious as that of Arabs, is a facade for nationalism and "should not be allowed to deceive us"; ibid., 70.

jective conditions or in the extent of the project's ultimate feasibility; in the end the vitalism of Baʿthism stemmed from this emphasis on a constellation of values almost entirely suggested by Arab-Islamic political culture. In contrast to his intellectual opponents, ʿAflaq had absorbed not only the vocabulary, but the grammar of moral reasoning followed by those he was addressing.

Even an advocate of pan-Arabism has to have whatever other beliefs he or she may hold, or whatever other actions undertaken, tested against the absoluteness of the basic norm of the Baʿthist moral system. This test is conducted not merely to establish the fitness of a person's entry into the party, but it is an "objective" test that establishes the fitness of membership in society as a whole—in the Arab nation conceived as a moral imperative.

The Baʿthist postulate that society depends for its very existence on having an unbreachable basic moral norm entails as a necessary consequence that all deviance is immediately and directly an act of treason. The new Arab order must be a seamless moral web. This is the fundamental source of the party's coherence, and its license to violence. Violence arises as an imperative prior to the establishment of societal rules; it springs from the very perfectionism of the Baʿth, which carries through into their concept of revolution. Struggle is an end in itself, and "profound change carries in it the meaning of violence."[47] Violence is not a matter of self-defence. With refreshing candor, ʿAflaq says that morality resides not only in the suffering and sacrifices of the struggling party, but in its cruelty as well:

> Our faith calls upon us to announce a division in the nation, because the nation . . . will not recapture that ideal unity which is today a matter of principle until it divides on itself.
> However, in this struggle we retain our love for all. When we are cruel to others, we know that our cruelty is in order to bring them back to their true selves, of which they are ignorant. Their potential will, which has not been clarified yet, is with us, even when their swords are drawn against us.[48]

The greater one's love for the nation—in other words the greater one's moral propensities as manifested in the intensity of the striving for Baʿthist excellence—the more necessary it is to be cruel when the occasion arises. Successful Baʿthi conduct must "engender fierce hatred until death towards those persons who represent a contrary idea. It is worth-

47. Ibid., 129.
48. Ibid., 103.

less for members of the movement to content themselves with combatting opponent ideas by saying: why bother with persons." Why is it worthless? Because "the antagonistic idea does not exist by itself; it is embodied in persons who must perish, so that it too may perish."[49]

The Baʿthi license to violence arises from the very morality of their conception of pan-Arabism. In other words it arises *before* any utterances on freedom, and in the very domain that is agreed to be their focus as a party. Moreover, it arises before the introduction of any socioeconomic criteria concerning the exigencies of development in a backward country and what this might entail in the way of limitations on freedom.

When Batatu quoted this last gruesome passage, he went on to say that it was the only instance of its kind, and no connection should be made between it and the brutalities of the Baʿth in power.[50] Kamel Abu Jaber ignored such passages, and vehemently argued that "ʿAflaq's conception of revolution precludes violence."[51] Norma Salem-Babikian weighs in against Eric Rouleau for daring to suggest that ʿAflaq "had Fascist tendencies," while Rouleau himself misses the forest for the trees in his hunt for the true socialists hidden within the Baʿth.[52]

Fouad ʿAjami, looking at the disillusionment of Baʿthist intellectuals in the 1960s from a different perspective, also drew unwarranted conclusions. How does one explain the regimes in Iraq and Syria on the

49. Ibid., 40–41. These passages were later deleted.
50. See Batatu, *Social Classes,* 739–40. Batatu characterizes ʿAflaq's ideology as "undisciplined eclecticism," and sees him as a humanitarian nationalist influenced by "the individualism of the Enlightenment, the democratism of the Jacobins, the youth idealization of Mazzini, the class standpoint of Marx, the elitism of Lenin" (p. 731). But ʿAflaq argued against "humanitarianism" and the "individualism of the Enlightenment," as has been shown. Generally too much is being made of Western influences on him. Finally, however eclectic ʿAflaq may have been, something about his ideas "worked." What? This is the central question which Batatu does not address.
51. Abu Jaber, *The Arab Baʿth,* 131 and 139. No one laboured harder than Jaber to make the Baʿth look respectable. Writing after the 1963 bloodbath in Iraq, Jaber says that Baʿthism is a peaceful and freedom-loving creed that has no interest in a one-party state but is "prompted by a desire to contribute to world civilization and humanity" (pp. 130–33). ʿAflaq, we are told, "means something new, uniquely Arab. This makes it difficult for Western political analysts, who at times take what they read at face value, to understand the writings of Middle Easterners. [They] . . . cannot fathom the intense emotional content of their words" (p. 9).
52. N. Salem-Babikian, "Michel ʿAflaq: A Biographic Outline," in *Arab Studies Quarterly,* Institute of Arab Studies & A.A.U.G., vol. 2, no. 2 (Spring 1980); 170. Rouleau, "The Syrian Enigma," 53–65, attributed noble motives to the anti-ʿAflaq Baʿthi Left that arose in the 1960s. He does not seem to have realized that this was the faction that presided over the 1963 bloodbath in Iraq against ʿAflaq's objections. The first person to note the violence inherent in early Baʿthist doctrine is S. G. Haim in her introduction to *Arab Nationalism* (London, 1962), 70.

basis that a party born in "youthful idealism" simply "surrendered to the intrigues and brutality of the military?"[53] After all, the comment is related to that conjuncture in which *stable* Baᶜthist polities came into being. The original "logic" of the party, on the face of it, seemed to be fulfilling itself. Reducing the Baᶜth to military coup makers loses the distinctive feature of Baᶜthism, particularly in a country like Iraq (a case might be made for differences between the Iraqi and Syrian Baᶜth). The loss of a few thoughtful souls does not illustrate the "bankruptcy" of Baᶜthist politics, and says nothing about the new political period that Baᶜthism inaugurated in the 1970s.

I had similar illusions. The problem is a reluctance to come to terms with the coherence of the Baᶜth. The problem is one of modern Arab politics as a whole. The reluctance to take ᶜAflaq at face value, or very seriously, stems in the end from the knowledge that if his ideas are in any sense "linked" to the practices of the Baᶜth in power, this could only happen because two further conditions were fulfilled. First, ᶜAflaq's early ideas had to have been followed through by later Baᶜthi leaders. Second, the Baᶜthi justification for violence, to be more than just the musings of an armchair philosopher, had to find a resonance among masses of people in Iraq and Syria. These were people who had nothing to do with the Baᶜth party at first, but would in principle have to become at least partly convinced of the necessity for its violence in order for any "linkage" to take place. The two conditions were eventually fulfilled in Iraq under the second Baᶜthi regime. Baᶜthi authority in Iraq assumes their fulfillment.

To conclude: Once political identity is accepted as belief in an absolute moral imperative, and once morality itself is seen as a striving for perfection towards an unrealizable ideal, then no aspect of conduct is in principle outside the purview of the political organization or the state. Moreover, there is no way to avoid the implication that such all-embracing interference is justified. Justice as the problem of arbitrating between claims on society (rights) never arises, and is not expected to arise. That kind of justice involves the a priori assertion of the moral inviolability of "human beings," which the Baᶜth reject. Nevertheless, even in the absence of all notions of human rights, deliberate violence over a prolonged period has to be justified (not merely rationalized) in the eyes of those who are its targets. Violence simply could not work for long without it. The moral imperative of Baᶜthism, bound up as it is with Islam, is

53. ᶜAjami, *The Arab Predicament*, 43.

now the only source of that justification. Morality and justice have become indistinguishable from each other just as they are in all religions and just as they have been considered to be throughout all of Arab-Islamic history.

Secularism or Confessionalism?

Many informed writers find a secular content in Ba'thi nationalism.[54] The party has taken steps on what looks like a secular course (for example, constricting religious and clerical prerogatives). Pan-Arabism is after all an overriding principle, and the party has never demanded conversion to Islam as a price of entry. In 1943, 'Aflaq merely wanted Greek Orthodox Damascenes to "see in Islam a nationalist education for themselves"; he left it to them to figure out the implications of this on their Christianity. By contrast, when the Lebanese Hizbollahis issued their manifesto in February 1985 they demanded the conversion of all Lebanon's Christians and called for a Shi'ite Islamic republic.

Clearly a Ba'thist and a Muslim fundamentalist do not meet on some very basic issues. Yet the Ba'th rest on the same absolutist moral foundations as do all religions; moreover, the Ba'th more than other pan-Arabisms single out Islam for deep-rooted ideological reasons and not out of expediency. How can we reconcile all this?

Those who call the Ba'th "secular" usually have in mind the view that modern nationalism, however ideological, is intrinsically secular regardless of immediate concessions it might be compelled to make to religious beliefs. The assumption is that time and the exigencies of a nation-state's boundaries will eventually "modernize" religious sensibilities by relegating them to a suitably subordinate role. The emphasis is therefore on certain formulations to the exclusion of others, or on the sorts of measures just mentioned.

SECULARISM

The problem begins with the meaning of "secular," or "secularism," in politics. If the word is limited to the institutional separation of a par-

---

54. Thus G. H. Torrey says: "'Aflaq being of Christian origin, has been compelled to establish his nationalism on a secular basis." See "The Ba'th—Ideology and Practice," *The Middle East Journal* 23 (Autumn 1969): 449. See also Abu Jaber, *The Arab Ba'th*, 129; and T. Y. Ismael, in *Iraq and Iran: Roots of Conflict* (Syracuse: Syracuse University Press, 1982), 30.

ticular religious doctrine from the affairs of state, then the Baʿth are secular in that the party does not attract clerics or involve them in politics.
Masses of people can after all remain religious in a genuinely secular
polity. In this formal definition of the term there is no (or very limited)
relation between the political and social implications of secularization. The price is confusion over the *source* of political obligation under
pan-Arabism.

In the historically Christian countries of the West that we know are
secular, secularization included the idea of politics as an arena that no
longer *existed* by virtue of any transcendent morality. Politics acquired
through secularization a radically new reason for existence. However
religious a population, once it has conceded this much by accepting the
new moral norm of tolerance among many moralities in a society constituted according to relative values and beliefs, then the formalism of
the previous definition takes on an entirely new meaning. One can say,
for example, that beliefs and moral convictions should occur on at least
two separate levels: private/personal and public/social. This separation,
which is at the heart of the Western conception of secularism in politics,
arose out of the growth of religious toleration following the religious
wars of the sixteenth and seventeenth centuries.

Religious toleration is by itself not enough, however preferable it
might be to all forms of moral absolutism. The moment that it is considered legitimate for even a few individuals not to believe in God, and to
follow their own judgement on matters of conscience, society is faced
with a new problem: How are moral norms for the justification of state
coercion to be ascertained in the absence of recourse to spiritual authority? Secularization (which takes many forms) is the answer that
Western civilization has given to this problem which arose in a Christian context from the institutional separation of state and religion.

The problem cannot arise in the same way when all that is involved is
the replacement of one religion with another, or mere tolerance between
religions (it being assumed that the main religions share enough of a
consensus on the transcendent origin of morality to form the moral underpinnings of an effective coercive system). With this qualification, a
truly secular and morally *legitimate* regime in the eyes of its populace is
unthinkable to all denominations and sects in the Middle East. For
however much a particular religion or sect objects to its domination by
another, all are united in the idea that in human affairs, systems that
relativize moral values, or ones that simply assert or presuppose them
(through the person of a Leader or say in a Bill of Rights) are themselves

immoral. In the Middle East, the religious group is still, to one extent or another, the raw material of politics. Identification with nation-state or social class remains at a disadvantage. Whatever illusions we might have held on this have been blown away by the Lebanese civil war and the Iranian revolution.

In the past the religious community preserved itself in the Middle East because it was a self-contained social unit. The communal consciousness fostered by the Ottoman millet system (a term that combined the meaning of nation and religious community) actually intensified in the nineteenth century as different powers assumed protectorships over communities, using them to gain influence. The subsequent dissolution of many of communalism's traditional roles through nation building and modernization may have in fact intensified its moral hold over the lives of otherwise modern Arab individuals. Many Third Worldisms look back with nostalgia to this "tradition" in the name of independence and the struggle against imperialism.

Baʿthist doctrine is firmly implanted in this Middle Eastern tradition in its view of the link between political and moral action so direct in the case of Islam. The moral absolutism of the Baʿth, however, is directed at a nonreligious end: the demarcation of national identity in a world that insists upon frontiers. For the Arabs this end is accessible through arguments about the primacy of the Arabs within Islam. ʿAflaq put it well when he said that it was the "force of Islam" that had the "new appearance" of pan-Arabism. From this standpoint, the Baʿth are anything but secular. The party found its ultimate justification in a broadly defined Arab-Islamic tradition of politics. Here is the relation between politics and society that renders the term secularism useless with respect to understanding Baʿthi politics.

But it is also important to keep in mind the broader moral basis of Baʿthism (going beyond Islam to embrace that which all sects in the Middle East have in common), because we also want to understand how the party was able to appeal *across* confessional barriers. The construction of political identity by reference to an unknowable absolute moral imperative may conflict with each established sect on this or that point (and in the emphasis on faith in the nation rather than God, it conflicts with all of them); nonetheless in the end the Baʿth succeed. No Arab communist intellectual, however dogmatic, could compete with the Baʿth on these kinds of ground rules. And no Western-influenced Arab could argue convincingly against ʿAflaq without addressing these fundamental belief structures, thereby alienating mass opinion. ʿAflaq's genius lay in having adapted from his environment a deeply absorbed religiosity so it fitted in a world no longer made up of religious denominations. He ideologized the consciousness underlying pan-Arabism in such a way as to borrow virtually nothing of the constellation of values associated with the European Enlightenment. His way of thinking attracted large numbers of Arabs *because* it placed no demands on their traditional mores, and because it fitted in with their view of the Arab place in history.

In another age he would have been one of the many seers, soothsayers, tribal outcasts, and prophets who have flourished in this part of the world for thousands of years. Such men came out of one religion, yet appealed across confessional fault lines. They worked within a tradition of religious-moral thinking that formed an overall referential framework understood and accepted by all denominations and sects. With the exception of ʿAflaq and the Baʿth, virtually everyone else compromised the relation of their modernizing project to religiosity; no one plumbed the depths as energetically or as sincerely as ʿAflaq.

From the standpoint of overthrowing the post-Ottoman order, it seems unlikely any challenge to the moral underpinnings of Arab politics could have worked. After all, the despised new regimes were set up by the French and British on the principle of the relativity of the moral values of the various religious sects. (This may have had something to do with why they were never accepted as legitimate. The exception, Saudi Arabia, never fell apart.) By stepping outside of Islamic doctrine, yet basing himself on its most fundamental normative rationale, ʿAflaq was able to provide a new and yet traditionally rooted justification for pan-Arabism that none of these illegitimate regimes could hope to match, largely because they were genuinely secular.

CONFESSIONALISM

Pan-Arabism is rooted not only in Islam, but in the Sunni sect that embraces the overwhelming majority of Arabic-speaking Muslims. An ideology based on the primacy of the Arabs within Islam logically falls back on that majority. ʿAflaq placed his stress on Muhammad and the first twenty years of the Islamic movement, with everything else "from conquests to civilization" present as a "seedling" in those years.[55] From then on Islam was contaminated by problems caused by the very success

55. ʿAflaq, *Fi Sabil*, 44.

of its appeal to non-Arabs. Shiʿism, by contrast, idealized the person of ʿAli, his line of descent, and his four-year role and demonized the last "purely" Arab Umayyad Caliphate based in Syria. Within Islam, Shiʿism has been the main contender to Sunnism. But because the creed consolidated inside Iraq alongside the unseating of Arab hegemony in the caliphate, Iraqi Shiʿism faced some formidable obstacles within Arabdom.

Shiʿism began as a movement of support for the leadership of certain Arab candidates in the caliphate, in opposition to the hegemony of Syrian Arab tribes ruling from Damascus. The revolt against the Umayyads combined Khurasani tribes from the Iranian northeastern highlands; Iraqi Shiʿism (the movement supporting ʿAli's descendants who it was hoped would rule from Kufa in Iraq); and the underground Abbasid movement whose claim to rule also originated in the House of Hashim (Muhammad's broader tribal family). Upon overthrowing the Umayyads, the Abbasids did away with their allies and quickly won over the broad base of Islamic clerical wisdom. However, the destruction of Syrian Arab tribal power was achieved by erasing distinctions between the original Arab conquering tribes and the new Muslims who came from the conquered populations of the Fertile Crescent, transforming the hitherto Arab character of the caliphate. The second Abbasid caliph founded Baghdad as the seat of a new caliphal order.

The historic schism between Shiʿism and Sunnism in Iraq originates in the position that Muslims took in relation to this Abbasid succession. Iraqi Sunnism emerged out of the acceptance of the Abbasid legitimacy. Iraqi Shiʿism emerged out of what used to be the most sectarian and dogmatic position within early Shiʿism (one that rejected all authority that did not start from the divinity of ʿAli and his descendants). Both creeds, however, formed alongside the elevation of the status of Iraq within Islam, primarily at Syrian expense.

This history bound together Iraqi Sunnism and Shiʿism within a single fatality. Iraqi Arabism was saddled with the problem of a tainted history; its very emergence coincided with the unseating of Arab primacy within Islam. The unquestionable Arabness of later Iraq never erased the proximity to Persia and the important role of Sassanian culture at the time of the Islamic conquest. Yet Arabism in Iraq was seen to flourish in the form of the remarkable achievements of Abbasid civilization at exactly the point that Persians started to supplant Arabs in Islamic politics.

Because sectarian Shiʿism, originally an all-Arab affair, could not turn to an Arabism outside Iraq (to Syria), or accept the ascendant Ab-

basid rulers in counterposition to whom its own identity had been established, a grave political identity crisis within Iraqi Shi'ism was born.
The rise of Abbasid absolutism in Baghdad underlined this crisis of
Shi'ism as a uniquely Iraqi phenomenon, one whose very exacerbation
coincided with Iraqi preeminence in both Arab and Muslim affairs.
Iraqi Sunnism on the other hand, which rode the crest of that preeminence, had a natural referential framework around which its own identity could coalesce and which more or less coincided with that of its Syrian predecessor.

Shi'ism continued to repudiate those it had cast into office, replay-
ing the story of its origins. Doctrinally it lacks the "worldly" flexibility
of the classical Sunni tradition. Instead of the caliph of Sunni Islam,
Shi'ism adopted the hereditary institution of the imam, an infallible di-
vine whose ancestry is traced to 'Ali. The various sects in Shi'ism await
the messiahlike return of the last imam because it will give rise to a new
and just age. Along with the absence of any practical programme for
rule, Shi'ism has refined a number of religious concepts and behavioural
injunctions related to political guilt, nihilistic opposition, and rebellion
(for example, the Muharram pageantry, flagellation, and martyrdom).
The affinity that Arab Shi'ites feel towards Iranian Shi'ism (some holy
sites are in Iran), in contrast with the Sunni tradition for whom the enmity between Persian and Arab runs deep, further emphasizes the incompatibility between Shi'ism and pan-Arabism.

However, Iraqi Sunnism and Shi'ism do not find their raison d'être in
doctrinal differences. Both creeds always have been held together in a
political embrace rooted in distrust and originating in the question:
Who am I? To an Iraqi Shi'ite, pan-Arabism and Sunnism go hand in
hand, just as for the Arabic-speaking Christian, pan-Arabism and Islam
are inseparable. On the other hand, what counts for a Syrian 'Alawite,
whose sect is Shi'i in origin and who is sitting in the Latakia province
rubbing shoulders against Sunni Turks, is the connection of his Arabness to Islam in general and not Sunnism in particular.

The first experience of pan-Arabism in Iraq was a diversion. Iraq did
not pioneer pan-Arabism or make any nineteenth-century contribution
to its emergence. Husri's memoirs testify to the fact that Iraqis in the
1920s were "alien" to pan-Arabism. The most prominent pan-Arabist
in Iraq in this period was after all a Syrian. When Faisal was displaced
from Damascus in 1920, he was cut off from a historical opportunity of
the first order. Iraq was not only more backward than Syria, but also its
ethnic and religious composition was at odds with a pan-Arabist project. Although the diversity of communities was just as great in both

countries, the mix was different. With independence in 1932 Iraq was made up of: 21 percent Sunni Arabs; 14 percent Sunni Kurds; 53 percent Shiʿi Arabs; 5 percent non-Muslim Arabic-speaking minorities; 6 percent other linguistic groups. Around the mid 1940s, Syria was made up of: 57 percent Sunni Arabs; 8 percent Sunni Kurds; 2 percent Shiʿi and Ismaʿili Arabs; 12 percent ʿAlawi Arabs; 3 percent Druze; 9 percent non-Muslim Arabic-speaking minorities; 9 percent other linguistic and ethnic groups.[56] These distributions of course do not reveal the regional, occupational, or urban concentrations that can affect political influence. Nor do they suggest the effects of major disruptions like rural-urban migrations and the settlement of nomadic tribes (estimated at 35 percent of the population in 1867, but 5 percent in 1947).[57] The repercussions of such changes on rootlessness and the attractiveness of millenarian politics in particular are considerable. Nevertheless, the percentages do demonstrate the profound sociological ill-suitedness of Iraq by comparison with Syria to be a springboard for pan-Arabism.

Much of the violence in modern Iraqi politics is attributable to the structural incompatibility between political goals and the confessional distribution of Iraqi society. In 1932 one-fifth of its population at most could be construed as a social base for pan-Arabism. Arabism was in the end bound to be perceived as the hegemony of a minority of Sunnis over Kurds, Shiʿites, and non-Muslims on terms set by this minority and designed to secure for it a new eventual majority.

Faisal's tolerance and sensitivity to this dilemma places him in a different category altogether from every other pan-Arabist to appear on either the Iraqi or Syrian political scene. Faisal's policies and their failure (along with that of the 1936–41 period) can be traced back to Iraq's fundamentally inappropriate confessional balance for any pan-Arabist project, no matter how attenuated (as in Faisal's case), or strident (as in that of the late 1930s).

The early experience of pan-Arabism in Iraq (1936–41) confirmed the historical affinity between pan-Arabism and Sunnism. Prominent politicians and the officer corps as a whole were overwhelmingly Sunni.[58] Shiʿite leaders were present mainly in Faisal's cabinets, the Ahali group,

---

56. Figures rounded off from those given in Gabriel Baer, *Population and Society in the Middle East* (New York: Praeger, 1966), 105 and 109.

57. M. S. Hasan, "Growth and Structure of Iraq's Population, 1867–1947," in *The Economic History of the Middle East: 1800–1914*, ed. C. Issawi (Chicago: University of Chicago Press, 1966), 157.

58. Tarbush identifies only one Shiʿite and two Christians, out of a sample of sixty-one officers in the Iraqi army in 1936. See *The Role of the Military* (London: Kegan Paul, 1982), table 6, pp. 79–82.

and the ICP. Rashid ʿAli himself came from the Gailani family of *sadeh* (men of religion who trace their descent to Muhammad), by far Iraq's most prominent Sunni family. What better symbol of the subtle identification of pan-Arabism and Sunnism could anyone invent other than the triumvirate that actually materialized in the climactic April–May events of 1941: Rashid ʿAli the politician, Haj Amin al-Husayni the Mufti of Jerusalem (a position second to none in the pecking order of Sunnism), and the four army officers (each one a Sunni).

From this experiment with pan-Arabism, Baʿthist politics drew practical lessons concerning Faisal's failure, the role of the army, coup making, and the utility of an antiimperialism of the Assyrian affair variety. To cope with its problems, ʿAflaq theorized a general doctrine that gave a license to violence, which powerfully arose from the very morality of the Baʿthi appeal. The confessionalism of the Baʿth also arose from their pan-Arabism and made its impact on non-Muslim minorities in both Syria and Iraq and between Muslims in Iraq in particular. In the 1940s, the party was explicit about its confessionalism. In power, a broader Arab leadership collapsed into control by one sect and even sub-subgroups of a minority sect (the Takriti clan in Iraq, and the ʿAlawite officer caste in Syria). However, ʿAflaq's writings were on the whole restricted to the general relationship between pan-Arabism and Islam, and occasionally came down hard against confessionalism in the name of that broader moral absolutism common to all religious creeds which he demanded they submit to. Here ʿAflaq can be given the benefit of the doubt because he managed to show Arabs how a party that takes the religiosity of the masses as its starting point can both appeal against confessionalism and yet *be* indelibly stamped with the mark of confessional politics.

SHUʿUBIYYA

The confessionalism of the Baʿth crystallizes in their use of that untranslatable, uniquely Arab concept: *shuʿubiyya*. Many pan-Arabists in addition to Satiaʿ al-Husri made use of this unstudied word.[59] The idea is steeped in Arab-Islamic history, ethnic hate, and mystifying ambiguity. Its mention makes a pan-Arabist bristle with suspicion. As in the comparison between Shawkat and ʿAflaq on national identity, it is in the vocabulary of hate, not "love," that the confessionalism of the Baʿth is best expressed.

59. Even as unlikely a candidate as Constantin Zurayq takes the term for granted. See *Al-Waʿy al-Qawmi*, 130.

'Aflaq and Arsuzi both defined it as the manifestation of foreign influences within Arabism.[60] The Ba'th used it vigorously against the local communist parties in the 1940s. A 1945 statement issued by the Ba'th Bureau on May 1, entitled "The Communist Party, Bulwark of Shu'ubism and Mouthpiece of the Foreigner," conveys the intense emotionalism of the word:

> The Russian victories evoke deeply buried hatreds in these *shu'ubi* remnants as they come to defy Arab sensibilities in the city of Damascus [a reference to a festival organized by the Syrian Communist Party]. They celebrate the victories of foreigners in meetings that end up in demonstrations in which Armenian songs are chanted. . . .
>   . . . The CP was alone in daring to call openly for friendship with Imperialist peoples, to make sacrifices out of love for them, to serve them, and to canonize their heroes, principles and victories, all of this under the excuse of equality between nations. They create false distinctions between the Imperialist government and their people, whom the Communists consider innocent of all the crimes of Imperialism. In this way the Communists have done things which the most degenerate reactionaries and traitors, themselves creations of the foreigner, have not dared to do. They celebrate France's national day (the 14th of July) on the Arab land of Syria, whose soil has not yet dried from the blood which French criminal oppression has spilled.
>   The CP is the most modern means for grouping the ethnic and confessional minorities in a common front with European imperialism against Arab nationalism.[61]

However, Iraqi pan-Arabists, more than the Ba'th in general, were always enamoured with the term. 'Abd al-'Aziz al-Duri, president of Baghdad University and Iraq's most prestigious historian, wrote an ideological source book in 1962 called *The Historical Roots of Shu'ubism*. Though ostensibly an academic exercise restricted to events in early Arab-Islamic history, Duri explained in the introduction that he had become motivated to write because "there have arisen [today] voices that . . . attack Arab consciousness and the concept of the Arab nation by inciting a *fitnah* [insidious plot] in the name of racism or regionalism."[62] This motivation is based on the same Sunni universalism previously discussed. The vocabulary of hate is couched in a Sunni pan-Arab grammar of appeal that is genuinely meant to be directed against con-

---

60. See the article by Arsuzi, "The Shu'ubi Current Under the Cover of Communism," in *Mashakiluna*. For a more sophisticated version that maintains the distinction between communism and *shu'ubiyya*, see 'Aflaq's 1944 article, "Our Position on Communist Theory," in *Fi Sabil*, 72. Also see his talk on "The Battle for Unity in Iraq" (ibid., 249), in which he refers to the uses that communists make of shu'ubism.

61. *Nidhal*, 1:61–62.

62. 'Abd al-'Aziz al-Duri, *Al-Judhoor al-Ta'rikhiyya lil Shu'ubiyya* (Beirut: Dar al-Tali'ah, 1962), 7.

fessionalism. Clearly *al-shuʿubiyya* is of less utility in those parts of the
Arab world where the confessional mix does not threaten Sunni hegemony—hence, the uniquely Iraqi fascination with the concept, acknowledged by Duri.

Who were the *shuʿubiyyun?* Duri says they were a political "movement" made up of diverse ethnic groups, stretching from one end of the
Islamic world to the other, united principally on the basis of their hatred
for the Arabs.[63] This movement began in the realm of ideas and came in
an Islamic guise, "using" early Islam against the Arabs by appealing in
the name of the Qurʾanic injunction for equality among Muslims. Only
later did it reveal its inspiration from non-Arab and even deeply anti-
Islamic sources (almost always Persian). The parallel between "using"
the idea of equality between Muslims as a weapon against the Arabs
and then, thirteen centuries later, calling "for friendship with imperialist
peoples . . . under the excuse of equality between nations," is never lost
on a pan-Arabist. The problem, however, as Duri himself implicitly admitted, is that "the movement" started, or at least was strongly supported, by the Arabs themselves during the Umayyad period.[64]

The more extreme the pan-Arabist, the more "false" is the portrayal
of the shuʿubi's faith in Islam, the less Arabs have anything to do with
the origins of the phenomenon, and the further back in history does the
movement originate. Duri is a model of reasonableness compared with
the Iraqi Baʿthi writer ʿAbd al-Hadi al-Fukaiki, who saw the first unorganized seeds of shuʿubism in pre-Islamic history in the course of "the
struggle between Arabs and Persians" (Fadhil al-Barak, the reader may
recall, set a date: 539 B.C.; see Chapter 1, p. 18.) In the first Muslim state,
these seeds became "those serpents of shuʿubi hate who spread their
poison . . . while remaining secretly attached to the religions of their fathers." Zoroastrians ("Fireworshippers"), Mazdeans, and Manicheans
(all Persian pre-Islamic religions) are the forerunners of all forms of *zan-
daqah* (freethinking or so-called atheist currents in the classical Islamic
period). They chose Iraq as a base from which to organize "furtively"

63. Ibid., 9–13, 120–27. *The Encyclopaedia of Islam*, 1st ed. (Leiden: Brill, 1927),
395, defines the *shuʿubiyya* as a definite "sect which . . . in general, despised and depreci-
ated the Arabs." The activities of this sect are described as covering a territory ranging
from Spain to Iran. Suddenly, without explanation, the entry refers to an "attitude,"
which is "connected with the Shiʿa and other schisms." At no point is it made clear that
there is a rather fundamental difference between an "attitude" and a "sect." The important issue ignored by the *Encyclopaedia*, as by all pan-Arabist writers, concerns the layers
of meaning compacted into the political use of a word that seems to have evolved to stig-
matize the political unseating of Arabs within Islamdom.
    64. See Duri, *Al-Judhoor*, 14–15, 21.

the penetration of Syria and the rest of the region. Under the Umayyads the shuʿubis form "secret societies," and from then on a semiconcealed war is waged between Arabism and its nemesis shuʿubism. A fascinating aspect of Fukaiki's argument is the contention that the struggle "clarified the Arabist idea, deepened Arab consciousness, and allowed the notion of Arabism to crystallize."[65] Not until this century did shuʿubism reach its "pinnacle" of achievement—the Arab communist parties.

Pan-Arabists tend to agree that after the Islamic conquests Arabness could no longer be defined racially, or by reference to some "pure" ethnic stock. This, in light of Duri and Fukaiki's "history," opens up a field day of possibilities. Were the *shuʿubiyyun* of bygone times who spoke Arabic and espoused Islam Arabs or not? Were they false believers? How does one organize a definite "sect" or "movement" stretching across the Islamic world, made up of diverse groups, and united only on the basis of hatred for the Arabs? Ideologically, shuʿubism is best understood as an idea that had to be invented whenever Arabism or Arabness became a problem; it is the idea of the enemy from within, the insidious, ubiquitous agent of a hostile outside whose presence is needed to reassure believers of what it is they are supposed to have faith in. God always came paired up with the devil, and no religion ever found a way around this. Just as history's shuʿubi was not only a Persian, today's shuʿubis in Iraq can be communists, minorities, and Shiʿites. But shuʿubis are by definition not any one of them and can be none of them. In general, pan-Arabists need to leave the satanic principle as vague and nebulous as their own faith is certain and absolute. They rely instead on insinuation and innuendo.

A remarkable instance of this is ʿAflaq's article "Us and Our Enemies," which extols the virtues of "Us" alongside an outpouring of vitriolic hate directed at "Our" enemies, all of which is couched in an uncharacteristically personalized language of abuse.[66] Neither antipode is ever once specified, as though ʿAflaq had decided to let his emotions rip, but on condition that impersonality remained vested in the anonymity of the pronouns he used. One is left with the eerie feeling that the intensity of the language was pitted against the vagueness of the objects described, as a deliberate incitement to the passions ʿAflaq wanted to bring

---

65. ʿAbd al-Hadi al-Fukaiki, *Al-Shuʿubiyya Wa al-Qawmiyya al-ʿArabiyya* (Beirut: Dar al-Adab, 1961), 37, 39, 42. After testing out several definitions of *shuʿubiyya*, Fukaiki settles on: "*Shuʿubiyya* is a word applied to every foreigner who hates Arabs, denies their glories, and prefers others over them out of hatred and jealousy" (p. 36).

66. ʿAflaq, *Fi Sabil* (article deleted in 1974 edition).

to bear on politics. Similar methods were constantly being used by the Iraqi media under the second Baʿthi regime.

Being through Organization

> In the conditions of the Arab nation today we need a party and a move-
> ment that represents in the first place the element of spirit. . . . The true
> party, the living party, the one that can perform its message for the Arab na-
> tion today, is the party that makes its goal the birth of a nation, or its renais-
> sance, on condition that this description is first realized in itself. In other
> words, the party must be a smaller version of the pure healthy and elevated
> nation that it wishes to resurrect.[67]

Originating in a reawakened Arab spirit, conducted through a "new generation," the nation-in-formation was going to get pounded into shape in that great crucible of twentieth-century politics: the party organization. Moreover, the united nation that *ought to be* is today constituted only in the corporal materiality of the party. The Baʿth realized that in order for violence to be effective, it had to have social organization. This is the fundamental intuitive idea of Baʿthism carried to its terribly coherent conclusion. Organization in the service of ideology, not ideology alone, was the only viable way to create the new citizen. A chasm separates the organization of the party from the society around it. From deep within its own resources, taken in calculated isolation from the rest of society, the party must become "the nation of revolution before it achieves the revolution of the nation."[68]

The unifying idea in this conception of the party is that of the degeneracy of the surrounding environment. In discussing the Baʿthist theory of organization, ʿAflaq contrasted the morality that needed to be inculcated in party members with the pitfalls that existed in the "sick" world outside. ʿAflaq argued that the party related to society in revolutionary times by building "bases, points of leverage and fortresses inside the reality that is filled with corruption, deficiencies, backwardness, ignorance and lack of firmness." He called these fortresses, to stress the need for them to be "very strong, to ward off corruption and external enemies."[69] In other words, Baʿthist islands of moral probity struggle ceaselessly to save people from the miserable creatures they have become.

67. Ibid., 92.
68. Ibid., 94.
69. Ibid., 119.

The state from a Baʿthist point of view is purely instrumental—"a body with no spirit."[70] Moreover, "speed is of the essence in a revolutionist movement."[71] Hence, there is no necessary connection between the size of the party and the goal of revolutionism, as in the Marxist conception of revolution. In 1955 ʿAflaq wrote that it was characteristic of the revolutionary stage in the nation's life that leadership remained in the hands of an enlightened minority, who "represents the people before the people expressly delegate them to undertake this representation."[72] Even in the early 1940s, before the party existed, ʿAflaq had said the nation was reducible to one man: the Leader.

In all of ʿAflaq's articles on the party, organized activism is placed at the foundations of individual and national identity. The unknowability of the pan-Arabist "mission" was thus ingeniously concretized.

> How do we unify the individuals of this nation who have been separated by selfishness, personal interests, and capitulation to illusions, despicable and violent differences, repulsion from one another and the cheap materialist life? How do we once again achieve the united nation . . . if not through fiery struggle across a difficult road in which every individual is forced to return to himself, to sink into his depths, to discover himself anew after experience and pain. At that point the true unity will be realized, and this is a new kind of unity different from political unity; it creates the unity of the spirit among the individuals of the nation.[73]

No matter how elusive the ideal of unity may have been in practise, or when viewed contemplatively, suddenly in the crucible of party organization it became real and deadly serious. The party member is "enchained and forced to be free to labour" for Arabism's goals, as he put it in another context.[74] A thwarted sense of individual identity was going to be reconstituted inside the political organization. The utility of ʿAflaq's distinction between "individuals" and "human beings" is now apparent. The party operates on individuals, not a deified notion of humanity. Only the resources of a party could extract from the "depths" of individuals the vitalism of their hitherto lost souls, thus transforming them into a life force for itself.

Once the party, and not Arab society at large, has become the locus

---

70. Ibid., 92.
71. Ibid., 129.
72. Ibid., 116–17.
73. Ibid., 102–3.
74. Ibid., 154. The formula may be taken from J. J. Rousseau in *The Social Contract*. Another point of contact between ʿAflaq and Rousseau's thought is the latter's notion of civilization (modernity) as a fall from grace into degeneracy.

of the nation-in-formation, then the holy grail of Arab unity loses some of its urgency. Facts on the ground are no longer a constraint. For Arab unity already exists in the form of the actuality of the party, and all that needs to be done is to extend it through one real society, and then through others. Irrationality has metamorphosed into the self-fulfilling rationality of quantitative party growth, which achieves for society something it cannot definitionally achieve by itself.

The action of believing, of having faith, is accompanied by the decision to forget the decision to believe. Party organization carries this logic a crucial stage further by resolving belief into habit and custom. The loss of the critical faculty, not simply a by-product of belief but an essential *condition* for beliefs to be taken seriously, henceforth becomes routine, first in the party organization, and then in society as a whole (to the extent that it gets to be organized on the same basis). Routinization in turn does away with the need to have fervour in one's faith, to believe actively that the party and Arab unity are one and the same thing. The outcome is a populace that is both gullible and cynical.

An illusory, hall-of-mirrors-like relation between fiction and reality is therefore inherent in the uniquely Baʿthist idea of "being-through-organization." This evershifting chameleonlike quality stays with the party in almost everything it says or does, in power or out. It is probably the most important and consistent characteristic of the movement's defences against an outside world that fills it with hate. If Baʿthism had to face up to an overpowering reality that was not of its own making—say, ruthless repression in opposition or a total rout in the Iraq-Iran war—then and only then would the party be in danger of internal decomposition (as opposed to infighting, which goes on all the time). In almost every other less dire situation, even the most unpalatable truths can be digested in fictionalized form.

THE LEADER PRINCIPLE AND PARTY
ORGANIZATION

The view that "the Baʿth of ʿAflaq and Bitar always favored some form of collective leadership" is false;[75] but it has an origin worth exploring. The 1974 edition of *Fi Sabil al-Baʿth* differs from the 1959 edition in that articles, pages, paragraphs, sentences, and phrases have

75. Salem-Babikian, "Michel ʿAflaq," 170. Abu Jaber and Majid Khadduri maintain the same view.

been systematically deleted or modified. The publisher's introduction hints at part of the truth in a reference to outdated texts and "inaccurate expressions such as using the term Marxism or Communism when what was meant was the Stalinist application or the local communist movement." [76] In fact, the changes relate primarily to the desire of the Ba'th to rewrite their history as it relates to communism generally and the Arab communist parties. But a secondary purpose of this exercise in self-censorship was the desire to obliterate 'Aflaq's early interest in European fascist ideas concerning leadership:

> The people everywhere are unable to understand any idea truly and quickly. That is why they look to living individuals in whom the idea is vested. It is to these individuals, and only to the extent of their moral worth and enthusiasm, that one looks to measure the value of an espoused idea.
> So if a group of educated, active and moral youth were to unite powerfully, according to a fierce discipline, and in accordance with a hierarchy of grades, this in itself is enough to guarantee their influence over the people. The holiness that these people endow upon their leader is in reality a sanctification of the idea which they wish to support and spread. To the extent that the personalities of these followers are strong and have moral value, the idea's chances of success will be that much greater. [77]

Alongside such formulations, consider the 1947 internal rules of the party creating a five-tiered structure culminating in the 'Amid, or Doyen of the party, who was of course 'Aflaq. The 'Amid had the power of appointment for all leadership positions, and was the marji' or highest authority on all policy questions. The functional hierarchy of organization (by area or workplace) was overlaid with a complicated and most revealing typology of members. Of the "natural" members, the 'Amid was certainly one; then there were "elected" members, "principal" members, and ordinary members who could only be upgraded upon the approval of the 'Amid. [78] These rules are never cited by authors who choose to "prove" the Ba'th's liberalism or its socialism on the basis of generalities in the 1947 party constitution.

Such writers focus instead on the 1954 internal rules of the party, a modified version of which still remains in effect. The organization was to be based now on small and vertically integrated cells of three to seven people (smaller than the average communist party cell). In Iraq, seven tiers replaced the previous five and all horizontal communication was

76. 'Aflaq, Fi Sabil, 3 (1974 edition).
77. From a deleted 1941 article in 1959 edition; ibid., 36.
78. This account of the 1947 internal rules is from Batatu, Social Classes, 744–45.

forbidden. Democratic centralism was established as the fundamental principle of organization, and the ᶜAmid was henceforth the secretary-general, with greatly diminished powers. ᶜAflaq as secretary-general had no powers of appointment, and his voice in the National Command, the highest decision-making authority, was one among several.

The establishment of the elective principle coincided with an even more complicated typology of members. In the place of "natural" and "principal" distinctions came the "active" member who was the well-sifted outcome of five other membership grades: organized supporter, second-grade partisan, first-grade partisan, candidate, and member-trainee. Active members could elect leaders and rise to responsible positions in the apparatus, whereas candidates and member-trainees could only vote on party policy; the rest had no party rights at all. Two of these grades were later innovations of the Iraqi Baᶜth, designed to control the flow of new members into the party in the early 1960s. The Iraqi branch emphasized organizational and security matters (the ICP, in comparison with other Arab communist parties, also distinguished itself in this area). By February 1963, there were 830 "active" members in Iraq and 15,000 people in the lesser grades; towards the end of the year the latter had tripled while the number of "active" members remained the same.[79] Full members constituted a mere 2 percent of the organization.

Would maintaining the 1947 rules have achieved more equitable results? Clarity sometimes has that effect. Clearly the language of Baᶜthism was changing in 1954, as symbolized also by the adoption of its new name, the Arab Baᶜth Socialist Party. But why were the rules changed? Many writers agree that the 1954 rules were inspired by the practice of the communist parties, then growing in influence in both Iraq and Syria. Communist prestige certainly accounts for the changes in terms, and for a new conception of the organization, however buried under levels of hierarchy and types of members. The Baᶜth, to give them the benefit of the doubt, were now genuinely concerned with providing a more "popular" justification for party policy. The will of the party had *to be seen* to be vested in all its members, equally considered. The idea of a "natural" member, or a Doyen, was not in the same spirit. However much of an ordeal it was to become a member does not alter the fact that a principle of legitimacy had changed. But the change in rules also meant that

---

79. Ibid., 1010. Abu Jaber puts the membership of the Iraqi Baᶜth in 1963 at 2,000 to 2,500, and all other categories "numbered well over 30,000"; see *The Arab Baᶜth*, 140, 144.

ᶜAflaq was being undermined and his status diminished. Some internal impulse must have opened the floodgates for a reconsideration of the party's rules. What was it?

In 1949 ᶜAflaq was imprisoned by Husni al-Zaᶜim, the leader of Syria's first coup. By some accounts he was tortured, by others merely threatened, and by yet others he was neither harmed nor threatened. At any rate, following his release an authentic letter bearing his signature was published. It addressed Syria's leader in obsequious language, asked for clemency, and announced ᶜAflaq's intention to retire from politics because "I believe that my mission has come to an end and that my method is not appropriate to the new era."[80] Baᶜthi followers were thunderstruck, and the party suffered a setback. ᶜAflaq has since maintained total silence on the affair. But clearly he had broken his own rules. By revealing himself as a fallible human being—not the Baᶜthist individual born in steel and fire that he extolled—he did something his kind of a leader can never get away with. His own tough standards consumed him.

In the 1950s ᶜAflaq's influence among Baᶜthists sharply declined in Syria, and the Baᶜth became a sorting house for new ideas, almost always drawn from the communist tradition. But in Iraq, ᶜAflaq's influence remained dominant: Orthodox Baᶜthism and ᶜAflaq were inseparable. Saddam Husain was formed on ᶜAflaq's writings, and his elevation to the Iraqi leadership, it is said, came through ᶜAflaq's intervention in the party struggles that followed the failure of the first Baᶜthi regime in 1963.

Imagine then this aging Doyen of the party who had lost his organizational grip and was on the verge of being forever purged from his Syrian home-base by a new breed of officer Baᶜthists. He was the complete opposite of his protege: physically slight, romantic, a prodigious tract-writer, organizationally inept, a philosophizer, and most important of all vulnerable in the exposure of his all too human fear of imprisonment and bodily harm. By contrast the young Saddam had made his mark inside the party as a tough and fearless assassin. He had all the qualities that ᶜAflaq needed to personify, but couldn't—ruthlessness, iron discipline, cunning, resolution, loyalty under fire, and physical stamina. Saddam Husain thus succeeded by the very same rules that Michel ᶜAflaq irrevocably broke, which only shows that however important a principle of legitimacy is, in the end it is not the most important thing.

80. Quoted in Batatu, *Social Classes*, 727.

Baʿthism and Communism

Baʿthi feelings towards the Arab communist parties are not in doubt. I stress the word "feelings" as opposed to say "political positions" because only in the emotional domain does total clarity exist in the first period of Baʿthism. The 1945 statement, for example, contains not a word on programmatic differences with the Syrian Communist Party. Certainly the communist parties did not support pan-Arabism. On the other hand, many other political currents were not pan-Arabist, and the communist parties were not all that vociferous or even explicit about their opposition to unity. In the 1960s many communists reversed their formal positions on Arab unity. It would of course be impossible to imagine a set of circumstances in which the Baʿth could do likewise, pan-Arabism being the fundamental defining principle of Baʿthism. Right from the start, therefore, the Baʿth were the nemesis of Arab communism. But what was it about the latter that so incensed them ideologically?

ʿAflaq left no one in any doubt: "Communism is Western, and alien to everything Arab," he said repeatedly in various ways. Marx may have "breathed into it some of his spiteful Jewish spirit," but the outcome was nevertheless that communism was the culmination of the "humanistic" impulse in European civilization, which first appeared during the Renaissance in the sixteenth century. This renewal of Greco-Roman civilization, ʿAflaq said, was integrated with the "abstract rationalism" of the eighteenth century and the technological advance of the nineteenth century to produce communism. "The European, whatever his nation, sect, social or political position, never feels as repulsed by communism as does the Arab," because all of these civilizational transformations "have absolutely no connection to Arab history, intellectual traditions, and way of life in either the present or the past."[81] Communism is inherently related "to everything that has entered Arab history from the outside and distorted Arab thought," including "the shuʿubi movements which appeared in the Abbasid period advocating equality in women and wealth, anarchy, sabotage, dissolution of family ties and religious teachings, and the debasement of Arab history, its heroes, and the qualities of the nation that gave rise to them."[82]

Despite this animosity, however, ʿAflaq never underestimated communist potential.[83] Communist theory would be opposed by practises

81. ʿAflaq, Fi Sabil, 71–72.
82. Ibid., 72.
83. See, for instance, what he wrote in Fi Sabil, 252, 71.

inspired by the Arab communist parties themselves. These had formed a decade or so before the Ba'th, and were the first modern parties in the post-Ottoman era oriented towards the downtrodden layers of the population. They were established on the principle of impersonal recruitment to a rounded program and a new style of politics. 'Aflaq's admiration for communist organization, in particular, was a long-standing conviction dating back to his stay in Paris. Whatever his intellectual indebtedness to fascism might have been in his early period, his knowledge of communist writings on organization and the concrete experiences of the Syrian Communist Party in the 1930s had convinced him of the efficacy of their methods.

Ba'thism and communism became the two antipodes of mass politics in Iraq after the overthrow of the monarchy in July 1958. The growth of the former took place at the expense of the latter in all realms. Between 1941 and 1958, the influence of the ICP grew considerably, reaching a peak in 1959 when it numbered around 25,000 active members and at least half a million organized supporters. By contrast, the Iraqi branch of the ABSP, which numbered barely 300 people in 1956, grew by its own accounting in the first year of the new republic to 1,200 "organized partisans," 2,000 "organized supporters," and 10,000 "unorganized supporters."[84] A comparable count for the ICP would probably exceed 1 million. In short the ICP had total command of the crowd in the streets, a new feature of the Iraqi political landscape after 1958. In that crucial first year, the ICP also controlled the Popular Resistance Force (a civilian militia), and virtually all the important unions and student and youth organizations. All this power was triumphantly displayed in the historic May 1, 1959, demonstration led by members of the party's central committee, most of whom were dead by 1968.

Ba'thi numbers held stable following their initial spurt of growth after 1958. They may even have declined in the first half of 'Abd al-Karim Qassem's regime (1958–63). The first sign that the party was becoming a force of some note on the street came with the Baghdad taxi drivers' demonstrations of March 1961, which were led by Ba'thi agitators. From 1961 to the fall of Qassem in 1963, the ABSP grew rapidly, gaining control of some unions and other mass organizations, leading strikes of even an economic nature, and generally capitalizing on the growing disenchantment with the Qassem regime. By contrast the ICP fumbled

84. Figures are from Hanna Batatu, "Some Reflections on the Decline of the Arab Left and of Iraq's Communists," *CCAS Reports*, Georgetown University, Washington, D.C. (1983): 2; and *Social Classes*, 816.

and stumbled once Qassem began taking the first of a series of measures against it in 1960. On the eve of the 1963 coup, the ABSP dominated whole quarters of Baghdad, and those towns of the central region that were favourably disposed to pan-Arabism because of their Sunni Arab composition. However, by February 1963 there were still only 830 "active" members and some 15,000 "organized supporters." Throughout, the Baᶜth never commanded in opposition the levels of support of the ICP during its heyday.

Nonetheless, the fact remains that a phenomenal turnaround in mass allegiances did take place in Iraq. If the May 1, 1959, demonstration is an apt symbol of the ICP's power at the beginning of the decade, by its end the appropriate counterpart was the first spectacle of January 1969, when Baᶜthi command of the streets was almost as total as the ICP's had been in 1959. The problem now becomes one of understanding how pan-Arabism made its comeback in the form of a stable and durable second Baᶜthi regime.

CHAPTER 7

The Legitimation
of Iraqi Baᶜthism

A Confession

> When I proclaimed for the first time [in 1969] the gross political and intellectual errors of the Iraqi Communist Party (ICP) Central Command [a faction of the ICP], many attacked and abused me. Others thought me driven to say things without true conviction. The matter, however, was no more than my coming to terms with errors through experience, debate, evaluation and long reflection. I believe that the profound progressive developments in Iraq since that date . . . and the developments in the Arab and international arena, have vindicated much of what I said then. Even my enemies in the Central Committee [the other faction of the ICP] have themselves been forced to recognize the exemplary revolutionary role of the ABSP in Iraq, and the enormous accomplishments it has brought to the masses. They entered a progressive front with the ABSP whose obligations they regretfully did not live up to.[1]

ᶜAziz al-Haj wrote his memoirs in 1979 in Paris, where he worked as the official Iraqi representative for UNESCO. In the passage he is reflecting on his public confession in 1969, which led to the deaths of scores of his former colleagues at the hands of the Baᶜth.

Until 1969 al-Haj's name was a synonym for the far left of Iraqi communism. He was born in 1926 to a poverty-stricken Shiᶜi Kurdish family. In the early 1940s, he joined the ICP, became a full-time militant, and rapidly acquired national fame as a Marxist intellectual, gifted publicist, and editor of the party organ, *Al-Qaᶜida*. He was arrested in 1948

---

1. ᶜAziz al-Haj, *Maᶜa al-ᶜAwam* (Beirut: al-Muassasah al-ᶜArabiyya, 1981), 28.

and spent the next ten years in prison. His statement to the investigating magistrate at the time proudly proclaimed his party affiliation, and boldly denounced the police for their brutality which he said would never deter the Iraqi people from the cause of communism.[2]

After 1958, al-Haj became a member of the central committee, and five years later he was organizing resistance to the first Baᶜthi regime from exile. Following his return, he became the focus of growing disaffection with the ICP leadership. The discontent came to a head in the wake of the 1967 war. In a vain attempt to forestall a split, al-Haj organized the "arrest" of all the other members of the central committee. By September 1967 two organizations emerged out of the ICP: ᶜAziz al-Haj's Central Command and the pro-Soviet Central Committee. Both naturally claimed to be the authentic heirs of the militant traditions of the ICP.

The Central Command called for "arming of the masses" and a "popular armed struggle in the towns and countryside." They wanted "a revolutionary popular democratic regime under the leadership of the working class." The Central Committee, on the other hand, denounced the "splitters" and their strategy of a "peoples' war." It called for "coalition governments" based on "united democratic fronts" of the revolutionary forces to combat imperialism, Zionism, and Arab reaction.[3]

After the 1968 coup, the Baᶜth offered both factions places in the new cabinet. The Central Command turned the offer down. An underground war of sorts broke out with the Baᶜth party organization over the following months. The bodies of communist militants started cropping up in dark alleyways and floating down the Tigris.[4] The Baᶜth denied responsibility for the killings. In fact they adroitly turned the ICP's accusations around, claiming they were part of a concerted effort to undermine their efforts to establish a national front of the progressive forces. The Central Command retaliated with "expropriations," "revolutionary holdups," and car bombings and even managed to strafe Saddam Husain's house.

The escalation of violence culminated in the capture of ᶜAziz al-Haj along with the whole politbureau and untold numbers of rank and filers, all of whom met a gruesome fate at the hands of Nadhim Kzar's

2. Mentioned in the biographical article by Abbas Kelidar, "ᶜAziz al-Haj: A Communist Radical," in *The Integration of Modern Iraq*, ed. A. Kelidar (London: Croom Helm, 1979).

3. See Hanna Batatu, *The Old Social Classes and the Revolutionary Movements of Iraq* (Princeton: Princeton University Press, 1978), 1070–72.

4. Ibid., 1098–99.

security forces. Two members of the five-man politbureau held out and died under torture. The rest broke down, and were brought on television to recant their sins against "the revolution." It is said of al-Haj that upon his arrest he exclaimed: "I can no longer bear torture, I will cooperate." On television he likened his career to "a bull charging a concrete wall."[5]

To see in the end of ʿAziz al-Haj nothing other than cowardice, betrayal, or, far worse, the unveiling of a deep-seated "revisionism" in his character is churlish and lacking in imagination.[6] The background of the man, to say nothing of the position he occupied in radical Iraqi politics, should alert us to deeper issues involved. Al-Haj's career spanned a quarter of a century during which the fortunes of Iraqi communism flourished (the 1940s), foundered but stood firm in the wake of sustained repression (1948–58), and finally got tested after 1958 and was found to be sorely wanting. This was a man whose youth was a bitter struggle won against odds unjustly imposed by his birthright; then came years of imprisonment in the prime of life followed by intense activism in a fluid situation as leader of a party that stood on the threshold of power, missed the boat, and saw its whole edifice of party-building come tumbling down not once but twice (1963 and 1968). The psychological breakdown of such a man—and for that matter the rest of his politbureau colleagues, all of whom were cast in a similar mold—cannot be separated from what they thought and stood for in the society they had consecrated their lives to changing. ʿAziz al-Haj's life, and his end, is a too perfect distillation of the spirit of his times for that. Here is a conversion to Baʿthism that has the ring of weariness *and* authenticity about it. Maybe al-Haj was able to see the writing on the wall long before most Iraqis because he had something to do with writing it.

The National Action Charter

While the Central Command was being hunted down, the Central Committee observed what amounted to a truce with the ABSP. As the regime's relations with the USSR and Eastern bloc countries improved, they began responding to Baʿthist overtures. On July 10, 1970, the ABSP announced a series of conditions, acceptance of which would en-

---

5. Kelidar, *Integration*, 186.
6. Efforts like this were made by Najm Mahmood in *Al-Siraʿ fi al-Hizb al-Shuyuʿi al-ʿIraqi wa Qadhaya al-Khilaf fi al-Haraka al-Shuyuʿiyya al-ʿAlamiyya* (Paris, 1980), 99–101.

title the Central Committee to join a "Progressive National Front." Among these conditions were: recognition of the ABSP "as a revolutionary, unionist, socialist and democratic party"; a statement on the historically progressive nature of the July 17, 1968, "revolution"; recognition of "the commanding role of the ABSP in the government, the mass organizations and the front"; the restriction of political activity inside the armed forces solely to the ABSP; an ICP commitment to persuade its "international extensions" to ally themselves with the Baʿth in other Arab countries; an "absolute rejection of the Zionist state," and the adoption of the idea of popular armed struggle against imperialism and for the liberation of Palestine; adherence to Arab unity "as the foremost and fundamental aim uniting all aims"; and reaffirmation of the necessity for a fundamental "socialist transformation" in Iraq.

The Central Committee regretted that the Baʿth insisted upon the idea of a "leader" party but affirmed that they had already defined the regime that came out of the "revolution" of 1968 as "patriotic." On Arab unity they had no differences. They resolutely objected to the Baʿthist formula on "socialist transformation" as "unscientific" because the country had not yet completed its "national-democratic revolution," and the Central Committee did not believe in "the burning of stages."[7]

In 1970, the regime made sweeping arrests of communists; then the death under torture of Central Committee member ʿAli al-Barzanchi and other local leaders followed. Negotiations stumbled. In April 1972, however, a fifteen year Iraqi-Soviet friendship treaty was announced. The event was greeted by the Central Committee as the realization of "one of the great aims" of the revolution, and within the month two Central Committee members entered government for the first time. In July 1973 the National Action Charter was signed by President Bakr in his capacity as secretary-general of the ABSP, and ʿAziz Muhammad in his capacity as first secretary of the ICP Central Committee. All the conditions set down in the July 1970 invitation of the ABSP were accepted by the ICP, now part of a "Progressive National Front" government that took its instructions from the all-Baʿthi RCC. For a while, the Baʿthist idea of freedom of political association took this hybrid form:

> It is our opinion that all Iraqis . . . should not feel that there is a contradiction in their belonging to other political parties and at the same time regarding the ABSP as their own party. This is because the ABSP is leading

7. From extracts in Batatu, *Social Classes*, 1103–5.

society and the Revolution and because it has proved to them that it is quali-
fied to be their own party.[8]

With the establishment of the National Front and the support of the
Central Committee, the regime launched its 1974 war against the Kurds.
Kurdish defeat in 1975 paved the way for the next ineluctable step. In
1976 Saddam Husain delivered this intriguing speech to an enlarged
meeting of the National Front, addressing his by-now thoroughly compromised partners:

> According to our information some brothers, especially from the Com-
> munist Party, still feel embarrassed when asked: "Are you with the regime or
> not? Are you with the Revolution or not?" Is it embarrassing for one to side
> with the great Revolution and its regime? The Revolution is cherished by
> every honest patriot and its major achievements are obvious to all. If there is
> to be any speculation about whether one is for or against the Revolution, it
> should be made in the context of goals [something the ICP had forfeited by
> signing the Charter], not that of details which should be criticized in a demo-
> cratic and objective manner.
>
> We should all criticize flawed details, but errors in details should not
> bring us into a psychological opposition to the Revolution and its regime. At
> the same time, however, the errors of the administrative apparatus should be
> neither a means nor a justification for pursuing party interests. . . .
>
> Supposing we Baʿthists reversed the case and started attacking the Com-
> munists in our speeches and through our media [as they were just about to
> do]. . . . [The ICP] would regard these as improper uses of the administrative
> apparatus and would try to put these tactics to their own advantage. What
> do you imagine would happen? Is such a state of affairs acceptable? If it is
> you can imagine how much you [the ICP] would lose. . . . We say this not
> out of vanity, but rather out of the conviction that our relationship with the
> masses is based on positive cooperation and mutual trust. That is why they
> would listen to our words.[9]

In effect, Husain has told the communists seated before him precisely
how the axe was going to fall in the coming months. This took the form
of admonishing them for an allegedly hostile psychological stance towards the Front. His argument was designed to exploit fears and doubts
that obviously existed in order to infer onto his victims precisely the actions he had already resolved to undertake himself. Accusations against
individual communists began late in 1976. The charge was political activism inside the armed forces, a clear breach of the conditions of the

---

8. Speech by Saddam Husain given on February 25, 1976, quoted in P. Mansfield's article in *Iraq: The Contemporary State*, ed. T. Niblock (London: Croom Helm, 1982), 68.

9. Saddam Husain, *One Common Trench? Or Two Opposite Ones?* (Baghdad: ABSP
pamphlet, 1977), 18–21.

Charter. Arrests and executions followed and by 1979 what was left of the ICP Central Committee was in prison or exile.

The Baʿthist triumph in securing the ICP's signature on the National Action Charter signified that the "revolution" the ICP had been struggling to realize since 1932 was in fact being led by an upstart. The July 17, 1968, "revolution" was recognized to be the legitimate continuation of the July 14, 1958, overthrow of the monarchy, the final "corrective" to the "errors and deviations" that had befallen that experience. This viewpoint was now concretely endorsed by all the prime actors in Iraqi mass politics. Nor was this some fleeting mistake of the ICP. The Charter, the culmination of years of hesitation and dialogue, obviously represented a watershed in the history and fortunes of the ICP no matter how communist leaders try to portray its significance today.[10]

How could they have been so naive? The very question begs the issue. After all they took five years to cross the Rubicon and sign that Charter. Nor were the leading personalities of the Central Committee cut from a different cloth than their Central Command counterparts. ʿAziz Muhammad was a Sunni Kurd and apprentice tinworker who had joined the party when he was fifteen years old. He too spent the decade 1948–58 in prison. These were experienced political men with a lifetime of political infighting and intrigue behind them. Their closest colleagues had been mercilessly cut down by Baʿthist goon squads in 1963. If that experience had grown dim, what about leading ICP members like Muhammad al-Khadri, Kadhim al-Jasim, ʿAziz Hamid, Thabit Habib, and ʿAli al-Barzanchi, all of whom died under torture between 1970 and 1971? To the leaders of the ICP, a seemingly inexorable political logic had set in, one that went beyond their own ideological blindness. It sucked the Central Committee like the Central Command before it into a course of action that men like this must have known was political suicide. Signing that document was endorsing a death warrant for the

10. From exile, ʿAziz Muhammad was asked whether in retrospect he still thought it had been correct to enter the National Front. After reaffirming the general principle of forming alliances with "national forces" in order to "advance the struggle against imperialism," he said: "We never said the National Front was final and that we would not face setbacks. We were under no illusions; we could see the Front was reversible. It is too easy to pass judgement on these matters if you are sitting abroad." The particular reason for the breakdown in relations was "the fact that the Baʿth engaged in a wholesale retreat from the positions we had agreed on." See MERIP Reports 97 (June 1981): 20–21. Taken at face value, his reply confirms that the Charter was so important to the ICP that notwithstanding their reservations about Baʿthi intentions, they felt compelled to take the plunge. If, on the other hand, they did have illusions, then the ICP leadership will have plumbed new depths of stupidity.

party, not only in the physical sense as events proved, but in the long-term political sense. Nonetheless, these men made their choice because in their eyes it had become necessary. In so doing their action not only confirmed the leadership of the ABSP, but also it conferred a seal of approval upon it.

Unlike its opponents, the ABSP always reached for the truly permanent questions of politics. Upon taking power in 1968, the ABSP knew it had "to build a genuine progressive front, not a mere formality." The party could not secure "respect" for its ideas, "nor win acceptance of them from the people . . . until it had morally and materially confirmed its leadership of the country's political life." [11] A strategic front provided that moral confirmation. It was also an interim step towards abolishing competing parties in the political arena. At bottom, all such "strategic" fronts dissolve the boundaries of parties in favour of a "Leader." And there can be no politics if there are no boundaries, as the Baʿth clearly understood. In the name of freedom, they only did to the Central Committee what violence had already done to the Central Command.

The End of Politics

ʿAziz al-Haj's confession and the National Action Charter are symbols for the general process of legitimation in the first years of the new regime. There was no shortage of recantations from various personalities in public life, most of whom confessed to being imperialist or Zionist spies, members of secret societies, agents or "economic saboteurs." A distinction exists, however, between cycles of terror related to an organization like the ICP, and those based on fabricated scenarios. The former conferred a "right" to be in power made by a real competitor in the political arena. ʿAziz al-Haj was the leader of a political organization engaged in armed struggle with the regime at the point of his capture. By contrast, a fabricated confession, for instance of the victims of the January 1969 hangings, took this right for granted and was designed to adduce "proof" of the organic relationship between Baʿthism and "its" masses.

All these legitimizing measures were prerequisites for the regime of terror that followed. From now on, political discourse was going to take place outside the confines of what was permissible, and this by general

11. *The 1968 Revolution in Iraq: Experience and Prospects* (London: Ithaca Press, 1979), 67–68. Henceforth ABSP, *Political Report.*

consent of the parties that had suffered the most. At this juncture politics as such came to an end. But instead of a vacuum, institutional violence took over—violence that could only reign supreme *after* all politics had ended.[12] The resettlement of Kurds, for instance, took place after their overwhelming defeat; and the deportations of two hundred thousand Shiᶜites to Iran had nothing to do with any real threat to the regime. The explosion in the size of the repressive apparatus and the ascendancy of a police state over the army also followed the end of politics, which can be dated roughly around 1975.

The peculiar feature of the second Baᶜthi regime, therefore, is that it developed ummistakable signs of a real social base (as measured by party growth, public support for Saddam Husain, more armed men, and statification) after all politics had ended and in an atmosphere of rampant violence no longer directed at real enemies, but at everyone.

From Classes to Masses: 1958–68

Baᶜthism's victory over the ICP was merely consummated by the National Action Charter and confessions like that of ᶜAziz al-Haj. Its roots lie further back in time. Moreover, the self-immolation of the ICP suggests that the idea behind a multiparty system was already thoroughly discredited by 1968. This was one outcome of the epic confrontation between Baᶜthism and Iraqi communism fought out after the fall of the Hashemite monarchy on July 14, 1958.[13]

The Baᶜth rightly see the principal progenitor of their 1968 regime in the events of 1958. And the decade 1958–68 is important because of the circumstances in which the party eventually took power. Unlike 1958, the 1968 coup faced an apathetic and partly demoralized atmosphere from which only the organized parties were immune. Not greeted with mass acclaim, the new regime had to orchestrate remedies for this lack of spontaneity. The absence of support, however, had no bearing

---

12. Hannah Arendt noted this necessary precondition in her analysis of totalitarianism. See *The Origins of Totalitarianism* (New York: Harcourt Brace and Jovanovich, 1973), 421–22. See also her essay "On Violence," in *Crises of the Republic* (New York: Harcourt Brace and Jovanovich, 1972), 153–55.

13. The idea for the section "From Classes to Masses" is indebted to Arendt's argument in chap. 10 of *The Origins*, 305–26. Along with Batatu, Uriel Dann's study of the Qassem years, *Iraq Under Qassem: A Political History, 1958–1963* (New York: Praeger, 1969), is the most comprehensive account of the years 1958–63. Phebe Marr's book, *The Modern History of Iraq* (Boulder, Colo.: Westview Press, 1985), is a competent recent political history; chap. 7 dealing with the years 1963 to 1968 is particularly good at capturing the atmosphere of the times.

on the ensuing revolutionism of the regime, which was made possible by the hegemony Baʿthist ideas had already acquired in Iraq. The groundwork for a new political and social order had been laid over the previous decade. The tired popular mood, which saw in the coup yet one more turn of the merry-go-round of military politics, could be excused its shortsightedness; its adherence to Baʿthist categories had left it without so much as a language with which to imagine what lay ahead. The point is not just that a regime of endemic violence came later (after 1975), but that violence by itself is unable to explain the long-term consolidation of Baʿthism. Like the ICP, the crowds in the streets and the public at large had first to convince themselves, however unwillingly, that they had no other alternative but to enter the Republic of Fear.

The first five years after 1958 were crucial in the turnaround of the public from the ICP towards the ABSP; 1968 was after all merely a re-enactment of 1963. The whole decade was thick with events that have been carefully studied by others. My only purpose here is to understand what happened to the sensibilities of masses of people. For this three events stand out prior to Qassem's downfall: the massacres in Mosul and Kirkuk in the spring and summer of 1959, both of which greatly tarnished the ICP's credibility; and the public trials of Baʿthists and other pan-Arabists after 1960, which greatly improved the ABSP's credibility.

The Mosul events were triggered by an abortive pan-Arab military revolt backed up on the streets by the ABSP. The ICP, which had got wind of the affair, organized with Qassem's approval a massive demonstration of supporters from all over Iraq. Some 250,000 people descended on the nationalist city of Mosul with its population of 180,000. The day after most of the outsiders had left, the military command in charge of the city proclaimed a pan-Arab revolt, and the Baʿth led mobs who burned down left-wing bookshops and an ICP meeting place. In the wake of the revolt's suppression, massacres involving widespread and public disfigurement of corpses were instigated by ICP supporters. The situation went out of control.

> For four days and four nights Kurds and Yezidis stood against Arabs; Assyrian and Aramean Christians against Arab Moslems; the Arab tribe of Albu Mutaiwat against the Arab tribe of Shammar; the Kurdish tribe of al-Gargariyyah against Arab Albu Mutaiwat; the peasants of the Mosul country against their landlords; the soldiers of the Fifth brigade against their officers; the periphery of the city of Mosul against its center; the plebeians of the Arab quarters of al-Makkawi and Wadi Hajar against the aristocrats of the Arab quarter of ad-Dawwash; and within the quarter of Bab al-Baid, the family of al-Rajabu against its traditional rivals, the Aghawat. It seemed as if

all social cement dissolved and all political authority vanished. . . . The struggle between nationalists and Communists had released age-old mechanisms, investing them with an explosive force and carrying them to the point of civil war.[14]

In Kirkuk a repeat version of the Mosul events occurred, pitting Kurds acting through their local branch of the ICP against their traditional rivals, the Turcomans.

Shortly after, in October 1959, a Baᶜthist hit team machine-gunned Qassem's car in broad daylight. The repression that followed led to considerable organizational dislocation, which lasted until 1961 when a new hardline "left" leadership took over. Although the leadership that had organized the assault disappeared from the scene, the actual participants in it eventually rose to a very privileged status in the party, the most notable being Saddam Husain. In spite of the party's internal problems, its public image was greatly enhanced by the trials of scores of Baᶜthis allegedly connected to the event. A selfless, fanatic, and fiercely militant image of Baᶜthism was flaunted by the militants in public; and when Qassem personally intervened in a show of clemency, as was his wont, the party ended up not only looking good, but with a new crop of heroes in its ranks.

The politics of the transformation in mass allegiances was sharply drawn up within days of the 1958 coup. The Baᶜth demanded unconditional unity with the newly formed United Arab Republic (UAR) of Egypt and Syria. On July 24, ᶜAflaq arrived in Baghdad to launch the campaign, emphasizing Iraq's role as the standard bearer of Arab unity. The ICP reacted by clinging onto Iraqi independence under Qassem, whom they proceeded to build up as the saviour of the nation and its "sole leader." In demonstrations, the communist taunt to Baᶜthi demands was *maku zaᶜim illa Karim* (there is no leader but Qassem). In a statement placarded throughout Baghdad on September 3, 1958, the ICP put forward this case:

> Today . . . when the masses of the Iraqi people . . . hear of the proposed merger, . . . they are filled with uneasiness . . . on account of the want of freedom of opinion and of party and social organization in the UAR. . . .
>
> The Kurdish people . . . too is worried about the fate of its national rights. . . .
>
> The Iraqi army and its brave officers . . . cannot, for their part, but be perturbed about the way in which the Egyptian and Syrian armies were united. . . .

14. Batatu, *Social Classes*, 866.

> Undoubtedly cooperation between the economies of Iraq and the UAR is possible to the utmost limits . . . but their merger . . . could only narrow the opportunities of the retarded Iraqi economy. . . .
>
> It is an error to say that before such a great objective as unity . . . negative results, however serious, dwindle in importance or that the interests of the part could be sacrificed in the interest of the whole, for if a merger would have an unfavorable effect on Iraq and would neither serve democracy in the UAR itself nor attract the sentiments of the other Arab peoples, what great interest could impel us towards it?[15]

ᶜAbd al-Karim Qassem was very popular; however vehement, the pan-Arabists were weak; and the ICP had solid roots inside Iraq which could get "sacrificed in the interest of the whole." These and other reasons help explain the ICP's rationale for a position that, retrospectively, looked like such folly to thoughtful commentators on Iraqi politics. More important, however, the ICP was being consistent with its own knowledge of Iraq as accumulated over a quarter of a century of militant activity. The problem was that the ICP's acquired knowledge was no longer relevant in the conditions of post-1958 Iraq.

THE ICP

The ICP began by looking for change in social inequalities and domestic injustices, like the *Ahali* group before it and the National Democrats in Qassem's government. The party saw itself as waging its struggle against a particular social class, the modern bourgeoisie and big landlords. By their own admission, this focus was not congruent with those who wielded power in the state or through the government. The separation made it possible for the party after 1958 to embrace Qassem who was perceived to be acting against the real social enemy.

Under the monarchy (1932–58), the distinction between state and ruling class was real, but of no great practical import. The state was in fact controlled at arm's length by big landowners and the modernizing bourgeoisie, as contrasted to the rule of military leaders (1958–68), or a single party (1968 on). The institution that made it possible for a whole social class to rule in the political sense of the word was parliament, as handed down by the British. Ramshackle and decrepit though it might have been, and notwithstanding interruptions, the parliamentary system after 1941 functioned to provide a forum restricted to the country's privileged and propertied elite. The collapse of the monarchy

15. Ibid., 829.

at the hands of its army brought down with it these two pillars that had sustained its rule: the hitherto ruling class in society was broken up, expropriated, and scattered, while the parliamentary system as a general form of government was shattered.

The class-centredness of the ICP was also confirmed by its view of itself as the party of the proletariat in alliance with other exploited or oppressed social strata. Membership was deemed to arise from an individual's identification with the interests of this exploited group. Excluded from the political process, the working class nonetheless had a defined or readily definable relationship with those other interest groups and classes that ruled economically, socially, and politically. Present in industry, manufacturing, and infrastructure, the numbers of workers grew significantly from the 1940s right through to 1958. Relatively speaking they remained miniscule; however, their presence encapsulated what it meant to be modern and catch up with the West. Under the monarchy the proletariat was an ascendant urban class that fascinated students, soldiers, underpaid civil servants, and even some junior officers. This was the ICP's "natural" constituency. Their exclusion from institutional politics caught the flavour of what was wrong with the monarchy. The element of voluntarism in joining the party, and the ICP's own sense of "mission," was thus acknowledged to be mediated by the existing social fabric and how it functioned, regardless of the fact that the ICP's ultimate goals entailed revolutionizing both this political system and the social relations it rested on.

Pre-1958 Iraq corresponded to the ICP's scenario in an important way. Over the years, countless political associations had formed, coalesced, dissolved, or reappeared under new names. Variously represented were landowners, tribal shaikhs, a modernizing bourgeoisie or aspirants in that direction, merchants, pro- and anti-British factions, religious communities, ex-Sharifian officers, pan-Arabists, liberal democrats, various nationalisms, authoritarian and leftist reformers. The list goes on. Inequality, and the extremes of poverty and privilege were on display, seen to reside in specific individuals and groupings. Injustice was in the air so to speak, not because it was greater or more real than in later years, but because notwithstanding repression, opinions could be held, judgements could be made, and the capacity to act in public was hard to suppress effectively. Political currents, newspapers, parties, interest groups, religions, and individuals had their own public space in which to jostle and joust against one another.

This was a world made up of self-conscious parts ("classes" in the

ICP's jargon), each incorporated inside a larger whole (administratively, economically, or socially) but not subsumed by this incorporation. Rough though they all were at the edges, classes, parties, movements, religions, and individuals fitted like pieces in a puzzle. A degree of self-awareness and autonomy arose from the very necessity to relate to an "other" standing outside of them.

Although legally banned in all the years of the monarchy, the ICP could not be eliminated in such conditions. With each bout of repression, it bounced back. The very act of banning the ICP enhanced its public status as the intransigent representative of the exploited and non-propertied groups excluded from formal representation. The mere existence of the ICP posed the question for society as a whole of the imperative for expanding democratic horizons, irrespective of the party's own decidedly undemocratic views on the subject. This was the ICP's real moral trump card under the monarchy, and the source of its wider legitimacy in the eyes of the general public.

All this changed after 1958. A world of "classes" collapsed in the wake of the eruption of the undifferentiated structureless mass into politics. Overnight the ICP became the party of the crowd on the streets, with a new kind of multifaceted, very diverse, and anarchically aggregated constituency. The relative weight of the working class had begun declining in the early 1950s as the state apparatus, the "services" sector, and the motley remainders of urbanization-without-industrialization began their secular expansion, boosted by new-found rentier sources of state income (oil revenues). People also rallied to the ICP for no other reason than that it was there, and they did so irrespective of the fact that they were workers, students, peasants, intellectuals, shopkeepers, or just marginal individuals lost among the hosts of rural migrants shacked up in miserable mud-hut dwellings around Baghdad. After 1958 Iraq's wealth-producing classes underwent an even sharper decline, which was only reversed by the Baʿth during the 1970s. A working class that had just begun to feel around "for itself" (before 1958) began to disintegrate even "in itself" (1958–68). Its former fragile sense of identity as a class collapsed completely, leaving the ICP's exhortations about working-class leadership suspended in a void of meaninglessness.

The ICP was intoxicated with its new supporters who corresponded to an emergent social phenomenon in Iraq as in many other Third World countries. But these masses were fickle, and Iraqi communists did not know how to handle them as evidenced by the Mosul and Kirkuk events. The problem was that they looked like the genuine article, the immense majority of the population, *al-akthariyya al-sahiqa,* and in the former scheme of things the ICP had merely been the leader of an important minority (the working class) whose very definition implied it was one of many classes. The new constituents had not been won over to the party in any meaningful political sense as their predecessors had been; they had simply rallied around it for any one of a number of disparate and usually superficial reasons. Their emergence on the political stage, alongside the breakup of the old ruling class and the dismantling of a parliamentary form of government, meant that the ICP was now inhabiting an unknown and strange new world whose distinguishing characteristic was the breakdown of all barriers between the identity of each part (be it a class, a group, an individual, a newspaper) and the experience of being fused into the mass. After 1958, the "parts" were losing the ability to "think" themselves separate from "the masses"; the walls of the self were disintegrating for individuals, parties, classes, and social groups.

The idea of the masses is the idea of community based on the undifferentiable dissolution of everyone into each other. It is a very attractive idea, rooted in the human urge for community, with manifestations in all the major religions, the experience of war, and of course politics. The ICP's Stalinist conception of socialism was built upon it (a classless, groupless, homogenized world made up of individuals who all have the same identity and therefore none at all). The masses as a sociological fact along with the masses as an idea of community swept up everyone into their wake from the summer of 1958 on. They remain ingrained in Iraqi political culture to this very day. However, the metamorphosis of classes into masses was only in accord with what the ICP hoped for in politics (its programme for the future); it did not fit in with what it actually *was* as an organization after a quarter of a century under the monarchy. Therefore, a chasm began to open up between reality and party political utterances, turning the latter into shibboleths in the eyes of more and more Iraqis. The September 1958 statement was the first step in that direction.

THE ABSP

By contrast with the ICP, the central point about Baʿthism was that their struggle was frontally directed at all institutions of the budding nation-state, focussing in particular on government and the levers of power. The Baʿth were not fixated upon any particular social class, neither the one that exercised power under the monarchy, nor some imagined alternative thought to be the ultimate historical agency working after 1958 in mysterious ways on all those dense military minds. Baʿthism derived its militantism and dynamic impulse as a movement from its clarity of purpose and identification of all failures of government with the "illegitimate" boundaries of the state. The two were always identical in their minds, and the argument was increasingly easy to make since there existed no consensus on the nation-state, particularly in the heyday of Arab nationalism in the late 1950s and early 1960s. Moreover, with the destruction of parliament there no longer existed the administrative scaffolding that organized the political interactions of classes and others. As classes were giving way to masses, the Baʿth, unlike the ICP, felt the pulse of the change.

"The role of the masses in the world has come of age," said ʿAflaq. "Contrary to what happened in the West, the revolt of the Eastern peoples carries in the first place a liberatory humanitarian character, because it is directed against imperialism. . . . And whereas oppression in the West falls only on classes, the East is made up of nations that are oppressed." [16] The Baʿthist idea of the masses shades into that of the nation; for them conceptually, class was not the relevant category in Arab conditions. Yet the communists as late as 1970 continued to emphasize class: "The working class is the developing class in our society. . . . [Its] vanguard role . . . increases continuously as a result of the enrichment of the content of the national-democratic revolution with new social meanings, and the ever deepening linkage of the revolution with the world revolutionary process." [17] By contrast, an intelligent piece of Baʿthi counterideology issued in 1973 by a government department charged with "educating the masses" made this argument:

> Is the contemporary Arab revolution one of a specific class, or a revolution of the Arab people with all its classes? Does this revolution aim to eliminate . . . specific classes? Does it look towards the dictatorship of the proletariat, for example? In the current historical period—in other words in the shadow of national division, Zionist invasion and imperialist domination—the Arab revolution cannot be the revolution of a class but of the nation directed at its backward, divided and exploited reality. . . .
>
> From [the Baʿth] standpoint the idea of the nation in the revolutionary

16. Michel ʿAflaq, *Maʿrakat al-Masir al-Wahid* (Beirut: Al-Muassasah al-ʿArabiyya, 1979), 49–50.
17. ICP Second National Conference proceedings, *Barnamaj al-Hizb al-Shuyuʿi al-ʿIraqi wa Nidhamuhu al-Dakhili* (Beirut: al-Nidaʾ publications, 1970), 57–58.

stage means those individuals, strata and revolutionary classes who form the materiel of the revolution. And by the people is meant those spontaneous and organized masses who form the base of the revolution. If within this framework it is the working class who is the primary class . . . then this simply means that its role is central . . . for an Arab revolution which is the embodiment of the unity of those classes, strata and individuals who are working for its goals.[18]

To the extent that there is a Baʿthi distinction between the categories of "masses" and "nation," it is in the following predictable direction: "The oppressed Arab masses, because of their oppression and victimization, represent the truth of the pure nation; also within them reside most of the strength of the nation and its abilities."[19]

In Arab affairs, the ICP faced the same dilemma it faced in domestic affairs after 1958, but from the opposite perspective. While not necessarily liking the inherited boundaries of Iraqi statehood, the ICP had nevertheless taken them for granted, accepting them in effect as the basis of a nation-state. With the destruction of the monarchy, this hitherto unproblematic assumption also got loosened from its anchorage in sociopolitical realities. The ICP's healthy pre-1958 focus on domestic injustices soon became uncomfortably wedded to a floundering engagement with all issues that transcended the boundaries of Iraq.

In practice, the "Unity Now!" demand of the Baʿth was pitted against an ICP formula for a federalist union of the Arab states. The position bore all the marks of hasty improvisation, and seems to have been conceived as a formality utterly lacking in inner conviction. ʿAmer Abdallah, for instance, the chief ideologue of the politburo, gave a public lecture in February 1959 that culled weighty "scientific" arguments to show that although the ICP itself was not against unity in principle, the process itself involved the most complicated dialectics.[20] In any case, genuine federalism presupposed the existence of well-developed regional nationalisms (Iraqi, Syrian, Lebanese, and so on). These did not exist as tangible realities any more than a deep-rooted pan-Arabist sentiment could be said to have existed in Iraq. Furthermore, Arab unity looked like it had been accepted in theory by the ICP, but was being hedged about for purely sectarian motives. The emphasis on internal de-

18. Ministry of Information, *Fi al-Fikr al-Ishtiraki (On Socialist Thought)* (Baghdad: al-Hurriyya Publications, 1973), 18–19.
19. ʿAflaq, *Maʿrakat al-Masir,* 17. The same idea is repeated in ʿAflaq's article "The Struggle For Unity is the Struggle of the Masses," which argues that "true" unity can only emerge "from below." See ibid., 148–52.
20. See Batatu, *Social Classes,* 830.

mocracy heightened the perceived element of hypocrisy in the ICP's position, particularly after what happened in Mosul and Kirkuk.

The pan-Arabists were winning the argument because they were responding to the real way in which Iraqi politics was changing, and they succeeded in putting the question on the agenda in spite of an overwhelmingly inferior status in the country. The strident call for instant unity with the UAR thus found a place by default; its very self-assurance served as an antidote to the prevarications of the Left. The belief that instant unity was a burning imperative for Iraq became for a while (1960–63) a marvelous substitute for the practical problems of real unity, particularly as it was fused with a single-minded intent to overthrow a regime that was declining in popularity.

Unlike the ICP, the Baʿth were a genuine secretion of the masses, with a politics tailored to the new political and social landscape of post-1958 Iraq. The parliamentary form of government was the only institutional mechanism that might have provided a countervailing measure to the emergence of the masses as a force at the bottom along with military men at the top. The political problem is created by the new hegemony of "the masses" as an idea of community and as a sociological reality. The entry of larger numbers of people than ever before into political action does not itself create a problem (unwieldy numbers is one reason for having a representative system in the first place). The mass sympathy extended to the Baʿthists on trial for the 1959 assassination attempt was one indication of how much and how fast the Iraqi public was changing. The ICP could not have reaped commensurate rewards from a shootout under the monarchy. The role of parties was reduced to clamouring for the attention of the masses at the expense of everything else. The rules governing politics were changing, and the Baʿth found themselves wallowing in a natural habitat.

Pan-Arabism's elegance as a formula lies in its utter simplicity, vibrant radicalism, and seemingly uplifting message for downtrodden Arabs. Instead of all the complicated and unwholesome specifics concerning people's real problems, apparitions from a glorious past were forged into present needs; and out of this revitalization, *ihyaʾ*, or renaissance, *baʿth*, a new generation was deemed to emerge in whom would be vested the spirit of Arabism. Self-centredness was cloaked in universalism and a stretching out of the hand of comradeship and antiimperialist solidarity to millions of other Arabs in far-off countries, none of whom were bound to each other by concrete ties of everyday life, economic interests, or even a common fate in the face of oppression. It is as though the very inchoateness and formlessness of the masses in one country were perceived to be their greatest virtue, then elevated to the status of an overriding principle—unity—embracing whole conglomerations of ever more separated masses from one Arab country to the next.

Pan-Arabism is that idea of community tailored to the masses as a sociological and phenomenological category. Like the idea of Arab socialism, also invented by the Baʿth, it pins down the object for whom everyone is asked to forsake their identity. In this way pan-Arabism is an enormous improvement on the pure idea of the masses as a community because it succeeds in turning into narcissism the outward-looking complete utopia of a molten world of brothers and sisters. As a way of thinking, therefore, pan-Arabism does have an awesome beauty, the kind of beauty that draws persons into its wonder like moths to a flame.

The Transmutation of Ideas

> We, the Communists, took up in the past isolationist attitudes towards the holders of the slogan of Arab unity. The formula that we put forth after the July 1958 Revolution was wrong. . . . We should not have raised a rallying cry contradictory to that of unity.[21]

The date was August 1964, barely eighteen months after the overthrow of Qassem and the decimation of the ICP at the hands of the 1963 Baʿthi regime. The ICP was making a major public turn, which, unsurprisingly, coincided with greatly improved relations between the UAR and the USSR. But the change had been in the air for some time and reflected more than a slavish adherence to the line from Moscow. The discovery of virtue in pan-Arabism entailed reassessing the ʿAref military regime that had overthrown Baʿthi rule in November 1963. The new regime was a stimulus to the struggle of the antiimperialist masses and a step in the direction of returning the country to "the caravan of Arab liberation." The inexorable logic of the ICP's turn was pursued to a bitter conclusion as the leadership renounced what it had stood for under the monarchy:

> It is erroneous . . . that Communists should continue to cling to political democracy as a condition for the support of any Arab unity. The question of democracy, including the issue of party life, can be solved within the course of the operation of unity itself with mass struggle, persuasion, and the persistent influence of the socialist camp upon the Arab leaders themselves.[22]

21. Ibid., 1037.
22. Ibid., 1037–38. The period 1963–68 was one of introspection and sharp swings in position inside the ICP, principally on the issue of Arab identity. The same debates were go-

When President ʿAref broke with Nasser and decided to embark upon a much-welcomed flirtation with open civilian rule (1965–66), the ICP detected "the hidden fingers" of British imperialism and the "oil monopolies." By such responses the ICP revealed the extent to which it now thought in pan-Arabist categories and had lost touch with popular sensibilities. In all thinking about politics, the idea of the masses held sway even though the masses were no longer a real force in the streets, and the public at large had turned away from the excesses of the Baʿth between February and November of 1963. When in 1969 ʿAbd al-Rahman al-Bazzaz, the prime mover under ʿAref of this democratic interlude, was accused of being a spy and horribly tortured under the second Baʿthi regime, what could the ICP see in this portent other than a vindication of their own previous accusations against him?

In the course of the 1960s the programmatic demarcation lines between pan-Arabism and communism wore very thin in the eyes of the public at large. The party that had been able, however inadequately, to criticize itself in 1959 for what happened in Mosul and Kirkuk was now firmly complicit in a conspiratorial view of things. Furthermore, this new thinking was increasingly wedded to a theorized devaluation of democracy. The moral high ground on which the ICP had rested under the monarchy was being frittered away even before the Baʿth came to power for the second time in 1968.

The transmutation of ideas between 1958 and 1968 broke up the seesawlike equilibrium between the two antipodes of Iraqi politics in a way that favoured the ABSP. What the Baʿth stood for in politics acquired status and even hegemony among all the intellectuals who saw themselves as the spokesmen of "the masses." Even if individuals were not yet leaving the ICP to join the ABSP, the legitimacy that had resided in the ICP was passing insensibly to their arch-enemies. The ICP as an organization remained a surrogate in the handover. There was after all a big historical legacy to pass on. The ICP was the oldest party in Iraq (founded in 1932), whose doctrines in the 1940s had "spread so widely in the big towns . . . that . . . nearly fifty percent of the youthful elements of all classes had been carried away by them."[23] Time was needed to effect the transfer.

Society at large was also having its options reduced. Whole chunks of

---

ing on the Syrian Communist Party. These have been published in a collection of documents entitled *Qadhaya al-Khilaf fi al-Hizb al-Shuyuʿi al-Suri* (Beirut: Dar Ibn Khaldun, 1972).

23. These are the words of the then chief of police, Bahjat ʿAtiyyah, quoted in Batatu, *Social Classes*, 465.

intellectual life were beginning to choke up long before the Baʿth came to power for the second time. Moreover, the language of politics was not only becoming the same; it was collapsing in on itself. Words were running into each other until they all meant the same thing. Distinction and nuance meant less in ideas; the ability to think politically was slipping.

Before 1958, ideas had moved in the opposite direction. No account of the Baʿth can afford to ignore the contribution then made by the local communist parties to the development of Baʿthi ideas. The communist theory of organization and notions of imperialism, socialism, and freedom all found a more coherent home within Baʿthism than pan-Arabism ever found inside Iraqi communism. In the course of the transference (and even before) the meaning of these three words was hopelessly corrupted. In general, language "becomes ugly and inaccurate because our thoughts are foolish, but the slovenliness of our language makes it easier for us to have foolish thoughts." [24] I shall now consider how the corruption of these three words gave rise to foolish thoughts.

IMPERIALISM

The link between state power and the perceived illegitimacy of the Iraqi territorial entity found a perfect pair of scapegoats in imperialism and Zionism, neither of which was directly shaping Iraqi political realities. Imperialism was appropriated from the formidable arsenals of Marxism beginning with Lenin. But this was a wholesale appropriation, not confined to Baʿthism, and linked to the most important new meta-ideology of the postwar period—Third Worldism. [25]

For the ICP under the monarchy, imperialism was always somewhat abstract: a force to be struggled against by solidarity with the USSR, for example, or by making friendship treaties and alliances with the socialist countries instead of the West. The Mandate system had been an indirect form of control by Britain, one designed with some kind of political independence at the end of the road. Inside Iraq, imperialism

24. From the essay by George Orwell, "Politics and the English Language," from *The Norton Reader* anthology (New York: Norton, 1984), 256.
25. The economics of this phenomenon has been discussed by Bill Warren in his book, *Imperialism: Pioneer of Capitalism* (London: NLB, 1980). Warren is a Marxist who became concerned with the acquisition by postwar Marxism of "a dual social character: it has become the philosophy simultaneously of socialism . . . and of modernizing nationalism" (p. 6). The key theoretical construct that made this possible, he argues, was the Marxist theory of imperialism from Lenin onwards.

manifested itself for the ICP in the shape of the local ruling class; its reality was given in the form of this class and no further implication of the idea was relevant to Iraqi politics.

Following the ICP's adoption of pan-Arabism and the 1967 war, imperialism loomed even larger in the ICP's mindset, becoming "the principal enemy of the national-democratic revolution." The old idea remained that imperialism had "natural counter-revolutionary allies inside the country among whom are the feudalists, the big landowners and the large bourgeoisie." [26] But none of these people existed any longer, having been nationalized or chosen exile. Therefore, as imperialism loomed larger in the mind, it had less substance on the ground by the ICP's own criteria for dealing with the phenomenon.

Zionism, on the other hand, had no natural place in the ICP's ideological universe. Their disorientation on this issue, like that of all the Arab communist parties, dates back to the USSR's call for partition in Palestine. The ICP's position on Zionism has shifted ground many times since 1948.

By contrast, in Baʿthist hands, imperialism was the cornerstone of an ideological system whose nexus was the post–World War I order in the Middle East. Politically this order was unquestionably the outcome of decisions taken by the victors in that war on the grounds of their self-interest. Once the premise of Arab identity is adopted (as opposed to Iraqi or Syrian), the concept of imperialism is no longer confined to a historical explanation for fragmentation; it naturally lends itself to becoming the ongoing reason for it (particularly in Iraq, where the search for a modern identity did not precede the breakup of the Ottoman Empire). This conjunction of reality with perception allowed Baʿthism in particular to imbue very powerful scapegoating attributes to the idea of imperialism, which metamorphosed from an ICP label for something with a supposedly factual content into the idea of the all-powerful outsider who is the source of all evil inside.

Zionism adds flesh to these poor bones. The insidious tentacles of imperialist influence are "proved" by all the Arab-Israeli wars, and failure in those wars points to the existence of a fifth column—Arab reaction, the local Jewish community, Kurds—in league with imperialism. Thus are generated the unholy triumvirate of colluding enemies—imperialism, Zionism, and Arab reaction—against which are arraigned all true forces of Arab national liberation. This most formidable explicative

26. *Barnamaj al-Hizb*, 57.

tool cannot be undermined once a few basic ground rules are accepted. Sooner or later every political question, no matter how localized, can be traced back to one or another schema revolving around this triumvirate, among whom of course imperialism occupies pride of place.

Ideologically, the main feature of the 1960s in Arab politics was the widespread acclaim given to this way of thinking. The conversion was going on even as pan-Arabism in the shape of Nasserism was being dealt a crippling blow in the 1967 war, and even as Baᶜthism was starting to divide into its Syrian and Iraqi components. Military defeat rebounded on the personal prestige of Nasser, it struck at the idea that "the progressive" Arab regimes could do anything about Israel, and it popularized armed struggle and revolution as alternatives. But it did not dislodge the fundamental underpinnings of a pan-Arabist view of the world. Neither the "Palestinianization" of the struggle against Zionism, nor the regionalization of Baᶜthism in Syria and Iraq, contradicts the adoption of a referential system of cause and effect in politics rooted in "imperialism, Zionism and Arab reaction." Examples of this adoption are numerous inside the left wing of the Palestinian Resistance movement after 1967, and can be found today in the explanations given for the Lebanese civil war from the Arab/Muslim side. Therefore, the legacy of pan-Arabism as a phase in postwar Arab politics lies not in its failure over half a century to achieve Arab unity but in the way it captured the high ground of all politics: the language and fundamental categories it is conducted in.

Naturally the fragmented reality of Arab states is bound ultimately to bear down hard on how the idea of pan-Arabism evolves. Mediations like this, however, become relevant in the light of the record of the Baᶜth in power (in the 1980s), not at the point at which they just grasped it (the 1960s). The distinction operating here is between the internal logic of an idea, and the realities it faces on the ground. The gap between these two in Arab politics is unusually large because of pan-Arabism's affinity with the Islamic heritage. In the absence of a clear-cut challenge to these underpinnings of a pan-Arabist reference frame, and given the fact of continuing Israeli expansionism (on the West Bank), it is unfortunately the case that pan-Arabism is likely to survive even a much further widening of this gap.

SOCIALISM

The ABSP is distinguished by the fact that it was the first movement in the Arab world to place the question of socialism side by side with that of the national question. It considered unity, freedom and socialism as principal goals which are organically linked. . . . The dialectical linkages between these three goals is the most brilliant and powerful feature of Baᶜthist ideology.[27]

At their founding conference in 1947, the Baᶜth adopted socialism as the model form of economic organization of the future united Arab state, following a major debate between the two hundred or so members who attended the congress—hardly a major force in Arab politics at the time. Baᶜthism's first decade was dominated by the necessity to assert its pan-Arab mission and differentiate itself from its principal enemy, the Syrian Communist Party. However, in the 1950s a much more intense debate focussing on a broader conception of socialism developed in earnest. Among other nationalists the Baᶜth are considered pioneers for their shift towards a greater emphasis on socialism as symbolized by the change of name in 1952 to the Arab Baᶜth Socialist Party. Unlike 1947 the new vision of Baᶜthi socialism went far beyond the idea of economic nationalizations grafted onto a purely pan-Arab nationalist content.[28]

The socialism of the Baᶜth was strongly influenced by the experience of the Soviet Union, which served as a model of a strong national state that leapt from the backwardness of Tsarist Russia to superpower status in a short time. However, in contrast to the Arab communist parties, Baᶜthist admiration for Soviet methods of social organization was coupled with the *nationalism* of Soviet Russia. ᶜAflaq liked to draw attention to Soviet conduct during World War II as proof of this nationalism. He coined "Arab Socialism" to differentiate what the Baᶜth wanted from the "Russian Socialism" of the USSR. Thus, once again an idea that looks slavish and parrotlike in the hands of the ICP emerges with an original and independent stature in the hands of the ABSP. The idea of Arab Socialism soon became common currency throughout the Arab world.[29] Today non-Baᶜthi Arab adherents have largely forgotten it originated with the Baᶜth.

27. Shibli al-ᶜAysami, *Hizb al-Baᶜth al-ᶜArabi al-Ishtiraki: Maᶜrakat al-ʾArbaᶜiniyat al-Taʾsisiyya* (Beirut: Dar al-Taliᶜah, 1978), 71. ᶜAysami is the assistant secretary of the National (pan-Arab) Command of the ABSP based in Baghdad.

28. This is what ᶜAysami meant in the previous quote. In general, one can only be precise about what the Baᶜth do *not* mean by socialism; over time it became harder to say what they thought the word meant in isolation from the ideas of unity and freedom. However, by the 1960s no Baᶜthi held a purely "economic" notion of socialism. For a generous recognition of the pioneering role of the Baᶜth in developing a "total theory" unifying socialism and pan-Arabism by a political opponent, see Basil al-Kubaysi's *Harakat al-Qawmiyyun al-ᶜArab* (Beirut: Dar al-ᶜAwda, n.d.), 70–71.

29. The sixth congress of the ABSP in 1963 debated replacing "Arab socialism" with "the Arab road to socialism." This congress marked the highpoint of the rise of a left current within Baᶜthism, which had assimilated a non- or even anti-Stalinist version of Marxism. The party had just come to power in two countries and the Left was at the helm

Many other Third World nationalisms have also equated socialism and the USSR. Socialism as an ideal in the Third World, as a symbol of hope for an equitable and just future, has become fused with the sordid reality of the USSR or China. Nor is separating the factories from the Gulags an exercise likely to touch people's hearts. In the Arab world, determining what is socialism is coloured by the absence of the alternative socialist traditions present in the West. In the consciousness of virtually every Iraqi, there is only one answer: Baᶜthi rule *is* socialism. No Iraqi can think any longer that the ICP's kind of socialism is going to be different from the ABSP's if the tables of power are miraculously turned in their favour; ironically, even the ICP ended up making this admission.

The Baᶜth have a fresh, vigorous, even messianic vision of a new order in society, whatever else might be said about their views on private property, the public sector, or ownership of the means of production. Revolution is a word they appended to socialism in their own inimitable way. Almost anything the Arab communist parties have said, or are capable of saying today, pales by comparison with the experience of Baᶜthism as a movement and in power. Hence, it is pedantic to latch onto a list of specific measures or policies that taken together could be defined as constituting the content of Baᶜthi socialism. For almost any such list, exceptions could be found and many qualifications required. Instead, Baᶜthi socialism is best understood in terms of a formulation like this:

> Socialism is a way of life, not just an economic order. It extends to all aspects of life—economics, politics, training, education, social life, health, morals, literature, science, history, and others both great and small.
>
> Socialism, freedom, and unity are not different names for different things . . . but different facets of one basic law from which they spring.[30]

---

in both. The Congress resulted in some very radical formulations on the revolutionary transformation of Arab society that exceeded in their originality anything produced by the Arab Communist parties. Yasin al-Hafiz, George Tarabishsi, and Fawaz Tarabulsi among others left the ABSP following ᶜAflaq's success in ousting the Left and overturning the programmatic innovations they had a hand in introducing. They continued to play an important role as Marxist intellectuals and leaders of far left groups that came to prominence after the 1967 war. Tarabishsi is the principal translator of Trotsky's writings into Arabic, and Tarabulsi founded the Organization for Communist Action in Lebanon. The Arab Revolution Group, formed by Iraqi exiles in Britain, had left Baᶜthist origins and was sympathetic to Trotskyism.

30. Quotations are from Munif Razzaz's influential 1957 article, "Why Socialism Now?" Razzaz was a leading Jordanian member of the party whose writings on socialism were probably the first systematic Baᶜthi attempt to go beyond ᶜAflaq's early writings. Taken from extracts in John Devlin, *The Baᶜth Party: A History From its Origins to 1966* (Stanford: Hoover Institution Press, 1976), 36–37.

From one point of view, this does not say much; ideas diluted to this extent have no taste. But if what counts is the sincerity of the intention, and the extent to which that sincerity was borne out by Iraq's experience since 1968, then reading backwards one can unlock, as Razzaz put it, "the one basic law from which they spring": the Baʿthi view of freedom.

FREEDOM

The Baʿth insist that freedom is always and unconditionally "in the interests of the masses" and can only materialize in "a state arising from their will." [31] One can scoff at the idea that the Republic of Fear in Iraq is such a state, or one can try to understand the important sense in which the Baʿth honestly believe their state is striving towards real freedom.

Freedom is in the interests of the masses because national sovereignty is; this identity is the starting point for the Baʿth, as it is for so much of the Third World. The whole of the antiimperialist rhetoric of pan-Arabism revolves around the idea of freedom *from* imperialism. Even in the broad trends of Arab political culture it has never had the Western connotation of personal sovereignty, or release of the individual from impositions on thought and action originating in the state or from society at large. This autonomy of the parts (individuals, groups, minorities, ideas) that make up a society also means the freedom to be left alone and to have the choice of not being part of the larger community (not absolutely, but in certain legally definable respects). These notions translate into a whole moral outlook on privacy, toleration, self-determination, the protection of minorities, and other issues of human well-being. But in the history of capitalism, personal sovereignty also took the form of the unimpeded right to exploit the labour of others. Generally, most types of Third Worldism have reduced all the complicated and civilizing ramifications of the idea of personal sovereignty into this last meaning. They have "skipped over" the kind of enlightenment that preceded modernization in the history of Europe. The emergence of fundamentalism and the broader obsession with *turath* (heritage) shows how fiercely such values are still being resisted in the Muslim world. Whatever the reasons, it is a fact that as large numbers of people from the Third World became drawn into political action, they did so by laying claim to their rights as collectivities of unfree nations able to un-

---

31. This is how ʿAysami begins his analysis of the Baʿthist meaning of *hurriyya*, freedom. See *Hizb al-Baʿth*, 69.

chain themselves only in counterposition to the idea of personal sovereignty now viewed exclusively as the selfish and rapacious creed of individualism inherent in capitalism and inimical to socialism. To this extent the Bathist view of freedom hardly departs from the norm in much of the Third World.

The "second aspect" of the Baʿthist concept of freedom, according to Shibli al-ʿAysami, "is characterized by the linkage of freedom to socialism, which means the rejection of bourgeois democracy which falsifies the essence of freedom and stabs it in the heart. We can say . . . that for the Baʿth party the liberal conception of freedom was contracting over the years to be replaced in a clearer way with the notion of popular democracy." [32] ʿAysami has placed the evolution of the party's view on freedom on exactly the same historical trajectory as the party's conception of socialism, which raises yet again the question of the relation between them. What is the sense in which freedom is no longer a negative freedom *from* outsiders (imperialism), but a positive freedom *for* something, whatever it may be called (popular democracy, socialism, Arab unity)? [33]

The second dimension of the Baʿthist idea of freedom shifts the focus from the obstacles placed upon action by the outside to the more fundamental question of who rules. Positive Baʿthi freedom derives from the desire to be self-governing and realize one's "true" interests. Ignorance, poverty, and, above all, the condition of being divided upon oneself are obstacles placed upon self-realization. Because of them a distinction arises between one's real condition with all the "false" and "corrupt" interests it generates, and the condition of being self-realized which coincides with the agent's "true" interests.

But the Baʿth also adhere to the Leninist idea that the interests of the masses can only be properly represented by the party organization. The party is the repository of the nation's "true" interests (otherwise called the "national will"), and the state is an instrument for their realization. Leadership is therefore a status that is given naturally because of who one is, as opposed to being earned formally through an interaction with others (in the course of elections, for instance). The ineluctable next

32. Ibid., 69–70. The phrase "liberal conception of freedom" is probably a reference to the early ʿAflaq who used to make the odd reference to individual freedoms whenever he was not discussing pan-Arabism. "Popular" or "people's" democracy is a synonym for freedom under socialism. Its content has been discussed for the second Baʿthi regime in Chapter 4, under "The Source of Authority."

33. This distinction in its general form is an old one in Western political thought, dating to the Renaissance or the Reformation. It can be elaborated upon in a number of different ways. I follow the general outline of Isaiah Berlin's argument in "Two Concepts of Liberty," in *Four Essays on Liberty* (Oxford: Oxford University Press, 1984).

step is a single party dictatorship, which is not something the ICP could fault the Baʿth with.[34]

"Bourgeois" democracy falsifies this second aspect of freedom because its exercise casts a shadow on "the compacted, interwoven unity" of the revolutionary party, as ʿAflaq put it, which is not made up of a "government that executes and a parliament that criticizes, attacks and objects." The party that is the nation in formation is founded on a "revolutionist psychology which if it is not achieved in the members of the party, falsifies it." These conditions of Baʿthi revolutionism strive always to collectivize the individual, "compacting" him into his comrades. The intention is to create inside the party the same all-fused mass that once stood outside and whose true interests the Baʿth champion. The difference of course is that the masses inside the party have a definite sense of purpose encapsulated in the party programme which they cannot have as consistently when they are outside surrounded by a whole world of baneful influences. This purpose tends to perfection to the extent that there are no blemishes on its singularity. The true interests of the masses, the "national will," are articulated by the party, and a "true road" leads the membership "to create in the party an atmosphere of activism, faith, enthusiasm and selflessness which overwhelms the good elements and the bad, and sweeps along everyone no matter what their mentality."[35]

Baʿthi freedom has become "socialist" because it is bound up with a comprehensive sameness implicit in the original building blocks that went into making "the masses," "the new society," the nation, or the party. These blocks were individually legitimated through an act of faith that brought them into the new community. The conditions for membership may have been subjective and ideological, but they were strictly the same for everybody. The equality the Baʿth seek in their members is stripped of all particulars and any sense that even blocks have individuality. In policy terms, equality of condition becomes "being a Baʿthi," along with the eradication of economic inequalities.

For the Baʿth, equality and the absence of autonomy start in the political realm and from there work into society. For the ICP the situation

34. Once in power, the criterion for having singled oneself out—whether originating in an ICP formula like *the* (one and only) party representing the interests of the proletariat, or an ABSP formula like the vanguard of the Arab revolution—makes little practical difference. Theoretically, however, the ICP can only end up erecting a dictatorship of the proletariat; the state it wants to lead is stuck with all the enemy classes inside it. The Baʿth, on the other hand, definitionally exclude everyone who is not among the struggling masses because voluntarism is their criterion for membership in the nation.

35. I am paraphrasing ʿAflaq's argument in *Maʿrakat al-Masir*, 54–56, from where all quotes are taken.

is reversed: objective economic inequalities that existed outside of itself while it was in opposition and in a well-defined class society constitute the nub of the argument against autonomy. The dictatorship of the proletariat takes away the freedom of action of other classes in order to constitute social equality.

In a variegated world, autonomy of the parts (individuals, groups, newspapers, parties) is the most fundamental precondition for political freedom. Nonetheless, this freedom is not secured for society as a whole simply because a set of actors becomes mature enough, and unimposed upon. The freedom to act politically as an autonomous agent, even more than the freedom to be left alone, must be formally secured; institutional structures *create* this kind of freedom, which otherwise does not exist. Without these "formal" structures, one is left with only a relationship of forces between warring parts, albeit autonomous ones.

Both autonomy and the kind of institutional freedom that presumes it dissolve when the idea of the masses takes hold: the idea of the collective dissolution of everyone into each other. Now, under the best of circumstances, the only kind of freedom that is logically possible is the freedom to act *as one* with the mass, and be sacrificed in its cause. Autonomy is no longer a condition for freedom because freedom has become a singular state of mind that ensures moral well-being once attained. Moreover, when "Unity" is understood as the compelling desire to be liquidated into the mass, it entails the casting away of all other forms of identity. In principle, therefore, pan-Arabism has to work at choking off all local nationalisms, and all other forms of identity (tribal, confessional, and even familial), because otherwise the principle of a disaggregated mass (one divided upon itself) would creep back into politics. In the Ba'thi mind, being at one with the mass is the norm against which all deviancy is measured and discarded for the sake of more freedom. This condition can be striven for. Even more important, it can be inculcated, which is why power always gives this kind of politics such a big charge.

In the public realm such total immersion is only occasionally found in a variety of "brotherhoods of men": secret societies, soldiers at war, heroes and martyrs, Nuremberg rallies, football hooligans, and even among a few comrades in struggle. Through such short-lived brotherhoods, individuals can experience an even more short-lived but nonetheless real sensation of ecstasy such as is felt by religious devotees in a world of sinners. Freedom, in this view of things, is this moment of ecstasy that is achieved when the mind has completely dissolved into "the other," forming what is in principle the absolutely perfect human mass. This is the essence of the freedom that was experienced by the raging mobs in Mosul, Kirkuk, and Baghdad in the summer of 1959 and winter of 1969. However rarely achieved and among however few saintly people, this condition is the Baᶜthist conception of true freedom because it is, from a certain point of view, the pinnacle of self-realization.

Here is a potent primordial force, present no doubt in all human beings. Maybe it springs from that magnificent human propensity for all-consuming and passionate love (the love of other persons, an idea, God, a nation). In politics, however, this force is never more present than when large numbers of men turn into masses, or desperately strive in that direction. And it achieves its moment of truth by eliminating the space that exists between the rest of us ordinary human beings. In this sense Baᶜthi freedom is total "unity"; at the same time it is an equalizing force of the most fundamental kind, and in its own language "socialist," because its unchecked course implies the obliteration of separateness, privacy, independence, difference, autonomy, variety, character, and personality.

The Baᶜth fervently believe in their slogan "Unity, Freedom and Socialism," which is why they inscribe it as a banner headline on every publication, in the streets, all over newspapers, at the front lines of their wars, in all their meetings and on the pictures of their leader. These signs are their chief identity symbols repeated ad nauseam to the point where too many people tend to forget the original intent behind it all; such people will also have forgotten that the Baᶜth are special because they insist upon this kind of freedom for all Iraqis, not some, but all of the time.

Conclusion:
The Final Catastrophe

Early in the spring of 1980 Saddam Husain began planning for war with Iran.[1] In March diplomatic relations were terminated; in April expulsions of Shi'i "fifth columnists" were stepped up; in July the Islamic regime foiled a coup attempt backed by Iraq. According to the Ba'th bits of territory in the Qasr Shirin area were taken in August. By September 11, some 130 square kilometres had fallen into Iraqi hands through military action.[2] On September 17, the Algiers treaty was officially renounced, and five days later full-scale war operations commenced with attacks on ten Iranian airfields.

Notwithstanding Iranian hyperbole about Iraqi intentions, observers are agreed that the regime was caught off guard when the invasion came. Border outposts at Bostan and elsewhere were poorly equipped, undermanned, and completely indefencible. Whatever the long-term expansionist dynamic of Iranian clericalism, at the time it was preoccupied with the intense conflicts building up between the Islamic Republican Party and Bani Sadr and his supporters. The hostage crisis was in full swing and tensions were building up between fundamentalist groups, Revolutionary Guards, and a decomposing army, many of whose upper echelon officers had just been executed. Thus while both sides were certainly engaging in inflammatory accusations and border violations in

1. This is the evaluation of Stephen R. Grummon, *The Iraq-Iran War: Islam Embattled*, CSIS, Georgetown University (Washington, D.C.: Praeger, 1982), 16.
2. According to K. McLachlan and G. Joffe, *The Gulf War: A Survey of Political Issues and Economic Consequences*, Economist Intelligence Unit special report no. 176 (London: 1984), 37.

the months preceding September 22, 1980, the notion that these could be used as a pretext for broader aims was undoubtedly in its origins solely a Ba'thist one.

Iraqi military strategy was initially conceived along the lines of an Israeli-type blitzkrieg. The whole operation was to be wrapped up in less than two weeks, in time for the coming Muslim feast. Militarily, the extent of the Iraqi miscalculation became apparent by the end of the first week of fighting.[3] The remaining course of the war can be broken down into: first, slower and more costly Iraqi advances culminating in the capture of Khorramshahr; second, stalemate lasting through the spring of 1981; third, an Iranian series of counteroffensives of varying effectiveness, which eventually succeeded in driving the Iraqis out of all Iranian territory in 1982; fourth, a three-year stalemate, marked by repeated Iranian human wave assaults against formidable Iraqi fixed defences; and finally the stage of slow, and very costly Iranian advances inside Iraq.

A Sense of Scale

By any reasonable criteria this has proved to be a very big war. Estimates of the dead range from 500,000 to 1 million.[4] The number who survive their wounds is considered low because of the intense heat and humidity, and inadequate medical backup. These casualties of six years of the Iraq-Iran war exceed those of all Arab-Israeli wars over the last forty years, inclusive of the 100,000 or so dead of the eleven-year Lebanese civil war; they are on a par with those of the Vietnamese war of national independence, which was, however, spread out over some twenty years. Several cities and many towns and villages have been destroyed, creating more refugees than were generated by the formation of the state of Israel.

The economic devastation caused by the fighting has attracted more

3. See the report from the Iraqi front line by D. Fairhall in *The Guardian*, October 29, 1980, entitled "Blitzkrieg Turns into Long Winter War." See also M. Woollacott in *The Guardian*, October 1, 1980.
4. The higher estimate is from D. Middleton's report in *New York Times*, September 23, 1985, and is based on estimates made in NATO capitals, which place Iranian dead at between 420,000 and 580,000, and Iraqi dead at 300,000. I have thrown in another 100,000 for the big battles since, particularly those of the Faw peninsula in February–March 1986. A report by L. Bushkoff places the "total casualty list" at 1.5 million; *Boston Sunday Globe*, September 22, 1985. All such "high" estimates are upward revisions of previously lower ones made by American sources in particular. It is entirely possible that the leaderships in Baghdad and Tehran will never know the human cost of their folly.

attention than its human cost. Billions of dollars in damage to fixed in-stallations, a monthly running cost of one billion dollars, "tanker wars," the prospect of decades of reconstruction in the future, and an all-consuming fascination with the vagaries of oil prices have created a cosy illusion of measurability. Maybe these are the numbers that contractors and foreign governments will benefit from at some point in the future. For them such preoccupations may in some sense be justified. But from the standpoint of the people doing all the fighting and the dying, "easy come and easy go" sums up a much healthier moral attitude to oil reve-nues, one common to many Iraqis. The opportunity cost of a barrel of oil has little to do with how people choose to live their lives, and this is a lesson that Iraqis and Iranians have learnt the hard way. Therefore, however awesome the destruction of physical assets, as consequences of the fighting they do not touch the heart of the "bigness" of this war.

Nonetheless, the Iraq-Iran war "floats" on the price of a barrel of oil in an important sense. Oil revenues make possible arms purchases, in-creasing the rate at which the combatants are able to kill each other. However, this is a relatively immobile war with the fighting largely con-fined to the border region. In such circumstances the numbers of people killed per unit of time has little impact on course or outcome of the war, other than at the limit where fresh supplies of bodies are no longer forthcoming, a limit reached by Germany in World War I.

Whole societies have been mobilized. Iraq is fielding over 1 million men, and every male under fifty-one was put on call in 1986. To supply such numbers under conditions where they do not forage for themselves is a major logistical problem involving a uniquely modern relationship between the armed forces and the community they are drawn from. Women are taking on economic and administrative functions on an un-precedented scale. In these conditions, the Iraqi economy still functions under an illusion of normality made possible because it was so cen-tralized in the first place. Long before the fighting started, strict controls were in place on imports, exports, distribution, consumption, and pro-duction. The fact is that for a long time the Ba'thist economy looked much the same in peace as it did in war, which probably signifies some-thing. Notwithstanding, the total social impact of war on Iraq should not be underestimated. During World War II, Britain took similar eco-nomic measures and lost in the end 400,000 people. In other words as-suming 300,000 Iraqi dead, the relative impact of this war on Iraq is already greater than World War II on countries like Britain, France

(600,000 dead), Italy (410,000), Czechoslovakia (415,000), and the Netherlands (210,000).[5]

But World War I is a more relevant comparison. The casualty rate in Britain, France, and Austria-Hungary was twice as high as in World War II. The dead were largely soldiers from the front, with few noncombatants. Immobility and a separation between the home front and the war front is a feature of World War I and the Iraq-Iran war (although to a more limited extent in the latter's case). Indiscriminate aerial bombardment of distant cities and civilian centres in the Iraq-Iran war was largely a psychological tactic in the first six years. Moreover, the conduct of the fighting bears an uncanny resemblance to World War I, a similarity aptly symbolized by the comeback of poison gas and the human wave strategy (not quite trench warfare, but close enough).

Fundamentally, however, the Iraq-Iran war, like World War I, is a first real war of the masses for the two countries engaged in it; it is about the mobilization of whole peoples, not merely the engagement of armies. Yet it is not a colonial war, nor an imperialist extension of some great power's zone of influence, or the offspring of machinations by insidious outsiders working through proxies of one sort or another. In sheer terms of scale, and mobilization of societal resources, the Iraq-Iran war is the first truly "great war" of the "Third" World. There has not been anything like it since the unfortunate idea of three worlds was first invented.

Moreover, there has not been anything like it in the long history of Iraqi-Iranian relations, just like there had been nothing like World War I in the history of Europe. That "Great War" lopped Europe off from its past in ways that Western civilization is still trying to understand. In a similar way the Iraq-Iran war is a modern war, launched by a highly organized bureaucratic state against one that underwent a revolution. Neither the aborted modernity of Iraq, nor the backward-looking revolution of Iran is explicable outside the history of what these countries became in the twentieth century, and why they turned out in this particular way. This is a momentous event that Iraqis and Iranians will eventually have to understand on the basis of the *new* polities they cre-

---

5. Total European dead in World War II was 30 million, but more than half was taken up by the Soviet Union alone. All figures are from Gordon Wright, *The Ordeal of Total War: 1939–1945* (New York: Harper, 1968), 263–64. Wright's exemplary focus on the whole societal involvement in the war effort is brought out in chap. 11, "The Impact of Total War." From the standpoint of Wright's criteria in this chapter, the Iran-Iraq war is a "total war," however different it may be in every other respect.

ated in a postcolonial and largely postimperial world. However much we may not like the regimes that have given us all this slaughter, the beginning of wisdom is the realization that, however unsavory, these are genuine offspring of our own societies and political traditions, not as these have evolved since time immemorial, but *in* the modern era. Like World War I for the masses that engaged in it, this war will cut deep into the modern consciousness of future generations of Iraqis and Iranians; it will shape their beliefs, attitudes, prejudices, and values for many many years to come.

The Problem of Cause

What caused the war? Three serious and yet finally unconvincing arguments have been widely circulated: they involve ethnic or racial hate; Shiʿi unrest in Iraq; and territory.[6]

1. Deep historically grounded feelings of enmity between the peoples of Iraq and Iran underlie the outbreak of war, even if they do not account for its timing. "Persian hatred of the Arabs . . . is so deeply embedded in the Iranian psyche," wrote Jasim Abdulghani, "that the Persians have forgotten almost all the various invasions except that of the Arabs."[7] This idea of enmity is deemed to originate in ethnic (Arab versus Persian) or racial (Aryan versus Semite) divisions. This view is very common on the Iraqi side, and it sometimes appears in journalistic accounts as a contributing "cause."[8]

The best evidence for it comes from the participants themselves. For example, initial Iranian reactions to the invasion made reference to

6. I dismiss as unserious the opinions widely held in the Middle East and propagated at one time or another by both protagonists, that either a "Persian-Israeli-American" plot was hatched in Tehran, or an "Iraqi-Israeli-American" plot was hatched in Baghdad. On such "causes," see David Hirst's report from Beirut in *The Guardian*, October 22, 1980, and Martin Woollacott's broader coverage on October 11 dealing with the attitudes of the Arab middle classes towards the war. See also the article by Richard W. Bulliet, "Time, Perceptions and Conflict Resolution," in *The Iran-Iraq War: New Weapons, Old Conflicts*, ed. Shirin Tahir-Kheli and Shaheen Ayubi (New York: Praeger, 1983).

7. Jasim M. Abdulghani, *Iraq and Iran: The Years of Crisis* (Baltimore: Johns Hopkins University Press, 1984), 2.

8. See for instance the book by Hasan Muhammad Tawalbeh, *Munaqashah fi al-Nizaʿ al-ʿIraqi al-ʾIrani* (Beirut, 1984), 60–61. Also see P. Hunseler, "The Historical Antecedents of the Shatt Al-Arab Dispute," and M. al-Najjar and N. Safwat, "Arab Sovereignty over the Shatt al-Arab During the Kaʿbide Period," both in *The Iraq-Iran War*, ed. M. S. Al-Azhary (London: Croom Helm, 1984). Daniel Pipes in his article, "A Border Adrift: Origins of the Conflict," in *New Weapons, Old Conflicts*, cites other examples; see pp. 4–8.

"backstabbing Arabs," and leaflets destined for the front got adorned with ancient poems denigrating the "uncouth Arab," who "drinks camel milk and devours alligator flesh." Never to be outdone in matters of this sort, the Baʿth talk and write about "barbarians," "fire-worshippers," and always "racist Persians." Saddam Husain has called for the "destruction of the Magus [a derogatory name for Zoroastrians]." The rule in Baʿthist propaganda is never to refer to Iranians, only Persians, who have historically always sought to extend their empire over other oppressed nations.[9]

Persian chauvinism towards Arabs is long-standing but overwhelmingly cultural in implication. When a Tehrani casually remarks that "the dogs of Isphahan drink ice-water, while the Arabs of the desert eat locusts," he has in mind a civilizational superiority with no overt political implication. Such attitudes persist among virtually all social classes of Farsi speakers and are applied with equal if not greater venom to all the other national minorities in Iran.

By contrast, in 1979 the clerics put considerable effort into "de-Persianizing" and "re-Islamicizing" Iran. Much of Khomeini's new jargon consists of Arabic words unknown to most Iranians before the fall of the Shah. Arabic replaced Western languages in the schools; the term "Sayyid" started to crop up in people's names; and the crescent replaced the ancient Persian emblem of the lion and the sun. Changes with an Arabic bent probably became more circumspect after September 22, 1980. Even when Khomeini "slipped up" with a reference to "backstabbing Arabs," or whenever he makes another one of his repeated calls for mass mobilizations against the army of Yazid (Saddam Husain), this imagery originates in sectarian Islamic historical themes (Shiʿi versus Sunni), and not Iranian racism or chauvinism. Khomeini was thinking of the Arabs in early Islam who called upon Husain the son of ʿAli to come and rule in Iraq, and then "sold him out" to the armies of Yazid, the son of Muʿawiyya who was himself a "usurper." Under the circumstances, this sectarian imagery stimulates Persian chauvinism. But the conclusion would still be that Persian racism, or Aryanism, played no role in the causation of the war, and only got deployed once the war started.

Baʿthi racism also has cultural roots, albeit weaker ones. The ʿajam are an inferior race of Muslims with an infirm hold on Islam. Princi-

9. The racist language that erupted at the start of the conflict was covered by Amir Taheri in a report in the *International Herald Tribune*, October 10, 1980. Bulliet, "Time," in *New Weapons, Old Conflicts*, gives other examples as part of an analysis concerned with evolving definitions and images of the conflict as held by the combatants.

pally, however, Ba'thi racism starts in the ideological-political realm through the production of tracts like Khairallah Tulfah's, *Three Whom God Should Not Have Created: Persians, Jews and Flies,* and the formidable efforts of policemen like Barak.[10] Ba'thism had to labour hard to inculcate among Iraqi Shi'is sentiments towards their coreligionists in Iran that were not given culturally or historically. In no other country were Arabs and Iranians so deeply intermingled. Persian "Aryanism" and Arab "Semitism" are of course myths with a toehold on reality located somewhere in the origins of languages, not peoples. Such elementary truths are validated by the reinvention in the modern era of the concept of *shu'ubism,* and the peculiarly pan-Arabist fascination with the idea of "the enemy from within." No doubt the usual dose of frictions can be found between Farsi and Arabic speakers whenever they lived together. But the very fact that these were not given politically, and had to be so vigorously ideologized, excludes them from being a cause of this war.

By the same token, this war, like all wars, bolsters the demonization of each side by the other. Today Khomeiniism is digging deep into Persian chauvinism while the Ba'th cultivate their racism. Once the bodies began piling up, both protagonists were able to dig where once they could only scratch, and then only if they were so inclined.

"History" has very little to say about this war other than to recall the greatest battle ever fought between Arabs and Persians on the plains of Qadisiyyah in southern Iraq (A.D. 636). This event produces intensely emotive imagery in Iraq where the war was officially called *Qadisiyyat Saddam.* The irony is, however, that the battle of Qadisiyya only succeeded in overthrowing the Sassanian empire because of how rotted through it had become, and historians are agreed that the Arabs won because Iranians abandoned their army in droves to join the Islamic advance. Moreover, Iraq was inside the Sassanian empire at the time (the ruins of its capital, Ctesiphon, are in the geographical center of modern Iraq). So this kind of history is made up of a heap of ironies and is not the "cause" of anything; it merely confirms, albeit negatively, how "modern" Iraqis and Iranians have become.

2. Once Iraq was put on the defensive, it became common to allege that Shi'i unrest inside Iraq, fomented by Iran, compelled the Ba'th to take defensive action to forestall the export of the Iranian revolution. The Ba'th had claimed right from the start that Iranian aggression took

---

10. See Chapter 1; also see the discussion in Chapter 6 on *shu'ubiyya.*

the form of 187 border incidents prior to September 22 but never provided a detailed account. By the mid-1980s, a new twist was introduced in the shape of claims by some Iraqi spokesmen that conditions of near civil war had prevailed inside Iraq in 1980. Analysts more attuned to the fixity of facts pointed instead to a few bombing incidents and the attempt in April 1980 on the life of Tariq ʿAziz, the deputy-premier. Such analysts do not deny the stability of the regime but contend, rather, that the 1979 Iranian revolution and Khomeini's intransigence created a psychological atmosphere that convinced the Baʿthi leadership that resolute defensive action was needed before it was too late.[11]

Notwithstanding Baʿthi paranoia, the view is untenable for various reasons. First, by the late 1970s the Baʿthi state was wealthier and stronger than any state has ever been in the modern history of Iraq, and it had crushed all organized opposition. Second, growing Shiʿi sectarianism inside Iraq was not principally a product of the 1979 revolution, even if this helped to foster it; sectarianism in the social and personal domain was produced by Baʿthism. Third, unlike Iran, this sectarianism was not overtly, or in the first place, political but reflected growing social and cultural antipathy between Sunnis and Shiʿis. Fourth, the relatively new Shiʿi political organizations (like *al-Daʿwah*), which probably received Iranian backing, were small and largely crushed *before* the outbreak of war.[12]

But if Shiʿi unrest was so pronounced, why go to war at all? The Baʿth did not declare war on Iran when the Kurds rebelled, and with the Shah's support. Instead, they took the initiative in negotiating the 1975 Algiers border accords. Also why launch the war from the overwhelmingly Shiʿi provinces of southern Iraq? And why attack with demands like the liberation of the whole province of "Arabistan," and the return to Arab sovereignty of three islands off the coast of the United Arab Emirates seized by the Shah in 1971? Baʿthi demands in September 1980 were tailored for rejection. Moreover, despite the great reversal of this war in 1982, Iraq's largely Shiʿite soldiery remained willing to fight. How could a regime lacking in authority survive its gross miscalculation apparently as strong as ever, and despite having cost its unwilling subjects untold misery and hardship? This is the most important question of this war from the Iraqi point of view. The mere fact that the question can be asked, however, demolishes the theory that Shiʿi unrest inside Iraq "caused" the Baʿth to go to war.

11. This is the theme of M. S. Al-Azhary's introduction to his book, *The Iraq-Iran War*.
12. See "Building Defences" in Chapter 3, "The Leader Syndrome" in Chapter 4, and "The End of Politics" in Chapter 7.

3. "The war resulted primarily from territorial disputes, especially the centuries-old conflict over the boundary at the Shatt al-Arab River."[13] Like so many other "causes," this view originates in Ba'thi justifications. Yet all the initial territorial justifications became negotiable once the Iraqi army was thrown out of Iran just as they were in 1975 when Saddam Husain initiated the Algiers accords with the Shah. The Ba'th were willing to leave the question of who was the real aggressor to international arbitration. Hints at reparations were made, and the Ba'th prepared to return to the prewar status quo unconditionally, thus frankly undermining the purposefulness of their original action. All of this flexibility improved Iraq's credibility, placing it in the position of the aggrieved party. Even Iranian anticlericalists, oppositionists without Ba'thist sympathies, react to their own regime's continuation of this war by conceding some legitimacy to the original Ba'thist territorial demands.

Obfuscation, deliberate or otherwise, surrounds this question of territory as a cause of the conflict. In the multitude of "evidence," political motivation is not easy to detect. Moreover, the practice of listing all issues in a shopping list of causes is a convenient substitute for the task of thinking them through.[14] Territory lends itself to this kind of abuse, particularly among Western writers inclined to favor Iraq in the war. Of the "causes" discussed so far, it is the most commonly held and yet in some ways the least convincing. Invariably, among proponents of the view, two separate questions get lumped together. The first, whether there is a territorial issue requiring resolution, I do not deal with. But if the answer to this question is affirmative, a second question arises: Was this issue in any way a "cause" for the war?

The most detailed exposition of the territorial argument appears in Tareq Ismael's *Iraq and Iran: Roots of Conflict,* an effort to justify the original Iraqi action by grounding it in a historically sound and legally ironclad territorial claim. At the same time it reinforces the claim that what exacerbated the conflict ideologically was the diametric opposition of nationally constrained secularism (by implication modernist and forward-looking) and messianic religious expansionism.

Ismael begins with the first peace treaty between the Ottomans and the Safavid empire in 1555, which was soon followed by a succession of

13. From Pipes, "A Border Adrift," in *New Weapons, Old Conflicts,* 4.
14. Examples of this are legion. William O. Staudenmaier finds "general precipitants" of conflict in culture, history, and Shi'ism versus Sunniism. "Specific precipitants" include Iran's attempt to export its revolution and Saddam's ambitions. Finally a "suitable spark" was at hand in the "smoldering Shatt al-Arab dispute." See his article "A Strategy Analysis" in Tahir-Kheli and Ayubi, *New Weapons, Old Conflicts,* 28. McLachlan and Joffe, *The Gulf War,* 36–37 lists five causes in "descending order of importance." And so on.

wars and other treaties culminating in the first "significant" 1639 treaty of Zuhab established by Sultan Murad IV who "drove the Persians out of Iraq."[15] Typically in all nationalist accounts conflicts between empires slip into such references to peoples. Anachronisms like this sustain the argument.[16] (Ironically they get caught by Western advocates of the same thesis. Daniel Pipes, for example, argued for territory as a cause, after criticizing the general Persian-Arab hostility thesis. But what can possibly link a Safavid-Ottoman border treaty in 1639 with Saddam Husain and Khomeini in 1980, other than some sort of "centuries-old" conflict between peoples?) With the Zuhab treaty, "the framework of future contentions over borders" was established.[17] Passing through other conflicts over "Arabistan," the author finally arrives at the first watershed treaty of Erzerum in 1823, which was to be the last boundary convention between indigenous powers, because "new [imperial] powers with different interests" were imposing themselves, and we all know how they handle border questions.

This momentous event in Arab-Iranian relations, which hardly anyone was aware of before the war started, is visually depicted with the first of six detailed maps showing that Muhammara (since called Khorramshahr) and Abadan were on the Iraqi side and the border followed the Bamshir River further east, establishing the whole of the Shatt al-Arab area as well as a small chunk of uninhabitable marshland between it and the Bamshir River as unequivocally Iraqi (even though Iraq was still a century away from existence). Ismael's sources that gave rise to this map are not shared with his readers, which is unfortunate, it being common knowledge that treaties between empires in this part of the world defined boundaries by the very blurred outlines of tribal space. Moreover, the tiniest of peeks into Iranian archives might just have revealed piles of similar cartographic adventures, with different results. In any case, the territory the professor assigned to Iraq according to the 1823 treaty represents less than 1 percent of the gross area of the province of Khuzistan (Arabistan), the whole of which was claimed by the Ba'th in 1980.

15. Tareq Y. Ismael, *Iraq and Iran: Roots of Conflict* (Syracuse: Syracuse University Press, 1982), 2.
16. An amusing case of this is the previously cited article by Najjar and Safwat on "Arab Sovereignty over the Shatt al-Arab during the Ka'bide Period." Pan-Arabist categories are deployed to give an account of tribal disputes four centuries ago. The authors describe how tribal allegiances swung backwards and forwards between the Ottomans and the Safavids while they remain blissfully unaware that any sort of a problem exists between their jargon and the facts that they themselves deploy.
17. Ismael, *Roots of Conflict*, 2.

Arabistan's boundaries have always been nebulous. Arabistan, or "the Ahwaz region," are terms the Baʿth use to designate something that includes the city of Ahwaz, but may or may not include the whole of the province that Iranians now call Khuzistan. If Arabistan is going to be defined by the presence of an Arab majority (which would be consistent with Baʿthi ideology), then the very unwelcome reception the Iraqi army got from those Arabs raises more problems. Moreover, by such criteria parts of southern Iraq, including Najaf and Kerbala, might be open to Iranian claims which would be reinforced by yet other justifications invented by the Baʿth to deport Shiʿi "fifth columnists."

Map two sets out another agreed boundary in 1847, but this one reflects "the commonality of imperialist interests with respect to stabilizing zones of influence."[18] It tosses Muhammara, Abadan, the Bamshir River, and the marshlands in between back to Iran, leaving the entire width of the Shatt to Iraq. Both sides reject this treaty today for the same reason, which does not dispose of it because Iraq's formal position is that while it is perfectly entitled to reject a treaty signed by the Ottoman empire—a party other than itself—independent Iran signed the treaty. The Iranian counterclaim carries the debate onto an even more elevated plateau; it appears that its representative, Mirza Mohammed ʿAli Khan, had not been authorized in 1847 to sign on its behalf. The "origins" of the conflict go on in this vein—with 180 pages of treaties, legal documents, explanatory notes, statements, and speeches appended to the text—until finally the author arrives at map six, which sets out an incontrovertible boundary lodged with the United Nations, and based on the March 6, 1975, Algiers agreement.

In 1975 Iraq formally conceded to an Iranian demand (first made in 1932) that the border be adjusted according to the *thalweg* principle, which translates into its running along the midpoint of the river's navigational channel. In return for this confirmation of shared sovereignty over a boundary river, the Shah would cease supporting Kurdish rebels in the north and both sides would respect each other's borders, putting an end to all violations. A few days before the September 1980 invasion, Iraq abrogated the treaty, and in summary form its formal posture on the outbreak of the war was as follows:

Iran had already abrogated the Algiers Agreement through 187 border violations, all of which had allegedly taken place in the four-month period preceding the war (any violation, Iraq claimed, nullified the entire

18. Ibid., 6.

document).[19] Numerous statements by Iranian leaders also proved their intent to "export" the Islamic revolution. It followed, once the treaty was abrogated, that the Shatt al-Arab waterway had to revert back to Iraqi sovereignty according to all previous agreements. All naval craft along the Shatt were henceforth to fly the Iraqi flag, and navigation fees should be paid to Iraq. In addition, the region of Ahwaz, or "Arabistan" had been wrongfully ceded in the second Treaty of Erzerum of 1847; its inhabitants were overwhelmingly Arab and their ancestry could be traced back to the Islamic conquest of Iran. Finally, the three uninhabited islands in the straits of Hormuz occupied by the Shah in 1971 should be returned to Arab sovereignty.

The Iraq-Iran war was not "sparked" by a unilateral Iranian action to grab territory. Therefore, if territory were at issue, it had to be a "cause" in the fundamental underlying sense that is, for instance, at the heart of the Arab-Israeli conflict. This is certainly the logic of the argument of Ismael, Pipes, and many others. But wars can be "caused" by trivial, even absurd reasons. Malvinas is a piece of rock inhabited largely by penguins and a few stalwart Britons left over from the days of empire. Yet many Argentines and Britons thought Malvinas worth having a war about. But did the Baʿth go to war over these territorial demands, however absurd and trivial they appear? In their own minds, was it chunks of territory and symbols of sovereignty they were after?

From the standpoint of the intrinsic merit of their claims as a "cause" of war, the largest (for Arabistan) was tailored for rejection and patently "ideological" as we have seen. (What the Baʿth would have done with "Arabistan" is anyone's guess; certainly they would not have hesitated in annexing the oil-rich province.) Similarly, the three-islands issue in the straits of Hormuz was conceived by the United Arab Emirates itself as an issue involving only it and Iran. The Baʿth had backed down on this one publicly in 1975. Hence, the decision to put the two claims forward in 1980 had to have been taken after the decision to go for a "total war" with Iran. Such demands are a barely concealed foil for plans to topple the Khomeini regime and bring about the breakup of Iran. Nor would they have considered the restoration of the monarchy. The thrust was wholly destructive, directed at the integrity of Iran, with as many of the pieces gathered into Baʿthist hands as possible. From a Baʿthist standpoint, such a real intent was by no means cynically "concealed" by the apparent self-righteousness of their territorial claim; it went hand in

19. Ibid., 27.

glove with a fervent and genuine ideological espousal of the latter. However, they still had to establish the "reality" of all their reasons before
fully and unambiguously proclaiming them as such—even the Ba'th
could understand the wisdom of such caution. Hence what they chose
to say the war was all about was truly plucked out of the thin air of
other people's credulity.

There remains the issue of sovereignty over Shatt al-Arab. Leaving
aside the formalities of the Algiers accords, it rankled the Ba'th to have
been forced to give this up in 1975. The Ba'th wanted to settle scores on
this one and felt the time was ripe. Granted that this might have been a
genuine motive for abrogating the 1975 treaty, and reclaiming title to
the whole Shatt, what was the point of the invasion on September 22?
Iraq had taken back by unilateral action on September 10 the only strips
of territory it still claimed under the treaty. There was no longer any
"territory" as such on the other side to conquer. The Ba'th had already
followed the Shah's example of 1971 when he unilaterally took over the
three islands in the Gulf. Under these circumstances, the whole thing
boiled down to whether Iranian vessels were prepared to fly the Iraqi
flag and pay navigation fees for a stretch of a few miles. But even for this
it was not necessary to invade because both before and after 1975 the
two sides could have packed their respective shores with artillery, and
pounded into oblivion anything with an inclination to float.

Qadisiyyat Saddam

Nothing in the self-proclaimed reasons for going to war explains
Ba'thi actions. Individually no claim was important enough, and as a
group they lose focus and dissolve into the sorts of disputes that many
neighbouring states have with one another. The name of the war is a
better clue to its "cause."

Qadisiyyat Saddam captures a mood that prevailed in Ba'thist circles
at the start of the fighting, a mood that had nothing to do with rancour
over possessions, competition for economic assets, greed for territory,
or alleged Iranian intentions. The regime was brimming over with self-
confidence and a sense of its own achievements; it was armed to the
teeth and capable of those great things that were given to it by "history"
and everything that the pan-Arabism of the Ba'th stood for. The time
was ripe for the Ba'th to take externally the kind of decisive action they
had already taken internally, to signify to the outside the rising preeminence of Iraqi Ba'thism in regional and Arab affairs. Ba'thist motives

were singularly political, derivative ultimately from deeply held ideological tenets to which they had given ample proof of their commitment. Of
course, economic, material, and strategic benefits (the oil-rich province
of Khuzistan, territory, and better access to the Gulf) would accrue
from victory, even if circumstances forced it to be a partial one. But
these considerations come afterwards, as a consequence of the extension
of Ba'thist power the imperative for which originated elsewhere. In
1980 exuberance was fused into the leadership of Saddam Husain, who
is the acknowledged architect of every move on the Iraqi side of this
war. There is a sense in which this is too obvious for the experts. If
pressed, no reasonable person would deny the obvious—that Saddam
Husain must have taken the irrevocable decision to launch a total war.
Nonetheless, the significance of the fact is frequently brushed aside.[20]

Saddam Husain exercised a very special kind of power. He had become an institution unto himself, one virtually without checks. His
leadership was related to the sentiments of the broad mass of Iraqis in a
complicated and yet resilient way as proven by the later course of the
war once the initial self-confidence had ebbed away. He presided over a
regime that had gradually, but nonetheless inexorably, changed all the
parameters affecting societal and state-organized violence. Eventually
expansion of the means of violence—army, police, security apparatuses,
networks of informers, party militia, party and state bureaucracies—
underwent the classic inversion: from being a means to an end, the
elimination of opponents and exercise of raw power, they became horrific ends in themselves, spilling mindlessly across the borders that had
once contained them. War, any war, it does not matter against whom, is
a not unlikely outcome of the unbridled growth of the means of violence, particularly when it is so structured as to compromise literally
masses of people in its terror. In this general "evolutionary" sense the
personality of Saddam Husain meshes in with a whole political system
that evolved such that someone like him needed to be created to act out
its imperative.

The absolutism of Saddam Husain's authority makes his person unusually important in this war. The absence of real *pressures* from within
Iraqi society, from Iran, from the world at large, or even from his own
party leaves those of us who would write about the "cause" of this war

---

20. Pipes, "A Border Adrift," does this, for example, in his only reference to Saddam's
role: "Assuming Saddam Hussein is not one to act rashly or foolishly—even critics acknowledge his pragmatism—one must conclude that he had serious reasons for making
war in September 1980." See Tahir-Kheli and Ayubi, *New Weapons, Old Conflicts*, 4.

with nothing to evaluate "objectively" and argue about. To substitute invented rationalizations for this state of affairs invariably plays into the hands of one or another side in a conflict that fortunately few people believe has a surplus of redeeming features. I think the whole question of how this war began resolves itself into what was passing through Saddam Husain's mind. Even though all judgements in politics "resolve" themselves inside the minds of the actors involved, the contention is that Saddam Husain's decision to wage war had an independent meaning to it because it was so fundamentally gratuitous. This attribute of the decision arose "historically," from the general evolution of Baʿthism as concretely manifested in the Baʿthist polity in Iraq. The point of this book as far as the Iraq-Iran war is concerned is to have described the conditions that went into making Saddam Husain's decision so gratuitous. However, the content of the decision, as opposed to its gratuitous form, was the action of the only genuinely free man in Iraq. There is no historical determinism arising from Baʿthist ideology or the nature of the Baʿthist regime that "propelled" Saddam Husain into making this particular decision and not any other.

A reason why determinism of this type is such nonsense is concerned with the problem of responsibility. The only political way of talking about the "cause" of any freely chosen action is in relation to pinpointing who is responsible for what. All other uses of the word "cause" can safely be left in the hands of experts when they debate each other after the important events have come to an end. Sooner or later Iraqis and Iranians will start asking themselves who was responsible for starting it all, and who kept the killing going. The important sense in which Saddam Husain "caused" and is responsible for the former is immediately clarified by the obvious fact that, notwithstanding his ongoing personal management of the Iraqi side of the fighting, he cannot be held responsible for the latter.

But, fortunately or otherwise, Saddam Husain chose to start a war for reasons that no analyst will ever be able to "prove." One can, for instance, argue with conviction that Iraqi Shiʿism did not represent a real threat inside Iraq; but no one can be half as convincing about the argument that Saddam Husain "thought" Shiʿism was or could become such a real threat, and launched a preemptive war to forestall the development. By the late 1970s such an argument was implausible. In its place I invite the reader onto a different journey into Saddam Husain's mind. Why did he follow up the 1979 purge with total war?

Imagine the scene that might have been in the summer of 1982, the scheduled date of the nonaligned nations conference in Baghdad. Keep in mind the face-lift that the capital city had begun undergoing once that venue was decided upon in the late 1970s. Hitherto neglected in favour of military expenditure, social control, infrastructural development, and petrochemical complexes, Baghdad was turned overnight into a giant urban construction site: road improvements, parks, new buildings, a crash subway system program, and massive redevelopment of urban areas. Contractors and consultants poured in from all over the world. Special legislation was promulgated removing all controls on selected projects of symbolic significance. The Baʿth were dressing up their power in elegant finery, and so they turned with a vengeance in the same direction they had once scorned when it was pursued to the exclusion of everything else by the Gulf countries. Consider the implications of a victorious Saddam Husain, recently host of the anti–Camp David Arab summit, receiving in this new Baghdad the mantle of Third World leadership from Fidel Castro (with echoes of Nasser and Tito reverberating in the background), disposing of "Arab" territory as the spoils of a fragmenting Iran, and master of the Gulf.

Here are dreams that can reasonably be inferred as having passed through his mind as he weighed up his options. They allowed the notoriously "cautious" Saddam Husain to translate well-founded self-confidence into megalomania. A demonstrably successful projection of Baʿthist power, no matter how slight, would have catapulted Saddam personally, and the Baʿthist movement generally, far beyond even Nasser's regional status during the peak of his popularity in the wake of Suez. Of course, Nasser's charisma, unlike Saddam's, derived from internal Egyptian accomplishments and took the form of a voluntary embrace by masses from all over the Arab world. Among them was the young Saddam Husain, who entered politics as a young teenager on the strength of that formative event. However, whereas Nasser in 1956 emerged in the wake of an invasion of Egyptian territory, after snatching a political victory from the jaws of military defeat, his alter ego Saddam Husain strode the pinnacles of absolute Leadership before he chose to set out and "make" his own Suez—not by standing up to imperialist powers and Zionist aggression, but by taking the initiative to launch an aggression that would achieve all this and more by breaking the spell of the 1979 Islamic revolution. Had the gamble succeeded, Saddam might have had all that Nasser obtained from 1956; in addition, a new fear and insecurity would arise from the certainty that he would lash out again sooner or later.

The distance between 1956 and 1980 is the distance separating one era's colonial expansionist wars from this new phenomenon that Saddam Husain inaugurated—the first completely indigenous "great war" of the Third World. For Saddamism is as important to Iraqi politics as Khomeiniism is to Iranian politics; it is a phenomenon rooted in violence, in the manipulation of the tools and means of violence to achieve expressly political ends. Saddamism is not plain thuggery, as many wrongly think; this is no Papa Doc or Idi Amin on the rampage. Saddamism is too political for that.

To understand the phenomenon of Saddam Husain in relation to "his" citizens, one must look beyond personal motivations into the broader societal preconditions and genuine authority that made it possible for a man like this to act out his dreams. For Iraqis the war raises a number of agonizing questions. Why has Saddam Husain, and the Baʿthist regime in general, not fallen despite the great reversal of this war in 1981 and 1982? Why has Iraq's largely Shiʿite soldiery not defected, and why have the Iraqi people as a whole remained willing to fight? How does a regime that so miscalculated in its original aggression and that has cost its population such misery and hardship, aside from forfeiting the future for generations to come, continue to survive apparently as stable as ever? Even if the regime were to fall tomorrow, these questions would remain valid for there is no turning back from the responsibility of this war and all its dead.

"The intimate connection between war and citizenship lies at the heart of the modern state," Fouad ʿAjami wrote of the 1967 defeat. War is always the acid test of legitimacy in a political order. The six-day war "revealed the failure of the Arab states to train and create modern citizens, to inculcate men with the will to fight and die for the state."[21] Granted that this sort of citizenry has not yet arisen in any Arab country, why has the "intimate connection between war and citizenship" taken such an original form in the Iraq-Iran war? Masses of Iraqis keep on dying for no palpably tangible reason that they can so much as identify to themselves, far less anyone else. Why?

In Iraq, the public has lost all sense of self; it exists only in the form artificially imparted to it by "its" regime. This was an outcome of statification, party growth, and all the other indices that have been discussed.[22]

21. Fouad ʿAjami, *The Arab Predicament: Arab Political Thought and Practice Since 1967* (Cambridge: Cambridge University Press, 1982), 32–33.
22. See "Numbers of Armed Men" and "Party and State" in Chapter 1. On the organization of masses, see Chapter 3.

The dissolution of Iraqi identity is the most fundamental explanation for why no connection existed in Baʿthist Iraq between military achievements and extending or withholding political allegiance. The Iraqi public's allegiance in the first years of the war was with the regime whatever it said, and not based on its stated objectives for the war or its performance on the battlefield. Before 1975 one would have been very hard put to find anyone inside Iraq who actually believed there was a "territorial" dispute with Iran. Certainly at the time of the 1975 accords most people were taken aback by the regime's volte-face. But this had nothing to do with Shatt al-Arab; it was for the most part directed at the dramatic overnight change in "line" towards the Shah's regime, and the three-islands issue in particular, which had been the subject of very intensive anti-Iranian campaigns for many years. The impression existed that the Baʿth had conceded something substantial in 1975, but it was more a question of loss of face and this irked no one more than the man who had brought it about: Saddam Husain.

In 1980 the situation changed suddenly, but only for a short while. The overwhelming initial enthusiasm for the war latched onto objects to venerate. People felt grievances they never knew they had before. But these, like the spies in the 1969 show trials, were momentary caricatures of broader societal presentiments that originated in the bond with Baʿthism, now crystallized in a new relationship to the person of Saddam Husain. Gradually this fixation waxed and waned with the presence of Iraqi troops on Iranian territory, and with the shifting sands of the formal Iraqi position on the war. The idea of "Saddam's crusade" stayed on, however, which attests to this union of Saddam Husain and his public and highlights the schism that existed between its stated aims and its original motivating dynamic.

Fear is the cement that holds together this strange body politic in Iraq. All forms of organization not directly controlled by the party have been wiped out. The public is atomized and broken up, which is why it can be made to believe anything. A society that used to revel in politics is not only subdued and silent, but profoundly apolitical. Fear is the agency of that transformation; the kind of fear that comes not only from what the neighbours might say, but that makes people careful of what they say in front of their children. This fear has become a part of the psychological constitution of citizenship. Fashioned out of Iraqi raw material, this fear is ironically the mainstay of the country's national self-assertiveness in the modern era. The violence that remained buried as a potential in the subconscious culture of society's groups surfaced, as this new kind of fear drove through all private space that once existed on the peripheries of families, boundaries of communities, or by virtue of status or class origin. The result was a true regime of terror whose deepest roots lay in the growing fear that people now had of each other.

These features of Iraqi society under the Ba'th shed some insight into what is after all the ultimate act of degradation, the final human catastrophe, a society held together because it cannot find light in the overthrow of those who plunged it into darkness. People's most primitive instincts of self-preservation warn them that a rout by Iranian forces would still result in a measure of Ba'thist victory snatched from the jaws of their own deaths in the form of the all-encompassing emptiness they would leave behind, an emptiness that could only result in untold paroxysms of slaughter. This hidden potential for even more violence inside Iraq could at some point in the future make the Lebanese civil war look like a family outing gone slightly sour. Nothing else explains the improved performance of the Iraqi army once the tide of war had decisively turned in favour of the Shi'ite clerics. The view that the pan-Arabism of the Ba'th inculcated a genuine Iraqi nationalism that has held the Iraqi army and polity together is flatly contradicted by the growth of confessionalism, family loyalties, ethnic hatred, and religious sectarianism in Iraqi society—which Ba'thism simultaneously inculcated and kept at bay, thus saving people from what they had become. In the face of this new Third-World style of barbarism, that much maligned simple Egyptian peasant-soldier who was able in 1967 to cast away his weapons on the Sinai desert and run away from it all is, to my way of seeing things, a paragon of virtue.

The Conduct of the War

By projecting itself beyond the confines of its own borders, Ba'thism exposed itself to a new kind of scrutiny, which highlighted the specificities of the regime. Initial Iraqi military strategy was determined by Saddam Husain and rigidly controlled from the top right through to the details. On occasion not even front-line commanders could explain their actions.[23] Military analysts were baffled at the conduct of the Iraqi armed forces—their timid use of overwhelming superiority in air power

---

23. For instance, see the on-the-spot report by John Kifner on the commander whose troops were engaged in building a highway across the desert outside Ahwaz. When pressed by journalists, he simply didn't know why he was doing this, and finally blurted out: "We are following the plan of the political leadership." *International Herald Tribune,* October 22, 1980.

and a marked unwillingness to commit infantry in situations where nothing else would do the job. One analyst concluded that the "primary reason Iran was not defeated at the outset of the war . . . lay in the inept strategy and tactics of the Iraqis, rather than the surprisingly fierce response of the individual Iranian soldier." [24]

Although this conclusion need not be shared, all experts who have reflected on Iraqi actions on the field find them strange. The initial three-pronged attack involving a big push into Khuzistan, a blocking move around the Mehran area, and the capture of Qasr Shirin in the north to counter any Iranian capability of moving onto Baghdad was militarily sound. The problem was in the thinking behind the main thrust into Khuzistan. The Iraqi army neither went for the cities, nor avoided urban areas with the idea of striking deep enough into Khuzistan in a classic World War II tactic to flush the Iranian army into the open. Instead they went for city encirclement, thinking that surrender would ensue from artillery bombardment supplemented by air attack. Even on a tactical level, the mobile heavy armour (in which Iraq had the edge) was not used by its armed forces to punch through defensive positions, or skirt around tenaciously defended obstacles (like cities). Sophisticated tanks were used as mere artillery, occasionally even buried in the sand for camouflage or protection; or else the Baʿth chose to use their armoured superiority in grossly inefficient ways, seemingly for the sole purpose of avoiding direct infantry combat. [25]

The common answer provided to explain Iraqi strategy on the taking of cities and their unusual way of deploying heavy armour is their supposed preoccupation with keeping casualties low. Iraq has after all one-third of the population reserves of Iran. In their first tactical success, the capture of Khorramshahr, for example, "the casualty rate . . . seems to have persuaded the Iraqi high command to lay siege to Abadan rather than attempt to capture it by house-to-house fighting." [26] But Abadan held out, and was used a year later as the springboard for the Iranian series of counteroffensives, which led to one Iraqi retreat after another. And so, a seven- to fourteen-day "blitzkrieg" turned into an endless "sitzkrieg":

24. William O. Staudenmaier, "Military Policy and Strategy in the Gulf War," *Parameters*, Journal of the US Army War College, 12, no. 2, p. 28.
25. In a major battle in 1985, the Iraqis used two full armoured divisions to crush an Iranian force that turned out to number 1,500 men. They took heavy losses because typically Iranian infantrymen would jump into foxholes and fire their RPG-7s at close range into oncoming tanks. See the report by John Kifner, in *New York Times*, February 28, 1986.
26. Staudenmaier, "The Gulf War," 29.

The Iranian front lines tend to be scenes of chaos and dedication, with turbaned mullahs, rifles slung on their backs, rushing about on brightly colored motorcycles encouraging the troops. Religious slogans are posted everywhere, and sometimes reinforcements arrive cheerfully carrying their own coffins as a sign of their willingness to be "martyred." There is little sign of military activity behind the combat area itself.

In Iraq, by contrast, the military zone extends for dozens of orderly miles of defenses behind the front with tanks and artillery dug into the dirt along the roadside, elaborate World War I–style bunkers and trenches, and dump trucks excavating grid-pattern defences.[27]

To think that Saddam Husain was so intent on avoiding casualties is naive. Why would a regime that had the loyalty of its public minimize face-to-face infantry contact by every strategem imaginable—indiscriminate bombing, heavy-artillery warfare, poison gas, vast defensive earthworks and artificial lakes, and mile upon mile of fall-back defences?[28]

The answer is not difficult to appreciate if one approaches the problem in a political rather than a military way. If fear is the cement that holds the Iraqi body politic and its soldiery together—not patriotism or Baʿthism as a positively embraced doctrine of some sort—then it follows that society as a whole is very vulnerable should that bond be loosened in any way. War creates unique conditions for the rise of an even greater fear of the enemy. For the Baʿth this poses more of an immediate threat to those bonds than a localized setback. If Iraqi soldiers become more afraid of the enemy in front than they are of the regime at their back, they will do what every other rational human being would do in their place: break ranks and run. This is what happened in every major Iraqi retreat of this war. It explains why there are at least three times as many Iraqi prisoners of war as Iranian, notwithstanding the completely different fighting strategies on each side (Iraqi armour versus Iranian manpower).

Fear, not "Soviet methods," explains the ponderously inflexible and ever so timid behaviour of Iraqi field commanders, another much commented upon feature of the fighting. The degree of bureaucratization or

27. Kifner, *New York Times*, February 28, 1986.
28. Among the more ingenious ideas that the Baʿth came up with to put distance between themselves and the Iranians is a fifteen-mile giant moat between half a mile to three miles wide. Billions of gallons of water were pumped from the Tigris and the Hawizeh marshes through a twenty-yard-wide canal, making the largest artificial lake in the Middle East. Mystery still surrounds the project, estimated to have cost in excess of $1.0 billion. The design, according to one expert guess, would give Iraq the capability of flooding Iranian land. See the reports in the British papers, *The Guardian*, July 31, 1984 and *The Sunday Times*, January 13, 1985.

state control of social life has by itself nothing to do with military performance as the case of Germany in both world wars proves (ironically Britain had the most rigid line of command in World War I). Saddam Husain understands what holds his own polity together, however much he may have misjudged the Islamic revolution of Iran.

Political insights, not military ones, are needed to understand what the Baʿth themselves thought they were doing when they first launched this war. Apparently, no specific Iraqi tactical military objectives existed that fitted into some broader military conception of how to fight this war. Certainly observers are agreed there was no alternative strategy in the event that initial assumptions were proved wrong. Saddam Husain must have believed that the mere shock of an Iraqi armed thrust into Iran was all that was needed to topple Khomeini or, at worst, force Iran into humiliating negotiations on his terms. When the Iranians did not collapse, his whole "strategy" fell into disarray.[29]

This ideological mode of thinking about military affairs was not confined to ground operations. For instance, on the first day of hostilities the Baʿth hinted that the oil sector should be exempted from attack; shortly after, Iranian gunboats took out the new computerized oil export terminals at the Iraqi port of Faw, and the Iranian air force bombed oilfields around Kirkuk and Mosul. All Iraqi oil exports were shut down temporarily, and by 1987 prewar production levels had still not been reached. Gulf outlets for Iraq have been out of operation for the whole duration of the war. As Iraqi oil production plummeted, Iranian output, which hit rock bottom at the start of the war, increased. Notwithstanding the crippling of Iranian refineries and other economic installations, Iraq was unable to check this strategic reversal in the accessibility to financial resources that took place on the third day of fighting. The Baʿth do not seem to have foreseen the remarkable ease with which the war could be extended to all economic installations, and took for granted a calculation on the Iranian side with which the latter were simply not prepared to oblige them.

Probably the most bizarre military decision of this war, however, concerns the use of the Iraqi air force. Just before September 22, the bulk of the Iraqi air force was dispersed across the airfields of the coun-

29. "Such a strategy is akin to developing a master plan in chess that culminates in a check mating sequence but which depends upon one's opponent making the "right" move so that the plan can be put into action." Grummon, *The Iraq-Iran War*, 18. Edgar O'Ballance, the military analyst, said the same thing. See his article, "The Iraqi-Iranian War: The First Round," *Parameters*, Journal of the US Army War College, 11, no. 1, (March 1981): 56.

tries of the Arabian peninsula barring South Yemen,[30] apparently to out-
smart the Iranians in the event that their capabilities in the air were still
a force to be reckoned with. The Ba'th were going to pursue a blitzkrieg
strategy, while making certain that they at least would not be caught
napping again; the paranoid obsession with Israeli tactics in 1967 is too
pathetic for words. When they did use their large air force, military analysts spilled much ink in the attempt to understand what they were
doing, even suggesting that their "command" of the air acted as a deter-
rent to surprise Iranian counterattacks on troop concentrations.[31] The
baffling absence of air support in ground operations, standard practise
since World War II, was thus explained by the fear that each held of
what they thought the other's air strength was. But maybe there was a
simpler military explanation: Iraqi air defences tended to shoot down
the wrong planes.[32]

The tendency to use the Iraqi air force primarily against civilian and
economic targets underscores this war's uncanny resemblance to World
War I, which became apparent with the massive Iranian human wave
assaults in the Basra region in 1982 and later on in February and March
of 1984. The consistency of pattern, however, extends to the war as a
whole, including the first Iraqi thrusts into Iranian territory and the organization of Iraqi defences in later stages. The paradox is that whereas
the character of the fighting in World War I was determined by the state
of military technique and equipment (artillery and fixed machine-gun
fire had become powerful enough to pin down infantry, but armour and
firepower lacked mobility), in the Iraq-Iran war the combatants were
engaging in a mode of warfare singularly unsuited to their equipment
and completely at variance with their training.

The problem is manifold. Lack of proficiency in the use of what is
growingly thought to be overly sophisticated equipment is one factor at

30. See Grummon, The Iraq-Iran War, 17. Also confirmed by W. Quandt in a different context. See, "Reactions of the Arab Gulf States," in The Iraq-Iran War: Issues of
Conflict and Prospects for Settlement, ed. Ali E. Hillal Dessouki (Seminar proceedings,
Princeton University, August 1981), 41.
31. See the comments of Drew Middleton in the International Herald Tribune, October 15, 1980; he later revised his estimation.
32. "In the middle of the desert, . . . we were shown parts of a wrecked fighter which
the Ministry of Information had swept together into an untidy pile and which our guide
described as the remnants of an Iranian Phantom. Their triumph turned into embarrass-
ment when a Polish correspondent politely pointed out that one of the pieces bore the
words 'emergency exit' in Russian, and that we were looking at the remains of an Iraqi
MIG fighter. Red-faced officials quickly shoved us back on the bus." Extended report by a
group of journalists in The Observer, September 28, 1980. On another occasion David
Fairhall reports "a big Russian-built Ilyushin 76 transport was shot down by its own side
while waiting to land at Baghdad." The Guardian, October 29, 1980.

the level of the individual soldier and lower-echelon command structure. But proficiency defects alone do not go far enough in explaining the regression; certainly they tell us nothing about the behaviour of the top command, or at the strategic level of decision making. There was a consistent blindness at work here that cannot be attributed to ignorance or sheer incompetence and stupidity. In the first six years of this war, neither side has been able to match a reasonably accurate assessment of the other's strengths and weaknesses, or even to learn from their own or each other's strengths and mistakes. At the start, this was mostly a feature of Iraqi military thinking; later on it became deeply characteristic of Iranian military "planning" (much license is required in the use of this word to describe Iranian military thinking). In effect it is the only consistent pattern of the first six years. The absence of military strategy when shared by both sides leads to gruelling slogging matches in which nothing is more expendable than human life—hence, the analogy with World War I.

Failures of judgement and overestimation of one's own capabilities happen in all wars; gross negligence and abject stupidity are very common; utter disregard for even one's own soldiery happens less frequently. But a consistent inability on both sides, and even at times unwillingness, particularly on the Iranian side, to judge the other realistically in order to map out an intelligible strategy for pursuing war aims that have as their final objective the more or less efficient overthrow of the adversary—this type of ingrained mental blockage is less common.

Saddam Husain's belated recognition that this was going to be a different kind of war than he had first imagined came in its third week, shortly before reservists were first called up for duty. Instead of soft-pedalling his war aims, however, he upped the ante, and took the decision to carry the war into civilian centres.[33] Apart from the aerial bombardment of cities, which had started earlier, the first ground-to-ground missiles were launched at Dezful coincident with the realization that the adversary was not going to just topple over.

> The rockets have pulverized three districts of the town, including hundreds of houses and shops. There is nothing left but piles of stones and ironwork.

33. Iraq's original war aims first escalated in a speech by Saddam Husain to the army on the occasion of 'Id al-Adhha, the Muslim feast. He called for the overthrow of the Khomeini regime in this language: "Truly, you are the sword of God on Earth and the heads you chop off are those of aggressive . . . backers of Khomeini, the maniac." Excerpts from the *International Herald Tribune*, October 20, 1980. At other times Saddam Husain has called for the arming of Iran's national minorities, the breakup of the "racist Persian" empire, and a holy war against Khomeini.

> Since the launching of rockets . . . the Iraqi artillery has taken over. It
> shells the town, but not the airbase every evening.[34]

The Dezful attacks took place in an atmosphere of frustration at the
leadership level, not defeat or even setback. Iraqi forces were still advancing, albeit far more slowly and with no apparent objective. Desperation, which so many commentators have wrongly used as an explanation for Iraq's resort to mustard and nerve gas later on in the war, was
wholly absent. Internally Saddam Husain was basking in war euphoria.[35] Militarily the bombing of towns and the pulverization of Dezful
was obviously counterproductive, greatly accelerating the massive Iranian recruitment drives.[36] Khomeini's call for an army of twenty million,
which had struck a false note before the invasion, was now able to take
on the status of a prophetic mobilizing vision.

Conducting a destructive war of this degree of hopelessness takes
two kinds of madness: to start it and to keep it going. I am concerned
with the former. A war in which only one side takes leave of their senses,
however, is very different from one in which both sides do. The differences reside in the number of casualties, the outcome of the fighting, the
essential nature of the war, and consequently the positions people feel
morally obligated to take for or against. It also profoundly affects the
judgement of those doing the dying, and their motivations for continuing to do so. With only one side pursuing an irrational strategy, the tendency to be demoralized, uneasy, and even rebellious, is reinforced;
once it is established that both are intent on such a course, and the war
for both has no tangible goals, the soldiery's resolve and ideological
commitment to its own side has to stiffen. For the Iraqi army, morale
was initially high on a wave of xenophobia and anti-Iranian chauvinism, but flagged appreciably with the breakdown of plans and stiff Iranian resistance; however, when the human wave strategy lost its initial
confounding novelty, and revealed itself as quintessentially ideological
and thus "strange," morale recovered. Analysts who persist in seeing the

34. Eric Rouleau, *The Guardian*, October 14, 1980. Reprinted from *Le Monde*.
35. See the report by James McManus from Baghdad on Saddam's risen standing entitled, "Hussein basks in war euphoria," in *The Guardian*, October 30, 1980. Four years
later morale was still "high among average Iraqis" according to Alex Paen's accurate if
naive report based on two weeks of travelling around sampling opinions; *Christian Science Monitor*, November 14, 1984.
36. Rouleau's report confirms this as do those of many other on-the-spot journalists.
"Listen to me well," an old peasant told Rouleau in Dezful, "we will hang on to this
ground with our nails. They can destroy everything, we will sleep in tents. Then we will
come back." *The Guardian*, October 14, 1980.

force of Iraqi nationalism in this recovery have not understood the com-pounded nature of the madness of this war.

Whenever Iranians fought in defence of their homes and towns, in effective isolation from the clerical leadership, by all accounts they did well against vastly superior odds. Nothing shook the Iraqi army more than the tenacious defence put up in Khorramshahr and Abadan. The character of such fighting is defensive and guerrillalike with snipers and scattered pockets putting up a sustained resistance to armoured and in-fantry advance. The nature of the combat was such as to place life at a premium, and so tactics evolved that tended to guard it. When the cler-ics took over, the military conception changed dramatically. The idea became to use the occasion of war to prove how good a Muslim one was; winning versus losing took on an entirely new meaning.

In Bostan the human wave attack led to an Iraqi rout and the capture of large numbers of prisoners. Rumour has it that officers and soldiers refused to mow down masses of people deliriously careering towards them. Whatever the truth in that story, it must be admitted that if a large enough number of people are prepared to commit suicide, then even in modern warfare almost any fixed position can be overrun. The problem is one of applied mathematics: an equation made up of numbers of people, the speed at which they can run, and the distance they have to cover on one side, versus the firepower and rate of delivery of the other. Using such "tactics" in the Basra region in the summer of 1982, the Ira-nians lost in two attempts a hundred thousand men and boys.[37] They failed to take the city and cut off the road to Baghdad. Nevertheless, with time on their side, a respectable flow of oil revenues starting to come in, an initial series of victories to bolster morale, and tested for-midable Iraqi fixed positions, they tried it again in the same location. In February and March of 1984, some five hundred thousand Iranians were amassed for what was billed as the "final offensive." In the initial battles that ensued (mercifully, the full-scale offensive did not materi-alize), the Ba'th used locally manufactured mustard and nerve gas against troop concentrations mixed in with raw, eager, and untrained teenage recruits. Reporters, allowed in for the first time since the first weeks of the war, have described scenes of carnage in language rarely found in modern journalism. "Carpets of bodies" and "hell on earth" are the sorts of phrases that cropped up in the reports of seasoned journalists to

37. From intelligence estimates cited in Drew Middleton's report in the *New York Times*, February 18, 1984.

describe the fighting around al-Qurnah, and what became known as the battle of Gzaeil. Iranian troops, revolutionary guards, and teenage "volunteers," all exhorted on by fighting mullahs, hopelessly rushed towards the Iraqi defences.

> The Iraqi guns kept up a heavy fire which cut down the Iranians like swathes of corn under a sickle. . . . Finally Iraqi armored units, driving across their own minefields, outflanked and routed the Iranians. . . .
> "We crushed the Iranians like insects," said an Iraqi soldier, jubilation showing through the exhaustion on his face. He squatted in a frontline trench he was sharing with three dusty Iranian corpses which, after two days, remained unburied. In the hot sun, the Iraqis' own dead still lay in the open where they had fallen, their limbs convulsed in death agonies. . . . This indifference to death . . . was hard to believe.[38]

Western reporters, however, arrived a few days after the fighting had subsided; one Iranian doctor on the front lines who was sent to Europe to accompany gassed victims, obviously shaken to his very depths, told of what he had seen: bodies left unburied, prisoners shot point-blank, the wounded left on the field to become carrion for desert jackals and vultures. Gone was the slightest implication of compassion if it had ever existed before. "I have seen young boys burned alive," he said. "I have seen Iranian and Iraqi boys tearing each other literally with their nails and teeth. It is raging hate against raging hate."[39]

In Lieu of a Conclusion

To say that the Baʿth and the clerical leadership in Tehran "took leave of their senses" and acted irrationally in pursuing even their own goals on the battlefield presumes some kind of shared sensibility on their part—not sagacity, wisdom, military experience, deep theoretical understanding, and certainly not compassion, but plain, run-of-the-mill common sense. This faculty is not an inner quality of the individual mind to do with abstract reasoning and reckoning with consequences; it is, as Hannah Arendt once observed, the series of judgements and perceptions we make as human beings who share the same world and gauge its real-

38. "After one telling battle in the marshes north of Basra hundreds of Iranian bodies were found floating in the brackish waters [after the Iranians sent a flotilla of five hundred small craft cross the marshes. They were cut to ribbons by helicopter gunships]. 'I have never seen carnage on such a scale,' said a seasoned TV reporter. 'After 500 bodies I stopped counting.'" Jon Swain, *The Sunday Times,* March 4, 1984.
39. *The Sunday Times,* February 26, 1984.

ity on that basis. It is therefore a profoundly political sensibility to do with human behaviour and affairs.

Both Saddam Husain and Khomeini possess common sense to a highly attenuated degree when dealing with their own self-made worlds. Their ability to assess their own human material in a consistently shrewd and calculating manner, surprising the pundits over and over again, raises two important questions: Why has the Iraqi regime not fallen or its Shiʿite soldiery defected in spite of the great reversal so early on in its course? And why is it that Khomeini continued to be successful in his mass recruiting drives despite unprecedented and militarily meaningless levels of casualties?

By the same token, when dealing with each other (or any other outsider), that same strength that each has when firmly implanted in his own world turns into a colossal weakness. The commonality to put it mildly was lacking; consequently the absence of simple common sense in Baʿthist Iraq and Islamic Iran is not a reflection on the sanity of those who made up these worlds, or those caught up in their vicelike grip. It is an outcome of the air of unreality that exists in the fictitious goals that their lives are sealed up in and being consecrated for.

Such goals have always existed at the heart of Baʿthism, both as a movement and in power. Normally their fictionality is screened from publicity, and the inner sanctum of Baʿthist fiction is hardly ever perceived as such. Once Baʿthism took power, and consolidated its authority by organizing the whole of Iraqi society, this fictional core of the movement got displaced into Saddam Husain's leadership.

However, even state power has its limitations for Baʿthism; it is constrained by a real border whose main implication is not that it delineates the frontiers of their nationalism, but that it acts as the terminus of their toehold on what is or is not real, and therefore capable of being sucked into the vortex of their kind of make-believe. The very extension of Baʿthist organization in Iraq—to the point where all internal opposition was eliminated and a regime of terror ensued that no longer had a rationality guiding so much as the selection of its victims—clogged up the original movement's vistas on reality such that it could no longer see anything that it had not made itself. The very success of Baʿthism's drive to complete its insularity and seal off the world, for so long a device to ward off the threats to its hegemony, turned against it; the conspiracies it had so mercilessly rooted out in the early years metamorphosed into dreams. The original fiction had been purely notional. Around this Archimedian point they had constructed a real universe that would no

longer expand unless they found and stood on this exact same point
that did not really exist; like Don Quixote, Saddam Husain set out to do
just that, while lacking of course every single one of that errant knight's
endearing qualities.

For Saddam Husain the world outside his grasp appears to him in a
guise other than that which presents itself to our common sense. He did
not need the Shah's ex-generals and Bakhtiar to tell him that the Iranian
revolution was rotten right through and the masses just awaiting his
signal to rise up in revolt. He knew that already, from "history," as his
choice of the name *Qadissiyah* expresses so aptly. Like the Iraqi masses
celebrating their victory over Zionist and imperialist conspiracies in the
January 1969 show trials, for Saddam Husain the "appearance" of the
Iranian revolution—the millions who marched, fought and died for it,
and the transferral of all their hopes and aspirations into the person of
Khomeini—was degraded at the outset. The world he had invented, and
forced into existence inside Iraq, posited it to be other than what presented itself politically, on the surface. The Khuzistani Arabs would wel-
come his liberating army, rise up in arms, and maybe even secede to Arabdom, their rightful inheritance, just as their ancestors had once done on
the plains of Qadissiyah at the expense of the mighty Sassanian empire.
That they did not do so, and even fought him tenaciously in the pre-
dominantly Arab provinces of Ahwaz and Khuzistan, was a testament
not to his error of judgement but to their treachery. A utopian pipe-dream
to dominate and break up Iran was thus congruent with yet another
conspiracy against Baʿthism; whether acting on the dream or the conspiracy always amounted to the same thing. This is why even if Saddam
went to war merely because he "thought" Iraqi Shiʿites represented a
threat, everything else I have said about this war would remain true; instead of acting upon delusions of grandeur, Saddam would have been
rooting out yet another conspiracy with about the same basis in reality
as all the rest.

Madness in this strictly political sense is expressed in the act of sub-
ordinating each particular incident, every development on the battlefield, each individual human life regardless of status, wealth, or rank,
and of course the sum of all lives to such indefinite, distant, and fictional
goals. Here are two warring world views that cannot help themselves in
their drive to take away from all of us that which we have in common.
When Saddam Husain tells the world that if it were within his power he
would start World War III before ever relinquishing office voluntarily—

and hence conceding forever the fictionality of his original war aims, something he does not have to do if they merely revert back into conspiracies—he means exactly that. With people like this, distinguishing between a genuine intention and a propagandistic flourish is inherently difficult. On the whole, however, they tend to believe their own utterances, and however monstrous a proposition might seem from the standpoint of our normality, it is essential never to indulge in the ostrichlike tendency to shy away from its insanity.

The difficulty arises when we try to understand their reasons from the standpoint of our commonness, or normality as human beings, and hence our notion of what makes sense and what does not. The extension of ordinary common sense into the world of Ba'thism and Khomeiniism does not work. Moreover, it can be pernicious. Thus, for example, in considering the use of poison gas, the assumption on the part of outside observers, Arab and Western alike, was that the Ba'th only resorted to this weapon out of desperation. Quite apart from the fact that the military situation on the ground was never as desperate as it was made out to be at the time, why not assume they did not poison Iranians earlier in the war and in greater numbers for no other reason than that the stuff was not available in adequate quantities? Gassing Iranians has residual benefits for the Ba'th, other than merely killing them; it dampens the ardour for martyrdom. It is one thing to die in a hail of bullets, gun in hand, careening across the plain with the name of the Almighty on one's dying breath; it is quite another to spend weeks having one's insides dissolve away on a hospital bed that is probably not available.

The use of chemical weapons of mass destruction poses the broader moral issue of what either side would have done had they possessed nuclear weaponry. Only grotesquely irresponsible minds could have had the slightest doubt that had Iraq possessed a bomb, it would have long since been detonated inside Iran. The meaning of mere possession of weapons of mass destruction—as distinguished from normal armaments designed for combat that has goals and a military strategy associated with it—originates in the firm intentionality to use them in whatever ultimate situation; hence, possession alone of weapons expressly designed for the wholesale slaughter of noncombatants is a perfectly adequate indication of criminal intent on the part of any government irrespective of its politics. However, to facilitate or even to acquiesce in the transfer of this kind of capability into the hands of a government whose power originates in an ever escalating threshold of institutional violence renders those responsible accomplices of the violence. Such is the position of all French governments that undertook to supply Iraq with this capability from 1975 on.

From this standpoint questions have to be asked regarding the meaning of a search for rationality in Saddam Husain's acts of war. Similarly, who are we to probe a clerical strategy in battle designed to protect the gains of His revolution, while shortcutting the arduous business of living with a certified one-way ticket to paradise? Can such a search shed light on the nature of this war, its broader regional significance? Or does it not by itself imply a refusal to accept this war for what it is and descend into their worlds and categories, thus further circumscribing and eroding the meaning of our own oneness as a species? All those who took positions in this war for one side or another, however critically, for whatever reason, and irrespective of when during its long course, entered and stayed in this moral abyss for as long as they held them. It does not matter why they did what they did, whether they were inside the countries or out, fighting or on the sidelines, or even who or what they are or were, because the essential point is that politics never had anything to do with this dimension of the deep-seated and terrifying insanity of the Iraq-Iran war.

Politics is the domain of public discourse and human interaction. Paradoxically this very domain, capable of causing such strife, itself gets extinguished once the killing begins. Politics ended between Iraq and Iran the moment the war began. It had ended inside Iraq much earlier, and this was related to how the war started. Therefore, far from this being a war that continues politics "by other means," as that great theoretician of warfare Clausewitz once wrote, it was the action of extending unbridled and mindless violence into new and uncharted frontiers. This is the essential nature of the Iraq-Iran war, a nature that arises from the deep-seated hostility that two world views have, not only to each other— then there might be hope, for maybe they are compatible with other world views—but also to everything human standing outside of them.

The two perfect symbols that sum up the meaning of the Iraq-Iran war are the human wave strategy and poison gas, neither of which lend themselves to a strategy in warfare designed around expressly political ends. Both fixate on death as an obviously nonpolitical end in itself, whether it be the purposeless slaughter of noncombatants or one's own soldiery. Ironically, poison gas and trench warfare (a different form of the human wave strategy) were inventions indissolubly associated with World War I—a war that gave us such monuments to human folly as the killing fields of Verdun, quite possibly the densest collection of corpses on the planet. The Iraq-Iran war has rightly been compared with this war, but usually for the wrong reasons. Poison gas and trench warfare in World War I were technical inventions that, coupled with long-range heavy artillery and the machine-gun, gave rise to the very special killing formula of that war. By contrast, symbols do not originate in matters of technique; in order to deserve the title they must go to the heart of the relations between people. In Baʿthist hands, poison gas is a way of killing that finds its source in the fear that binds that society together. The Iranian human wave strategy is its perfect counterpart; it is the celebration of death not for purposes to do with this life, but for an idea about the hereafter. Therefore, while poison gas and the human wave strategy are symbols that point to the fundamentals of the Iraq-Iran war, the same cannot be said about their place in World War I.

In his novel *A Fable,* set in World War I, William Faulkner depicted a scene in which a French division commander undertakes an attack that only he and the senior command knew beforehand was doomed. The regiment assigned mutinies at the precise moment of the attack; to a man the soldiers refuse to leave the trenches. As if by a prearranged signal, the division and then the whole French front follow suit. The parable resides in the fact that the Germans do not grasp the opportunity to press their counterattack; no one ever finds out quite how or why, but the whole German front simultaneously freezes up. Baffled officers keep up appearances by firing artillery barrages at the empty spaces between the two front lines. A group commander explains: "We can permit even our own rank and file to let us down on occasion; that's one of the prerequisites of their doom and fate as rank and file forever. They may even stop the wars, as they have done before and will again; ours merely to guard them from the knowledge that it was actually they who accomplished that act." [40] The terrible meaning of the Iraq-Iran war lies in the insight that such a scenario is unimaginable. It is not a matter of likelihood as it was for Faulkner—the literary power of his imagery stems from its extreme unlikelihood; it is rather a question of absolute unmitigated inconceivability.

When fighting over things (territory, oil reserves, navigation rights, strategic assets) or even projections of state power beyond acknowledged frontiers, actors the world over remain capable of rational judgement, at least abstractly and on the whole. Because lifeless things are at

40. William Faulkner, *A Fable* (New York: Random House, 1978), 45.

stake, the calculus of cause and effect makes it just barely possible to imagine French and German soldiers in World War I finding more that binds them in their fate than separates them in material interest, patriotism, or anything else. Moreover, the "relationship of forces" between two powers that war is capable of changing, temporarily or otherwise, is a calculable political reason for engaging in it. That is not to say the outcome can be known in advance of the fighting, or that uncertainty and error are not built into the decision making; rather it is to say the decision to go to war and the manner of conducting it stem from a series of political judgements in which correspondence to reality—or accuracy of assessment—is in principle coveted by, and accessible to, the combatants; and their actions as a consequence can be more or less accurately read through these judgements. These wars are "the continuation of politics by other means"; thus, those doing the dying may actually acquire the knowledge that those managing their deaths are always so keen to keep tucked away.

Conversely, if that which appears to constitute one side's innermost being is at war with what appears to the other side to constitute their innermost being, the already slim hope of finding a commonality is, to say the least, greatly reduced. On the face of it, the Iraq-Iran war presents itself, both in its origins and in what has sustained it, as the titanic clash of two men locked in a fight to the finish. This does not go far enough only because the dominant political attribute of each man is his unprecedented concentration of authority deriving in the one case from fear and in the other from faith. Fear and faith are among the most elemental and primordial of all human drives; under certain circumstances they have the force to make men die in droves for no other reason than that they cannot imagine doing otherwise. They have conferred onto the personal will of these two men the deadly power unleashed by the decisions of this war. The final meaning of a war like this, one it shares with the Lebanese civil war but none of the Arab-Israeli wars, resides in the simple truth that its mere occurrence has taken away from all of us yet another chunk of an already battered humanity.

Appendix

APPENDIX 1. PURGES OF HIGH-RANKING OFFICERS,
BAʿTHIST OLD GUARD AND POLITICIANS OF
MINISTERIAL OR HIGHER RANK SINCE JULY 17, 1968

Name	Date Purged	Method Used	State Position After July 1968	Regular Occupation	Party Affiliation
Abdul Razzaq al-Nayef	July 30, 1968	Arrested, then exiled. First assassination attempt in London 1973. Gunned down in London, July 1978	Prime minister; member of RCC, July 17–30	Army officer	None
Ibrahim al-Daud	July 30, 1968	In Jordan at time. Stayed in exile	Minister of defence; member of RCC, July 17–30	Army Officer	None
Nasir al-Hani	November 1968	Taken by group of Baʿthists at night. Body found in ditch riddled with bullets	Foreign minister	Career diplomat; scholar; literary critic	None
Ibrahim Faysal al-Ansari	December 1968	Dismissed, then arrested, accused of conspiracy. Sentenced to twelve years imprisonment	Chief of Army General Staff	Army officer	None
ʿAbd al-Rahman al-Bazzaz	October 1969	Tortured and sentenced to fifteen years imprisonment for "spying for Israel"	None	Career diplomat and scholar	None
ʿAbdul ʿAziz al-Uqaili	1969	Arrested and sentenced to death	None	General in Army	None

Name	Date	Fate	Position	Background	Ba'thi status
Hardan al-Takriti	October 15, 1970	Dismissed from all positions. Assassinated in Kuwait on March 30, 1971	Deputy premier; minister of defence; deputy commander in chief of the Army; member of RCC	Army officer	Ba'thi since 1961
Hasan al-Naqib	October 1970	Dismissed and made Ambassador in Spain. Retired from Army	Deputy chief of Army General Staff	Army officer	Ba'thi after 1958
'Abdullah Sallum al-Samarra'i	1970	Dismissed from all positions, then made ambassador to India	Minister of information; minister of state; member of RCC	Party man	Ba'thi from the 1950s (member of Regional Commands)
Salih Mahdi 'Ammash	September 28, 1971	Dismissed from all positions, then made ambassador to Finland	Deputy premier; minister of interior (1968–70); member of RCC	Army officer	Ba'thi since 1952 (member of Regional and Pan-Arab Commands)
'Abd al-Karim Mustafa Nasrat	August 1971	Stabbed to death at his house	Minister	Army officer	Ba'thi from late 1950s
'Abd al-Karim al-Shaikhli	September 28, 1971	Dismissed and appointed to UN. Later assassinated in his car	Foreign minister; member of RCC	Party worker	Ba'thi (member of Regional and Pan-Arab Commands)
Fuad al-Rikkabi	November 1971	Murdered in prison	None	Engineer	Ba'thi since 1950; party leader 1952–58

(continued next page)

(APPENDIX I, continued)

Salah 'Umar al-'Ali	1972	Dismissed. Made ambassador to Sweden	Minister of guidance; member of RCC	Party worker	Ba'thi (member of Regional Command)
Hammad Shehab	June 30, 1973	Killed by Kzar in coup attempt	Minister of defence; chief of Army General Staff; member of RCC	Army officer	Ba'thi after 1968
Nadhim Kzar	July 8, 1973	Executed	Chief of Internal Security	Party worker	Ba'thi since 1950s
Muhammad Fadel	July 9, 1973	Executed	Head of Ba'th Military Bureau	Army officer	Ba'thi
Na'im Haddad	July 1973	Imprisoned	?	Party worker(?)	Ba'thi (member of Regional Command)
'Abd al-Khaliq al-Samarra'i	July 1973	Sentenced to life imprisonment. Shot in July 1979 purges	Member of RCC	Municipal Clerk became party theoretician	Ba'thi (member of Regional and Pan-Arab Commands)
Hasan Mustafa	1974–75	Imprisoned	General in Army	Army officer	Not known
Saddiq Mustafa	1974–75	Imprisoned	General in Army	Army officer	Not known
Taha Shakarchi	1974–75	Imprisoned	General in Army	Army officer	Not known
Husain Hayawi	1974–75	Dismissed. Appointed military attache in Pakistan	Commander of Air Force	Army officer	Not known
Dawood al-Janabi	mid-1970s	Dismissed	Commander of Republican Guard (elite units in Baghdad)	Army officer	Not known

Name	Date	Fate	Position	Profession	Party Status
Dr. ʿIzzat Mustafa	March 1977	Dismissed. Kept under house arrest	Minister of health (1968–69); minister of labour (1976); minister of municipalities (1977); member of RCC (1968–77)	Physician	Baʿthi since late 1940s, early 1950s (member of Regional Command)
Ahmad Hasan al-Bakr	June 1979	Placed under house arrest. Gradually stripped of all positions	President; commander in chief of Army; minister of defence (1973–77)	Army officer	Baʿthi since early 1950s (Secretary General Baʿth Regional Command; member of Pan-Arab Command)
Muhyi ʿAbd al-Husain Rashid	July 20, 1979	Forced to "confess" to RCC, then shot along with whole family	Secretary of RCC	Party man	Prominent Baʿthi (member of Regional Command)
Khaled Abed Osman	July 1979	Executed	Minister of Kurdish affairs; member of RCC		Baʿthi
ʿAdnan Husain	July 1979	Executed	Deputy prime minister and chief of President's Bureau; member of RCC		Baʿthi (member of Regional Command)
Mohammed Mahjoub	July 1979	Executed	Minister of education; member of RCC		Baʿthi (member of Regional Command)

(continued next page)

(*APPENDIX 1, continued*)

Mohammed ʾAyeh	July 1979	Executed	Minister of industry; member of RCC	Baʿthi
Ghanin Abdul Jalil	July 1979	Executed	Chief of vice-president's office; member of RCC	Baʿthi (member of Regional Command)
Muhammed ʿAyish	July 1979	Executed	Member of RCC	Leading party organizer	Baʿthi (member of Regional Command)
Adnan Hamdani	July 1979	Executed	Director general of president's office; minister of planning (1976–79); member of RCC and Committee on Oil Affairs	Lawyer and party man	Baʿthi
Riyadh Ibrahim	June 1982	Executed	Minister of health	Party worker	High-ranking Baʿthi

SOURCES: In addition to sources already mentioned, see Abbas Kelidar, "Iraq: The Search for Stability," *Conflict Studies* (London: The Institute for the Study of Conflict, 1975), 1–21. This appendix is not definitive because it relies on names that have been published abroad.

Index

Chronology

The chronology is intended as a guide to the text and for reference by readers not versed in the events of Iraqi political history.

THE MANDATE YEARS (1918–32)

October 3, 1918: Ottoman rule over the Arabs symbolically ends as the Bedouin army of Faisal, the son of Sharif Husain of Hijaz, and leader of the Arab revolt against the Turks, enters Damascus.

June 2, 1920: Widespread tribal uprising in Iraq against British military rule.

July 24, 1920: French forces oust Faisal and occupy Damascus. The French Mandate over Syria begins.

August 27, 1921: The British install Faisal as monarch in Iraq under Mandate from the League of Nations. He is accompanied by an entourage of Iraqi supporters from the days of the Arab revolt. Satiaᶜ al-Husri, a Syrian pan-Arabist thinker, arrives with Faisal and gradually takes over the educational system.

October 10, 1922: The Anglo-Iraqi Treaty, which sets out the scope of Britain's involvement in Iraqi affairs, is signed.

November 16, 1930: The Iraqi parliament ratifies a new Anglo-Iraqi treaty, which sets a date for the termination of the British Mandate over Iraq on conditions favourable to Britain.

THE MONARCHY (1932–58)

October 3, 1932: The independent state of Iraq is formally admitted to the League of Nations.

December 13, 1932: The first communist proclamation appears in Iraq written in longhand by "Fahd," the future leader of the Iraqi Communist Party (ICP).

August 1933: The Assyrian Affair. The army under General Bakr Sidqi initiates a pogrom of the Assyrian community with the support of the government and against the express wishes of Faisal. Sidqi becomes a national hero.

September 8, 1933: King Faisal dies to be succeeded by his son Ghazi, a keen supporter of the army's actions against the Assyrians.

October 29, 1936: Bakr Sidqi overthrows the government in the Arab world's first military coup. He promises widespread social reform. The left-wing Ahali group enters government.

April 28, 1937: Saddam Husain is born in the desert town of Takrit.

August 11, 1937: Sidqi is assassinated by army officers. Six more coups follow in quick succession ending in 1941.

April 1, 1941: Four pan-Arabist generals proclaim a state of emergency. A government of National Defence headed by Rashid ʿAli al-Qaylani and the generals is formed and immediately supported by the Axis powers. Pro-British Iraqi politicians flee.

May 1941: Fighting breaks out on May 2 between British forces newly landed in Basra and the Iraqi army. On May 19 the Iraqi army is routed. Rashid ʿAli and the generals escape to Tehran on May 29. The regent and pro-British politicians are reinstalled.

June 1, 1941: Several hundred Iraqi Jews killed in riots involving disgruntled junior officers of the Iraqi army.

July 24, 1943: A group of less than ten people, calling themselves The Arab Baʿth movement, issue their first programmatic statement in Damascus.

April 1947: The first congress of the Baʿth party is held representing a membership of a few hundreds. In Iraq, Baʿthist ideas are brought by Syrian teachers in 1949, and the first organizing efforts begin in 1951.

January 20–27, 1948: Massive urban uprising against the proposed Portsmouth treaty with Britain. The ICP emerges as the main organizing force.

February 14–15, 1949: Fahd and two other leaders of the ICP are publicly hanged in Baghdad.

1956: Nasser nationalizes Suez, and Egypt is invaded. Soon after, the young Saddam joins the Iraqi Branch of the Arab Baʿth Socialist Party (ABSP) as it is now called.

MILITARY RULE (1958–68)

July 14, 1958: A secret organization of two hundred "Free Officers" overthrows the monarchy in a coup acclaimed throughout Iraq. The populace fills the streets hours after the first shots are fired. Parliament is abolished and the army purged. A People's Court under Colonel Fadhil Abbas Mahdawi is set up to try the members of the ancien regime. Brigadier ʿAbd al-Karim Qassem who executed the coup emerges as prime minister and commander in chief.

July 24, 1958: Michel ʿAflaq, founder of the Baʿth party, arrives in Baghdad calling for instant unity with the newly formed United Arab Republic. In opposition, the ICP projects Qassem as the sole leader.

September 30, 1958: ʿAbd al-Salam ʿAref, a Free Officer of pan-Arabist persuasion and organizer with Qassem of the 1958 coup, is removed from his posts as deputy premier and minister of interior. He fails in a personal attempt on Qassem's life and is arrested on November 4. In December ʿAref is publicly tried in Mahdawi's court. The falling out between Qassem and ʿAref draws attention to the irreconcilability of the pan-Arab and Iraqist trends among the coup makers of 1958.

March 1959: Disaffected pan-Arabist Free Officers from the Mosul garrison organize a revolt against Qassem, which is crushed. Communist supporters go on a rampage. Hundreds of suspected Arab nationalists are killed and bodies mutilated. The conflict takes an ethnic and communal character. In its wake Qassem purges more nationalists and Baʿthists.

May 1, 1959: Historic demonstration of about half a million people calling for Communist representation in government.

July 1959: Turcomans are massacred by Communist Kurds in the city of Kirkuk. Qassem now launches a wave of arrests of ICP members that continues through August.

September 1959: The writings of Michel ʿAflaq are collected and published for the first time under the title, *Fi Sabil al-Baʿth.*

October 7, 1959: A Baʿthist hit team fails to assassinate Qassem. A member of the team, twenty-two-year-old Saddam Husain, escapes to Syria and then goes to Egypt. Seventy-eight Baʿthists implicated in the incident are brought before Mahdawi's People's Court. Their defiant militancy leaves a deep impression.

January 1, 1960: Qassem announces that all political parties will be legalized, but ICP is rebuffed. Anticommunist measures continue until the end of the regime.

March 1961: Baʿthi agitators lead important demonstration against the Qassem regime.

September 1961: The Iraqi army launches its first major offensive against the Kurds in mountainous terrain. By the spring of 1962 a costly full-scale guerrilla war had developed, which Qassem could not win.

December 24, 1962: The Baʿth successfully organize a nationwide strike of all secondary-school and university students, which continues until the fall of the regime.

February 8, 1963: A Baʿthist coup overthrows Qassem amidst several days of terrible street fighting. The first Baʿthi regime is installed. Its nine-month rule is marked by a relentless settling of accounts with communists and their fellow travellers. ʿAbd al-Salam ʿAref becomes President.

November 18, 1963: Following bitter infighting between moderate and radical factions of the Baʿth, ʿAref overthrows the first Baʿthi regime. He is supported by moderate Baʿthist officers. The Baʿthi militia controlled by the civilian wing of the party takes to the streets and is crushed by the army. ʿAref appoints Ahmad Hasan al-Bakr, a former Free Officer and long-standing Baʿthi, vice-president. But gradually all Baʿthis are eased out of the new military regime, which leans towards Nasserism.

February 1964: Michel ʿAflaq recommends the elevation of Saddam Husain to the Regional Command of the Iraqi branch of the ABSP.

July 14, 1964: Comprehensive nationalization laws are promulgated as a step towards Arab socialism and unity with Egypt.

April 18–August 6, 1966: Prime Minister ʿAbd al-Rahman al-Bazzaz negotiates a temporary end to the Kurdish war, tries to curb army privileges, and bring about an atmosphere reminiscent of the old regime.

June 1967: The six-day war brings military catastrophe to the Arab world. All officer-led regimes are discredited.

September 6, 1967: The Baʿth lead a large demonstration against the new ʿAref regime. They call for action against the fifth column responsible for the June defeat.

September 17, 1967: The ICP splits into two organizations: the Central Command faction led by ʿAziz al-Haj and the pro-Soviet Central Committee faction.

July 17, 1968: In alliance with non-Baʿthi army officers, the ABSP organizes a successful coup that overthrows the ʿAref regime.

THE SECOND BAʿTHI REGIME (1968–80)

July 30, 1968: The Baʿth cast out their former allies in a second carefully planned coup. Supreme authority passes to the Revolutionary Command Council (RCC) chaired by Ahmad Hasan al-Bakr, secretary-general of the ABSP, who also becomes president and commander in chief of the army. Saddam Husain, already assistant secretary-general of the party, becomes deputy chairman of the RCC in charge of internal security.

February 1969: ʿAziz al-Haj, leader of the ICP Central Command, is arrested and makes a public confession, which leads to the capture of the whole politbureau.

August 8, 1969: The Kurdish village of Dakan in Mosul is the scene of a major army atrocity. The war against the Kurds is being stepped up.

October 1969: Former prime minister, ʿAbd al-Rahman al-Bazzaz, is tortured and imprisoned for fifteen years on charges of being a Zionist agent.

December 14, 1968: Iraqi television presents graphic details of an alleged Zionist spy ring involving Iraqi Jews that had been broken up in Basra.

January 5, 1969: The new regime's first batch of "spies" are brought for a public trial. Seventeen defendants, including thirteen Iraqi Jews, are hanged in Liberation Square amidst speeches and much fanfare. Hundreds of thousands of people attend the spectacle.

January 21, 1970: The regime reports that a new conspiracy is foiled. Within a week forty-four people have been executed.

March 11, 1970: A Manifesto on Kurdish autonomy is published amidst much fanfare. On paper the Kurds are granted more rights as a nationality than ever before. The fighting stops and the Baʿth government gains time to consolidate.

July 10, 1970: The ABSP announces conditions for the Communist party to join it in a Progressive National Front. The ICP Central Committee prevaricates.

August 1971: ʿAbd al-Karim Nasrat, early Baʿthi and organizer of the militia that was used in the overthrow of the Qassem regime in 1963, is stabbed to death in his house.

October 15, 1970: Hardan al-Takriti, prominent officer Baʿthi and former member of the RCC and deputy premier and minister of defence, is gunned down in Kuwait.

September 1971: Iraqi state security fails in an attempt to assassinate the Kurdish leader, Barazani.

November 1971: Fuad al-Rikkabi, the leader of the Ba'th from the inception of an Iraqi organization until 1959, is murdered in prison.

April 1972: Iraqi-Soviet Friendship Treaty is announced.

May 1972: Communists enter the government for the first time.

June 1972: The Iraqi Petroleum Company is nationalized.

July 8, 1973: Nadhim Kzar, chief of internal security, is executed along with at least thirty-five others in the wake of an attempted coup.

July 1973: A National Action Charter first announced in 1971 is signed by the ABSP and the ICP, in which the latter accepts all the July 1970 conditions.

January 1974: The eighth regional congress of the ABSP is held in Baghdad. Its Political Report assesses the past and projects Ba'thist intentions.

March 1974: Following the collapse of the 1970 Kurdish Autonomy accords, all-out war breaks out. The Kurdish towns of Zakho and Qala'at Diza are razed to the ground. Hundreds of thousands of Kurds flee the cities. Brutalities break all previous records.

December 1974: Five Shi'i 'ulama' are executed for unknown reasons.

March 6, 1975: The Algiers agreement between the Iraqi Ba'th and the Shah's regime in Iran is promulgated. Iraq formally concedes to Iranian territorial demands in return for the Shah's support against the Kurds. The Kurds' lines of supply are cut off. Kurdish resistance crumbles. The government launches its policy of mass Kurdish deportations and resettlement.

February 1977: Shi'i clergy head a demonstration on the religious occasion of 'Ashura' in the city of Karbala. Some two thousand people are arrested and eight more 'ulama' executed. Mass deportations into Iran of Iraqi Shi'i fifth columnists commence around this time. By the late 1970s some two hundred thousand Iraqis have been dumped inside Iran, stripped of their nationality and property.

October 1978: Khomeini expelled from Iraq.

February 1979: The Islamic revolution in Iran.

June 1979: Saddam Husain becomes president. Ahmad Hasan Al-Bakr is stripped of all positions and placed under house arrest.

July 1979: Massive purge of top Ba'thi command. Muhyi Rashid, secretary of RCC, forced to confess and then shot along with whole family. One-third of the members of the RCC are executed. By August 1, some five hundred top-ranking Ba'thists are said to have been executed.

April 9, 1980: Mohammed Baqir al-Sadr and his sister Bint al-Huda, symbols of the Shi'i opposition in Iraq, are executed.

September 22, 1980: Saddam Husain launches full-scale war operations against Iran.

Compositor: G & S Typesetters
Text: 10/13 Sabon
Display: Sabon
Printer: Maple-Vail Book Mfg. Group
Binder: Maple-Vail Book Mfg. Group